Please remember that this is a library book,
and that it belongs only temporarily to each
person who uses it. Be considerate. Do
not write in this, or any, library book.

JUVENILE DELINQUENCY
Causes, Patterns, and Reactions

JUVENILE DELINQUENCY
Causes, Patterns, and Reactions

William B. Sanders
SAN DIEGO STATE UNIVERSITY

HOLT, RINEHART AND WINSTON
NEW YORK   CHICAGO   SAN FRANCISCO   DALLAS
MONTREAL   TORONTO   LONDON   SYDNEY

The authors wish to thank the following for permission to reprint their photographs:
p.   1 Courtesy of Sam Teicher
p. 23 Courtesy of Bob Adelman
p. 40 Courtesy of Bob Adelman
p. 62 Courtesy of Bob Adelman
p. 80 Courtesy of Micheal Kagan, Monkmeyer Press Photo Service
p. 96 Courtesy of Bob Adelman
p. 126 Courtesy of Sam Teicher
p. 150 Courtesy of Charles Gatewood
p. 183 Courtesy of Wide World Photos
p. 213 Courtesy of New York City Police Department
p. 230 Courtesy of Sam Teicher
p. 253 Courtesy of Bob Adelman
p. 269 Courtesy of Sam Teicher
p. 286 Courtesy of Sam Teicher

Library of Congress Cataloging in Publication Data

Sanders, William B   fl. 1974–
  Juvenile delinquency.

  Bibliography: p.
  Includes index.
  1. Juvenile delinquency. 2. Juvenile justice,
Administration of. I. Title.
HV9069.S25 1981   364.3'6   80–18550
ISBN 0–03–040776–1

Dedication

This book is dedicated to my great-uncle Bert who met his untimely end while attempting to rob one of the gold stages that ran between Hangtown and Sacramento, California, in the late eighteen hundreds.

Preface

The study of delinquency is as much a matter of addressing the right questions as it is of finding the right answers. In this book I have attempted to raise those questions and find the answers so as to provide an introduction to juvenile delinquency. The questions raised have been sociological ones dealing with theory and research in the area of delinquency. The purpose, though, has not been to leave the student hanging onto unanswered questions. Instead it has been an attempt to put a clear order to the study of delinquency. By clearly stating the salient issues and problems in delinquency, we are able to keep on the right track and not go running off in every conceivable direction that the study of delinquency may take us. The purpose is to focus, not narrow, our perspective on delinquency.

In order to achieve the goal of a focused study of delinquency, I have divided the book into three major parts: theory; patterns; and societal reaction. It is true that all of these parts are interrelated, but I think that students can better understand delinquency if we discuss each part separately. At the same time, however, once we understand the separate parts, there is no reason to insist on their separation, and so while discussing one part we can show its relationship to another. By first discussing theories of delinquency, it is possible to raise salient questions and formulate these questions as focal points. In other words, by beginning with theory, we provide a roadmap for further inquiry. Next, in discussing patterns of delinquency, we can see there are very different types of behaviors that constitute what is called "juvenile delinquency." Having focused our line of inquiry in the theory section of the book, students can examine the patterns in terms of the questions raised by theory. Not only does this help in understanding the various patterns of delinquency, but it also assists in understanding the purpose of theory. The third major section deals with the societal reaction to delinquency in the form of the juvenile justice system. Here again we isolate an important element of delinquency study and at the same time see that the causes of delinquency as well as the patterns are related to what society sees to be "delinquent."

In the final chapter in the book, I have tried to show the relevance of theory and research to "doing something" about delinquency. Sociologists who engage in pure theory and research play a vital role in understanding delinquency, but few students understand how this knowledge can be employed to deal with delinquency. The most practical thing that can be done in developing programs to work with delinquents is to have good theory and research behind the programs. There is a simplified self-report survey in the

Appendix to use with college students as a device to show how one type of research into delinquency can be done.

In deciding how to write the book, there has always been a split in textbooks as either "serious" or "frivolous." The "serious" books tend to present materials in such a way as to be dry, humorless, and technical, while the "frivolous" ones have attempted to "talk to the student" by using baby-talk. Rather than searching for a golden mean between the two, I attempted to write in what I considered to be a clear, expository manner using interesting examples to clarify and expand points. Since delinquency itself is an interesting subject, this was not too difficult. However, interesting stories about delinquency can be found in the newspapers, and so at the same time I tried to show how a sociological understanding of delinquency can expand one's knowledge. To this end, concepts are introduced *as* concepts. The language of sociology need not be a mysterious jargon, and I do not think concepts are. Employed properly, sociological concepts are an aid to understanding, not a hinderance. In this book, I simply tried to use concepts to clarify, not impress.

The point of view of this book is one that attempts to get close to delinquent behavior. There really is no place on a "radical-reactionary" continuum where this book belongs and what political ax-grinding there may be is a discussion of different viewpoints. The focus is on the "delinquent occasion" where actual delinquency occurs. This position is mid-point between a macro-level structural–cultural approach and a micro-level social–psychological one. An entire chapter is devoted to this point of view, a quasi-theoretical position that seems to have been overlooked in the study of delinquency. Being midway between the macro- and micro-level approaches, it serves to benefit and clarify both levels.

In preparing such a book as this, there are many debts of gratitude. First of all, there are my students who taught me how to explain things to them, all the while keeping me honest. Their efforts are still continuing. Dr. Charles Frazier of the Universtiy of Florida did a great deal to better my understanding of control theory, and Professor Felix Berardo, also of the University of Florida, allowed me access to his files on runaways. Donald Cressey and Don Zimmerman were mentors whose past efforts will always be appreciated. Many others provided me with information that I employed in one way or another, but there were so many with so much that I only hope they know who they are for they are too numerous to list. I thank them collectively. The editors at Holt, Rinehart and Winston were always helpful, especially Jim Bergin, Frank Graham, and Patrick Powers. The senior project editor, Fran Bartlett, provided the fine sanding to what had been one big rough edge. Through this, as well as all other past efforts, my wife Eli and sons Billy and David were understanding and helpful in ways that cannot be quantified.

Contents

1 The Phenomenon of Juvenile Delinquency

INTRODUCTION

As we begin our study of juvenile delinquency we must first get a clear idea of exactly what we are going to examine. Even though most people have a vague idea of what constitutes delinquency, the most common and popular ideas tend to be stereotypes rather than precise images. Since this book is about delinquency, we will begin with an overview of what delinquency is and the way we will approach our examination of it.

The first thing we will consider is the scope of delinquency. This will include a look at the kinds of activities that are considered delinquent. Some of these, such as gang shootings, obviously constitute delinquent behavior. Others, however, such as minor juvenile-status offenses like truancy, are obscure, and many people do not even realize that these too are violations of laws. Later in the book the different types of delinquency will be examined closely; in this chapter we will simply point out the different types of behaviors that can be considered delinquent.

Second, we will focus on the legal and social aspects of delinquency as well as the sociological perspective that we will take in this book. The legal elements of delinquency refer to laws that define delinquent behaviors and the kinds of offenses they constitute. The social elements refer to how the legal definitions of delinquency are applied in social interaction. Taking the legal and social features of delinquency, we will develop a sociological definition of delinquency that we will employ in our study. This will provide the sociological viewpoint to be applied in understanding delinquency.

The next step involves the methods used to measure delinquency. In order to explain delinquency, it is necessary to observe its patterns and trends. By understanding how delinquency is measured we can assess the validity of any theory that is used to explain it. If an inaccurate or biased measurement is employed, it follows that any explanation based on that measurement will also be inaccurate.

Finally, we will look at that period in life we all pass through—that transitory period squeezed in between young childhood and adulthood. These are the years in which delinquency occurs; by understanding something about youths at this point in time we can shed light on the nature of delinquency.

THE SCOPE OF DELINQUENCY

The range of activities that can be considered delinquent is wide and varied. On the most serious end of the scale are those that violate the criminal law, and on the least serious end are juvenile-status offenses. Serious criminal

offenses—felonies—are the least common but most notorious types of delinquent activities committed by youths. These include violent crimes such as
murder, rape, robbery, and assault. About 10 percent of all juvenile arrests
are for violent crimes, and it is estimated that between 5 and 11 percent of
all serious delinquent acts are of this nature.[1] A more common juvenile felony
is some type of property crime, such as grand larceny, burglary, or automobile
theft where no violence is involved.

Petty offenses are a far more common type of violation of the criminal law.
These include smoking marijuana, shoplifting, and malicious mischief. Most
of these offenses go undetected, and those that are uncovered usually do not
result in arrests. Moreover, when such offenders are caught, they are often
sent home instead of arrested.[2] As a result, most petty offenses remain "hidden," so that it is difficult to say what proportion of delinquency is in this
category. However, judging from the various measures we do have, we can
safely say that over 90 percent of all criminal delinquency is of this petty
nature.

The third type of activity that comes under the umbrella of delinquency
is the juvenile-status offense. Youths who commit offenses that apply only
to juveniles are considered juvenile-status offenders, a category that includes
runaways and truants. As we will see, the juvenile-status offense is the most
encompassing of all acts for which a youth may be arrested, and the range
of activities that covers such offenses is enormous.

A number of years ago I worked with juveniles in a detention center. In
order to indicate the scope of the different types of offenses that juveniles
commit, from serious to petty, I shall introduce a number of illustrations
drawn from that experience. Since that time new laws regulating juvenile-
status offenders have been passed, and such offenders are not as likely to be
placed in detention today as they once were, but the illustrations will show
the range of behaviors that can be considered delinquent.

A few of the youths were in detention for serious offenses, but most were
there for relatively petty matters. The most serious offender was a 15-year-
old bank robber from an upper-middle-class background whose father was
a university professor. The boy was exceptionally intelligent and told me how
he had disguised himself as a 21-year-old to avoid detection. The pictures
from the bank's cameras showed a boy that appeared quite different from the
one I met, and judging from what the youth told me, he probably would have
escaped detection had not a friend informed on him. More typical of those
arrested for serious offenses were lower-class minority youths picked up for
assaults or robberies, usually of liquor or convenience stores. In large urban
areas many of the muggers who prey on old, weak, and isolated victims are
juveniles.

The next most serious group of offenders I met were boys and girls arrested
for property offenses. Most of the girls were in the detention center for
shoplifting, but the boys had committed everything from burglary to auto

theft. A young-looking 13-year-old boy who had been arrested for auto theft explained that he would steal a car and "low-ride" up and down the street until the car ran out of gas. His excursions consisted of first stealing the car, "scooting way down in the seat," then popping the clutch, jerking the vehicle quickly forward. He simply kept repeating the operation, and for him it was an enormous amount of fun.

Virtually all of the status offenders I met were locked up for running away from home or being out of their parents' control. One boy, who had a note from his parents allowing him to hitchhike up the coast, was arrested for being "out of control." When the parents of another boy who had left home unannounced learned that their son had been arrested as a runaway they told the juvenile authorities they did not care to have him return. Another run-away was a 16-year-old girl, a habitual status offender, who had been bounced from one foster home to another. The court decided that she was not being cared for properly by her mother, who was separated from her husband, so the girl had been made a ward of one set of foster parents after another. She generally did not like her foster parents, so she would leave them and return to her mother, who would have the juvenile authorities place her daughter in detention until she could be placed in another foster home. When the girl found a foster home she liked, she would still run away because she knew she could stay in the home for only a year before being placed in a new home. In this way, she explained, she would not become too attached to the foster parents before her stay was terminated at the end of a year.

LEGAL ASPECTS OF DELINQUENCY

The first consideration in distinguishing delinquency from other forms of behavior involves legal issues. For an act to be delinquent there must be some legal statute that prohibits or demands certain actions. For example, there are laws that prohibit stealing by anyone, juvenile or adult. Other laws demand certain behaviors, such as attending school, but this law applies only to youths.

Even though all criminal laws apply to both juveniles and adults, juveniles come under a different set of laws than do adults. The differentiation between adults and juveniles is based on age, but the legal age varies from state to state. In 33 states and the District of Columbia the maximum age over which the juvenile court has original jurisdiction is 17 years.[3] Therefore, until a person is 18, he or she is legally a juvenile. In twelve states the maximum age of original juvenile court jurisdiction is 16 years, and in six states the age is 15.[4] Thus a 17-year-old in Columbus, Mississippi, who broke the criminal law would come under the original jurisdiction of the juvenile court. But if the youth crossed the Tombigbee River into neighboring Alabama and committed the same crime, he or she would come under the jurisdiction of the adult court.

In certain instances a juvenile can be tried as an adult, especially if the individual has a long record and has committed a serious crime. For example, if a 16- or 17-year-old has been arrested several times for assault or armed robbery, even though the juvenile court has *original* jurisdiction, the criminal or adult court can have the *final* jurisdiction in the case. If the juvenile is tried in an adult court, he or she can receive an adult penalty. Likewise, a person over the age of original juvenile court jurisdiction can be turned over to the juvenile court for adjudication, but for the most part the "legal age" determines whether the individual will go to adult or juvenile court.

Finally, in some states the legal age for juvenile status is different for different areas of behaviors. At age 18 in California, for example, a person is considered to be an adult in every area but possession of alcoholic beverages. Thus, a 19-year-old in California who is caught with a six-pack of beer can be arrested and tried in an adult court for being under age! This "limbo age" is most common in states where the maximum age of original juvenile court jurisdiction is relatively low.

Legal Definitions

The legal definitions of youthful violations and violators are typically split between what are considered delinquents and status offenders. By and large, a delinquent is anyone who has broken a criminal law, while a status offender, as we have seen, is a juvenile who has broken a law that applies only to juveniles. We will examine the statutes of California, Pennsylvania, and Florida as examples of typical juvenile laws.

California. In California the juvenile laws come under what is called the Welfare and Institutions Code, as opposed to the Penal Code. Two sections of the Welfare and Institutions Code, Sections 601 and 602, summarize the state's legal definitions of juveniles and delinquents. Section 601 provides that

> Any person under the age of 18 years who persistently or habitually refuses to obey the reasonable and proper orders or directions of his parents, guardian, custodian or school authorities, or who is beyond the control of such person, or any person who is a habitual truant from school within the meaning of any law of this state, or who from any cause is in danger of leading an idle, dissolute, lewd, or immoral life, is within the jurisdiction of the juvenile court which may adjudge such person to be a ward of the court. [Amended Ch. 1748, Stats. 1971. Effective Mar. 4, 1972]

Given a literal reading of this definition of juvenile-status offender, there is an immense range of possible actions for which a juvenile can be arrested. For example, the 17-year-old boy mentioned earlier who was arrested for being "out of control" even though he had a note from his parents was picked up on the basis of this law. The police reasoned that if the youth were hitchhiking and not in the same county as his parents, he was not in his parents' control, even though they permitted his travel. By this same reasoning a child could be arrested for habitually not cleaning up his or her room. Since telling their children to pick up their rooms is a "reasonable" and "proper" order on the part of parents, habitually refusing to do so *could* be interpreted as a status offense. (I hasten to add, however, that I have never met a youth arrested on charges of having a messy room.)

The other major California statute regulating the treatment of juvenile delinquents groups all other possible offenses together. Section 602 of the California Welfare and Institutions Code reads:

> Any person who is under the age of 18 years when he violates any law of this state or of the United States or any ordinance of any city or county of this state defining crime or who, after having being found by the juvenile court to be a person described by Section 601 [see above], fails to obey any lawful order of the juvenile court, is within the jurisdiction of the juvenile court, which may adjudge such person to be a ward of the court. [Amended Ch. 1748, Stats. 1971. Effective Mar. 4, 1972]

All juveniles who commit any criminal act are charged under Section 602. Juvenile murderers and malicious mischief makers are charged under the same section. Even though young murder suspects are treated differently from juveniles who shot at windows with air rifles, the legal charge is the same.

Pennsylvania.   Pennsylvania's juvenile law (Public Law 1433) is similar to California's. The pertinent sections state:

> (2) The word "child" as used in this act, means a minor under the age of eighteen years. . . .
> (4) The words "delinquent child" include:
>   (a) A child who has violated any law of the Commonwealth or ordinance of any city, borough, or township;
>   (b) A child who, by reason of being wayward or habitually disobedient, is uncontrolled by his or her parent, guardian, custodian, or legal representative;
>   (c) A child who is habitually truant from school or home;
>   (d) A child who habitually so deports himself or herself as to endanger the morals or health of himself, herself, or others.

Subsection 4a is essentially the same as the California Section 602, and subsections 4b through 4d are the same as the California Section 601.

Florida.   Florida's definition of juvenile-status offenders and delinquents is similar to those of California and Pennsylvania. Chapter 39 of the Florida statutes states:

(11) "Child in need of supervision" means a child under the age of 18 years who:
    (a) Being subject to compulsory school attendance, is truant from school.
    (b) Persistently disobeys the reasonable and lawful demands of his parents or other custodians and is beyond their control.
    (c) Has run away from his parent or other custodian.
(12) "Delinquent child" means a child who commits a violation of law, regardless of where the violation occurs, except a child who commits a juvenile traffic offense and whose case has not been transferred to the circuit court by the court having jurisdiction. (1974–1975)

The wording of the laws in California, Pennsylvania, and Florida is different, but the theme is almost identical. The same is true for the other 47 state laws regulating juvenile behavior. Essentially, juveniles come under the jurisdiction of the juvenile court either for a status offense or for violation of a law. Now that we can see what *may* constitute a delinquent act and define a delinquent person, we need to examine how delinquency is typically handled on a day-to-day basis in our society.

SOCIAL ASPECTS OF DELINQUENCY

In developing a sociological understanding of delinquency, we will focus on certain features over others. A key sociological concept is that of *social interaction,* that is, what the actions of an individual are in relation to the actions of others, such as two people taking turns talking. Therefore, we will consider how the social reality of delinquency is created as people interact with one another.

On one level we can say that delinquency is any act that violates the delinquency laws[5] and that a delinquent is anyone of juvenile age who engages in such acts. If we consider the broad aspects of the delinquency laws, it is difficult to imagine any young person who could *not* be said to have violated some part of the law—and that would mean that all of us have probably been delinquents at one time or other. Surely, if we closely examined any single juvenile's biography, we would very likely find some act that could be interpreted as a violation of delinquency laws. For example, a group of youths hiking in a rural area crossed a farmer's field without permission. In a strict legalistic interpretation, we could say that the juveniles had violated a law by trespassing and so had committed a delinquent act.

If we continue this reasoning and say that any juvenile who commits a delinquent act is a juvenile delinquent (as is explicitly stated in the Pennsylvania and Florida laws), then the youths who trespassed are indeed delinquents. Following this further, we see that since it is unlikely that anyone can grow up without doing *something* that can be assessed as being in violation of the law, then by this purely legal definition most if not all juveniles are also juvenile delinquents.

In reality, however, we recognize only certain juveniles as being delinquent, and it is unrealistic to say that all juveniles are delinquents. One problem with this purely legalistic view is that it assumes that delinquent acts exist in the world independent of social interpretations of these acts. It is the assessment of an act that makes it delinquent, not the act alone.[6] Using our example of the hikers who trespassed on the farmer's land, we will examine the different possible assessments of the act by the people involved. First, the youths may or may not see the action as an offense. If they do, they may simply regard the action as "wrong," "naughty," or "sneaky" but not illegal. Similarly, the farmer may assess the hikers' action in a number of ways. He might recall that he did the same thing in his own boyhood and disregard the trespassing. On the other hand, he might worry about the possibility of a civil suit should something happen to the young people while on his land and therefore call the police to arrest them. If the police are called, they may not see the trespassing as in any way constituting delinquency and may simply tell the youths to go home and stay off private property in the future. Or the police may view the event as serious and arrest the juveniles. If the youths are arrested and taken to a detention center, the probation department may or may not see their behavior as warranting court action. Whatever the decisions, clearly numerous interpretations of the action must be made for it to be treated as "really delinquent." Therefore, to understand delinquency we must consider its interactional as well as its legal aspects.

DELINQUENCY DEFINED

Having considered both the legal and social implications of a delinquent act, we must include both aspects in our definition. This will be a *sociolegal* definition of delinquency:

> *Juvenile delinquency is the characterization of an act by a juvenile as a violation of delinquency laws.*

The person who takes an action that might be characterized as delinquent will be referred to here as the *actor* and those who assess the action in terms of delinquency as *others*. Since an individual may assess his or her own behavior, the actor can simultaneously be both actor and other.[7] That is, if an actor characterizes his or her own behavior as violating the delinquency laws even though nobody else is around, the act can be considered delinquent. For example, if the youths who trespassed on the farmer's land had tried to avoid detection for fear of being arrested, they would have been characterizing their own actions in terms of the law. But the farmer who owns the land might have seen the situation as perfectly innocent, and the notion that the youths were violating the law may never have entered his mind.

However, by our definition, since at least some of the people involved viewed the act in terms of a violation of the law, we can speak of the act as delinquent.

Often, there is uncertainty as to whether an act is delinquent or not. This is especially true when the judgment involves the *intentions* of the actors. A common but petty delinquent activity is malicious mischief, but depending on the nature of the mischief, it can be considered serious or minor. Depending on the assumed intentions of the juveniles who are engaged in malicious mischief, others will either see the behavior as intentionally malicious or as the more or less accidental result of carelessness. For example, if a police officer sees a group of boys start a landside onto a roadway, he might approach them with the intention of arresting them for malicious mischief. The boys may explain that the landside was an accident and volunteer to clear away the rocks. If the officer believes them, he or she reassesses the act as not being a violation of the law. Therefore, even though the act was initially characterized as a violation, it is reformulated as an "accident." The assessment in this case was that the act was an accident and not delinquent, and so by our definition the act would not be delinquent. Under the same circumstances if the police officer did not accept the boys' account and had arrested the youths, the act would have been considered a delinquent one.

DELINQUENT DEFINED

Now that we have defined a delinquent act, we will define a delinquent actor, or juvenile delinquent. The immediate temptation is simply to define a delinquent as anyone who engages in a delinquent act based on our definition of delinquency. Here, however, we are dealing with a *social identity* rather than a *social action*, and even though the two are related, they are not the same thing. A social identity refers to the way in which a person is typically identified by others, while a social action is an activity interpreted in terms of social interaction.

In order to see the difference between committing a delinquent act and being a delinquent, consider how others would view a group of high school students arrested for drinking. The act has been socially and officially defined as delinquent, but is not really atypical of juvenile behavior. The youths' parents, friends, and probably even their probation officer would not be likely to view the juveniles as "real delinquents," but instead as simply some "kids who got into trouble." On the other hand, consider a boy who hangs around with a delinquent gang but for some reason has never committed a delinquent act. Because of his associations, others are likely to identify the boy as a delinquent. Even though he has never been seen breaking the law, others are likely to assume that he simply has not been caught. What is important in defining a delinquent, then, is not so much the actual commission of delinquent acts but the assumptions that others make about the individual.

Given the above considerations, we can define a delinquent as follows:

A juvenile delinquent is anyone whose character, biography, and actions are assessed in terms of his/her having committed delinquent acts.

The definition does not imply that there is no connection between committing delinquent acts and being identified as a delinquent. Indeed most juveniles who are identified as delinquents are judged as such on the basis of their having violated the law. However, far more juveniles engage in delinquency than are identified as delinquents. Moreover, as Kai Erikson[8] has noted, most people who are identified as deviant spend the vast majority of their time engaging in nondeviant activity. A boy who takes part in gang fights once or twice a year but is otherwise not a delinquent is going to be identified as a *bona fide* delinquent. Therefore, it is more than just the delinquent act itself that results in the label delinquent.

A further example will help clarify the difference between committing a delinquent act and being a delinquent. Suppose a girl is caught shoplifting. If the store manager calls the girl's parents instead of reporting the incident to the police, the act will not be considered an "official" delinquency, even though clearly it is considered delinquent. The girl's parents might say that the shoplifting "isn't like her" or otherwise deny that the act and their daughter's character have anything in common. Therefore, they do not assess their daughter's past and future behavior in terms of her being a delinquent.

On the other hand, in another set of circumstances, the girl who shoplifted could be assessed as typically engaging in delinquent behavior. The store manager catching the girl may decide, "I'm going to stop this *delinquent* and have the police lock her up." The police will then be likely to set up an official record of the delinquent act, attaching the act to the person. The girl's parents may speak of their daughter's delinquent act as "just like her" or may say, "We're not surprised." The girl's future behavior, such as getting poor grades or staying out late, may be judged in terms of her "being a delinquent," and this second course of action by others—unlike the first course of action for essentially the same behavior—labels the girl as a delinquent. The mere act of delinquency was insufficient for the girl to be judged *a delinquent.*

As we have seen in discussing delinquent acts and identities, actors and others define behaviors and people as delinquent. The question that arises in these definitions is exactly *who* is doing the labeling and the defining. For example, driving down the street a man and his wife see some juveniles standing on the corner. The man turns to his wife and says, "Look at those delinquents hanging around the corner." In such a case it is highly unlikely that the man's comments to his wife or even to the juveniles is going to have much impact on the identity or actions of the youths. But if a mother tells her daughter that she is "a no good little tramp," or a police officer uses his power of arrest to take a youth into custody for a delinquent act, the words and actions are going to have a great deal of impact. Therefore, in considering delinquency and delinquents, *consequential others* are those who engage in the kinds of definitions relevant to our concerns. The concept of "consequential others," borrowed from Erving Goffman's concept of "consequentiality,"[9] refers to the fact that *anyone's definition that has a significant effect on another's actions, including the labeling of the individual's actions or identity, is a consequential other.*

AMOUNT, DISTRIBUTION, AND MEASUREMENT OF DELINQUENCY

How much delinquency is there? Who commits delinquency? What kinds of delinquencies are most common and least common? What changes in the patterns of delinquency have occurred over time?

As we have pointed out, just about every juvenile has engaged in at least one delinquent act, and most have been involved in more. It does little good, however, to say that virtually every juvenile engages in delinquency. We need to know something about the patterns of delinquency and delinquents so that we can determine if there are certain conditions that are associated with delinquency. For example, if we find that there is more delinquency per capita in cities than in rural areas, then we can examine the conditions that are unique to urban areas to isolate the factors that contribute to delinquency. But if we do not have an accurate picture of delinquency in urban and rural areas, then we have no basis for comparison and analysis. Likewise, we need to know something about general patterns of delinquency so that we can tell whether there have been any changes in the frequency and distribution of delinquency as well as identify trends. Without such information we cannot know if there was more juvenile delinquency in the 1970s than in the 1960s. Likewise, by noting the patterns of the past, we can begin to understand emerging patterns in the 1980s and predict into the 1990s.

Official Statistics

As a point of departure we can look at the official statistics generated by the police, courts, and corrections departments. The most widely used official statistics are based on the number of crimes reported to and recorded by police departments as well as arrest records. From these data it has been estimated that over half of the major property crimes—burglary, larceny, and auto theft—are committed by persons under 21 years of age.[10] Since this estimate was made on the basis of arrests, it may be that juveniles are more easily caught than adults, especially for high-visibility crimes such as "joy riding." If this is the case, then inferences based on police data probably overestimate juvenile involvement in such crimes. On the other hand, we know that the police often give young offenders a "break," often taking them home to their parents rather than arresting them.[11] To the extent that juveniles "get off" in such offenses, juvenile involvement in property crimes is underestimated. Moreover, since we know only that the persons arrested were under 21, we do not know how many were juveniles because most states define juveniles as under 18. How many were between 18 and 21?

Being Noticed.   Additionally, we must consider the process whereby people come to the attention of the police and thus become statistics in official data. One study found that white victims were less likely than black victims to demand that an arrest be made in delinquency situations.[12] Since blacks are usually involved with black victims and whites with white victims, a greater proportion of black juveniles are arrested because black victims are more likely to demand that black delinquents be arrested. Thus, when we consider that 41 percent of black 15-year-olds in Philadelphia have official delinquency records,[13] we cannot be certain to what extent those figures reflect delinquent activities among inner-city black youths and to what extent they indicate the black community's demand for the police to exercise their arrest options in delinquent situations.

Furthermore, it has been found that "tough-looking" lower-class black youths are more likely to be arrested than the "clean-cut" boys—namely, middle-class white youths.[14] As a result, we would expect that black youths in situations where just the youth and the police officer are present would be more likely to be arrested than white youths. Thus, since the arrest records and the statistics derived from those records are based on actual arrest and not merely encounters, the statistics compiled by the police are as much a reflection of their own policies and practices as they are of the incidence of delinquent activities and reports of such activities.

Detention Data.   On the other end of the scale of official statistics are those based on juveniles in detention. This population is supposed to represent the "real delinquent group." It is argued that by studying the "hard-core" delinquents we can better understand the underlying causes of all delinquency. For example, from 1971 to 1973 the juvenile population in public detention decreased by more than 16 percent, from 54,729 in 1971 to 45,694 in 1973.[15] Can we say that the "hard-core" delinquents decreased by 16 percent? If we did, it would be inaccurate for two reasons. First, during the period between 1971 and 1973 there was an increase in diversion programs aimed at getting juveniles out of detention and putting them into community-based programs.[16] Second, a large proportion of youths who were locked up in detention before the advent of diversion programs, including half of the girls, were there for juvenile-status offenses rather than serious delinquency. Thus the notion that because youths are locked up they are "hard core" is a misinformed idea centering around the official reaction to delinquency.

A further problem in studying incarcerated juveniles as an appropriate population for explaining delinquency lies in the differential patterns of youths who are placed in detention. Goldman reported that of those youths arrested by the police, 33.6 percent of the white youngsters were referred to juvenile court (and possible detention), while 64.8 percent of the arrested black youngsters were referred to court.[17] Likewise, in a study of juveniles who were detained in Denver, Colorado, it was found that minority youths and youths from lower socioeconomic groups were more likely to be detained than white youths and those from higher socioeconomic groups.[18] Thus, if we study just the detained juveniles, we are likely to prejudice our explanations and understandings of juvenile delinquency, since the populations in detention facilities are a reflection of juvenile justice practices as well as the patterns of delinquency.

What Official Statistics Tell Us.   Using official statistics for estimating the frequency and distribution of delinquency is perhaps better than sheer speculation or reliance on sensationalist accounts of crime and delinquency in the media and popular literature. It is important to understand, however, that official delinquency statistics are *not* a random sample of all delinquency. This is true for several reasons. First, certain delinquent acts are more likely to be reported than others—typically the more serious over the less serious. The result is that a disproportionate amount of more serious offenses makes up the total picture of delinquency. Second, official policies toward juvenile delinquency change over time, and delinquency statistics reflect these changing policies. Third, certain groups are more likely than others to come to the attention of juvenile authorities, and as a result there is a biased population of "official delinquents." There are additional problems associated with official statistics, such as manipulation of records for fiscal considerations, but for now it is enough to recognize the three we have mentioned. At the same time, while we know that the official statistics are biased, those juveniles who come to be "officially recognized" as delinquents do make up the bulk of socially defined delinquents. Thus even though there is a great deal of bias, official statistics do tell us something about the way in which society selects its delinquents.

Victimization Surveys

Recognizing the problems with official statistics, delinquency and crime researchers have sought new ways to study the frequency and distribution of crime and delinquency. One technique is the *victimization survey,* which involves surveying a sample population to determine what proportion has been victimized by crime. Interviewers ask people whether they have been the victims of crime, the types of crimes, and whether they reported the incidents to the police. The survey data can be compared with the police data to determine what proportion of crime in an area is reported to and recorded by the police.

Since victimization surveys do not differentiate between delinquent and criminal activities, it is still necessary to use general estimates to determine the amount of delinquency. For example, persons who are burglarized are unlikely to know whether the burglar was a juvenile or an adult. However, by examining typical juvenile crimes, such as car theft and petty larceny, we can get a better idea of the actual amount of certain delinquent acts. For example, bicycle theft is a typical form of juvenile larceny, and one victimization survey found that only 53 percent of all bicycle thefts were reported to the police.[19] According to police records, there were about 13 bicycle thefts per 1,000 population, but the victimization survey showed that there were about 24 bicycle thefts for the same population, or almost twice what had been reported. Likewise, another victimization survey found that larcenies occurred at the rate of 80 per 1,000 while the police data showed only 15,[20] or five times less. Based on arrests, it is estimated that half of all larcenies are committed by juveniles. If this is the case, victimization surveys show that there is far more delinquency than estimates based on official statistics. This means that in order to understand the patterns of delinquency, it is necessary to take into account the "hidden delinquency" as well as the official statistics.

Crime Ratios.   One value of victimization surveys in increasing the validity of police statistics is that they set up a ratio of known to unknown crimes. For example, with the information that the ratio of known to unknown larcenies is one to five (1:5), and we know that 378 larcenies were reported to the police in a certain week, we can estimate that five times that number, or 1,890 larcenies, took place. Further, by estimating the proportion of juveniles typically involved in various crimes we can obtain a more realistic idea of how many delinquent acts have been committed. Thus, if on the basis of victimization-survey ratios we estimate that there were 1,890 larcenies in a week and that 50 percent involved juveniles, then 945 larcenies were instances of juvenile delinquency.

Self-Report Surveys

Another device that researchers employ to determine the frequency and distribution of juvenile delinquency is the *self-report survey*. Unlike the victimization survey, which samples victims of crime and delinquency, self-report surveys sample juveniles who have been involved in crime and delinquency. By having youths fill out questionnaires asking them about various juvenile-status offenses and delinquent acts, it is possible to get an estimate of the proportion of the juvenile population that has been involved in a number of different delinquencies. The report of the President's Commission concluded that 90 percent of all young people have committed at least one act for which they could have been brought before juvenile court.[21] Many of the offenses to which youths admit are relatively trivial, yet they are serious enough in the eyes of juvenile authorities to require court action.

Drawbacks.   The major problem with the self-report survey is its lack of a standardized format. Different surveys use different questions or deal with the same question in different ways. As a result, when different instruments are employed it is often difficult to compare one group of juveniles to another or the same group over time. Police statistics were drawn up along the lines of the FBI's *Uniform Crime Report,* and victimization surveys follow the standardized, if unwieldy, format employed in government surveys. Any comparisons made between self-report surveys must be done on the basis of specific questions and/or groupings. For example, in a 1972 study[22] students were questioned about a wide variety of offenses, broken down by school class; another study comparing the same group in 1971 and 1973 grouped all students together and concentrated only on drug use.[23] In the first study there was an increase in the proportion of students who had used marijuana as their class grade moved up, so that depending upon the grade used for comparison, there would be different results. The 12th-graders reported that 41 percent had used marijuana, but only 18 percent of the 11th-graders reported having tried the drug. In the second study 34 percent of the students in 1971 had tried marijuana, and 37 percent of the 1973 group had. In order to compare the two studies, the first done in Indiana and the second in California, it would be necessary first to average the percentages of the Indiana study. Doing this, researchers found that 19 percent of the Indiana group had tried marijuana and compared to the California group had less marijuana use among junior and senior high students.

Since the above example involved only *one* question, and the findings had to be recalculated in order to make that comparison, the usefulness of standardizing self-report questionnaires is obvious. Unfortunately, no such format exists at this time, and many of the studies using self-report surveys are interested only in a specific form of delinquency, necessitating specialized formats. The Appendix of this book contains a general self-report survey covering the major forms of delinquency discussed in this text. The form is very simple and is designed to be employed by virtually anyone, even those without a methodological background.

Patterns Confirmed by Self-Report Surveys.   Self-report surveys can still help to gauge the patterns of delinquency, but they must be used cautiously and generally. First, virtually all self-report surveys have found that far more youths have been involved in delinquency than are officially labeled delinquent. This is not to say that the delinquency problem is far greater than we realize based on official statistics, especially detention statistics, but there is a good deal of selectivity in who does and does not become labeled.

A second pattern confirmed by self-report surveys is that fads involving delinquency change over time. For example, in a 1958 study [24] only 3 percent of the high school students reported that they had ever sold or used a narcotic drug of any kind. Compared with the Indiana and California studies cited above, along with an additional study conducted in Illinois,[25] there is fairly clear evidence that there was a definite increase in drug use among juveniles, especially among middle- and upper-class white youths. Of course, it did not take self-report surveys to inform the public that drug use among teenagers was on the rise, but such devices were able to tell us more specifically the nature of the change that was taking place.

Other variations in juvenile delinquency measured by self-report surveys include differences based on sex, social class, age group, and area of the country. Combined with victimization surveys and official statistics, self-report surveys have added to our knowledge of the phenomenon of delinquency. As with the other instruments, however, we still must refine and develop our techniques, and our conclusions must be stated with more than a grain of humility.

CHANGING PATTERNS OF DELINQUENCY

As we just saw, there was a clear change in the patterns of juvenile drug use in the mid-1960s, and there have been changes in other areas of delinquency as well. When a new form of delinquency is first identified there is great public concern—even panic—and either it goes away or becomes accepted and gradually integrated into social mores. When white middle-class youths first began using marijuana there was an outcry for tougher drug laws, but only 10 years later such conservative states as Mississippi had passed laws decriminalizing marijuana, making possession of the drug punishable only by a fine.

Fads and Cults

Other fads and styles of the past that are now viewed as either passé or a part of mainstream life include everything from rock and roll to the hippies. When Elvis Presley introduced his style of rock and roll many groups believed that his influence was decisively "delinquent," but during later Presley performances before devout fans who had teen-aged children themselves, the earlier fears appeared quaint. Similarly, few Californians recall the widespread distaste for surfers, yet many southern Californians in the early 1960s were greatly upset about the "surf bums," and the police, business people (many of whom refused to hire any youth who admitted to surfing), and the general public saw surfing as a path to delinquency. Further shocks came with the hippies, who not only smoked marijuana and took LSD but openly admitted and advocated such activities. They wore long hair and turned their backs on the Establishment, making parents wish their children would take up the wholesome sport of surfing. In the later 1970s when many of the styles introduced by the hippies had become either out of date or part of conventional society, former hippies were outraged by "punk rock" and the violence of its songs and actions.

Other fads that were seen as a positive move away from delinquency also cropped up, but many of them were later seen to be "going too far" away from conventional morality. For example, when the "Jesus Freak" movement started, many of the early converts were youths looking for meaning they had otherwise not found, especially in drug use. However, many of the cults that emerged were seen as fanatical and undermining of parental authority. Especially singled out as a target were such groups as the "Moonies" and similar cults that demanded and got total dedication from their followers, even though there is little evidence that such movements contributed to delinquency. When over 900 followers of Jim Jones committed mass suicide in Guyana, virtually all of whom were Americans and many of them juveniles, the religious groups outside of the conventional ones were seen as a great danger to youths.

Meanings of Fads.   In order to understand patterns of delinquent behavior as new fads and forms of delinquency emerge, it is important to understand the meanings of the acts that come to be seen as delinquent. On the one hand, the acts have meanings for the juveniles, which may or may not be shared by others who observe these acts. For example, when people were upset by the surfers the meaning that the appearance of a surfer took on for certain segments of the community was that of a dangerous youth—a delinquent. The surfers, on the other hand, saw different meanings in their activities and life-styles. What for the surfers was "having fun" was for others "disgusting, delinquent behavior." On numerous occasions the police were called on the basis of the meanings the observers held. To the police who arrived on the scene the surfers would explain the events in terms of their own meanings, no matter what they were actually doing. Whatever behaviors others found "disgusting" were so viewed because it was the surfers who were engaging in them much as because of the nature of the activities themselves. For example, surfers drinking beer around a beach fire and engaging in horseplay might well be seen as delinquent behavior, but if a fraternity group (excluding the denizens of "Animal House") were doing the same thing, the scene would more likely be seen as only slightly naughty and not warranting a call to the police. For the police, the surfers' actions might hold the meanings formulated by the complainants—or, less frequently, of the surfers themselves. If the police interpreted the situation in terms of what the complainants saw, they could charge the surfers with anything from disturbing the peace to malicious mischief, based on the meaning of the situation, not just the situation itself.

Since meanings are generally social ones because they are shared by a segment of society, we can expect to find patterns of meanings as well as patterns of delinquent activities. Viewing the smoking of marijuana as something engaged in by "dope fiends" and viewing it as "less harmful than alcohol" imply two quite different meanings of the same activity. As the pattern of meanings change from the former to the latter, so too will the social meanings of marijuana smoking and delinquency. Youthful marijuana smokers today are not seen to be "hooked on dope"; instead, they are more likely to be thought of as "experimenting," "being naughty," or simply "getting high." The former meaning implies delinquency while the latter suggests a Huckleberry Finn mischievousness. Thus, we must be careful in the study of juvenile delinquency to understand the activities in terms of the appropriate meanings linked to them.

Summary

The answer to the question, "How much delinquency is there?" is not a simple one. We cannot rely on police and court records, because they reflect only crimes reported and youths arrested. Less than 4 percent of the juvenile population appears in court in any given year,[26] but we find in examining self-report surveys that almost all youths engage in delinquent acts for which they *could* be brought before juvenile court. Further, the victimization surveys show that far more crime is committed than is reported, but we can only guess, on the basis of arrests, at the proportion committed by juveniles. We know that juveniles in general are likely to commit at least some delinquent acts and that the nature of the acts as well as the volume changes over time. However, we still cannot say exactly how much delinquency exists. What we do know is that almost every juvenile commits a delinquent act at one time or another and that only a fraction of these offenses are brought before the courts. Therefore, there is a massive amount of activity characterized as delinquent, of which the police and court records reflect very little.

DELINQUENCY AS A TRANSITORY AND PERMANENT PHENOMENON: A SITUATIONAL PERSPECTIVE

 The juvenile phase in life that we all pass through lasts only a few years. The majority of youths who engaged in delinquency, including those who are officially recognized as delinquents, grow out of it, however, as they mature and become social and legal adults. In part this is because they are no longer subject to juvenile-status statutes, but those who engage in typical crimes committed by juveniles, such as petty larceny, vandalism, and battery (fist fights), also give them up as they grow up. In this respect delinquency is transitory in a person's life—like acne, it is a plague of juveniles that goes away with maturity.

On the other hand, delinquency appears to be permanent over time. Ever since the American Revolution, and indeed since well before then, every generation of juveniles and just about everyone passing through this in-between stage of life has fallen into delinquent situations with greater or lesser intensity. For some individuals it is merely a single stumble, and for others it is a leap into the official records, but delinquency is a definite pattern among juveniles.

Because delinquency is not peculiar to just a few juveniles, we will not be concentrating on the question of what went wrong with a youth. Rather, we will concentrate on the occasions where juveniles come into delinquent occasions. We will *not* divide the juvenile world into delinquent and nondelinquent youths, but instead the focus will be on the delinquent and nondelinquent *situation.* As social occasions, we can begin to understand why youths enter into such activities, and at the same time why they grow out of them. The social occasions of delinquency during the juvenile years are transgenerational, and while the forms and fads may differ, the delinquent situations remain; only the actors change. In this way we can understand why delinquency is both transitory and permanent.

At the same time that we will investigate the delinquent situation, we will be concerned with how involvement in such situations leads to the label of delinquent. By using the concept of the delinquent occasion, we can see that there is a difference between engaging in juvenile delinquency and being a juvenile delinquent.

An Approach to Delinquency

The situational perspective taken in this book is a sociological one, and as a result we will give most of our attention to the interactive, institutional, and organizational aspects of delinquency. However, given this perspective, there are several ways we may approach the phenomenon. We can attempt to be humanistic, hard-nosed, objective, detached, or involved. None of these approaches guarantees a successful understanding of delinquency, and each has its merits. Therefore, rather than adopting an approach that necessarily excludes or includes a given course of action, we will take an *open approach.* This implies the investigation of evidence from many different viewpoints, but at the same time we will maintain a focus on the delinquent situation so that we can keep track of the important elements of delinquency.

Our own biases are difficult to overcome, and this is especially true with a subject matter such as delinquency. Remembering our own delinquencies, we are prone to be forgiving and understanding in the sense that we forgive or forget our own misbehavior, and we may attempt to "understand" all delinquency from this viewpoint. Conversely, we encounter examples of the terrible carnage caused by juvenile thugs who are released by the courts. This may have us examine delinquency in terms of vengeance, demanding stiffer penalties. But the truth of the matter is that whether we see juveniles who engage in delinquency as misunderstood children who need guidance or young "punks" who require firm punishment is irrelevant. Our love or hatred of juveniles or their actions will not aid our understanding. As we will see later in the book, the harshest punishment may lead to violent delinquency, and the most humane intentions may lead to the most perverted punishment. What is important is that we examine delinquency in the same way that we would look at any other social phenomenon. We must go deep into the delinquent occasion, and at the same time stand back and look at the overall patterns of these occasions. We will find poverty, broken homes, arbitrary arrests, racism, and terrible suffering by both victims and delinquents, but these obvious, and often journalistic, renditions often hide the roots of the problem. We find massive delinquency in middle- and upper-middle-class youths who have complete homes, plenty of money, and the skin color we typically assume to minimize delinquent activity. A middle-class morality and bias of sorts exists when we jump on the opportunity to cite poverty as the cause of crime and delinquency, wagging our heads at the sight of poor youths in juvenile court. Some people even assume that the poor really do not mind delinquency, but the poor, especially those in minority groups, are the greatest victims of violent delinquency, and they very much mind crime and delinquency.

The problem lies in what people *avoid* looking at in attempting to explain delinquency. The tendency is to gloss over that which disproves a favored position and magnify evidence that goes along with what we already think. For this book, we will take a critical look at numerous facets of delinquency and examine as much evidence as possible, especially the overwhelming data concerning hidden delinquency, which while mentioned in studies of delinquency, has been ignored for its theoretical importance. Moreover, we will operate within a framework so that we do not simply marshall a number of facts without meaning.

SUMMARY

In this chapter we began by looking at the scope of delinquency, seeing that a wide variety of juvenile behaviors can be considered to be delinquent. The bases for the different delinquencies are the laws that define juvenile-status offenses and juvenile criminal offenses, and these laws are subject to a social filtering through interpretations. From these foundations a definition of delinquency and delinquents was developed that accounts for both the legal and social elements that must be considered in any study of juvenile delinquency. We examined the various measuring techniques delinquency researchers use and learned that rather than being an isolated anomaly among a small segment of society, delinquency is widespread. Therefore, it is necessary to consider the juvenile years as a period in one's life during which delinquent occasions are encountered. We developed the concept of the delinquent occasion and situation, leading us to investigate the social circumstances in which delinquency occurs rather than examining only the delinquent actor. Throughout this book we will use the idea of the delinquent occasion as a primary focal point, but at the same time we will look at the social forces that lead certain juveniles to one form of delinquency or another. In this way it is hoped that we can understand both the situation of delinquency as well as the delinquent actor.

NOTES

1. Paul A. Strasburg, *Violent Delinquents: A Report to the Ford Foundation from the Vera Institute of Justice* (New York: Monarch, 1978), p. 41.
2. Donald J. Black and Albert J. Reiss, Jr., "Police Control of Juveniles," *American Sociological Review, 35*:63–67 (February 1970).
3. National Criminal Justice Information and Statistics Service, *Children in Custody: A Report on the Juvenile Detention and Correctional Facility Census of 1971* (Washington, D.C.: Law Enforcement Assistance Administration, 1974), p. 1.
4. *Ibid.*
5. Don C. Gibbons, *Delinquent Behavior,* 2d ed. (Englewood Cliffs, N.J.: Prentice-Hall, 1976), p. 5.
6. Clayton Hartjen, *Crime and Criminalization* (New York: Praeger, 1974), pp. 5–8.
7. Herbert Blumer, *Symbolic Interaction: Perspective and Method* (Englewood Cliffs, N.J.: Prentice-Hall, 1969).
8. Kai Erikson, "Notes on the Sociology of Deviance," *Social Problems, 9*:307–314 (Spring 1962).
9. Erving Goffman, *Interaction Ritual* (New York: Doubleday, 1967), p. 159.
10. President's Commission on Law Enforcement and Administration of Justice, *The Challenge of Crime in a Free Society* (Washington, D.C.: Government Printing Office, 1967), p. 55.
11. Black and Reiss, p. 64.
12. *Ibid.,* pp. 65–66.
13. National Institute for Juvenile Justice and Delinquency Prevention, "City Life and Delinquency" (Washington, D.C.: Department of Justice, April 1977), p. 1.
14. Irving Piliavin and Scott Briar, "Police Encounters with Juveniles," *American Journal of Sociology, 70*:206–214 (September 1964).
15. U.S. Department of Justice, *Children in Custody* (Washington, D.C.: Government Printing Office, May 1975), p. 1.
16. Andrew Rutherford and Robert McDermott, *Juvenile Diversion* (Washington, D.C.: Government Printing Office, September 1976).
17. Nathan Goldman, "The Differential Selection of Juvenile Offenders for Court Appearances," in Arthur Niederhoffer and Abraham S. Blumberg (eds.), *The Ambivalent Force* (New York: Holt, Rinehart and Winston, 1976), pp. 183–187.

18. Lawrence Cohen, "Who Gets Detained? An Empirical Analysis of the Pre-Adjudicatory Detention of Juveniles in Denver" (Washington, D.C.: Department of Justice, 1975), pp. 18–19.
19. William B. Sanders and Brian McCarthy, "Survey of Crime Victims," in William B. Sanders (ed.), *The Sociologist as Detective* (New York: Praeger, 1976).
20. President's Commission, p. 21.
21. *Ibid.,* p. 55.
22. Max J. Mobley and Richard M. Swanson, *Indiana Youth Survey,* Vol. 2 (Carbondale, Ill.: Center for the Study of Crime, Delinquency, and Corrections, n.d.), p. D-31.
23. Donald W. Bowers and Lynn White, *Behavior and Attitudes: A Longitudinal Perspective* (Turlock, Calif.: California State College, Stanislaus, n.d.), pp. 10–12.
24. James F. Short, Jr., and Ivan F. Nye, "Extent of Unrecorded Juvenile Delinquency: Tentative Conclusions," *Journal of Criminal Law, Criminology, and Police Science, 49*:296–302 (Nov.–Dec. 1958).
25. William B. Sanders, "Drug Use among Suburban Midwest High School Students," unpublished consultant paper prepared for Palos Township Youth Council, Illinois, 1970.
26. Office of Youth Development, *Juvenile Court Statistics, 1972* (Washington, D.C.: Department of Health, Education and Welfare, 1974), p. 11.

2 Explaining Delinquency

INTRODUCTION

In this chapter we will begin to examine the problem of how to explain delinquency. Essentially this will involve an examination of theories of delinquency, but we will also need to consider delinquency in the larger context of both deviance and crime. Additionally, we will look at some early explanations to provide an analytic and historical context for the sociological theories to be discussed in Chapters 3 and 4.

First, we will focus on the concepts of deviance and crime, showing the similarities and differences between these concepts and that of delinquency. In Chapter 1 we saw the various legal and social nuances of delinquency, and we must consider these in relation to the more general issues of norm violation and law violation as they apply to deviance and crime.

Second, we will see what is necessary to provide an adequate explanation or theory of delinquency. While there are many explanations for delinquency, we must establish criteria by which we can measure the validity of the different theories offered.

Third, we will examine various early explanations of crime and delinquency, including a number that are still used today. By employing the criteria used to assess the adequacy of theory, we will isolate these explanations to determine to what extent they are useful in understanding delinquency.

DEVIANCE AND CRIME

Social norms refer to guides or rules of behavior for people in given situations at given times.[1] Violation of norms is *deviance.* Deviance spans a broad range of behaviors, from minor norm violations such as public nose picking to major offenses such as multiple ax murders. Moreover, there is a great deal of situational relativity in deviance, and what is perfectly acceptable in one situation is outrageous in another. Mundane sexual relations in private situations is considered perfectly normal, but in a classroom situation the same activity would be met with incredulity and severe sanctions. What is deviant, too, depends upon the group one is with when the question of deviance arises. Smoking marijuana is illegal, and as such it violates a norm, but among many groups anyone who refuses to take part in the activity, no matter what the situation, is considered deviant by the marijuana-using group.

In the study of delinquency the question of deviance revolves around violation of the larger societal norms and conformity to peer-group norms. If a youth commits an act for which he or she receives social sanctions in terms of the juvenile justice system, we are dealing with a form of societal deviance. However, if the societal deviance occurred because a youth was conforming to peer-group norms, then it would be difficult to argue that we are dealing with deviance *per se.* Rather, we have a dual set of norms—the larger norms of society, including legal ones, and the norms governing juveniles, which may or may not be in conflict with general societal norms. In addition, we may find all types of subcultural norms governing different groups of adults and juveniles. Therefore, we must give a good deal of attention to the context of actions in order to assess the *sense of norm violation* for both those who break the rules and those who make judgments about the rule violators.

Compared to deviance, crime is far more specific and is not subject to the same kind of group relativity in society as is deviance. Crime refers to the violation of a formal societal norm or law.[2] Defined legally, a crime is an offense against the state punishable by a fine, imprisonment, or some other specified penalty.[3] The key to this definition is that the violation of the law is *punishable by the state,* and the act is considered to be *against the state.* This means that persons who have committed crimes have committed offenses against society as a whole, and punishment is in the name of all the people.

Crimes differ from deviance in that the latter covers a far broader range of offenses, including crime, and an act of deviance can be taken to be against either individuals or groups. Further, the laws of a society apply to all people in that society, whereas norms may apply only to some groups and not others. For example, shoplifting may not be a violation of the norms of a juvenile group, but it is against the law and therefore is a crime.

Ideally, in a democratic society laws are supposed to reflect the collective will of the people. Enacted by elected officials in national, state, and local jurisdictions, criminal laws should reflect important social norms. In a pluralistic society with many different groups and interests and vastly different amounts of power for both individuals and groups, however, we find that most laws represent the interests of the powerful more than they do the will of the whole.[4] In later chapters we will see that the laws governing juveniles were formulated and enacted in the interests of small powerful groups. It is important, therefore, to understand from the outset that while many laws do represent the ideal of collective sentiment, there is no necessary connection between the law and a popular consensus of what is right and wrong.

The differences between crime and delinquency lie more in degree and societal response than in formal substance. All crimes are also delinquent, but as we saw in Chapter 1, delinquency includes both crime and juvenile-status offenses. But since status offenses have the same official character as criminal laws and are legally constituted in the same way, they differ from criminal laws only in that many tend to be less specific and more encompassing. In addition, punishment is not attached to them in the same way as it is specified for criminal acts. Juvenile-status offenders typically will become wardships of juvenile court, while criminal laws specify fines, prison terms, or other specific punishments for violators.

We will see that the more general theories of deviance cover explanations that apply to all types of norm violations, including delinquency. Likewise, criminological theories account for much of what we seek to explain in delinquency, but they are still somewhat broader in that they include all forms of criminal violations, many of which are not applicable to juveniles, such as white-collar crimes. In examining theories of delinquency, while we will find many elements of deviance and criminological theory, we will see that there are aspects that pertain only to juvenile delinquency.

CRITERIA FOR AN ADEQUATE THEORY OF DELINQUENCY

In our examination of theories of delinquency we need some measuring stick by which we can judge the adequacy of theory. The essential question a theory must address and answer is, *Why is a delinquent form of behavior taken as opposed to a nondelinquent form*? Depending upon its assumptions, a theory will either attend to this basic question or not and focus on one set of concerns or another. Therefore, not only does a theory tell us what questions to ask, it also indicates what is important to examine in attempting to understand delinquency. For example, the early theories we will examine at the end of this chapter focus on biological and developmental aspects of delinquency, while sociological theories take into account everything from peer-group pressure to societal reaction to delinquency.

At the outset we must take care to avoid the fallacy of explaining delinquency through the goals expressed in delinquent acts.[5]

For example, we might ask why some runaway girls turn to prostitution. One answer that prostitutes themselves often give is that they do it for the money. Such a statement explains the delinquent activity by the payoff. Since academics are often chided for overlooking the obvious, it might seem that explaining prostitution in terms of financial reward isn't so far from the truth. However, if we think for a moment, we will see that people do a lot of things "for the money." Students go to school so that they can enjoy profitable careers, and most people would not remain in their jobs if there were no financial incentive. Thus if we say that prostitutes are in their profession "for the money," we are not differentiating their behavior from that of people in noncriminal or nondelinquent professions. In other words, we do not explain anything about delinquency if we take general goals as the cause of delinquent actions, for those same general goals are met through nondelinquent behaviors.

This is not to say that we must ignore goals in delinquent behavior, because different delinquent acts may reflect different goals, and even similar delinquent acts can achieve dissimilar ends. For example, gang fighting might reflect an individual's desire to achieve a reputation, while shoplifting might represent thrill-seeking. Or some juveniles might steal cars for "kicks" while others do so for the financial payoffs. Thus even though we can differentiate types of delinquency by understanding the different goals that may be involved—and this itself is important in understanding delinquency—we cannot point to the goals as the causes of delinquency.

What Theories Must Explain

Theories of delinquency must address two basic problems. First, they must account for the patterns of delinquency. This refers to explaining the forms, frequency, and distribution of delinquency. Second, theories must explain a particular juvenile's involvement in delinquent activities. Gibbons summarizes these issues as follows:

> The first has to do with the development of explanations of the *kinds and amounts of delinquency* observed in a society or among different societies, while the second revolves about the discovery of the processes involved in the *acquisition of delinquent behavior patterns by specific youths*. Two questions are asked about delinquency: (1) What elements of social organization or social structure are responsible for the rates and patterns that are observed, and (2) what results in delinquency on the part of some youngsters and nondelinquency on the part of others?[6]

If both of these questions can be answered by a theory, then we know that the theory is sufficient to explain delinquency.

However, a third element should be added to these two. This is an explanation of the criminalization process in delinquency.[7] By criminalization process we mean the ways in society by which (1) a juvenile or act becomes officially defined as delinquent and (2) statutes are enacted designating certain acts as delinquent. The first aspect of the criminalization process refers to patterns in the application of the laws regulating delinquent behavior, while the second has to do with the official mechanisms for law making. For example, we may find that middle-class youth are less likely than lower-class youth to be officially sanctioned by the juvenile courts. This pattern is important, because in studying delinquency we may erroneously conclude from looking at court records that lower-class juveniles are more likely to be involved in delinquency. Therefore, if a theory fails to account for the application of delinquency status to juveniles or their acts, it may mislead us into a false understanding of the process of delinquency. The second aspect of the criminalization process deals with the actual procedures involved in the creation and dissolution of statutes regulating delinquent activities. It is important to examine these procedures because they define the actions that can be applied in the first part of the criminalization process as well as because delinquency statutes are sociolegal creations. For example, we will see with biogenic theories of crime that it is sometimes assumed that delinquents have some kind of biophysical malfunction. This malfunction is used to explain delinquency, but the extent to which we realize that the definers of delinquency are made up of social factors, we will not be misled into thinking that biological problems are the causes of delinquency. For example, suppose that a state lowers the juvenile age from 17 to 16. This would mean that 17-year-olds would no longer be subject to juvenile-status offenses. Obviously, the change in the law would have no biological effect on the 17-year-olds, but it would change their social status, legally, from juveniles to adults, and therefore, it would be impossible for them to commit juvenile-status offenses. Any theory that fails to take into account the fact that laws are socially created and dissolved risks making unwarranted assumptions about those who break the laws.

EARLY EXPLANATIONS OF DELINQUENCY

When discussing early explanations of delinquency, we will be focusing on the background of these theories and their implications in modern theory. However, since we will be dealing primarily with sociological theory, we will give some examples of more recent ideas and research in the biogenic and psychiatric/psychoanalytic theories.

Biogenic Theories

Early Theories.   Today biogenic theories are largely discredited as general explanations of crime, but the early biogenic theorists, notably Cesare Lombroso, deserve credit for their early insights and the role they played in bringing a scientific perspective to the study of delinquency and criminal behavior. Lombroso attempted to explain criminal and delinquent behavior through atavism, or the idea that primitive genetic forms recur in certain criminal individuals.[8] As evidence for this theory Lombroso presented anatomical measurements he had made of prisoners convicted for various crimes—for example:

> Commencing with the most important study, that of cranial activity of criminals, it is clear from the measurement of the circumference that a small number are of very large circumference (1 @ 580, 1 @ 550, 2 @ 560, and 2 @ 520), the others of ordinary circumference (8 @ 530, 13 @ 520), and that there is also a rather remarkable number of circumferences which are almost microcephalic: 39 out of 65, namely, 19 @ 510, 8 @ 490, and 12 @ 500.
>
> As for measured capacity in cubic centimeters, I am only perfectly certain about 40 males. Out of these 40, the average capacity is 1389 which, if compared with the normal average, works out to be clearly much lower. Generally, thieves show an even lower capacity (1321) compared with murderers (1415).[9]

What is significant is that Lombroso was among the first to measure systematically some aspect of criminals. His atavism hypothesis was not presented without empirical data, and he went to lengths to compare different types of criminals on the basis of different physiological dimensions. Goring later showed Lombroso's theory to be false because in his study Goring found no difference between the measurements of prisoners and those of the general population.[10] Yet the type of study initiated by Lombroso paved the way for scientific inquiry into the causes of crime.

Modern Theories.   Contemporary biogenic theories point to more sophisticated physiological anomalies, but their essential hypothesis is the same as Lombroso's, namely, that a biological malfunction leads to behavior that is in violation of the law. A few years ago, for example, the discovery of an extra Y chromosome in certain prison inmates generated a flurry of investigations. The XYY pattern of chromosomes in males, it was claimed, leads to increased aggressiveness resulting in more criminal activity among these men than in those with normal chromosome patterns. Richard Speck, who was convicted of murdering eight nurses in Chicago, who did not have the XYY chromosome pattern, was somehow linked with evidence that the XYY chromosome produced violent crimes. However, careful analysis by Richard Fox in one study,[11] and by Theodore Sarbin and Jeffrey Miller in another,[12] showed that imprisoned males with the XYY chromosome were less violent and aggressive than male inmates with normal chromosome patterns. Additionally, XYY criminals, it was found, were more likely to have been convicted of property crimes than violent crimes.

The appeal of biogenic theories lies in the possibility that crime, like physical illness, can be cured if a biological cause can be located. One can imagine the benefits of producing a "thief serum" or a "runaway pill" that would cure delinquent shoplifters and runaways (or a "political lotion" that would end crime in high places). However, as we noted earlier, there is a difference between socially and biologically determined behavior. This is not to say that physiological factors do not cause changes in behavior. The slaughter on the nation's highways is largely caused by drunken drivers whose reactions are impaired by the effects of alcohol. Obviously, if people did not drink and drive about half of all traffic deaths would not occur. Similarly, violent family fights are often precipitated by the use of alcohol, as are numerous homicides. It is also clear, however, that most of the time that people drink they do not commit crimes. Manslaughter caused while a person was driving while intoxicated most likely would not have taken place had the person been sober, and if alcohol had not impaired the biological function of the driver, then there would have been no vehicular manslaughter. Yet this is not to say that the alcohol by itself caused the manslaughter. First, many under-aged youths drink, and many of them kill or are killed while driving drunk. The fact is that they break the law when they drink. Their drinking is not caused by a biological element, but more likely by a social one—for example, a party where everyone is expected to drink. Furthermore, drunken driving is a crime. Again, the alcohol is not a cause of the crime but a condition of the crime. Persons who are caught driving with a certain level of alcohol in their systems will be charged with driving while intoxicated. The law holds people responsible for drinking, but it does not hold the alcohol responsible for the condition of those who drink. The assumption is that the effects of alcohol are known to those who use it, and so they are responsible, and in that sense cause their own condition.[13]

Other biological impairments over which the individual has no control, such as mental retardation, are sometimes used to illustrate the biogenic argument. Likewise, brain tumors, spinal and nerve damage, syphilis, and similar diseases create abnormal behaviors that are sometimes criminal. These conditions can certainly be said to cause the abnormal behavior that is observed. The biogenic theorists argue that crime can similarly be linked to other more subtle biogenic conditions if we were willing to search hard enough for these causal factors.

Problems with Biogenic Theories.   The biogenic argument contains two major fallacies. First, criminal behavior by persons with diseased or damaged organs is random and undirected. That is, no pattern of criminal or delinquent acts has emerged that can be linked to specific biological problems. Second, most delinquent acts are committed by youths who have no such impairments. If a person can be shown to be incapable of telling right from wrong due to a biological abnormality, then the individual is not held criminally responsible for the act and will not be charged with a crime. Thus legally the individual is not criminal or delinquent but "mentally ill." But even if delinquent acts were not excused because of organic impairment, very few delinquent acts are committed by persons who suffer from such conditions. Thus, the rejection of biogenic theory is not merely a definitional rejection but an empirical one based on the condition of those who commit delinquent offenses.

Psychogenic Theories

Unlike biogenic theories, psychogenic theories are a heterogeneous category. Gibbons divides these theories into three groups: (1) psychoanalytic theories, (2) personality theories, and (3) psychopathic theories.[14]

Psychoanalytic Theories.   At the heart of psychoanalytic theories is the work of Sigmund Freud. Essentially, these theories view delinquent behavior in terms of basic unresolved drives and instincts that lie hidden deep in the human psyche. When these basic drives are in conflict, abnormal behavior, including delinquency, may be the result. The usual approach to these behavior problems is psychoanalysis, which focuses on delving deep into the individual's past experience to uncover the unconscious conflicts.[14]

By and large, psychoanalytic theories have been dismissed on the grounds that they cannot be tested. Gibbons adds that we should not concern ourselves too much with psychoanalytic theories because today they are infrequently used anyway. While it is true that psychoanalytic theories are essentially not subject to empirical testing, to say they are not in current use in one form of another is not altogether accurate.

Many schools of social work are still heavily influenced by psychoanalytic theory, and there has been a re-emergence of certain Freudian ideas in sociobiology. Since social workers and probation officers trained in social work have an influence on juvenile courts, psychoanalytic theory still has an impact on the field of juvenile delinquency. One researcher states that the purpose of applying psychoanalytic theories "is to help the judge understand individual cases, make diagnoses, offer recommendations on dispositions, and treat offenders placed on probation."[15] Robey sees the female runaway as motivated by the girl's desire to "ward off the unconscious threat of an incestuous relationship with her father"—or what in Freudian analysis is known as an Electra complex.[16]

The problem with psychoanalytic theory is not so much that it is a poor theory for explaining delinquency but that its application can *cause* problems for the juvenile. If a child is deemed to have deep-rooted problems but cannot afford the high cost of private psychoanalysis, institutional treatment is often seen to be a "healthy" alternative. However, such "help" can lead to institutionalization and all of the accompanying problems (see Chapter 12) that it implies. Moreover, since psychoanalytic treatment has not been demonstrated to have consistent results, it can become an obstacle in the way of other approaches to the problem of delinquency.

As a final note on psychoanalytic theory and any other theory that points to hidden forces that cannot be tested by empirical means, it is important to question what a theory can show us. As in astrology, anything that psychoanalysis says can be "shown" to exist if one uses it as an interpretive scheme for looking at what is being "shown."[17] If I tell a person that he or she has some kind of "hidden" or "unresolved" complex that is linked to an undesirable behavior, two things occur. First, I tell the person that he or she is not personally responsible for the behavior, so that the individual is relieved of the responsibility and accompanying guilt. Second, I give that person his or her entire experience to examine for "proof" of what I tell them. By saying that something happened in the past that was a problem that went unresolved, I provide the person with every conceivable frustration that people normally encounter in life.[18] The result is that what I "show" them is merely another way of looking at what they have already seen. The theory cannot provide us with observable indicators that can be measured or processes that can be shown to occur in recurrent and typical fashions. Thus, we must judge a theory by what it can show us—that is, what it can show us that can be *seen*.

Personality Theories.   The second group of psychogenic theories derive from nonpsychoanalytic premises and base their conclusions on empirical evidence. However, like psychoanalytic theories, personality theories tend to build their explanations by defining their subject matter. For example, the following definition of a runaway was cited in a psychiatric journal:

> Individuals with this disorder characteristically escape from threatening situations by running away from home for a day or more without permission. Typically they are immature and timid and feel rejected at home, inadequate and friendless. They often steal furtively.[19]

The psychiatric definition includes the *cause* of the behavior, and from .t the theory is implicit. Since runaways are legally defined, and age differs from state to state for juvenile status, a 16-year-old leaving home in Alabama would not suffer from this "disorder" because juvenile court jurisdiction ends at age 15 in that state. In neighboring Mississippi, however, where the adult age is 18, the youth would be diagnosed as a runaway. The definition fails to take into account the legal aspects of the violation, assuming that leaving home is a "disorder."

However, the most widespread feature of personality theories is their use of personality tests. From the results of IQ tests, the MMPI (Minnesota Multiphasic Personality Inventory), and the Rorschach inkblot test administered to labeled delinquents, personality theorists have attempted to develop a profile of the delinquent personality. Compared to psychoanalytic theories, which provide no propositions that can be tested, the personality testers begin with very little theory and attempt to develop explanations by examining inferred personality traits from the patterns of test results.

Before examining the findings that test the personality theorists' explanations, it is important to consider the implications of their methods. First, by dealing with labeled delinquents, or persons who have been adjudicated delinquent, the theorists take a skewed sample of those actually involved in delinquency. Labeled delinquents represent only those youths who have passed through the juvenile justice process, and the tests may merely reflect the decision making of the juvenile justice system and not the juveniles involved in delinquency. For example, in the preparation of the social history report, juvenile probation officers base their recommendations in part on psychiatric reports, which may include psychometric test results (see Chapter 11). The extent to which the probation officer employs the tests to recommend a juvenile for detention as opposed to probation or release in parental custody guarantees that labeled delinquents who are tested in detention facilities will exhibit certain personality profiles on personality tests. Thus, there is a self-fulfilling prophecy in selecting out labeled delinquents through the use of psychometric devices and then measuring delinquent personalities with the same tests.

A second error that is possible in measuring delinquency on the basis of comparing labeled delinquents with a control population is that the testers may measure social or cultural characteristics and not individual personality attributes. As we pointed out in Chapter 1, poor and minority-group youths are far more likely to become labeled delinquents than their white, middle-class peers. If the control group does not reflect the same ethnic-socioeconomic mix as the labeled delinquent group to which it is compared, the differences that show up on the personality test may reflect the ethnic-socioeconomic differences between the poor minority group making up the labeled delinquent group and the white, middle-class control group.

These problems can be controlled by using the tests in combination with self-report surveys and samples that are comparable on the basis of socioeconomic status. However, there is a third problem of measuring delinquency on the basis of personality tests when comparing any group of labeled delinquents, especially those in detention facilities. It is quite possible that those who are in detention develop certain personality characteristics as a result of the detention experience. As we will see in Chapter 12, the detention for juveniles is often traumatic, and it is likely that the experience significantly alters what is measured on personality tests. Thus, again it is possible that the tests are measuring the effects of the juvenile justice process and not the individual personality characteristics of those who are labeled delinquent or commit delinquent acts.

Obviously, we cannot evaluate the validity of personality theories on the basis of invalid research, and it would be unfair to reject personality theory on the basis of such data. By the same token, unless personality theory research addresses critical issues, one has difficulty accepting findings that "show" a relationship between personality and delinquency.

Turning now to research in this area, we see that the case for personality theory is very weak. And given the methodological criticisms listed above, even the supportive findings are questionable. Beginning with an early study of personality and delinquency, Healy and Bronner,[20] examining a sample of 153 juveniles with a control group of nondelinquent siblings, presented data showing a number of interesting relationships between selected items considered to be roots of personality distortion. For example, they found that 91 percent of the delinquents suffered from major emotional disturbances while only 13 percent of the control group did. However, in the same study, Healy and Bronner found some astounding things about the control group. For example, the delinquents were three times as likely as the control subjects were to have belonged to the Boy Scouts or Girl Scouts, 50 percent more likely to be fond of reading, and were 100 percent more likely to be characterized as great readers. The control group showed about a 30 percent greater likelihood of avoiding companionship and a more than seven times higher likelihood of displaying "distinctively submissive tendencies." In the control group 41 youths were described as "notably quiet, placid, subdued, etc.," while none in the delinquent group were so described. Depending on what one considers to be a good or bad personality trait, one can draw different conclusions about healthy personalities and delinquency. Given the proportion of nondelinquents who were described as "subdued," it would appear that the personality theorists are viewing being comatose as part of normal personality development. The avoidance of companionship displayed by the control group points to what can be considered "antisocial" tendencies, but the researchers claim that only 13 percent of the control group suffered from major emotional disturbances. In his study of psychiatric diagnoses of adolescents, Hakeem found that given the wide variety of diagnostic styles and concepts employed, the personality differences among delinquents could better be explained by the variation in diagnostic devices used by psychiatrists than by variations in the personalities of the delinquents.[21] By the same token, we can see that depending on how the Healy and Bronner findings are read, we can find greater personality disorder among either the control or delinquent group.

Two general studies of personality findings and delinquency suggest that there is a weak, at most, relationship between personality and delinquency. Schuessler and Cressey found that most of the studies they examined had doubtful validity, and there was no single personality trait that differentiated delinquents from nondelinquents.[22] Waldo and Dinitz in a later study, found that based on the Minnesota Multiphasic Personality Inventory (MMPI) delinquents and nondelinquents could be differentiated in 81 percent of the studies that used this test.[23] Even this later assessment of personality studies, however, found them to be far from conclusive.

Ironically, Sutherland and Cressey concluded that the best general study of personality and delinquency was the 1936 Healy and Bronner study mentioned above.[24] As we pointed out, the Healy and Bronner study could be easily interpreted to show that the control group made up of nondelinquent siblings of delinquents demonstrated characteristics that were more abnormal than those of the delinquents. Moreover, since the personality theorists have been unable to improve on the Healy and Bronner study for over 40 years, it is doubtful that this line of thought will prove fruitful later on without a thorough revamping of both theory and method.

Psychopathic Theory. The final psychogenic theory we will evaluate is psychopathic theory. To call this approach a theory is perhaps a misnomer, for we are dealing with a psychiatric category variously called psychopathic and sociopathic personalities. Concerning exactly what a psychopath or a sociopath is, there is considerable disagreement, and the only apparent accord involving the application of this concept in delinquency is that it is a vague concept with little empirical support to link the condition to delinquency.[25]

According to psychiatric understandings, the psychopathic or sociopathic personality lacks normal feelings of obligations to conform to social norms.

This definition is not taken from a psychiatric dictionary, because there appears to be no single definition on which psychiatrists agree. Carson found 202 terms used more or less synonomously with "psychopath," but generally psychopaths and sociopaths are considered to be people without moral constraints who do what they please.[26]

The main problem with the concepts of sociopath and psychopath as explanations of delinquency lies in the reality of delinquency and delinquents. Erikson's observation that delinquents spend relatively little of their time engaging in delinquent activities is not taken into account by these theories.[27] Furthermore, as we will see throughout this book, there are several different types of delinquent activities as well as changing patterns of delinquency. Psychopathic and sociopathic personalities, while not out of touch with reality, are still considered to be out of touch with social morality. This being the case, they would have to commit far more delinquent acts and engage in a far wider variety of delinquent acts to meet the requirements of the psychiatric definition of psychopathic. Moreover, Thomas Scheff has pointed out that for every psychopath who is in some kind of institutional care, there is at least one who is not receiving any care at all, yet not getting into trouble with the law.[28] This suggests that even those who fall into the psychiatric category of psychopathic personality do not engage in the massive deviance the definition of the category would suggest.

Furthermore, Matza has made two important observations regarding the commission of delinquent acts.[29] First, he points out that delinquent activities are committed only in certain situations, and that juveniles who are credited with the most delinquency consider certain situations to be clearly inappropriate for delinquent activities. This suggests, following Goffman's[30] formulation, that delinquency is norm-governed to the extent that there are mutually understood situations in which it is appropriate to engage in delinquent activities. The situations may be spontaneous, such as the looting in New York City's 1977 blackout, or they may be anticipated, such as a planned gang fight. It is clear, however, that most youths conform to situational expectations in committing delinquency or in refraining from doing so. Since this is the case, it is doubtful that all but a few would fit the psychopathic image of a youth engaging in delinquency whenever he or she felt like it. Second, Matza has pointed out that there is a *moral* consideration in delinquent acts.[31] For the most part he found that juveniles in subcultures of delinquency held to conventional morality and in the course of committing delinquent acts felt obligated to neutralize the negative moral implications of their acts. If delinquents fit the psychopathic of sociopathic model, they would have no sense of morality to neutralize or justify their actions. Yet since juveniles who engage in delinquency are cognizant of what others think of them, they cannot be said to be divorced from all moral standards of conduct.

Clearly, then, psychogenic theories of delinquency provide us with little to account for delinquency or to show a definite causal relationship between delinquency and psychogenic forces. One could call for further research to clarify the relationship, if one exists, between psychogenically grounded concepts and delinquency. What appears to be necessary, however, is a reformulation of theory in this area and a consideration of the effects of social sanctions on the psychological states of juveniles. New theory in the area of psychiatry and psychology has begun to address some of these issues, especially the social forces that are intertwined with psychological states. So far, however, there has been little consideration of the effects the criminalization process has on the individual who becomes an official delinquent. Instead of asking whether certain psychological states lead to delinquency, we should ask if the labeling process of juvenile justice leads to certain psychopathological behaviors.

Multiple-Factor Approach

Before we discuss sociological theories in Chapter 3, we must consider a popular misconception in explaining delinquency. What has been called multiple-factor theory is not in fact a theory but instead an approach to delinquency that attempts to locate factors which appear to be related to delinquency.[32] The argument put forth by the multiple-factor theorists is that no single cause has been or will be found that explains all delinquency; therefore, we should seek the different factors that are related to delinquency and perhaps be able to explain different types of delinquency according to different factors.[33] The Gluecks' study of delinquency, which compared delinquents and nondelinquents on the basis of 100 overlapping items or "factors," exemplifies this approach and best illustrates the problems associated with it.[34] Certain factors were found to be related to delinquency as measured by comparing the likelihood that a given factor was more apt to be found among delinquents than among nondelinquents. Delinquents, for example, were more likely to be from broken homes than nondelinquents. Some factors may affect some juveniles and not others, and some factors associated with delinquency in some youths may not cause delinquency in others. In other words, the multiple-factor approach essentially says that a lot of different things can cause delinquency. Its adherents point out that this broad approach is superior to theories that examine only one or a small number of factors.

The first problem is that simply throwing a lot of factors into a pot and saying that some are more associated with delinquency than others doesn't tell us much. In other sciences if we were told that "a lot of things" are associated with a biological, chemical, or physical process without being given an explanation of the relationships among the factors, we would not be in a position to predict the effect of any one factor. If we are told that sunlight and water are associated with plant growth, that association is explained in terms of the relationship between water bringing minerals to cells, which produce sugar through photosynthesis, which is stimulated by sunlight. However, anyone who has house plants knows that too much water or too much sunlight can ruin a plant. Thus, if we are not told the relationship between the water, the sunlight, and the plant's growth, our understanding of the process is very limited.

This leads to the problem of theory in the multiple-factor approach. Theories are made up of interrelated propositions that explain relationships among concepts. Any theory acknowledges variables that will affect the phenomenon described and explained by the theory.[35] Multiple-factor theory confuses single "factors" with single "theory." Most theories do not have single "factors"; rather, they include a single set of propositions with several variables.[36] Thus, if we say that social class and family are related to delinquency, our theory must show the interrelationships among the three concepts. However, if we simply say that social class and family are factors in delinquency, we are not explaining the relationship between social class and family or how these two factors are related to delinquency. As a result, we cannot predict delinquency as well as we could if we understood the relationship—any more than we could expect to have healthy house plants if we only knew that water and sunlight are factors in plant growth but did not know their relationship to each other or to the plant.

Finally, factors that may be associated with delinquency may have no causal relationship to delinquency. For example, the populations of juvenile detention centers contain a disproportionate number of minority youths. We may conclude that there is a relationship between race and delinquency. However, unless we understand the relationship between the juvenile justice system, social class, associational patterns, and other variables related to ethnic status, such conclusions are unwarranted. For example, in Holland, a disproportionate number of Surinamese youths are found in juvenile prisons, but unless we understand the social situation of the Surinamese in Dutch society, we cannot claim that the people from Surinam are delinquent.

SUMMARY

In this chapter we have attempted to understand how to go about the task of understanding juvenile delinquency. By establishing guidelines by which to measure the adequacy of theory, we can evaluate a theory in terms of its ability to explain (1) patterns of delinquency; (2) individual involvement; and (3) societal reaction in the form of citizen and official treatment of delinquents. Without these criteria it would be much easier to "explain" delinquency, but we would have false explanations and no way of knowing when an adequate explanation was available. By the criteria established, in addition to research studies and simple logic, the biogenic and psychogenic theories were found to be very weak explanations. Likewise, we see that the so-called multiple-factor approach, which attempts to incorporate just about anything that appears to be related to delinquency, is also lacking, even though it considers biogenic, psychogenic, and sociogenic variables.

The expectation at this point is that a well-integrated theory of sociological origins is the answer to all the problems, and we should not consider biogenic, psychogenic, or combination theories at all. This is not the case, for no student of delinquency can afford to ignore new findings in biogenic or psychogenic studies that can demonstrate, by the criteria for an adequate theory, new insights. Moreover, we cannot ignore efforts that take into account more than a single dimension, especially if such efforts constitute theoretical integration.

In the next three chapters, however, we will concentrate on sociogenic theories to the exclusion of biogenic and psychogenic explanations. In this way we will focus on the many important sociological dimensions of delinquency and see whether the sociological theories are any better than those examined in this chapter. To some degree, we will meet many of the same problems in fulfilling the stated criteria that we found with psychogenic and biogenic theories. However, we will also obtain new insights, though not without flaws, that will open up vistas for further exploration and understanding.

NOTES

1. Arnold Birenbaum and Edward Sagarin, *Norms and Human Behavior* (New York: Praeger, 1976), p. 1.
2. Edwin H. Sutherland and Donald R. Cressey, *Criminology*, 10th ed. (Philadelphia: Lippincott, 1978), pp. 8–12.
3. Hazel Kerper, *Introduction to the Criminal Justice System* (St. Paul, Minn.: West Publishing Company, 1972), p. 30.
4. Richard Quinney, *Class, State, and Crime* (New York: David McKay, 1977).
5. Sutherland and Cressey, p. 82.
6. Don C. Gibbons, *Delinquent Behavior*, 2d ed. (Englewood Cliffs, N.J.: Prentice-Hall, 1976), p. 90.
7. Clayton Hartjen, *Crime and Criminalization* (New York: Praeger, 1974), p. 8.
8. Cesare Lombroso, *L'Uomo Delinquente* (Milan: Hoepi, 1876).
9. *Ibid.*
10. Charles Goring, *The English Convict* (London: His Majesty's Stationary Office, 1913).
11. Richard S. Fox, "The XYY Offender: A Modern Myth?" *Journal of Criminal Law, Criminology and Police Science*, 62:59–73 (1971).
12. Theodore R. Sarbin and Jeffrey E. Miller, "Demonism Revisited: The XYY Chromosomal Anomaly," *Issues in Criminology*, 5:195–207 (1970).
13. David Matza, *Delinquency and Drift* (New York: Wiley, 1964), p. 96.
14. Gibbons, p. 160.
15. Ames Robey, "The Runaway Girl," in Otto Pollact and Alfred Friedman (eds.), *Family Dynamics and Female Delinquency* (Palo Alto, Calif.: Science and Behavior Books, 1969), pp. 127–137.

16. *Ibid.,* p. 127.
17. Harold Gerfinkel, *Studies in Ethnomethodology* (Englewood Cliffs, N.J.: Prentice-Hall, 1967).
18. Thomas S. Szasz, *The Myth of Mental Illness* (New York: Hoeber-Harper, 1961).
19. Richard L. Jenkins, "The Runaway Reaction," *American Journal of Psychiatry, 128*:168–173 (1971).
20. William Healy and Augusta Bronner, *New Light on Delinquency and Its Treatment* (New Haven, Conn.: Yale University Press, 1936).
21. Michael Hakeem, "A Critique of the Psychiatric Approach to Crime and Correction," *Law and Contemporary Problems, 23*:650–682 (1958).
22. Karl F. Schuessler and Donald R. Cressey, "Personality Characteristics of Criminals," *American Journal of Sociology, 55*:476–484 (1950).
23. Gordon P. Waldo and Simon Dinitz, "Personality Attributes of the Criminal: An Analysis of Research Studies, 1950–65," *Journal of Research in Crime and Delinquency, 4*:185–201 (1967).
24. Sutherland and Cressey, p. 165.
25. Sutherland and Cressey; Gibbons, pp. 85–87; Stephen Schafer and Richard D. Knudten, *Juvenile Delinquency: An Introduction* (New York: Random House, 1970), pp. 257–258.
26. Hulsey Carson, "The Psychopath and the Psychopathic," *Journal of Criminal Psychopathology, 4*:522–527 (1943).
27. Kai Erikson, "Notes on the Sociology of Deviance," *Social Problems, 9*:307–314 (Spring 1962).
28. Thomas J. Scheff, *Being Mentally Ill* (Chicago: Aldine, 1966), p. 50.
29. Matza, pp. 33–64.
30. Erving Goffman, *Behavior in Public Places* (New York: Free Press, 1963).
31. Matza, pp. 69–98.
32. Sutherland and Cressey, pp. 67–72.
33. Ruth Shonle Cavan and Theodore N. Ferdinand, *Juvenile Delinquency,* 3d ed. (Philadelphia: Lippincott, 1975).
34. Sheldon Glueck and Eleanor Glueck, *Unraveling Juvenile Delinquency* (Cambridge: Harvard University Press, 1950).
35. Jonathan H. Turner, *The Structure of Sociological Theory* (Homewood, Ill.: The Dorsey Press, 1974).
36. Albert Cohen, *Delinquent Boys: The Culture of the Gang* (Glencoe, Ill.: Free Press, 1955).

3 Delinquency and the Social Structure

SOCIOGENIC THEORIES

Given the problems with biogenic and psychogenic theories in explaining delinquency, a number of theories were developed that began to question the social structure and situation of delinquents and delinquency. Noting that criminal and delinquent behavior patterns were found under certain conditions and in certain areas more frequently than in others, sociologists began looking at the social milieu of delinquency. Could it be that the problem lies not with the individual but in the social conditions or situations in which the person lives? Would a biologically and psychologically sound person placed in the same social structure engage in delinquency? Or would an otherwise normal juvenile in certain social conditions develop psychological problems or behavior patterns that would lead to delinquency?

Sociological explanations of delinquency focus on the social structure—the major institutions that mold society, its values, and its norms. First, we will examine explanations that center on one of society's most basic institutions —the family. While this explanation is not a theory proper, it was an early attempt to focus on an individual's environment rather than on his or her genes or psyche. Next, we will examine Merton's theory of anomie, wherein the values and norms of society are analyzed in terms of institutional demands and possibilities. Third, we will look at subcultural theory, which focuses on delinquent values that are developed around structural forces which place certain groups at a disadvantage. Finally, we will consider conflict theory, which sees certain groups in conflict as a function of basic economic institutions.

To examine these theories we will apply the same criteria we did in Chapter 2. We will be asking whether a theory accounts for (1) the patterns of delinquency; (2) the social-psychological aspects of an individual offender; and (3) the criminalization process. Each theory will be presented in turn, along with empirical evidence that either supports or refutes the theory. With this approach we will be able to evaluate each one thoroughly, both to see whether it meets our criteria and to determine if it is supported by research.

The Broken-home Explanation

A factor that seemed promising in explaining delinquency was the home of the delinquent. In homes from which one or both parents were absent because of death, divorce, or desertion, the child was seen to be deprived relative to those who had the advantages of a complete, stable family life. The amount of delinquency "caused" by broken homes was not specified, but since a number of studies showed that delinquents were likely to come from broken homes,[1] it was believed that broken homes must have something to do with delinquency. Glueck and Glueck found that 60.4 percent of the delinquents and 34.2 percent of the nondelinquents they studied came from broken homes.[2] The Gluecks' study was based on matched pairs of delinquents and nondelinquents: the sample of delinquents was selected on the basis of juvenile records. Since the courts consider home life in making decisions about the disposition of delinquents,[3] those who come from broken homes are more likely to be made wards of the court. Therefore, it is possible that the Gluecks' study was based on a self-fulfilling prophecy. The courts believe that juveniles from broken homes are more likely to be delinquents; therefore, they are more likely to make them wards of the court. Hence, in a sample based on those judged delinquent by the courts, one is likely to find an overrepresentation of juveniles from broken homes, because of court practices.

In an examination of the data on delinquents from broken homes, Toby found that the broken home had a greater impact on younger (preteen) juveniles than on older ones.[4] Poorly integrated families did not provide the control over the younger juveniles that well-integrated families did, but neither type of family had much control over older, more mobile youths. According to Toby, young juveniles who lacked the control and direction that can be offered by a complete family were more likely to drift into delinquent activity. In summarizing numerous studies of family cohesion and delinquency, Rodman and Grams point out that family control is the most significant factor in preventing delinquency.[5] If the parents lack control of their children because they pay little attention to the children or because the children regard them as unfair, the socialization of the children is incomplete, and instead of taking on the general social values, they come to take on delinquent values.

Writers have also attributed delinquency to poor home life defined on the basis of the disciplinary techniques used. The Gluecks found that families which used firm but kind techniques in disciplining their children produced the fewest delinquents, while families using either lax and erratic measures or overstrict techniques were more likely to produce delinquency.[6] Parents who provided affection for their children had the fewest delinquent offspring, while the children of parents who were indifferent or only sporadically affectionate were likely to develop a poor image of authority figures, insecurity, and overall frustration with family values—conditions that tend to foster delinquent values and activities.

More recent works on broken homes and delinquency have shown finer variations between other factors and the broken home. Datesman and Scarpitti, for example, showed that the relationship between broken homes varied between the sexes depending on the type of delinquent offense with which a juvenile was charged.[7] Female delinquents who appeared in family court were more likely to be from broken homes than males if they had been charged with a family-related delinquency, such as running away or incorrigibility. Male and female delinquents who were charged with property crimes, however, were equally likely to come from broken homes.[8]

While the broken-home explanations of juvenile delinquency clearly left a great deal to be desired and were never developed into a full-scale theory, they paved the way for an examination of the social conditions of delinquency. The fact that the studies on home life and delinquency found relationships between external social conditions and the conduct of juveniles showed that delinquency did not stem merely from biological or psychological factors and prompted researchers to look still more closely at the social milieu of the delinquent.

Moreover, broken-home theories of delinquency were often nothing more than multiple-factor theories with the broken home being one of the factors. Furthermore, the broken home was seen to be a problem that led to psychological problems, usually glossed over as "frustrations," and these frustrations led to delinquent activities. Thus, even though the broken-home theory brought a social institution to the attention of delinquency research, so much of it was couched in psychological concepts that it hid the social significance in the family-youth relationship.

Uncertain Evidence.   The empirical evidence backing the broken-home approach is fairly consistent in showing that delinquents are more likely to be from broken homes than nondelinquents. There is a big difference, however, between demonstrating co-variation and showing a casual relationship. Furthermore, while juveniles labeled delinquent are more likely to come from broken homes, most juveniles from broken homes do not engage in delinquency, and many from unbroken homes do. Finally, as we pointed out earlier, the juvenile justice system tends to select out those from broken homes. Those who are deemed by juvenile court to "need" the court's help are more likely to be from broken homes than children from unbroken homes. Since the juveniles that are studied in detention centers are more likely to be from broken homes, the erroneous conclusion is that delinquency is caused by broken homes. As a result, the broken-home theory has been rejected as a general explanation of delinquency.

Further research on the relationship between broken homes and delinquency needs to concentrate on (1) the use by the juvenile justice system of the broken home as a criterion for placing a juvenile in detention; (2) delinquency as measured by self-report surveys and the differences in reports of delinquency by juveniles from broken and unbroken homes; and (3) developing propositions stating the conceptual variables surrounding home life and their relationship to one another and to delinquency. If this is done, not only can the concept be meaningfully tested, but it may be possible to develop a relationship into a theory.

Structural Theory

One of the first theoretically sophisticated explanations of crime and delinquency was developed by Robert Merton, who pointed out how the structure of social values leads to a high rate of property crimes among the working class.[9] According to Merton, just about everybody wants the "good things in life," as identified by society. The mass media, especially television, present us with a cornucopia of material things which we are told we must have. Success and happiness are often measured in terms of whether or not we have these material goods, which Merton calls "culturally prescribed goals."

At the same time that the members of society are directed toward these goals, they are given a set of rules, or "socially sanctioned means," for the achievement of these goals. For example, we are told that it is good to become rich, and we are also advised that only certain avenues should be taken to gain wealth. It is socially correct to get a job and save money to buy material things, but it is wrong to rob a bank even though the money from the bank robbery will be used to realize the culturally prescribed goals.

The problem is that the social structure blocks certain members from attaining these goals in acceptable ways. Certain occupations provide only enough income for the essentials, leaving little or no surplus for the "good things in life." Groups whose occupational status and overall situation prevent them from attaining the necessary resources are "blocked" from realizing these goals. The American social structure has room for only a limited number of people to reach positions from which they can begin to attain the culturally prescribed goals. Even though the American ideology and mythology stress equal opportunity to "make it," there are just so many niches in the social structure that allow goal attainment. For example, in a large corporation, there are so many executive positions, so many staff positions, and so many assembly line positions. Even if everyone in the corporation is of equal ability and works equally hard, there are only a few who will fill the executive positions.

Furthermore, equal opportunity is a myth. Those from higher socioeconomic backgrounds typically have far more opportunity to go to college and learn the necessary skills for higher-paying jobs. Many lower- and working-class members cannot afford to send their children to college, and even if they can, the children are less likely to have been brought up with the idea that college is important. Moreover, persons from wealthy families, whether or not they go to college, are more likely to get good jobs since their parents are in positions to know the "right" people to help them. Many of the sons and daughters of the wealthy are assured of positions in the family business no matter what their educational background is.

Adaptations. Merton outlines a number of possible responses to this state of affairs. A person can try to stay within the socially provided boundaries in attempting to realize the culturally prescribed goals, by working, saving, and so on. This line of adaptation, called *conformity,* represents the ideal adaptation in a stable society.

Second, an individual can accept the culturally prescribed goals but reject the institutionalized means of achieving them. This adaptation is typical of societies in which there is an overemphasis on success goals and structural barriers to reaching the goals for certain segments. Merton refers to this mode of adaptation as *innovation,* a term that generally denotes positive action but here refers to not following the rules for goal attainment. This mode of adaptation is especially relevant to a study of delinquency, for essentially it refers to breaking the law. For example, a juvenile may steal (rejection of institutionalized means) a car (cultural goal) or commit some other property crime to get money.

A third adaptation, *ritualism,* refers to one who accepts the institutionalized means while rejecting the cultural goals. Some individuals scale down their expectations below the cultural standards while holding onto the socially correct means. In this way, they don't risk getting into trouble for breaking the rules, and at the same time they're not frustrated by failure to meet the high expectations of the cultural goals. Examples are the frightened bureaucrat who plays it safe but never rises in the bureaucracy. He holds tenaciously to what he has, rigorously conforming to the rules, but he has no expectations of advancement.

Retreatism, the fourth mode of adaptation, applies to individuals who reject both the culturally prescribed goals and the means. In a sense these individuals are aliens, for they do not feel themselves a part of the society in which they live. Skid row bums and chronic heroin users (junkies) exemplify this mode of adaptation. They do not expect to attain cultural goals, nor do they conform to the institutionalized norms. Young dropouts who give up the values and norms of the Establishment are the juvenile counterparts of these bums and junkies and constitute a significant segment of the delinquent population.

In the final adaptation, *rebellion,* cultural goals and social norms are rejected and new ones are established in their stead. The difference between retreatism and rebellion is that in the latter the goals and norms are replaced, while in the former they are merely rejected. The rebel substitutes new ideologies for the old and strives toward the new goals by new means. Among the young, the counterculture, hippie movement, and radical movement represent rebellion.

Conformity and ritualism are relatively unimportant for our analysis since they involve law-abiding behavior, but the other three adaptations are useful in examining juvenile delinquency, for each represents a form of activity that can be characterized as delinquent. Merton's main point is that the social structure gives rise to these different adaptations. Various deviant adaptations emerge because of the frustrations produced by the social structure.

Thus, delinquency has a pattern and is not merely a set of random responses to frustration by individuals. People in certain parts of the social structure experience more frustration than others, and when we compare those who are deemed delinquent with those who are not, we find an overrepresentation of the underprivileged, disadvantaged, and poor. In other words, those who are most likely to experience frustration because of their position in the social structure are most likely to be judged delinquent. Self-reported crime surveys also show that while almost everyone commits some crime, crimes are more prevalent among the lower socioeconomic strata.[10]

This theory explains why more crime is committed by the disadvantaged, but does not account for the various types of delinquencies or for the patterns of delinquent behavior; it explains "too much" delinquency. Given that structural frustration causes delinquency, why is it that only a relatively few members of the lower socioeconomic strata commit delinquent acts frequently? Why are boys ten times more likely to engage in delinquent acts than girls in the same social position?

Further, while Merton's theory does explain why some may adopt innovation (for example, shoplifting) and others choose retreatism (for example, drug use) as a mode of adaptation to frustration, it does not explain why some innovators choose shoplifting and others choose armed robbery, or why some retreaters prefer to use drugs and others alcohol. It does not show why drug use replaced alcohol use as the most popular form of retreatism for the young.

Double Failures.   Richard Cloward provided a "repair" of sorts for structural theory by pointing out that for some youths illegitimate as well as legitimate means may be blocked.[11] As Cloward notes, a boy may be denied membership in a delinquent gang because the gang members don't think he is tough enough or that he has some other defect. Thus, the boy is denied access to the delinquent activity generated in the gang. Other illegitimate means are similarly limited. Those who are blocked from both legitimate and illegitimate means are considered to be "double failures," unable to make it either way.

Cloward's contribution to Merton's theory helps to explain why not all lower-class members and other structurally frustrated individuals turn to illegitimate means. "Double failures," he claims, are likely to take on a retreatist mode, rejecting *both* legitimate and illegitimate means *as well as* the culturally prescribed goals. Without access to any means of achievement, they tend to abandon goals and simply sink into the apathy of retreatism.

Limitations.   Empirically, structural theory is supported by patterns of officially produced delinquency and the findings of self-report surveys showing greater reports of delinquency among the lower socioeconomic classes. As we have already pointed out, however, the theory accounts for too much delinquency in lower-class segments of society and does not explain why there is so much in the upper classes. Cloward's contribution in accounting for the double failures lends some support to Merton's basic thesis, but it is insufficient because it predicts far more retreatism than is found in the lower classes, and it still fails to explain, on the basis of structural theory, why females commit so little delinquency. Most lower-class girls do not follow a retreatist pattern of behavior, and so it is not the case that they have "tried delinquency" and have "failed," thus taking on retreatism.

Furthermore, since structural theory does not adequately explain the criminalization process in delinquency, even the evidence that supports the theory is open to question. We know that most juveniles commit delinquency, but we also know that mainly minority and lower-class youths come to be labeled official delinquents. Since structural theory derives its support from pointing out the high proportion of lower-class youths who are involved in delinquency, its base of evidence is founded on a skewed representation of delinquency because the juvenile justice process tends to "select out" lower-class youth. By not accounting for the impact of the juvenile justice system and the criminalization process, structural theory ignores the fact that the supporting evidence is produced by differential societal reactions to delinquency and not by differential rates of delinquency.

Subcultural Theory

Cloward's insight that there is a delinquent opportunity structure in addition to a legitimate one led to his development, with Lloyd Ohlin, of a theory of delinquent gangs.[12] The Cloward-Ohlin theory puts its main emphasis on the structural conditions that lead to *lower-class* gang delinquency, but it also explains the development of other delinquent subcultures. A delinquent subculture, in this context, is a group that fosters beliefs legitimizing delinquent activities. When the experience of frustration is a collective one, as is the case with lower-class juveniles, the response to the socially created condition is likely to be collective as well; thus Cloward and Ohlin saw delinquent gangs arising out of blocked opportunities to cultural goals. The gangs are "forced" to take illegal measures to realize these goals because their opportunities to use legitimate means are limited or nonexistent. In lower-class enclaves, therefore, in addition to adult criminal rackets, juvenile reactions to blocked opportunities develop in the form of delinquent gangs.

As the gangs develop, they come to rationalize their activities. Instead of seeing their delinquency as "bad" or "wrong" they evolve their own beliefs and values, which do more than merely reduce guilt. Risk-taking in the form of delinquent behavior comes to be seen as a sign of manliness, and those who will not engage in delinquency are characterized as "sissies" and "punks." Since there are positive connotations associated with "manliness" and negative images with "sissies" and "punks," the illegal actions that show "manliness" have social rewards in addition to any crime payoff there might be. Likewise, those who abide strictly by the law are given negative status. Thus, in delinquent subcultures both the norms for achieving status and the goals are different from those of the larger social order. What is considered proper and decent in the larger society is turned on its head, and numerous illegal activities are seen as intrinsically good.

In addition to spelling out how criminal subcultures begin and flourish, Cloward and Ohlin explain how different types of delinquent subcultures develop in lower-class areas. They identify three types—criminal, conflict, and retreatist—each based on the integration of supporters of conventional and deviant values as well as on the integration of people at different age levels. In all three subcultures legitimate channels to success goals are closed, but in the *criminal subculture* there is a good deal of opportunity through illegal routes. Racketeers, pimps, and others who have achieved success illegitimately are regarded by lower-class juveniles with admiration. To a youth who has little hope of becoming a banker, lawyer, or doctor, the racketeer is impressive, as the following statement makes clear:

> Every boy has some ideal he looks up to and admires. His ideal may be Babe Ruth, Jack Dempsey, or Al Capone. When I was twelve, we moved into a neighborhood with a lot of gangsters. They were all swell dressers and had big cars and carried "gats" [guns.] Us kids saw these swell guys and mingled with them in the cigar store on the corner. Jack Gurney was the one in the mob that I had a fancy to. He used to take my sis out and that way I saw him often. He was in the stick-up rackets before he was in the beer rackets, and he was a swell dresser and had lots of dough. . . . I liked to be near him and felt stuck up over the other guys because he came to my home to see my sis.[13]

The boy's conception of and relationship with the racketeer illustrates how those who hold deviant values are used as role models by youth. The relationship is not unlike that between a nondelinquent youth and an adult in a legitimate pursuit to which the youth aspires.

The criminal subculture requires a stable community organization; wild juveniles engaging in gang conflict and other destructive activities are likely to be strongly disapproved of in such a subculture. Beginning in apprenticeship criminal positions, juveniles are required to discipline themselves and work their way up in the rackets in much the same way that a young businessperson is required to work his or her way up in a company.

Where stable community organization does not exist, a *conflict subculture* is likely to emerge. If the local criminals are disorganized and cannot provide an orderly route to success through crime, there is little chance that the transition from young delinquent to adult criminal can be made. A disorganized, unstable community cannot provide the illegitimate opportunities that a criminal subculture can; at the same time it cannot provide legitimate opportunities as can a stable middle- or upper-class community. Because of community disorganization, there is little direction, and the conflict subculture emerges.

In part, conflict subcultures have developed because of the government's attempts to clean up the slums. When old tenement houses are bulldozed and housing projects for low-income people are set up, a community is often scattered and thereby disorganized. The stability provided by the network of neighborhood relationships is distributed as different families are bureaucratically allocated new housing in the projects.

Without the opportunity structure provided in the criminal subculture, such virtues as self-discipline and conformity to community standards are no longer valuable. Frustration due to lack of opportunity is often vented in the form of violence. The status of having either legitimate or illegitimate "connections" is replaced by individualistic status based on personal bravery and a willingness to demonstrate "heart." Typically "heart" is realized through risk-taking behavior such as fighting or breaking the law. In this context, violent gangs emerge and juvenile gang warfare increases. As long as the opportunity structures remain closed the violence is unchecked.

Finally, the *retreatist subculture* is exemplified in the drug-using cultures of the lower class and, more recently, the middle class. As in Merton's definition of retreatist behavior, both cultural goals and legitimate means are abandoned. While retreatism initially appears to be an individualistic mode of adaptation, Cloward and Ohlin show that much retreatist behavior is a collective phenomenon. A good example is the middle-class drug subculture that emerged in the 1960s, in which a collective life-style centered around the use of psychedelic drugs and rejection of the established values.

As we have pointed out, Cloward and Ohlin explained that many of those who joined retreatist subcultures of lower-class drug users were "double failures" who had not been able to attain success goals through either legitimate or illegitimate means. In the conflict subcultures, only some were able to attain a good "rep" (reputation) and the status that went with it. Those who failed, having also failed to achieve status through legitimate channels, withdrew and turned to drugs. In conflict subcultures, sometimes violent gangs would shift from fighting to drug use, thereby taking on a collective retreatist adaptation. Those who entered the retreatist subculture entered an organized world of drug traffic and connections in addition to a world view supporting drug use.

While this seems to be an accurate description of lower-class drug-using groups, the process of "double failure" does not appear to describe the development of the middle-class drug subculture. Those who entered the "hippie" subculture were highly educated and had access to legitimate means to success goals. During the 1960s jobs for college graduates were plentiful and material comfort was virtually guaranteed, yet they were more likely to become "hippies" than the lower-class youth who were denied these advantages. Many who joined the youth subculture centered on drug use were disillusioned with material success goals and sought something more meaningful. They were not "failures" in the sense of not having access to means of achieving cultural goals.

Delinquency as Nonutilitarian Behavior

Another theory that attempts to explain the emergence of delinquent subcultures was put forth by Albert Cohen.[14] Like Cloward and Ohlin, Cohen pointed out that lower-class juveniles were denied opportunities to achieve middle-class goals and came to see their failures in terms of various social barriers. However, whereas Cloward and Ohlin emphasized utilitarian goal-seeking through illegitimate means, Cohen's main focus was on nonutilitarian behavior by lower-class juveniles.

Cohen explained that working-class juveniles were aware of the legitimate success paths in American society; however, they were equally aware of their limited chances of obtaining the goals implied in middle-class values. Instead of taking illegitimate means to achieve success goals, they turned the middle-class values and norms upside down. Such violent acts as unprovoked beatings and school vandalism achieved no ends in terms of middle-class success goals, but they did give the delinquents status. Status deprivation was the main problem working-class boys had to cope with, since they were denied the opportunity to achieve status in the conventional system. In the same way that illegal activities allowed boys in the conflict subculture described by Cloward and Ohlin to achieve a "rep," so nonutilitarian acts gave working-class youth a way of "being someone," of achieving *some* status even though it was not recognized as such by the larger society.

What is important about Cohen's theory is that it accounts for delinquent activities that appear to have no purpose. By providing something other than a middle-class measuring rod, Cohen was able to show that seemingly "senseless" acts of destruction and violence do have a purpose in terms of the subcultural values available in the lower and working class. Instead of being nonutilitarian, these "hell-raising" activities serve to achieve status for the juveniles who engage in them.

Like the Cloward-Ohlin theory of the retreatist subculture, Cohen's theory is based on lower- and working-class delinquency and does not adequately account for middle-class delinquency. The conditions described by Cloward and Ohlin as well as the social situation and reaction explained by Cohen fit only disadvantaged youths and do not explain the drug-using subculture consisting largely of middle-class youth.

Middle-Class Delinquency.   In order to deal with the growing delinquency among middle-class youths, Cohen formulated a theory of middle-class juvenile subcultures that promote delinquent values and activities.[15] As in his explanation of lower-class subcultures, he looked to the social structure and the structure of opportunities for his explanation. After World War II the opportunity structure for middle-class youths expanded as never before. In the prewar years, even middle-class youths had to work hard and defer gratification in order to obtain success goals, but in the postwar period youths from middle-class backgrounds could successfully pursue success goals without deferring gratification. As opportunities for success increased, there was no need to wait until one had attained a secure position to begin enjoying the fruits of the American dream. Juveniles in growing numbers had access to automobiles or even had cars of their own. Thus they were no longer tied to the home or under the supervision of their parents. Like their parents, young people were beginning to find new adventures and were exploring innovations in having fun. Premarital sex became increasingly common, and the introduction of birth-control pills banished or at least diminished the fear of unwanted pregnancies. All the while, there was little concern over "making it" in American society, for the opportunities appeared to be unlimited.

At the core of the youth culture was the hedonistic pursuit of fun, excitement, and enjoyment with peers. With the new affluence to provide the resources for this pursuit and with parents' desire to display this affluence by giving their children the status symbols previously reserved for independent adults, there was a breakdown in the traditional insulators against delinquency. Additionally, as the economy entered a phase dependent on huge consumption, the mass media encouraged the hedonistic values of the youth culture, not only for youths but for their parents as well. The Protestant ethic of compulsive hard work, which had dominated America in an earlier day, came to be rivaled if not replaced by the "have fun-stay young" ethic of Madison Avenue. Parents who did not allow their children or themselves the pleasures of an affluent society were characterized as old-fashioned and "square"; thus the breakdown of the traditional barriers against nonproductive free-time activity was also effected among parents. The urge to direct their children toward single-minded productive activity lessened as parents were encouraged to loosen up and enjoy themselves more as well.

The delinquency generated by this hedonistic pursuit of happiness did not involve an intentional reversal of values, as did the lower-class delinquency described by Cohen. Instead, by imitating and exaggerating adult values as depicted in the mass media, youth transformed adult resources into toys, and their playful handling of adult status symbols was seen as delinquent.[16] For example, automobiles were used not only for functional transportation but also for the thrills of racing and speeding. Furthermore, juveniles were subjected to legal sanctions for indulging in such pastimes as drinking and sex, which were not illegal for those holding adult age status. Middle-class youths were more likely to see their violations of the law as a mere imitation of their parents' behavior; in their view, their actions were not bad, the laws were unjust.

The development of subcultural theories has several important implications for understanding delinquency. First, it set the stage for further theories about delinquency. Later we will discuss theories of conflict and of differential association, both of which interact with subcultural theories in explaining delinquency. Second, subcultural theories pointed out the normal social processes involved in delinquent activities. Some subcultures were in no way delinquent or criminal.

Subcultures of Delinquency.   A critique of the subcultural approaches developed by Cloward and Ohlin and Cohen was set forth by Sykes and Matza[17] and later elaborated by Matza.[18] The subcultures envisioned by Cloward and Ohlin and Cohen were essentially oppositional ones in that they were directly at odds with conventional culture.[19] Miller, following Cohen's lead, went so far as to state that lower-class delinquent subcultures were autonomous value-sustaining entities, largely unaffected by conventional culture and values.[20]

Sykes and Matza pointed out that juveniles in high-delinquency areas often use what they describe as "techniques of neutralizations"[21] to justify delinquents acts.* It was reasoned that if juveniles who live in a delinquent subculture use rationalizations to excuse delinquency, they must have some kinds of ties to conventional culture and its system of values. This is because in a delinquent subculture, where the values are in opposition to conventional values, there is no need to justify actions that are in violation of values the youths do not hold.

Matza suggested an alternative formulation of delinquency and subcultures based on the characteristic of *publicity.*[22] Rather than a delinquent subculture, Matza referred to settings in which the commission of delinquency is common knowledge among a group of juveniles as a *subculture of delinquency.* This type of subculture was not in opposition to conventional culture, but instead it was accommodating in that it embraced parts of conventional culture but allowed for delinquent activities under certain circumstances.[23] This reformulation of the notion of delinquent subcultures explained why delinquency, even in the most delinquency-prone areas, was not taken up by all juveniles or to the extent that the other subculture theories would have us believe.[24] Moreover, it is a notion that brings middle-class delinquency as described by Cohen somewhat closer to lower-class delinquency.[25]

In pointing to differences between middle- and lower-class delinquency, even if we can now see that the difference is not so great, we are still talking about *class* differences and not the difference between the status of a juvenile and that of an adult. All that the subculture theories appear to do is identify

---

*In the next chapter, in discussing social control theory, we will elaborate Matza's theory and the techniques of neutralization.

aspects of working- and lower-class values, or what Matza identifies as sub-terranean values, which appear to be more prevalent among certain groups than others.[26] Since the prevalence almost invariably shows up in the lower classes, subcultural theories come to be nothing more than theories of class differences. Those of Cohen, Miller, and Cloward and Ohlin suggest a conflict value orientation toward conventional culture, whereas Sykes and Matza's view of subcultures suggest an accommodating orientation. All of these sub-cultural theories, however, point more to class differences among juveniles than to differences between juveniles and adults.

Subculture of Juvenility

Here an alternate orientation toward the study of delinquency and subcul-ture is suggested. Following Matza's lead, we will look at the concept of subculture along the lines of publicity and contend that we are dealing with an accommodating subculture whose values are largely conventional ones. However, instead of positing a subculture of delinquency, I would like to suggest a *subculture of juvenility* in which are couched certain delinquent values.

The subculture of juvenility is centered around the life situation of the juvenile, namely, economic dependence, compulsory education, and the legal status of a juvenile. In this life situation the juvenile develops certain values that are divergent from those of the conventional value system, even though in most cases the values of juveniles reflect those of their parents and general ethnic-socioeconomic position.

In Chapter 5 we delve into the situational structure of juvenile life and its relationship to delinquency. Here, however, we will look at empirical evi-dence that supports the concept of a subculture of juvenility as a more useful understanding of juvenile delinquency than either that of delinquent subcul-tures or subcultures of delinquency.

First, as was pointed out in Chapter 1, virtually every juvenile engages in delinquency. Furthermore, the peak age for crime is during adolescence.[27] Once a person "leaves" the status of a juvenile, either through a full-time job, marriage, or some similar passage, his or her crime and delinquency drop significantly.[28] Since what juveniles "leave" when they pass from being juve-niles is the status of juvenile, they also leave the subculture of juvenility—not necessarily a subculture of delinquency.

In a study of juvenile drug use, it was found that only 20 percent of the juveniles in two midwestern high schools had used marijuana.[29] However, the same study found that 50 percent of the juveniles claimed to have a "close friend" (not merely an acquaintance) who had used marijuana. Since students from the upper socioeconomic families were the ones most likely to have tried marijuana, it was not the case that a lower-class group of students constituted a subculture of delinquency. Given that the knowledge of the violation was widespread, judging from the number of students who had a close friend who smoked marijuana, and assuming that others knew of the violation even though they did not have a close friend who used marijuana, we can characterize the delinquency as an aspect of a subculture of juvenility.

Throughout this book we will be examining different forms of delinquency. Most of the delinquency we will look at is committed by typical juveniles who are not labeled as delinquent; and given certain situational understandings of particular violations, the delinquent acts are accepted by the subculture of juvenility. These delinquent activities change with time, and those that juveniles accept at one time they do not at other times. For example, during the early 1960s marijuana use was not acceptable as a part of the subculture of juvenility; however, since the late 1960s it has been acceptable and even encouraged among juveniles. Likewise, the "toughness" that accompanied styles of the 1950s was rejected in the late 1960s among juveniles for a more "loving" and "meaningful" style. However, with the growing violence in "punk rock" reflecting a *Clockwork Orange* mindlessness, we may see a new wave of violence become acceptable in the subculture of juvenility.

As a final note, it is important to understand that not all delinquent actions are tolerated by this subculture of juvenility. Not only do styles change, but there is also a sense of appropriate discretion in matters of delinquency. Smoking marijuana in class, for example, would be negatively sanctioned not only by school authorities but also by students. In this way the subculture of juvenility defines and controls delinquency, and the delinquency that is outside of this subcultural definition is seen as deviant delinquency. By focusing on what juveniles themselves allow, we can account not only for the widespread incidence of delinquency but also for its control and direction. Deviant delinquency, or delinquency that is considered inappropriate in the context of the subculture of juvenility, is relatively scarce, and unless it becomes a part of the subculture, as did marijuana smoking, it accounts for only a minute part of the total amount of delinquency.

Conflict Theory

As subcultures develop, the likelihood increases that they will evolve norms that diverge from and conflict with conventional values. The extent to which there are different values among cohorts, in turn, points to the development of distinct subcultures. For example, as young people come to see themselves as a unique group with its own norms and values or even an entire life-style that is different from their parents', a youth culture forms. Slogans such as "Don't trust anyone over thirty" suggest a distinct separation between young and old and also show that some conflict exists between the age cohorts.

According to Simmel, some conflict is an attempt to achieve an end, but other disputes are merely expressions of frustrations with no other end than to vent aggression.[30] The first type of conflict is termed *realistic* in that the conflicting parties are clashing with a goal in mind. For example, if two rival gangs fight over the right to a piece of territory, we can call the conflict realistic in that it is directed toward a specific result—namely, control of the territory. In contrast, when two parties are in conflict simply because one of the groups is using the other to release its frustration the conflict is *unrealistic.* Hilter's use of the Jews as a scapegoat for Germany's problems is an example of unrealistic conflict, because there the aggression had no true object.

In examining the conflict between the youth culture, especially those involved in the life-style that emerged around drug use, and the larger society, do we find it to be realistic or unrealistic? The laws contain negative sanctions for marijuana use, and anyone who uses marijuana therefore comes into conflict with the larger society in the form of the juvenile and criminal justice systems. On the one hand we can say that the conflict is realistic because one side is attempting to maintain the drug laws and the other side is attempting to flout them. On the other hand, the conflict is unrealistic because the goals for maintaining the laws are unclear. Similarly, when young men began to wear long hair, they found themselves in conflict with the bulk of the adult population, and there appeared to be no reason for the dispute. The same was true with the music of the young. Initial reactions to rock 'n' roll were extreme; many adults claimed that it signaled the downfall of Western civilization. The styles and fads of the young frequently evoke conflict between young and old.

Criticism and conflict were not in a single direction, however. During the civil rights movement of the fifties and throughout America's involvement in Vietnam, adult values and life-styles came under violent attack by the young.[31] The American dream of material affluence and the values of the Establishment were rejected by the emerging philosophy of youth. Adults were characterized as hypocritical and shallow, voicing the values of a Judeo-Christian heritage while engaging in racial, social, and economic discrimination, and compulsively pursuing material affluence at the cost of humanistic values. Thus, not only did adults attack the new values developing among the young, the young assaulted the old values of their parents.

In their desire to express the new freedom, the young often came into conflict with the delinquency laws. As we pointed out, the marijuana laws were violated with increasing frequency, and the life-style of youth came into conflict with other laws as well, especially those reserved for the young. For example, numerous youths were leaving home without their parents' permission or knowledge, thereby breaking the laws pertaining to parental control over children. Juveniles who left home to join the youth culture in such rallying points as Haight-Ashbury in San Francisco, the Sunset Strip in Los Angeles, the East Village in New York City, and Oldtown in Chicago were subject to control by the juvenile court. Likewise, since the young no longer saw sex as something to be postponed until marriage, a number of female juveniles came under the jurisdiction of the juvenile courts.

It would seem initially that this reaction by the adult institutions might hinder the development of the youth culture; however, many theorists believe that conflict creates solidarity among the emerging outgroup—in this case youth. According to Karl Marx, conflict creates cohesion within each warring faction.[32] As the conflict increases, members of each group become increasingly aware of their common situation in relation to their adversary. That is, they come to identify with one side or the other rather than adopt an individualistic orientation. Since the battle lines were drawn between the young and the old, age status put people in one camp or the other. Furthermore, individual problems come to be interpreted in terms of group troubles, or, to paraphase Marx and Engels, each collective moves from being a *class in itself* to a *class for itself*.[33] A class in itself is a group of people who share a similar fate in life but are unaware of their common interest. They have no class consciousness. However, as members of the classes come to see their common interest, they come to act in terms of their unique class status. They see the problems of those in like circumstances as their own problems, and the source of their problems are identified in terms of their adversary's actions. In the case of youth, when they attempted to exercise their new values, they were subjected to the sanctions of the adult establishment, and this was seen as a threat to all youth. Thus, rather than perceiving individualistic violations of basically just laws, the youth culture interpreted the laws as a means of maintaining the status quo by keeping youth in line. Law violations were therefore regarded not as delinquency but as a consequence of adult repression of the values of the youth culture.

The development of the youth-adult conflict along the lines suggested by Marx was destined to some form of cooptation, however. As youths become older, they move socially and economically into the adult world and eventually come to be part of that world. Many of them bring the new life-styles along with them, and some of the conflicts of values and norms are thus dissipated. At the same time, as they grow older the laws regulating juveniles no longer apply to them. If a young man wishes to travel, for example, he can do so after he reaches legal age without becoming a ward of the court. Youth, as a class, is something one "grows out of," and the conflict between the youth and adult cultures, unlike racial conflict, has the feature that one group inevitably joins the other after a certain period of time.

One of the signals of the death of a strong and active youth culture was the apparent end of the war in Vietnam in 1974. When American soldiers left Vietnam, the protest movement more or less fizzled out. The war had been a rallying point for young people, and when it ended, so too did much of the spirit of solidarity among the young. The war's end also coincided with an economic slump, and job opportunities declined for college graduates, and even more so for high school graduates. Students sank into apathy and thereby left a void in youth leadership, which had been provided by college-age youths. Young people came to see one another as competitors in a depressed job market and lost the sense of identity that was generated during the antiwar movement.

Another event that lessened the conflict between young and old came from an unexpected quarter. A major aspect of the youth culture had been disillusionment with the government's willingness to respond to the needs of young people. They distrusted governmental institutions and saw little input in decision making. When the Watergate scandal broke and grew, more and more people came to share this view of government. However, instead of inciting new mass demonstrations by the young, it merely confirmed what they had believed all along. As the adult world came to the same conclusion, young and old joined in their distrust of government. Instead of increasing conflict, the Watergate affair came to reduce conflict between young and old.

A key point for understanding conflict explanations of juvenile delinquency is that differences in the treatment of cohorts lead to different conduct norms as well as different values and life-styles.[34] The implication, of course, is that to the extent that there is social differentiation, there will be conflict. Juveniles are differentiated from adults in numerous ways, and this differentiation leads to conflict. The process of social differentiation for juveniles has two sources: the restriction placed on juveniles by adults, and the life-styles and interests developed by the youths themselves. Special juvenile laws designed to protect and control the young set them off from the adult world, and this discrimination puts juveniles in a position to develop their own independent interests and norms. Schools, especially junior high schools and high schools, serve as collection points where youth can develop a unique identity apart from the adult world. Ironically, schools are supposed to be places where youth is prepared for the adult world, but because educational institutions for the young keep them apart from the adult world, they function to socialize juveniles into the youth culture and therefore into conflict with adults.

Critical Theory. More recently, conflict theory has been reformulated by the "critical theorists." The general theory in this area was developed by Richard Quinney,[35] and its specific applications to juvenile delinquency have been put forward by, among others, Anthony Platt.[36] The critical theorists have stressed the conflict between classes that emerge in a capitalist society and the criminal laws imposed by the powerful on the powerless to maintain the institutions of the powerful. Chapter 11 will consider in detail Platt's analysis of the emergence of the juvenile court, but here we present the basic general theory of crime developed by Quinney and its implications for the study of delinquency.

The following six propositions comprise the basic theory of critical thinkers:

1. Crime is a legal definition of human conduct that is created by agents of the dominant class in a capitalist society.

2. Definitions of crime are composed of behaviors that conflict with the class interests of the dominant economic class.
3. Definitions of crime are applied by the class that has the power to shape the enforcement and administration of criminal law.
4. Behavior patterns are structured in relation to definitions of crime, and within this context persons engage in actions that have relative probabilities of being defined as criminal.
5. Conceptions of crime are constructed and diffused in the course of communicaton.
6. The social reality of crime is constructed by the formulation and application of definitions of crime, the development of behavior patterns in relation to these definitions, and the construction of conceptions of crime.[37]

The critical theory as applied to juveniles has special relevance to the laws exclusively regulating juveniles—the juvenile-status laws. Compulsory education and the attendant truancy laws are seen by the critical theorists as devices for preparing youths for positions in the capitalist labor market and centers for socializing youths to the capitalist ideology. The laws reflect the control that the powerful exert over all segments of society and even take away from the more traditional socializing institutions, such as the family.

The apparent flaw in this thinking lies in the fact that the juvenile laws apply to all segments of society, and not merely children of the nonelite. If the laws discriminate against juveniles, which they clearly do, then they discriminate against youths of all classes. Logically this is true, but empirically it is not, and by examining which children are arrested and sent to detention and which are warned and sent home to their parents, we see that the children of the upper classes receive favorable treatment. This is predicted by the critical theory in Quinney's proposition 3, which states that the law is applied by those with power. In Chapter 11 we will examine evidence which demonstrates that children of the upper social strata receive very different treatment at the hands of the law than do children of the working and lower classes.

The conflict predicted by the critical theorists lies in the reaction to the laws by those who are most affected by them in society. Again turning to the juvenile-status laws, we can see that they are a source of major conflict—if conflict is measured by arrests of juveniles for these offenses. Until recently, since a number of states have made juvenile-status offenses nondelinquent for first offenses, the majority of the girls and a large proportion of the boys in juvenile detention were there for status offenses. The direction of the laws specifically against juveniles and their position in society constituted the source of conflict.

In summary, the conflict perspective has developed from viewing conflict as a normal form in the work of Simmel up through the neo-Marxist approach of the critical theorists. The social differentiation between juveniles and adults heightens the conflict, even if conflict already exists between social classes. However, as Matza noted in discussing subcultures of delinquency, the differences between the subcultures and the dominant culture appear to be something other than conflict. We could say that the conflict is specifically over certain laws that are imposed upon the powerless juveniles by the power structure, and therefore the differences and conflict are not general. But Matza was dealing with cultural differences and values, while the conflict theorists are dealing more with structurally imposed differences created in the form of different social classes and unequal distribution of power and wealth. The core of the conflict lies in the ability of one group to impose control over another group and not necessarily differences in values, which on their expressed state, may be very similar for the different segments. The social differentiation may lead to different values, as the subcultural theorists argue, but for the conflict theorists the values are secondary to the structural differences. The life experiences accompanying social differentiation in relation to one class over another are the source of conflict, and since juveniles are differentiated socially and legally, they are more likely to come into conflict with the law than other segments of society.

SUMMARY

The key element that links the various structural explanations is *social differentiation.* The differentiation may be based on anything from different family structures to differentiations based on power and wealth. In order to focus on juveniles and juvenile delinquency, it has been suggested that we consider a *subculture of juvenility,* for it is the differentiation between adult and juvenile that gives juvenile delinquency its specific and unique form. Moreover, the other structural theories tend to be more general, being used to explain criminality and deviance as well as delinquency.

In later chapters we will investigate the institutional structures that mold the subculture of juvenility, especially the legal institutions. For now, however, it is sufficient to understand that these institutions differentiate juveniles from adults, shaping a common experience and world view among juveniles. This is not to say that the subculture of juvenility *causes* delinquency, but rather it forms delinquency into the style it has. By studying the extent to which the subculture of juvenility *allows* various forms of delinquency, ones that change from time to time, we can explain and understand the structural elements of delinquency.

NOTES

1. Elmer H. Johnson, *Crime, Correction and Society,* 3d ed. (Homewood, Ill.: The Dorsey Press, 1974).
2. Sheldon Glueck and Eleanor Glueck, *Unraveling Juvenile Delinquency* (Cambridge, Mass.: Harvard University Press, 1950).

3. Aaron Cicourel, *The Social Organization of Juvenile Justice* (New York: Wiley, 1968).
4. Jackson Toby, "The Differential Impact of Family Disorganization," *American Sociological Review, 22*:502–512 (October 1957).
5. Hyman Rodman and Paul Grams, "Juvenile Delinquency and the Family: A Review and Discussion," Appendix L of *Task Force Report: Juvenile Delinquency and Youth Crimes,* President's Commission on Law Enforcement and Administration of Justice. (Washington, D.C.: Government Printing Office, 1967), pp. 188–221.
6. Glueck and Glueck.
7. Susan K. Datesman and Frank R. Scarpitti, "Female Delinquency and Broken Homes: A Re-assessment," *Criminology, 13*(1):33–55 (1975).
8. *Ibid.,* pp. 53–54.
9. Robert K. Merton, *Social Theory and Social Structure* (New York: Free Press, 1957).
10. Stanton Wheeler and Leonard S. Cottrell, *Juvenile Delinquency: Its Prevention and Control* (New York: Russell Sage Foundation, 1966).
11. Richard A. Cloward, "Illegitimate Means, Anomie, and Deviant Behavior," *American Sociological Review, 24*:164–176 (1959).
12. Richard A. Cloward and Lloyd E. Ohlin, *Delinquency and Opportunity: A Theory of Delinquent Gangs* (New York: Free Press, 1960).
13. Clifford R. Shaw, "Juvenile Delinquency: A Group Tradition," Bulletin of the State University of Iowa, no. 23, N.S. no. 700, 1933.
14. Albert Cohen, *Delinquent Boys* (New York: Free Press, 1955).
15. Albert Cohen, "Middle-Class Delinquency and the Social Structure," in Edmund W. Vaz (ed.), *Middle-Class Juvenile Delinquency* (New York: Harper & Row, 1967).
16. Ralph W. England, Jr., "A Theory of Middle-Class Delinquency," in Edmund W. Vaz (ed.), *Middle-Class Juvenile Delinquency* (New York: Harper & Row, 1967).
17. Gresham Sykes and David Matza, "Techniques of Neutralization: A Theory of Delinquency," *American Sociological Review, 22*:664–670 (December 1957).
18. David Matza, *Delinquency and Drift* (New York: Wiley, 1964).
19. *Ibid.,* p. 35.
20. Walter Miller, "Lower Class Culture as a Generating Milieu of Gang Delinquency," *Journal of Social Issues, 14*(3):5–19 (1958).
21. Sykes and Matza.
22. Matza, p. 30
23. *Ibid.,* p. 40.
24. *Ibid.*
25. Cohen, "Middle Class Delinquency and the Social Structure."
26. Matza, p. 63.
27. Daniel Glaser, *Crime in Our Changing Society* (New York: Holt, Rinehart and Winston, 1978), p. 156.
28. Delbert S. Elliott, "Delinquency, School Attendance and Dropout," *Social Problems, 13*: 307–314 (Winter 1966).
29. William B. Sanders, "Drug Use among Suburban Midwest High School Students," unpublished consultant paper prepared for Palos Township Youth Council, 1970.
30. Lewis A. Coser, *The Functions of Social Conflict* (New York: Free Press, 1956).
31. Daniel Yankelovich, *The New Morality: A Profile of American Youth in the 70's* (New York: McGraw-Hill, 1974).
32. Karl Marx, *Poverty of Philosophy,* H. Quelch, trans. (Chicago: Charles H. Kerr, 1910).
33. Karl Marx and Friedrich Engels, *Manifesto of the Communist Party* (Chicago: Charles H. Kerr, 1888).
34. Thorsten Sellin, "Culture Conflict and Crime," *Bulletin 41,* Social Science Research Council, 1938.
35. Richard Quinney, *Criminal Justice in America: A Critical Understanding* (Boston: Little,

Brown, 1974); *Criminology: Analysis and Critique of Crime in America* (Boston: Little, Brown, 1975).

36. Anthony Platt, *The Child-Savers: The Invention of Delinquency* (Chicago: University of Chicago Press, 1969). "The Triumph of Benevolence: The Origins of the Juvenile Justice System in the United States," in Richard Quinney (ed.), *Criminal Justice in America: A Critical Understanding* (Boston: Little, Brown, 1974).

37. Richard Quinney, *The Social Reality of Crime* (Boston: Little, Brown, 1970), pp. 15–23.

4 Delinquency, Social Situations, and Interaction

DELINQUENT PROCESSES

In Chapter 3 the emphasis in explaining delinquency was on the social structure. Here we will examine explanations that point to more immediate elements in social life. The structural theories pointed to macro-structures, while the theories we will look at now concentrate on the micro-structures and the social processes within these structures. In a certain respect, these theories can be seen as a fine tuning and adjustment of structural explanations because they all acknowledge the effect of social structure on delinquency. At the same time, however, they indicate that structural theories paint with too broad a brush. Thus we need to understand the micro-structures and processes to see how delinquency is patterned the way it is.

The three major theories we will examine are (1) social control theory, (2) differential association theory, and (3) labeling theory. We will also briefly look at differential anticipation theory, which combines control and differential association theory.

Social control theory focuses on the external social situation of the individual and examines how social control is either in force or broken. It is a theory of *soft determinism* in that individuals are not compelled to commit delinquency but rather find themselves in situations in which they are not bound by social control mechanisms and then *choose* whether or not to commit a delinquent act.[1] In differential association theory, on the other hand, the emphasis is on the *learning* of delinquent behaviors from others, and depending on one's associations, a juvenile is more or less likely to commit a delinquent act. Finally, labeling theory concentrates on the *societal reaction* to delinquency. The labeling theorists show how the stigma of "juvenile delinquent" can lead to further delinquency by separating certain juveniles from others.

SOCIAL CONTROL THEORY

Social control theory explains delinquency largely in terms of the external social situation of the juvenile.[2] It is the inability of society to control juveniles, either through internalized values socialized into individuals or external control, that provides the situation which allows delinquency. Control theorists are careful to state that they are not pointing to causes of delinquency in the same way as other theories do, but instead they are dealing with the social situations that provide the possibility of delinquency. Linden and Hacker[3] point out that control theory views individuals in society as having a good deal of freedom from societal ties and obligations in comparison to other sociological theories of delinquency. By identifying the social situations in which the ties are the weakest and the sanctions for violation are least likely to be subjectively experienced by the individual, control theorists attempt to map out and explain the patterns of delinquency.

Frazier has identified six major control theorists—Emile Durkheim, Albert Reiss, F. Ivan Nye, David Matza, Walter Reckless, and Travis Hirschi.[4] Each of these theorists identifies different aspects of control over individuals in society and the conditions under which the controls fail to be effective. Rather than reviewing all of these theorists, we will concentrate on the works of David Matza and Travis Hirschi as representative of the control theorists' contribution to the understanding of juvenile delinquency.

David Matza.   In most theories of delinquency the individual is viewed as compelled and controlled by circumstances over which he or she has no control or choice. Matza characterizes this view as "hard determinism" and suggests an alternative image of delinquents centered around the concept of "drift."[5] The individual is neither wholly free nor wholly constrained, but rather is in a state somewhere in between. As Matza states:

> The image of the delinquent I wish to convey is one of drift; an actor neither compelled nor committed to deeds nor freely choosing them; neither different in any simple or fundamental sense from the law abiding, nor the same; conforming to certain traditions in American life while partially unreceptive to other more conventional traditions; and finally, an actor whose motivational system may be explored along lines explicitly commended by classical criminology—his peculiar relation to legal institutions.[6]

This view implies some amount of will and choice in the individual, but at the same time recognizes the social forces surrounding the person. It is the midpoint between freedom and control.

In the subculture of delinquency juveniles commit a good deal of delinquency, but not as much as they would were they committed to delinquency implied in the notion of a *delinquent* subculture. In the situation of drift, the individual is free to commit delinquency, but whether he or she does or not is a matter of choice, not compulsion. This explains why delinquents are not committing delinquency all the time and why later, as they mature and come to be less in a state of drift, they stop committing crimes.

The state of drift is an episodic and situational one.[7] Drift is the episodic release from moral constraint in which the delinquent does not feel obliged to keep from violating social and legal norms. This does not mean that during these situations the delinquent must engage in delinquency; rather, during drift, he or she is free to do so. Most of the time delinquents either feel constrained to abide by conventional morality or they are distracted by something else requiring their attention and therefore do not engage in delinquency. In still other situations they are under the surveillance of others who would provide external controls over their actions. As a result, even the most delinquent youths commit only a few delinquent acts in comparison to the time they spend in law-abiding, nondelinquent activities.

When youths do commit delinquent acts, they are not expressing values that are contrary to conventional morality; instead, the situations are defined in such ways that the offenses are negated. Generally, offenses are negated by formulating the circumstances of the act as justifiable in much the same way that any crime is seen as justifiable. First, a delinquent act may be justified as an instance of *self-defense*.[8] As a legal defense, claiming self-defense is valid if one can show that there was an immediate danger to oneself. However, delinquents have a different conception of what constitutes an immediate threat. For example, a youth might present a threat by calling another a "punk." To allow such a remark to pass without taking offense is, in the delinquent's view, to be subjected to further remarks or even assaults. Likewise, if an outsider, especially a youth from another gang, trespasses on one's gang's "turf," then attacking the foreign gang member is seen as a matter of self-defense. Of course, these conceptions are outside of the legal definitions of self-defense, but they serve to show a delinquent version of an attachment to conventional morality.

Two further legal-like negations on the part of delinquents include claiming *insanity* and *accident*. Since delinquents view being "mixed up" or neurotic as unmanly, the insanity defense for delinquent acts implies a temporary state caused by intoxication or anger.[9] To commit delinquency while "bombed outta my mind" or "gone crazy with anger" releases the individual from responsibility and explains the action in a way that maintains the person's general acceptance of conventional values. Likewise, negating an offense on the basis of an accident is given a peculiar twist in the context of the subculture of delinquency. First, for the subcultural delinquent accidents include recklessness.[10] Matza summarizes the subcultural conception of recklessness as follows:

> An act either is intended or not. Recklessness is a state of mind which either implies intent or it does not. Clearly, I am reckless. I do not deny that. I did not bother to foresee the consequences of my line of action. But how could I? I am reckless. It's not a crime to be reckless. It's like being a wild child.[11]

Thus, given this conception, anyone or anything that happens to get in the way of the subcultural delinquent is the accidental victim of recklessness, like a runaway truck roaring down a hill.

A second type of accident absolving responsibility for delinquency is the *accident of circumstance*.[12] In this case fate guides one's fortunes, and there is little to be done to alter fate. The subcultural delinquent is thus a victim of fate, and the intent of committing a delinquent act is absent. The extent to which the delinquent experiences himself or herself as effect (that is, guided by fate) instead of as cause, he or she is rendered not responsible. This puts the individual into a state of drift in which he or she is free to commit delinquency.[13] In many ways the subcultural delinquent's position is the same as the positivistic conceptions held by criminologists who strip the individual of will and account for all delinquency in terms of the conditions surrounding delinquents. Matza's conception differs, however, in that he is talking about the delinquent's subjective viewpoint; the delinquent is thrown into a state of drift where delinquency is possible, not mandatory.

In an earlier work with Sykes, Matza outlined a set of five distinct techniques of neutralization.[14] These techniques serve to maintain the sense of moral worthiness by relieving the delinquent of responsibility. Sykes and Matza contend that delinquents do not create a separate set of values but instead develop "techniques of neutralization" by which they rationalize and justify actions that in some circumstances they would condemn.[15] Essentially, delinquents believe in the laws they violate, but they neutralize potential feelings of guilt by means of various techniques that justify their lawbreaking.

Five techniques of neutralization are identified. Delinquents may adopt a *denial of responsibility,* blaming their activities on conditions over which they have no control, such as their social position, family, or associates. They may become adept at using psychological and sociological theories in denying their responsibility. For example, a juvenile may claim that he did not have a father and because of this turned to a delinquent gang for a masculine identity. Second, they may adopt *denial of injury,* claiming that their delinquent acts are not really harmful. Gang violence, for example, may be defined as a private quarrel not harmful to innocent bystanders in the same sense that boxers in a match do not strike out at the audience. A third technique of neutralization is *denial of the victim.* The victim is characterized as having deserved whatever happened to him or her, perhaps because he is a homosexual, an unfair teacher, or a storekeeper who engages in shady business practices. Delinquents may also *condemn the condemners,* shifting the focus of their wrongdoing to those who condemn them. Thus they charge that the police accept bribes, teachers engage in favoritism, and others are pious hypocrites. This technique changes the subject and the impact of accusation, functioning to relieve the assault on the juvenile's self-image. Finally, delinquents may *appeal to higher loyalties,* claiming that they are sacrificing the demands of the larger society to higher loyalties to friends and neighborhood solidarity. They come to characterize themselves as caught between the loyalty they owe the legal order and the more immediate allegiance they owe to those close to them.

The techniques of neutralization attest to the delinquents' acceptance of general social values and do not stand as a set of subcultural values. They develop as a means of coping with the guilt generated by violation of the internalized norms and values of the larger society. However, the collective acceptance of these techniques as justification for delinquency does suggest the development of a delinquent enclave in society. Sykes and Matza point out that these techniques do not always succeed in relieving delinquents of guilt, for they may not be sufficiently isolated from conforming society to accept such techniques as valid. Those who are isolated from the values of larger society may not need to employ any techniques of neutralization at all. What is important about the Sykes-Matza thesis is that it explains how the mechanisms of social control may lose their effectiveness in compelling compliance with the social norms. The extent to which such techniques are employed with social support points to some type of delinquent cohort and collective world view. At the same time, the absence of techniques of neutralization among delinquents suggests the existence of a delinquent subculture, for it is the internalization of conventional social norms and values that makes such techniques necessary.

In summary, Matza states that subcultural delinquents are not wholly alienated from conventional values, nor do they randomly and constantly commit delinquent acts. Rather, when in the state of drift they are freed from conventional norms so that they may choose to commit delinquent acts. Drift is episodic, not constant. When a delinquent act is committed the act is justified by techniques of neutralization. These techniques serve both to placate the actor's conscience and to set the stage to allow delinquency. The general negations of offense further excuse delinquent acts in a similar way that legal exceptions to *mens rea* (criminal intent) do. The fact that negations and neutralization techniques are employed suggest that there is at least some attachment to conventional morality.

Travis Hirschi.   Hirschi has identified elements that bond the individual to society and constrain him or her to conform.[16] Unlike most other control theorists, he gives almost no credit to internalized norms and values as explanations of social conformity. Linden and Hacker characterize Hirschi's position as follows:[17]

> control theory "sees in the delinquent a person relatively free of the intimate attachments, the aspirations, and the moral beliefs that bind most people within the law."[18] Thus, the delinquent is not viewed as being tied to a different value system or even to deviant peers, but is seen as being relatively free of ties to society. "If a person does not care about the wishes and expectations of other people—that is, if he is insensitive to the opinion of others—then he is to that extent not bound by the norms. He is free to deviate."[19]

Thus, for Hirschi, it is important to identify what in society constrains the individual from delinquency and not the factors in the delinquent's background or associations that lead to internalized norms and values moving the individual toward or away from delinquency.

The first element identified by Hirschi that bonds the individual to society is *attachment.*[20] By attachment Hirschi means the links of an individual to others. The extent to which one is attached to others links one with society and its norms and obligations that force conformity. Frazier equates Hirschi's understanding of attachment with that of Emil Durkheim's stress on the sharing of collective conscience that comes through the attachments to society.[21]

Second, the individual is bonded to conformity through *commitment.* The more an individual is committed to conventional society and positions in society, the more he or she stands to lose through deviation. For example, a youth may enjoy smoking marijuana. But as he begins a career, starts a family, and increases his status in the community, the costs for being caught smoking marijuana increase. While for a juvenile being caught smoking marijuana may mean paying a fine or being placed on probation, the offender will not be rejected by his or her peers, and he or she will probably not be thrown out of school. As the individual becomes committed to conventional society and adult status in that world his or her values and attitudes toward marijuana may not change, but the person comes to realize that the costs are so great for the violation that he or she quits marijuana. Thus, since most juveniles are not committed to society to the extent that adults are, they are less constrained to conform.

Third, Hirschi points out that *involvement* constrains individuals to conform. Involvement refers to the extent to which one is engrossed in conventional activities and routines. A person who is working and involved in family and community activities during a good part of his or her free time has little time in which to engage in delinquent activities. The opportunities for delinquency are far less frequent.[22] Juveniles, however, are far less involved in and tied to such involvements, so that they have more time for subordinate involvements that may be delinquent.

The last element identified by Hirschi that binds the individual to conventional norms are *beliefs.* One may understand the conventional values of society, but one may not necessarily believe in them. Whenever the beliefs are weakened, delinquency is possible, but this is a situational condition and not a constant that is internalized in personality. Unlike differential association theory, which we will examine next, Hirschi does not contend that the beliefs are determined by peer association and that there is a fundamental difference between conventional and delinquent youths. Rather, there are circumstances in which social control over an individual is such that the person no longer believes in following the social norms.[23] However, combined with attachment, beliefs come to account for what other theorists treat as "internalized norms and values."[24]

Control theory provides us with a way of accounting for the situational nature of delinquency. Patterns of delinquency that are not adequately explained by other theories—namely, the episodic nature of delinquency even among subcultural delinquents—can be accounted for by control theory. The theory can also account for the social-psychological state that allows delinquency in the concept of "negation of offense." The criminalization process is taken into account to some extent by Matza,[25] but the focus of the discussion is on the juvenile justice system from the point of view of the subcultural delinquent and not on its impact in defining delinquency. Nevertheless, since control theory focuses on external controls such as the juvenile justice system, we can say that control theory does address the criminalization process.

The problem that control theory wrestles with and never quite seems to explain adequately is the role of internalized norms and values. This dilemma is outlined by Frazier:

> Internal controls are either internalized norms opposed to deviance or personally pragmatic decisions making deviance impractical. External controls rest in the influence others, groups, and institutions have on the individual. While the two general sources of control probably never exist exclusively of one another, they frequently vary considerably in relative strength. Internal controls, which are in large part a product of external controls, are usually considered to be the most effective given the weakness of controls outside the person.[26]

To the extent that external controls are weak and internal controls are a product of external controls, *internal controls must be weak.* There is a circular argument here—and if one is strong, the other is implied to be strong, and vice versa. The control theorists are vague on this point of internal control, and where they attempt to be specific, they are thrown into a tautology.

To a great extent control theorists are encountering the same problem Durkheim faced. In his early writings Durkheim stressed the constraint on individual behavior by pointing to external controls in the form of social sanctions. In his later writings, however, Durkheim realized that at least some individuals in society must have internalized social norms and values in order for them to impose sanctions on others. That is, if no one had internalized social values, there would be no one to impose sanctions for violating the norms implied in the values.[27] In Chapter 5 we will re-examine this problem and attempt to incorporate control theory into another framework that will resolve the problem of internal and external control.

Empirical examinations of control theory generally confirm the basic tenets of the theory. In examining the life histories of 50 career criminals, Frazier found that control theory accounted for more deviance than either socialization theory or societal reaction theory (labeling theory).[28] Tittle found that the fear of sanction in different situations constrained individuals to conform, confirming the most basic aspect of control theory.[29]

One study by Linden and Hacker, which combined control theory with differential association theory under the title of "affective ties," found that neither differential association theory nor control theory could predict delinquency separately as well as the two theories could when combined.[30] The investigators measured the ties youths had with nondelinquent youths, delinquent youths, and their parents. Those who had stronger ties with their parents and nondelinquent youths were less likely to engage in delinquency than those who had strong affective ties with delinquent youths. Control theory was tested in that ties to the conventional order were measured, and differential association was tested by measuring ties between delinquent youths.

Control theory has shed a good deal of light on the problem of delinquency, explaining how we can understand the episodic delinquency of the great majority of juveniles and at the same time why even the most delinquent youths commit delinquent acts only under certain circumstances. The emphasis on forces external to the individual give it a uniquely sociological character. Control theory, however, still needs clarification with respect to the role of internalized norms and values. With further development of the theory, or with synthesis with other principles of social behavior, this approach offers considerable promise.

Differential Association Theory

In situations that are "ripe for delinquency" there must be someone who recognizes the "ripeness." That is, someone must *define the situation* as possibly being delinquent. Even in the drift situation, in which a youth chooses whether or not to commit a delinquent act, the individual must recognize the situation as offering the possibility of delinquent rule violation.[31] Several years ago while visiting Holland, on noticing that the Dutch did not lock their bicycles, I thought, "Someone might rip off their bikes." That is, I defined the situation as possibly delinquent. Apparently, however, there were few Dutch who would have defined the situation in the same way. If they had, either they would have locked their bicycles or there would have been a rash of bicycle thefts. Other Americans also noted the unlocked bicycles and remarked that it was nice that in Holland the people did not have to worry about theft the way we do in the United States. Why was it that the Americans immediately defined the situation as having delinquent possibilities and the Dutch did not? Differential association theory attempts to answer this question.

Differential association theory assumes that crime, like any other behavior, is learned, and it is learned in social interaction.[32] The learning of criminal behavior, however, involves learning more than the techniques, for many crimes, such as shoplifting, require little substantive knowledge. More important is learning the attitudes that favor breaking the law. By associating with others whose attitudes favor law violation, individuals come to learn these attitudes. Thus, if most of an individual's associations are with people who habitually break the law and who express attitudes that justify their activities, he or she is more likely to become delinquent than is someone who associates with people who do not break the law and who disapprove of law violation.

Given this theory, why don't all police and prison guards engage in criminal and delinquent activity, since they associate frequently with law violators? As Sutherland and Cressey point out, the nature of the association is as important as the fact of social contact. Whether a person will take on criminal or anticriminal behavior patterns depends on certain variables describing the association. Some associations are more *frequent* than others. If one spends most of one's time with delinquent gangs and very little with law-abiding juveniles, one is more likely to take on the attitudes of the delinquent gang members. The *duration* of the association is also important: the longer the association, the more likely one is to pick up the attitudes of the others. The third factor is the *priority* of association—how early in life the individual is exposed to criminal or noncriminal attitudes. The earlier the exposure to criminal behavior patterns, the more likely the person is to engage in criminal activities. Finally, the *intensity* of a relationship determines whether the association is close or casual. If a juvenile has close ties with delinquents and casual ties with nondelinquents of the same duration, he or she is more likely to take on the attitudes of the delinquents.

It is important that differential association theory points to the availability of criminal (or delinquent) *behavior patterns* in a given social milieu. These behavior patterns exist independent of any single cohort that may engage in the activity. For example, a delinquent gang may exist for several generations; while the people who occupy the various positions in the gang change, the behavior pattern of the gang may persist. Through differential association a given juvenile is more or less likely to come into contact with the pattern of delinquent gang activity. Depending on his or her peers, the individual will come to see the delinquent activity in the gang as a good or a bad thing. If a boy lives in a neighborhood where membership in delinquent gangs is taken for granted as an aspect of growing up, he is more likely to take on a positive orientation to gang activities and attitudes than if he grows up in an area where nondelinquent peer relationships are available.

Additionally, differential association theory points out that delinquency is very much a social as opposed to an antisocial activity. In an area in which there is massive delinquent activity, a youth who shuns social relationships and acts as a loner is less likely to become delinquent than a more gregarious youth. If a boy wants to pursue his own interests alone, he is less likely to join a delinquent gang and engage in delinquent activity than is a peer-oriented youth.

To get a thorough idea of differential association theory, we should look at all of its propositions, set forth by Sutherland and Cressey:

1. Criminal behavior is learned.
2. Criminal behavior is learned in interaction with other persons in a process of communication.
3. The principal part of the learning of criminal behavior occurs within intimate personal groups.
4. When criminal behavior is learned, the learning includes (a) techniques of committing the crime, which are sometimes very complicated, sometimes very simple; and (b) the specific direction of motives, drives, rationalizations, and attitudes.
5. The specific direction of motives and drives is learned from definitions of the legal codes as favorable or unfavorable.
6. A person becomes delinquent because of an excess of definitions favorable to violation of law over definitions unfavorable to violation of law.
7. Differential associations may vary in frequency, duration, priority, and intensity.
8. The process of learning criminal behavior by association with criminal and anticriminal patterns involves all the mechanisms that are involved in any other learning.
9. While criminal behavior is an expression of general needs and values, it is not explained by those general needs and values, since noncriminal behavior is an expression of the same needs and values.[33]

It appears that most of the theory is accounted for in terms of learning and associations, and the various propositions elaborate the manner in which learning takes place. However, the last proposition appears to stand by itself, and further explanation of this very important postulate is necessary. To explain it let us consider an example. Let's say that some boys want to go fishing (a value) and require fishing poles and tackle. In order to obtain the necessary gear there are a number of tactics they can employ. They can ask their parents for the money to buy the fishing equipment, they can work and earn money to purchase it, or they can engage in some illegal activity to acquire it. Whatever activity they choose will be for the *same* value and need (the wish to go fishing and the need for the gear); therefore, if they engage in delinquent behavior to realize their goals, we cannot say that the desire to go fishing *caused* the delinquent behavior, for the same desire presumably could have been realized through nondelinquent means. That is, we cannot explain delinquent behavior by pointing to the ends of the activity, for there are legal routes to the same ends. Similarly, it is tempting to explain bank robbery by saying that the robbers wanted the money. Well, everyone wants money, but not everyone robs a bank. We must ask, rather, why given individuals choose criminal or delinquent *means* to realize their needs and values. In this way we explain the delinquent activity instead of general social needs and values.

There have been a number of criticisms of differential association theory, which have generated several empirical tests of the theory's propositions and a good deal of debate as well as insight. We will look briefly at some of the criticisms of the theory, examine empirical studies, and discuss the theory's importance in accounting for juvenile delinquency.

Criticisms of differential association spring from numerous sources. Some criticisms, such as the charge that the theory neglects individual differences,[34] are aimed at sociological theories in general, but since the theorists are attempting to account for *patterns* of crime and not individual criminals this charge is not relevant. A second criticism is that while differential association theory accounts for a good many criminal patterns, there are several types of crimes which it does not adequately explain. For example, embezzlers appear to act alone in the commission of their crimes and do not appear to associate with other violators of financial trust.[35] In many respects this criticism appears to be valid, especially since Donald Cressey, who was instrumental in the development of the differential association theory, carried out the research on financial trust violation. However, some other crimes that at first appear to be exceptions to differential association theory are found, upon closer examination, to be consistent with the theory. So-called compulsive crimes such as criminal homicide were thought to be exceptions to the theory; however, the "compulsive" nature of these crimes appears to be simply another theory of crime.[36] Luckenbill found that, far from being compulsive, homicides follow a consistent pattern of development. Further, they occur only on certain kinds of social occasions, and only when the sequence that leads to homicides is available and appropriate to the occasion.[37] Thus, this criticism of the differential association theory was found to be based on a misconception of certain types of crime, or, as Cressey pointed out in the case of embezzlers, a partial understanding of the theory.[38] Even though embezzlers act alone, they learn in social interaction the rationalizations, techniques, and everything else necessary for committing their crime. Finally, differential association theory has been criticized for not accounting for the origin of crime. While the theory shows how crime is passed on from one cohort to another, it does not explain how the criminal behavior pattern began. This is true: it is necessary to couple differential association theory with subcultural theories to explain how criminal behavior patterns originate. By the same token, however, the subcultural theories are dependent on differential association to explain the maintenance of the subculture.

The research designed to test differential association has had mixed results. In a self-report survey of juvenile drug use, the researchers found that the reason most often given by juveniles for trying illegal drugs was the desire to be "in" with their peers.[39] This supports the contention implicit in differential association theory that delinquent behavior is dependent on peer group attitudes. Similarly, in another self-report survey of high school students, it was found that almost 99 percent of those who had smoked marijuana had a close friend who had used the drug.[40] Furthermore, a number of studies have found that delinquent activities are typically committed by groups of two or more juveniles.[41] Reiss and Rhodes attempted to find out whether boys in close friendship groups share the same specific patterns of delinquent behavior.[42] In their study, which focused on the *intensity* variable in differential association, they found that the probability that an individual will commit a specific delinquent act depends upon the commission of the act by his friends. This supports differential association theory. However, they also found that the salience of association as a variable itself varied with social class and with types of crime. Working-class delinquents were more likely to have associates who committed similar crimes than were middle-class delinquents. Also, those who committed the more serious crimes (for example, robbery) were less likely to have close friends who had done the same thing.

Differential Anticipation

A relatively new theory, developed out of differential association theory and social control theory, is differential anticipation theory.[43] This theory directs attention to the following key concepts:

1. *Social bonds,* both anticriminal and procriminal, that each individual develops in life, which create stakes in conforming to the standards or expectations of others so as to please rather than alienate them;
2. *Differential learning,* by which tastes, skills, and rationalizations are acquired that determine whether success and gratification are achieved in criminal or in alternative activities;
3. *Perceived opportunities,* reflecting not just social bonds and differential learning but the possibilities of law-violating or conforming behavior that a person observes—that is, the assessments of prospects and risks.

This theory provides explanations of the external constraints emphasized in social control theory and the learning of criminal and anticriminal behavior patterns and attitudes in differential association theory. At the same time, however, it stresses the importance of examining the rationality of the actor in deciding to commit a crime or not based on the situational elements as perceived by the actor. This provides a model of humans whereby they are not totally compelled by social forces to commit crimes even though they are greatly influenced to choose to do so in certain social situations. Moreover, it provides a frame of analysis for accounting for different types of crimes committed by different groups of people. A good deal of research is necessary to further develop and test this theory, but since it is empirically based, it shows a good deal of promise in explaining delinquent actions.

Labeling Theory

In the discussion of an adequate definition of delinquency and delinquents (Chapter 1), we saw that unless someone defines an activity as delinquent, no delinquency exists. Similarly, when we talk about a delinquent, we refer to someone who has been labeled as such by the juvenile justice system. Once a person has been labeled, he or she is often forced to play that assigned role even though he or she may prefer another course. Labeling theory focuses on the *interactive* aspects of deviance because it takes into account not only the delinquent activity and performer but also the others who come to define the situation and the actor as delinquent.

To understand this theory, it is important to know a little about *symbolic interactionist theory.* First, labeling theory assumes that all reality is grounded in the symbols we use to talk about it, or, as W. I. Thomas put it, "If men define situations as real, they are real in their consequences."[44] For example, if some juveniles are playing in front of a house when a bird flies against a window and breaks it, then flies away, the juveniles may be blamed for the broken window. If the juveniles are believed to be responsible for the act, the police may be called, and as a consequence of this definition of the situation the juveniles may be labeled delinquents. Now, we might say that they were falsely accused, but the point is that their innocence of the act does not alter the consequences. They have been defined as delinquents, and on the basis of this definition they are treated as such.

A second important concept is that of the "looking-glass self." Essentially, this concept, developed by Cooley, holds that people come to see themselves as they are defined by others.[45] Thus, if juveniles are seen by others as stupid and lazy, they are likely to come to see themselves in the same way. Furthermore, since people act in terms of their self-identity, the definition of self is instrumental in determining behavior. A juvenile whose self-conception is that of a stupid and lazy student is more likely to act stupid and lazy than one who sees himself or herself as intelligent and hard-working. Similarly, a juvenile who has been labeled delinquent is more likely to commit acts that are consistent with this identity than a youth who has not been so labeled.

Now we can appreciate some basic tenets of labeling theory. First, Lemert has distinguished between primary and secondary deviance.[46] *Primary deviance* is the original act that is defined as deviant by others. Any number of social, cultural, psychological, and physiological factors can cause this original offense.[47] More important is *secondary deviation,* an adaptation to the societal reaction to primary deviation in terms of social roles, social identity, and processes in fixing a person in a deviant category. For example, let's say a girl is caught shoplifting. She enters a transformation process from a nondelinquent to a delinquent. First, the juvenile justice system judges her delinquent and places her in a social category along with all other delinquents.

Goffman refers to the label of "delinquent" as a *stigma* and to the process by which a person is discredited as stigmatization.[48] This process serves to separate the stigmatized individual from nonstigmatized others, and it also puts those with a like stigma into social contact with one another. That is, stigmatized individuals are isolated from everyone except others who are stigmatized. The girl who has been stigmatized for shoplifting will be cast in the role of a delinquent, and her parents, friends, and teachers may come to treat her somewhat differently than before. Sometimes this treatment is blatant and sometimes subtle, but when it exists the stigmatized individual can sense it. For example, as one convicted criminal noted:

> You know, he didn't see this as an insulting remark at all: in fact, I think he thought he was being honest in telling me how mistaken he was. And that's exactly the sort of patronizing you get from straight people if you're a criminal. "Fancy that!" they say. "In some ways you're just like a human being!" I'm not kidding, it makes me want to choke the bleeding life out of them.[49]

As labeled delinquents are gradually isolated from nondelinquents, they are forced into association with other delinquents. Parents tell their children not to associate with "bad kids," images of delinquents are exaggerated so that association with them is undesirable, and what began as a social sanction for norm violation becomes a force making it extremely difficult for the delinquent to avoid further deviation. The extent to which an individual is caught up in this process suggests secondary deviation.

It should be noted that the process beginning with official labeling does not inexorably lead to secondary deviation. Depending on social status and resources, the individual can fight even repeated attempts to fix a stigma. For instance, one young man who was charged with first-degree burglary and arson had considerable resources behind him to fight off the stigma of a criminal.[50] His mother hired an expensive criminal attorney who was able to have the charge reduced to second-degree burglary and to have the arson charge dropped completely. The young man was placed on probation and fined even though he had been in trouble with the law on several other occasions. Someone with fewer resources may not have been able to avoid imprisonment and the stigma of a convict. Additionally, friends and relatives of the young man called the victim and berated her for having brought the charges and thus caused the burglar's problems! No one in the young man's circle saw him as being delinquent because of his actions; instead they somehow redefined the event to emphasize the victim's willingness to report the crime.

Labeling theory at first may seem to tell us not so much about the patterns of delinquency as about the process whereby one comes to be seen as delinquent. However, as Becker points out, the power to label people criminal is the power to determine their fate.[51] As we have noted, almost all juveniles commit delinquent acts, but only a few are officially judged to be delinquent. Members of minorities and the poor are more likely to wind up in the official statistics as being delinquent. Lacking power in the form of either financial clout or knowledge, the disadvantaged in society are less able to fight the official labeling process. Because of this lack of power, and not necessarily because of their greater delinquent activity, the disadvantaged are overrepresented in the official statistics. Moreover, given the process of secondary deviation, since members of minorities and the poor are more likely to be labeled delinquent, they are more likely to be forced into the role of a delinquent and thereby actually be involved in more secondary deviation. Thus, there is a self-fulfilling prophecy. The minorities and the poor may not commit any more primary deviance than the affluent, but they are more likely to be labeled delinquent. The labeling process leads to secondary deviation, which leads to further delinquency, and thus the disadvantaged come to commit more delinquent acts.

The labeling perspective is limited in explaining initial deviance. By linking this theory with other theories that share the symbolic interactionist framework, such as differential association, we can account for more delinquency. The most significant contribution of labeling theory is that it forces us to examine the influence of others in creating delinquency instead of regarding delinquency as something that exists in a vacuum. Labeling theory shows that those who define the situation, either officially or unofficially, have an important role in creating the social reality of delinquency. It thereby further demonstrates the social nature of delinquency in society and refutes the notion that something must be pathologically wrong with juveniles for them to commit delinquent acts. Finally, labeling theory accounts not only for the patterns of delinquency and the social-psychological process of becoming delinquent but also for the role of the juvenile justice system in delinquency.

SUMMARY

In this chapter we have seen a number of different explanations for juvenile delinquency. Each has its strengths and weaknesses, but none appears to meet completely our criteria in adequately accounting for (1) patterns of delinquency; (2) social-psychological states explaining individual acts; or (3) the criminalization process. Social control theory provides us with good explanations of certain patterns and social-psychological conditions, but it is weak in explaining why the juvenile justice process reacts to certain groups while ignoring others. Labeling theory gives us a good deal of insight into the criminalization process, patterns of official delinquency, and the impact of the delinquent label on the individual and his or her reaction to it, but it tells us little about primary deviation. Differential association theory can account for patterns of delinquency and can even explain why different groups engage in specific forms of delinquency along with the social-psychological elements of delinquency, but it is weak in explaining why only certain groups of delinquents are held accountable for delinquency.

At this juncture many students will be tempted to opt for either a synthesis of theories or a multiple-factor theory that will explain everything. We have already seen why a mutiple-factor theory would be a serious mistake, and so we won't waste time with that option. On the other hand, if we take the key elements that appear to be consistently valid in each theory and construct a new theory that integrates all of these elements we might be able to develop a "new" theory that will account for delinquency. The problem is that we might find that the key elements of one theory are inconsistent with those of another theory. For example, social control theory denies that differential association is an important element in explaining delinquency. However, if we take a new framework and integrate the principles into it, then we can transform the character of the elements so that they can be consistently integrated. Such a synthesis provides us with a new way of looking at delinquency from a sociological point of view, and it directs our attention to aspects of delinquency that are ignored under any single perspective.

In Chapter 5 we will refocus on delinquency and raise questions that have been unasked in the study of delinquency. At the same time, we will attempt to integrate a number of principles that have been laid down in the theories we have examined. Such an effort is both new and cumulative, and we hope it will open new doors in understanding delinquency.

NOTES

1. David Matza, *Delinquency and Drift* (New York: Wiley, 1964), pp. 9–12.
2. Charles E. Frazier, *Theoretical Approaches to Deviance: An Evaluation* (Columbus, O.: Charles E. Merrill, 1976), p. 49.
3. Eric Linden and James C. Hacker, "Affective Ties and Delinquency," *Pacific Sociological Review, 16*(1):27–46. (January 1973).
4. Frazier, pp. 49–71.
5. Matza, p. 27.
6. *Ibid.,* p. 28.
7. *Ibid.,* p. 69.
8. *Ibid.,* pp. 75–81.
9. *Ibid.,* p. 84.
10. *Ibid.,* p. 85.
11. *Ibid.,* p. 86.
12. *Ibid.,* pp. 87–90.
13. *Ibid.,* p. 89.
14. Gresham Sykes and David Matza, "Techniques of Neutralization: A Theory of Delinquency," *American Sociological Review, 22:*664–670 (December 1957).
15. *Ibid.*
16. Travis Hirschi, *Causes of Delinquency* (Berkeley: University of California Press, 1969).
17. Linden and Hacker, p. 29.

18. Hirschi, Preface.
19. *Ibid.*, p. 18.
20. *Ibid.*
21. Frazier, p. 66.
22. Hirschi, p. 22.
23. *Ibid.*, pp. 23–26.
24. Frazier, p. 66.
25. Matza, pp. 100–179.
26. Frazier, p. 102.
27. Talcott Parsons, *The Structure of Social Action,* Vol. I (New York: Free Press, 1937).
28. Frazier, pp. 209–221.
29. Charles Tittle, "Sanction Fear and the Maintenance of Social Order," *Social Forces, 55.* (March 1977).
30. Linden and Hacker, pp. 35–36.
31. Edwin H. Sutherland and Donald R. Cressey, *Criminology,* 5th ed. (Philadelphia: Lippincott, 1978), p. 80.
32. *Ibid.*, pp. 80–83.
33. *Ibid.*
34. Gwynn Nettler, *Explaining Crime* (New York: McGraw-Hill, 1974), p. 196.
35. Donald R. Cressey, *Other People's Money: A Study in the Social Psychology of Embezzlement* (Belmont, Calif.: Wadsworth, 1971).
36. Donald R. Cressey, "The Differential Association Theory and Compulsive Crimes," *Journal of Criminal Law, Criminology, and Police Science, 45:*29–40 (June 1954).
37. David F. Luckenbill and William B. Sanders, "Criminal Violence," in Edward Sagarin and Fred Montanio (eds.), *Deviants: Voluntary Actors in a Hostile World* (Morristown, N.J.: General Learning Press, 1977), pp. 88–156.
38. Cressey, *Other People's Money,* pp. 147–151.
39. Don Bowers and Lynn White, "Behavior and Attitudes of Students: A Longitudinal Perspective" (Turlock, Calif.: California State College, Stanislaus, 1974), mimeographed.
40. William B. Sanders, "Drug Use among Suburban Midwest High School Students," unpublished consultant paper prepared for Palos Township Youth Council, Illinois.
41. Clifford R. Shaw and Henry D. McKay, "Social Factors in Juvenile Delinquency: A Study of the Community, the Family, and the Gang in Relation to Delinquent Behavior," in *Report on the Causes of Crime* by the National Commission on Law Observance and Enforcement, Vol. 2, No. 13, Chap. 6 (Washington, D.C.: Government Printing Office, 1931). Thomas G. Eynon and Walter C. Reckless, "Championships at Delinquency Onset," *British Journal of Criminology, 2:*167–168 (October 1961).
42. Albert J. Reiss, Jr., and Lewis A. Rhodes, "An Empirical Test of Differential Association Theory," *Journal of Research in Crime and Delinquency, 1:*5–18 (January 1964).
43. Daniel Glaser, *Crime in Our Changing Society* (New York: Holt, Rinehart and Winston), pp. 126–127.
44. W. I. Thomas, *The Unadjusted Girl* (Boston: Little, Brown, 1923).
45. Charles Horton Cooley, *Human Nature and the Social Order* (New York: Scribner's, 1902).
46. Edwin Lemert, *Social Pathology* (New York: McGraw-Hill, 1951).
47. Edwin Lemert, *Human Deviance, Social Problems and Social Control* (Englewood Cliffs, N.J.: Prentice-Hall, 1967), p. 40.
48. Erving Goffman, *Stigma* (Englewood Cliffs, N.J.: Prentice-Hall, 1963).
49. T. Parker and R. Allerton, *The Courage of His Convictions* (London: Hutchinson, 1962), p. 111.
50. William B. Sanders, *Detective Work: A Study of Criminal Investigations* (New York: Free Press, 1977).
51. Howard Becker, "Whose Side Are We On?" *Social Problems, 14:*239–247 (Winter 1967).

5 Delinquent Occasions

INTRODUCTION

In this chapter we will take a new look at juvenile delinquency as we look at the *moments* during which delinquency is committed. This will involve conceptualizing the social circumstances in which delinquent acts are most typically found and explaining why some circumstances are more likely than others to lead to certain delinquencies. At the same time, we will attempt to see how these delinquencies come to be noticed and labeled. Finally, we will examine these delinquent moments in terms of the social-psychological concepts of identity and character, showing how certain risk-taking behaviors constitute "character tests" and "thrills" for juveniles. Throughout this chapter we will make extensive use of Erving Goffman's works and his underlying assumptions about social action.

To begin our examination, we introduce the concept of the "social occasion" and differentiate between types of occasions to show how some are more open than others to the commission of delinquent acts. Next, we will show that juveniles are more likely than adults to find themselves in the kinds of occasions in which law violation is common. To a great extent we can see the connection between the routinization of juveniles' lives and the subculture of juvenility discussed in Chapter 3. We will then examine how involvement in certain kinds of delinquency comes to be noticed and labeled as "trouble," leading to the definition of the situation as "delinquent." Thus, rather than merely pointing out that some youths who commit delinquency are labeled while others are not, we will consider the relationship between the nature of the offense and the labeling process. In order to show why juveniles even consider certain typical delinquencies, we will tie together delinquency with images of self that can be achieved through delinquency.

SOCIAL OCCASIONS

Initially we need to define our terms and spell out how we are going to frame the problem of delinquency. The most important concept before us is that of the social occasion, which is defined as *an affair, undertaking, or event bounded by time and place within which many situations and gatherings form, dissolve, and reform.* [1] In order to understand the significance of the term as Goffman uses it, it will be helpful to look at some examples. Consider two very different social occasions—a classroom occasion and a party occasion. During typical classroom occasions we expect a limited number of situations to arise that normally come up during class. The instructor may lecture, conduct a discussion, or give a test. All of these situations may arise and dissolve during classroom occasions, and we more or less expect them. On the other hand, a party occasion holds a number of different situations, and the situations have not only different forms but a different texture. For example, drinking and dancing are party situations but are not found in the classroom occasion. Discussions also take place at parties, but they are quite different from those in the classroom. They are not limited to a specific topic, and they are not formalized and sequenced.

There is nothing unusual about the examples above, and most people understand what to do in one type of occasion or another. However, many people do not realize that occasions structure our actions and are powerful social forces which control our behavior. Consider what would happen if during class a student began acting as though he or she were at a party. People would think the person crazy, and if we considered behaving that way ourselves, we can imagine the powerful constraints that would keep us from doing so. Other social occasions force us to act in one way or another, and most of the time we conform to these expectations. Deviations are usually minor ones, such as talking in class or boring someone at a party by talking about class.

We can now begin to frame our examination of delinquency in terms of the social occasion. We will begin by examining the occasions on which delinquent acts almost never occur, and then those on which such acts are likely to take place. We will not be concerned with the personalities involved, but instead we will concentrate on the occasion in which *any personality* would be more or less likely to engage in a delinquent act.

Tight and Loose Occasions

From a relatively young age children come to know those occasions on which they can run free and play and those on which they must sit and be quiet, squirming uncomfortably. They come to learn that appropriate behavior depends on the situation, and behavior that may be tolerated in one situation may be admonished in another. Conceptually, we can begin to see occasions as being either *tight* or *loose*.[2] In the most general terms, loose occasions are *informal* and tight occasions are *formal*. While the notions of looseness and tightness are relative to one another and to larger social circumstances, we can use them as starting points in our examination of social occasions and delinquency because they serve to differentiate basic forms of social action.

More specifically, we can understand loose occasions as those that permit a diversity of activities, with the boundaries regulating appropriate behavior only roughly defined. The timing of events is not strict, and one may move from one involvement to another with relative ease. By contrast, tight occasions have strictly defined boundaries regulating appropriate involvement for participants. Events are typically precise and follow a set sequence and order.

Returning to our examples of the classroom situation and the party, we can see that the former is a tight occasion and the latter is a loose one. Behavior during class is precisely bounded, involvements are limited to a certain set of ordered activities, and a definite sequence and time schedule are followed. Parties, on the other hand, tend to be just the opposite. Involvements are generally only vaguely outlined, sequencing is often random and only generally timed, and the texture of the activities is informal. There are, of course, continuums of looseness and tightness, and many normally tight occasions may display features of informality, such as certain avant-garde, unstructured educational programs, and many parties are so formal that they can be considered tight occasions. On the whole, however, there are certain occasions of a given class that we consider tight and others we consider loose, relative though they may be. By examining the extent to which delinquency occurs in one type of occasion we can understand the relationship between delinquency and social occasions.

Juvenile Routines and Occasions

In examining the distribution of tight and loose occasions in society and in the lives of its members, we are faced with a hypothetical situation because there has been no research on this subject. However, we can estimate the amount of time one spends in tight and loose occasions by examining what people typically do in a normal day. For juveniles during the school year a typical day involves going to school in the morning until about three o'clock in the afternoon, with the time from the end of school until dinner occupied by school-related activities such as sports or clubs, a part-time job, or free time. Evenings are taken up by homework, other school-related activities, including sports or clubs, or free time. The extent to which time is "free" suggests the lack of commitment to tight occasions.

Compared to an adult's daily rounds, especially parents who are involved full time with either commitments to a job or work in the home, a juvenile is far more likely to be a participant in loose occasions. The loose occasions for adults, moreover, are loose in the sense that they are relatively less structured, but they do not constitute free time. Everything from attending luncheon meetings to making necessary house repairs occupy much of an adult's time in occasions generally considered loose, and because of the compelling nature of these activities, they cannot be considered free. However, in relation to tight occasions, they allow some freedom.

Given this comparison and the assumptions being made about the distribution of loose and tight occasions, we can now begin to hypothesize about juvenile delinquency and involvement in loose occasions. For reasons we have seen, juveniles are more likely to be found in loose, unstructured occasions than are adults, and the extent of delinquent behavior can be explained to a significant degree by such involvement. We have already seen that juveniles engage in more violations of certain criminal laws than do adults (for example, auto theft, larceny), so that the next question we must address is whether or not most of the typical juvenile crimes occur in loose occasions.

In order to address this question, a study was conducted to determine the kinds of occasions which prompted calls to the police.[3] Obviously, such a study has limitations because it cannot assess all crimes. For example, white-collar crimes virtually always happen during work, which constitutes a tight occasion, and since crimes in this category are rarely reported to the police, we cannot say that the study was a sample of all crimes. However, the study should give us an accurate assessment of crimes handled by the police, and since the police constitute a critical element in the labeling process, the study can provide us with an understanding of the occasions on which labeled crimes and delinquent acts occur.

An examination of 289 police mobilizations for all types of incidents for which people called the police or for which the police responded on their own initiative determined that 84.1 percent of the occasions were loose and only 15.9 percent were tight.[4] As expected, most of the calls for police services came in during occasions in which people were not under rigid constraints. Typical of such loose occasions was "life at home," where families let down their hair and drop the constraints necessary in the workday world. Over a quarter of the calls involved loose occasions in the home. Almost 40 percent (39.7) of the incidents necessitating police mobilizations were in "the streets," where human traffic interacts outside of any bounded set of specific norms directing involvements.[5] This area is the favorite area for juveniles who want to be out of the home, where they may not feel constrained from yelling and screaming at their parents but do feel constrained by their parents' presence. Other settings available to juveniles are typically tight and constraining in one way or another, and so "the streets," and the relatively loose occasion of the streets, constitute settings in which juveniles are often found.

We have not said that loose occasions cause delinquency, but it can be said, in a very specific sense, that tight occasions can prevent delinquency of certain types. In the classroom, at work, or at other relatively formal gatherings people are constrained to behave in a law-abiding manner. These constraints order involvements in such a way as to preclude the opportunity to become engaged in typical forms of delinquent activities, such as fighting, smoking marijuana, and other acts that are highly visible. On the other hand, the kind of delinquency that occurs in tight occasions is usually of low visibility and is not sanctioned by the involvement of the police. For example, in a victimization survey it was found that most retail businesses experienced problems with employee theft. Juveniles working in department stores, drug stores, and other retail businesses who steal from the business do so during tight occasions. The survey found, however, that only 10 percent of the known cases of employee theft were reported to the police.[6] Usually the business would fire the employee who was caught pilfering, or if the theft was minor, the employee would simply be reminded to record any purchases on his or her account. Thus, while neither kind of occasion can be said to cause delinquency, it is clear that tight occasions provide little opportunity for highly visible acts that will draw the attention of the police, while the opposite is true of loose occasions. Moreover, the kind of delinquency that takes place in tight occasions is not publicized, and the sanctions taken are informal. As a result, we should not be surprised to find that the delinquency which comes to the attention of the police is likely to occur in loose occasions.

THE FORMULATION OF TROUBLE

In order to understand the dynamics of the social occasion in relation to delinquency, we need to examine the processes involved in occasions in which delinquency may occur. We have mentioned that different occasions make greater or lesser claims on our involvement. Specifically, we can examine the allocation of involvements in terms of dominant and subordinate involvements.[7] *Dominant involvements* are those that have claims over an individual's activity and attention above all others on a given occasion. For example, during class, the dominant involvement is the material being presented by the instructor, and students are expected to give their attention to the class topic over all other possible involvements they may have. *Subordinate involvements* are those in which one may become engrossed while the dominant involvement is suspended. Before class begins, for example, students can become mutually involved with one another, talking, comparing notes, or engaging in minor horseplay. These subordinate activities are suspended when class begins and the dominant involvement demands their attention.

In loose occasions, the dominant involvement is not well defined, or there may be no single dominant involvement. As we have pointed out, the boundaries for appropriate behavior are broad and vague, and deviations from a single appropriate focus of attention are difficult to sanction because there is no dominant involvement to redirect one's attention.

As a result of the lack of specific norms regulating involvements, there is greater opportunity to fall into activities that are delinquent. This is not to say that youths during loose occasions have to fall into delinquency, but following Matza's notion of "drift," they are freed from the constraints to conform to the law.[8] There may be pressures to commit delinquent acts in loose occasions—for example, occasions in which youths are smoking marijuana and everyone present is expected to take part in the group ritual. We certainly can see, however, that pressures to smoke marijuana would not exist in a tight occasion such as a church ceremony. Anyone who was slipped a lighted marijuana cigarette during a church service would probably refuse it with shocked demeanor and an incredulous, "Are you crazy?" Thus, even the opportunity to pressure youths into delinquent acts depends on the occasion in which the pressure is applied. Even "hard-core" delinquents realize that there is a time and place for everything.

At the same time that we can begin to see the effect the occasion has on controlling youths who are looking for an opportunity to commit delinquent acts, we need to understand the relationship between the normally nondelinquent youth and the occasions in which delinquency can flourish. In contrast to the youthful hustler who is looking for a seam in the social fabric to breach,[9] the nondelinquent youth is attempting to stay out of trouble but is more or less handed delinquent opportunities on a golden platter. In tight situations the few opportunitites presented are easily resisted, but in loose occasions the opportunities are relatively abundant and resistance is less firm. In the company of other nondelinquent youths, a juvenile is probably less likely to get into trouble than in the company of youths who normally engage in delinquency. It is unlikely that a youth will smoke marijuana unless he or she is with someone who does, because the opportunity to engage in the delinquent act depends on having access to the drug and knowing what to do with it.[10] Thus, while delinquency depends on the occasion, it also depends on *those present in the occasion,* and to the extent that the occasion makes delinquent opportunities available, a youth is more likely to become involved in a delinquent act.

Occasional Trouble

The extent to which an act is delinquent or not depends on the kind of situation in which the act occurs. In Chapter 1 we examined the ways in which an act can be characterized and pointed out that only by meeting certain characterizations can an act be viewed as delinquent. At first we might conclude that delinquency is far more likely to be defined as such in tight occasions because appropriate and inappropriate behavior is strictly defined. Yet, as we have seen, most calls for the police occur in loose occasions, letting us conclude that the constraints of the tight occasion limit delinquency. Thus, in tight occasions, there is less to define as delinquent.

There is a problem with concluding that there is less delinquency in tight occasions because of rules that dominate those occasions. We must examine the kind of delinquency that does occur. A girl or boy employed in a department store who regularly steals merchandise does so in such a way that there is no deviation from the dominant involvement. For example, part of a girl's job as a clerk in the dress department is to ring up sales and place purchases in bags. If the girl wants to steal something, all she has to do is to enlist a cohort to come into the store and buy something so that she can slip into her friend's bag an extra pair of pants, a blouse, or a skirt. The girl's involvement, for all to see, appears to be in line with the dominant involvement of the occasion and her job. There is nothing readily visible to characterize her as out of line and possibly delinquent. The extent to which a juvenile can engage in delinquency in tight occasions depends upon his or her position and involvement in that occasion.

We can now begin to see the relationship between an act being noticeable in a situation and being considered possibly delinquent. To understand this relationship, we must understand the concept of "trouble." First, there is "normal trouble," or the kind of trouble that is expected in a situation and that is routinely dealt with.[11] Technological breakdowns—flat tires, burnt-out light bulbs, jammed cash registers, overloaded computers—serve to illustrate the little troubles that people encounter all the time, that they expect, and that are repaired with only minor, if inconvenient, interruptions in the normal flow of events. They are noted only in passing and come to constitute more than minor irritations only if the routines for handling the problems fail. If the burnt-out light bulb happens to be in a movie projector and there is no available replacement, the trouble is seen as more than normal trouble. Someone is going to be held accountable for not having a spare bulb, and depending on the importance of the film being shown, the consequences will vary. The interruption during the showing of a training film might be seen as a reprieve from boredom, while the same trouble at a major motion picture premier would be considered a near catastrophe. Its ability to cause a major change in the routine of the occasion defines trouble as normal or real. The more the trouble changes the routine, the more it comes to be noticed.

In the social sphere, trouble may be viewed in much the same way. Boys on street corners who make embarrassing remarks to passing girls constitute normal trouble for the girls, which they can routinely manage by ignoring both the boys and their comments. However, if the boys begin grabbing the girls, the trouble becomes more than normal. On certain occasions, such as Mardi Gras in New Orleans, there is more toleration for these physical advances, and at parties people tend to let pass what in other occasions would be viewed as real trouble. But in occasions where the trouble is controlled and well defined, we tend to see breakdowns occurring in the technological sphere rather than in the social one. Social control has no influence over breakdowns in machinery other than to force people to have repair equipment available for malfunctioning parts.

Since we have said that the ability to cause trouble is dependent on how noticeable one's actions are in the context of a given occasion, we should expect more trouble in tight occasions because these situations have the most bounded norms of involvements. But since tight occasions also carry more constraints, it is less likely that people will be able to act out noticeably disrupting behavior. Therefore, we will examine a number of different types of loose occasions to uncover their structure and their relationship to visibly delinquent activities.

Family members at home are in a typically loose occasion, free to express themselves vocally and unconstrained by the restrictions of public occasions.

Violence on these occasions includes child abuse, wife and husband beating, and assaults by children on their parents. Police who are summoned to these incidents typically attempt to define them in terms of order maintenance; especially if the people are not hurt, no one wants to treat the disruption as a criminal matter.[12]

However, if parents define the situation to the police by calling their child incorrigible, the police can suggest or take actions that lead to the definition of the juvenile as incorrigible. The loose occasion of family life at home allows for the expression of feelings that can lead to mutual screaming and assaults. To a great extent neighbors ignore these incidents, but sometimes they call the police, either because the fight has become too bothersome to ignore, it is one of a continuing series, or because they fear for the safety of those involved. The point is that the loose occasion provides the social conditions for these outbursts, which are not allowed in other occasions. For example, family fights in tight occasions, such as dining in a formal restaurant, are rare.

Another loose occasion presents itself after school for youths not involved in part-time jobs, club activities, or sports. "Hanging out" is an involvement that can mean several different things and is loose in that "anything can happen." Usually it involves going somewhere that is out of sight of parents and looking for "something to do." Sometimes "something to do" involves a legitimate activity such as a game of basketball, but at other times the activity is delinquent. Getting together with friends to smoke marijuana may constitute "something to do," as may going to a shopping center to shoplift. Later we will examine these different delinquent involvements separately, but for now we will simply point out that they occur during loose occasions.

The visibility of the activities youths engage in is partly due to their location. Stinchecombe has pointed out that one reason the police arrest lower-class persons more frequently than individuals from other classes is that the former lack access to private space.[13] The Skid Row derelict is a prime example of one who has great visibility due to lack of private space.[14] Similarly, juveniles have relatively little access to private space where they can be unobserved by their parents or school authorities. As a result, their activities are more likely to occur in public where they are far more visible.

Another aspect of the visibility of juveniles in loose occasions has to do with disruptions of public order. Fist fights, malicious mischief, vandalism, and other violent forms of delinquency are not easily overlooked unless they are hidden in nonpublic arenas. In public, these kinds of actions tend to disrupt the normal course of events.

Finally, juveniles in loose occasions are more visible because they are singled out for attention. Security officers in department stores are more likely to keep an eye on juveniles than on adults because they assume that youths are more likely to engage in shoplifting. Similarly, the police may more readily question youths because their involvements are less predictable than those of adults, who are usually engaged in involvements dominated by tight occasions. Public life is regulated by involvement structures, and the extent to which it is dominated by tight occasions it is orderly. Being orderly, it is not particularly noticeable, for the activities of the individual are hidden in the patterns generated by the occasion. Individuals who are not part of an orderly, predictable pattern tend to stick out or be picked out for special notice. Because young people are more likely to be in such circumstances, they are more likely to be subjected to delinquent characterizations by others. Moreover, youths in such occasions are more visible in demeanor and style and are not as likely as adults to engage in sophisticated control moves.[15] They also stick out from adults by their clothes, and their bounce, swagger, and awkwardness is self-consciously displayed.

In summary, the behavior of juveniles is not constrained in the same way as that of adults. The constraints are not merely in terms of the sanctions that others apply in a Durkheimian sense. Rather, they are occasionally applied in terms of the situations and occasions in which constraints are made sensible. Because of the way their lives are structured, juveniles are thrown into more occasions than are adults which are not tightly bounded by norms. These loose occasions offer the opportunity, or choice, in Matza's terms, to choose to engage in delinquent acts.

At the same time that much of their world is made up of loose occasions, from the standpoint of juveniles these occasions cut into the tight occasions of others. In a department store where the employees can be said to be in a tight occasion, given their dominant involvement, the occasion is for the juveniles a loose occasion. The same may be said for many adult shoppers, but they see themselves as being "between tight occasions" and their accompanying responsibilities. Thus for adults the matters external to an occasion overshadow the occasion itself.[16] As a result, adults are constrained even in loose occasions by the tight occasions they have just left or will later enter. By comparison, then, juveniles are far less constrained in loose occasions than are adults.

"Something To Do"

It is not sufficient to say that merely because juveniles are more likely to be in loose occasions they are more likely to engage in delinquency. Fads and styles of delinquency change over time, and we must account for these patterns and forms. Obviously, it is important to understand why marijuana was used only by lower-class youths before the mid-1960s and by virtually all classes of juveniles since the late 1960s. It is more important, however, to understand the basic characteristics of delinquency that transcend styles and fads. Thus we must examine what different forms of delinquent acts have in common.

To begin our analysis, we will go back to the loose occasion and examine the kinds of activities that take place in it. We will consider the idea of "something to do," and then look for connections between "something to do" and delinquency. In order to examine this question, we will employ Goffman's theory of "action."[17]

To Goffman, people are actors and the world is a stage.[18] Using the resources available to them, men and women carry on performances, and on the basis of these performances, others make judgments about their moral character. On the one hand, we come to see ourselves according to how others treat us, but this treatment can be manipulated through impression management in our performances. Our appearance, including our dress, gestures, and posture, tells others who we are, and they are obliged to treat us in terms of the claims we make through this appearance. By the same token, if we put on any given performance, we are expected to back it up with certain other activities. For example, if a young man wants to be seen as intelligent he may carry certain books, use a polysyllabic vocabulary, and present all the other props associated with being a scholar. However, if he does poorly on exams and papers, others will come to see him as a phony who cannot back up his claims. The incongruity between his appearance and his ability calls into question his moral character, and his claims to future identities may be difficult to make convincingly.

In the context of Goffman's dramaturgic framework, identities are made (and unmade) in social situations. Instead of being something that follows a person around as a constant, identity has a situational character. For example, a juvenile may be seen in school and classroom situations as "dull," "slow," or, in the parlance of educational newspeak, "educationally handicapped." The same juvenile, however, may be a gang leader in his neighborhood, and when he's with his gang, engaging in gang activities, he is seen as "tough," "brave," and full of "heart." His appearance and even his general performance may not be substantially different in the two situations, but the different audiences and contexts dictate the sense that is to be made of the performance.

As the youth grows up, his situational performances and the identity he develops in those situations come to be increasingly consequential, for more and more others are making judgments about his moral character.[19] That is, each situational performance is assessed in terms of who and what the juvenile *really* is. Is the kid who talks tough *really* tough, or is he just a bigmouth? Does he have the heart to pull it off, or is it just talk? What kind of stuff is this person made of? These questions are asked not only by others who make judgments as to moral character but by the individual of himself. The problem is how to establish and maintain character.

In conventional middle-class society, juveniles' moral character is established by doing well in school, and the character tests are administered by teachers. Similarly, the tennis court, ski slope, surfing beach, and bedroom are settings where young people can prove themselves. The gang youth, on the other hand, does not have the resources or the interest to go skiing or surfing. Further, only a limited number of young people will be chosen to play on the varsity team and to participate in other groups where membership is evidence of a strong character. In other words, there are limited resources in middle-class settings for character building by lower-class juvenile males.

Since identities are made in situations, it is necessary to create and enter into situations where moral character can be established. To show courage, one needs a situation where courage can be demonstrated. Likewise, other attributes prized by gang members, such as "coolness"[20] and "smartness," require situations where one can show others unequivocally that one is "cool" and "smart."[21] It is not enough to tell others of one's courage, as we have shown. What is difficult about making identity claims is having others honor them, especially when the claims involve moral character. Furthermore, the situation must be a real test of these attributes and not one in which the attributes are questionable. For instance, it is not difficult to maintain "coolness" and composure when one is not threatened, and if a youth performs coolly in any number of safe situations it tells us little of his or her ability to carry off the same performance when there are strong urges to the contrary. It is one thing to remain calm and cool during a normal class period but quite another when the school catches fire and everyone is beating a hasty retreat to the exits.

If juveniles waited around until their school caught fire to demonstrate those prized attributes, there would be few opportunities to establish character. However, by creating and seeking out risky situations in which conduct is seen to be a reflection of one's character, they have not only greater opportunity to show what they are made of but the added status that comes from searching for trouble instead of merely waiting until it comes along. Goffman uses the term *action* for situations that are created and entered into for the purpose of establishing moral character.[22]

Now, action can exist and be created just about anywhere. Familiar places include gambling houses, racetracks, and roller derbies. However, these places are typically reserved for adults, and even though gang members have no problem gaining access to such settings, they do not have the same character-establishing possibilities as situations the members can create for themselves. Likewise, certain occupations promise action, notably police work, firefighting, and the military, occupations in which one's mettle is routinely tested and demonstrated. However, these occupations too are reserved for adults.

On the other hand, stealing cars, gang fights, and similar risk-taking activities provide lower-class youths with situations in which they can show the world that they have real courage, coolness, and smartness. The resources for creating action are those that happen to be available, and since opportunities to commit theft and engage in fights are the most readily available to lower-class youths, these are the situations they enter to establish moral character. Unlike their professional counterparts, however, who commit theft and violence as a source of income and take precautions to avoid detection, gang members who engage in these same activities knowingly make them risky.[23]

For example, when asked if he did much joy riding, one gang boy responded as follows:

> Yeah. When I was about thirteen, I didn't do nothing but steal cars. The guy that I always stole with, both of us liked to drive so we'd steal a car. And then he'd go steal another car and we'd chase each other. Like there would be two in our car, two in the other car, and we'd drive by and stick out our hands, and if you touch them then they have to chase you. Or we'd steal an old car, you know, that have the running boards on it. We'd stand on that and kick the car going past. Kind of fun, but, uh, it's real dangerous. We used to have a ball when we'd do that other game with the hands though.[24]

Obviously, no professional car thief in his right mind would engage in this kind of behavior. Thus, gang members not only transform their resources into props for demonstrating character but also transform normal criminal activities, in which there is a good deal of risk to begin with, into even riskier situations.

Attempts by the criminal and juvenile justice system to put a stop to these character-building events typically have the effect of making them more enticing. "Getting tough" with juveniles makes the risks of engaging in delinquencies even greater. As the risks increase, so does the value of the delinquent activity, for one must demonstrate greater courage, coolness, and smartness in order to pull it off. This logic is direct contradiction to the theory of law enforcement, which contends that increasing the risks reduces the likelihood of risk-taking activity. If there is a high value placed on character and if character is best demonstrated by taking risks, then the higher the risks, the better they are for showing off moral character. Hence, in the context of the high subjective value or utility placed on "action," the juvenile justice system provides not a deterrent to delinquency but a spur.

The delinquent behavior generated by the attraction of action situations is by no means limited to theft and fighting. During the youth movement of the 1960s, which included the free speech movement, antiwar protests, and the civil rights movement, there was a good deal of action.[25] College students, and to a lesser extent high school students, engaged in pitched battles with the police, not only risking their freedom but putting their physical welfare and their careers on the line. Leaders of the movement were not above challenging dithering followers to show that they had the "balls" to engage in civil disobedience or outright revolution. Moreover, in campus turmoil, the presence of the police was more likely to incite riot than to quell it. For example, at San Francisco State College, most of the students were politically apathetic. However, when the police department brought the tactical squad to the campus to put down a demonstration, many uncommitted students joined in the protest. Most accounts of the troubles at San Francisco State tended to blame the police for harassing innocent students, thus forcing them into the ranks of the protesters. However, it can also be said that the police activity provided an opportunity for students to demonstrate that they were courageous and willing to protect "their" territory. Moreover, as was amply shown in the mass media, a number of reputations were made during the movement, and in no small way the situations generated by the movement provided the necessary social ingredients for character building.

Another arena of character building for the young was the drug culture. "Acid trips" came to be an adventure in which one could "show one's stuff," and the real and imagined dangers of using LSD provided the necessary risks for demonstrating moral character. As Goffman has noted, "Interestingly, there is currently available through LSD and other drugs a means of voluntarily *chancing* psychic welfare in order to pass beyond ordinary consciousness. The individual here uses his own mind as the equipment necessary for action."[26] The challenge of "try it if you're not chicken" may not have led legions of youth to drugs, but it was incentive enough for a substantially large number of juveniles.

Besides the possibility of showing off character, a further feature of action is the excitement of the situations. To demonstrate coolness as well as other valued character attributes it is necessary to be at least somewhat agitated. This inner agitation provides a thrill that is not available in mundane activities. Finestone describes the "kick" as

> any act tabooed by "squares" that heightens and intensifies the present moment of experience and differentiates it as much as possible from the humdrum routine of daily life. Sex in any of its conventional expressions is not a "kick" since this would not serve to distinguish the "cat" from the "square," but orgies of sex behavior and a dabbling in the various perversions and byways of sex pass muster as "kick." Some "cats" are on an alcohol "kick," others on a marijuana "kick," and others on a heroin "kick."[27]

By transforming the everyday routine into an adventure, young people are not only able to say something about themselves as unique individuals but can also have fun. Delinquency occurs in these situations to the extent that the kicks are characterized as breaches of delinquency laws. In part the kick comes from the fact that delinquency violations are seen as exciting, and in part it is due to the fact that many exciting activities, pursued merely for excitement, happen to be against the law. This is not to say that delinquency is necessarily sustained, although it certainly can be, through action-seeking, for some adventures that begin as a kick may become a habit or a necessity. What is important to understand is that youths in their quest for action may (or may not) engage in delinquencies and that these acts are more likely to be expressive and thrill-provoking than instrumental.

Studies of gang violence have found not only that gang members enhance their moral character or "rep" by seeking out action-type situations but also that maintaining individual as well as collective honor is an ongoing concern for gang members.[28] This leads to situations in which character is made or reaffirmed. Horowitz and Schwartz found that when a gang member or a gang as a whole was verbally or otherwise derogated, the gang felt that it had to fight the detractors or lose face.[29] Typically, this meant a gang fight between the gang whose honor and moral character were questioned and the gang that derogated it. In turn, the gang fight situation provided an occasion on which members of the warring gangs could demonstrate individual strength of character. Therefore, two purposes are served by clashes between gangs. The collective honor of the gang is defended, and at the same time individual members can build their "rep." All this is provided by gang rumbles in addition to the excitement they generate.

With this analysis of "action," we can speculate that one way to fill up a loose occasion with "something to do" is to engage fate, to take a chance to prove oneself. The payoff is not only the thrill of the risk and the high resulting from a rush of adrenalin but also the establishment of self-worth. All of one's resources have been brought to bear and employed in a total involvement of being and self. The moments that we remember best and relive are those in which the chips were on the table and we challenged fate. Out of all of our past experiences, we accumulate days in mundane routines, and only by racking our brains can we recall any single such day. But virtually every risk is easily remembered and symbolically recalled time and again. Our hands were full of fate, and at that time we had "something to do."

SUMMARY

We examined the structure of the occasions in which juveniles find themselves and focused on the delinquent event and situation. We are not saying that delinquency is merely one way of satisying a general need, for Sutherland's dictum is important to remember—delinquency cannot be explained by general needs and values because those same needs and values are realized through nondelinquent means. What is important is the means available to youth for realizing these general needs and values. To the extent to which they participate in loose, unstructured occasions, and to the extent to which "something to do" in these occasions violates the law, we can begin to see that the choice is one of means and opportunities, not just ends. To be sure, a number of youthful activities that fill in the unbounded occasions are legal and constitute "action," but the boundaries of the loose occasions allow greater leeway than do tight occasions where constraints are defined and present.

Furthermore, a situational approach to the study of delinquency cannot forget certain principles of sociology. The principles of differential association and labeling cannot be ignored, for the former explains the participation in a behavior system and the recurrent forms of nonindividualistic delinquency, and the latter accounts for the criminalization process. As we have pointed out, however, even the most committed delinquent engages in delinquency only on certain occasions, and those juveniles labeled delinquent did *something* that could be labeled delinquent. The situational approach forces us to examine delinquent events in the context of a juvenile's situation, both in general terms and in specific instances. Combined with other principles of delinquent studies this approach provides a holistic understanding of the phenomenon of delinquency.

NOTES

1. Erving Goffman, *Behavior in Public Places* (New York: Free Press, 1963), p. 18.
2. *Ibid.*, pp. 198–215.
3. William B. Sanders, "Police Occasions: A Study of Interaction Contexts," *Criminal Justice Review,* 4:1–13 (Spring 1979).
4. *Ibid.*, p. 8.
5. *Ibid.*, p. 11.
6. William B. Sanders, "Victimization Survey of Retail Businesses," unpublished survey, University of Florida, Gainesville, Winter 1975.
7. Goffman, *Behavior in Public Places,* p. 44.
8. David Matza, *Delinquency and Drift* (New York: Wiley, 1964), pp. 27–30.
9. Leroy Gould, Egon Bittner, Sheldon Messinger, Kris Kovak, Fred Powledge, and Sol Chaneles, "Crime as a Profession" (Washington, D.C.: Department of Justice, 1966).
10. Howard Becker, "Becoming a Marihuana User," *American Journal of Sociology,* 59:235–242 (November 1953).
11. Erving Goffman, *Frame Analysis* (New York: Harper & Row, 1974), pp. 307–344.
12. James Q. Wilson, *Varieties of Police Behavior* (Cambridge, Mass.: Harvard University Press, 1968). William B. Sanders, *Detective Work: A Study of Criminal Investigations* (New York: Free Press, 1977).
13. Arthur L. Stinchecombe, "Institutions of Privacy in the Determination of Police Administrative Practice," *American Journal of Sociology,* 69:150–160 (September 1963).
14. Jacqueline Wiseman, *Stations of the Lost* (Englewood Cliffs, N.J.: Prentice-Hall, 1970).
15. Erving Goffman, *Strategic Interaction* (Philadelphia: University of Pennsylvania Press, 1969).
16. Erving Goffman, *Encounters* (Indianapolis, Ind.: Bobbs-Merrill), p. 29.
17. Erving Goffman, *Interaction Ritual* (New York: Doubleday, 1967).
18. Erving Goffman, *The Presentation of Self in Everyday Life* (New York: Doubleday, 1959).
19. Goffman, *Interaction Ritual.* Carl Werthman, "The Function of Social Definitions in the Development of Delinquent Careers," *Task Force Report: Juvenile Delinquency and Youth Crime* (Washington, D.C.: Government Printing Office, 1967).
20. Stanford Lyman and Marvin B. Scott, *A Sociology of the Absurd* (New York: Appleton-Century-Crofts, 1970).
21. Werthman, p. 155.
22. Goffman, *Interaction Ritual,* p. 185.
23. Werthman, p. 156.
24. *Ibid.*, p. 157.
25. Marvin B. Scott and Stanford M. Lyman, *The Revolt of the Students* (Columbus, O.: Charles C. Merrill, 1970).
26. Goffman, *Interaction Ritual,* p. 201.
27. Harold Finestone, "Cats, Kicks and Color," *Social Problems* 5:3–13 (July 1957).
28. Walter Miller, "White Gangs," *Trans-action* (September 1969), pp. 11–26.
29. Ruth Horowitz and Gary Schwartz, "Honor, Normative Ambiguity and Gang Violence," *American Sociological Review, 39*(1):238–251.

6 Juvenile-Status Offenses

INTRODUCTION

Juvenile-status offenses are unique offenses in that they can be committed only by juveniles. These offenses result in nothing stolen, no one assaulted, and no illegal drug taken, but they are commonly given the designation "delinquent," and juveniles are placed on probation and even incarcerated for them. In this chapter we will examine the juvenile-status offense in the context of delinquency and societal reaction. After defining juvenile-status offenses, we will look at their general frequency and distribution. Next, we will discuss the changes in the laws of some states that were designed to remove the delinquent stigma from status offenses, and the effects such changes have had on juvenile-status offenders (JSOs). Finally, we will look at the different major forms of JSOs—sex offenders, runaways, and truants.

Juvenile-status offenses fall into two categories. They may involve the violation of certain ordinances that apply only to juveniles, such as curfew, truancy, and alcohol and tobacco laws. Some cities, for example, have ordinances that prohibit juveniles but not adults from being out after certain hours in the evening. The other category of juvenile-status offenses involves youths charged with being "out of control"—runaways, children who will not obey their parents, young people who are experimenting with sex. An unmarried 17-year-old who has sex with her boy friend is subject to legal sanction under the juvenile statutes, but the girl's 18-year-old sister who does the same thing with *her* boy friend will be left alone because she is beyond the age of a juvenile in most states.*

Now we might ask if JSOs should be included in a study of juvenile delinquency since they have committed no crimes. Moreover, we might suspect that the courts are more lenient with JSOs than with other delinquents and that JSOs are therefore less likely to be officially labeled delinquents and incarcerated or placed on probation. Surely a girl or boy who commits an "adult crime" is more likely to receive harsh punishment than one who merely runs away from home or experiments with sex. We would expect that most of the "hard-core" delinquents who are placed in reformatories would be from the ranks of juveniles who commit crimes such as burglary, assault, and drug use.

When we look at the data, however, we find that a large proportion of those labeled delinquent are JSOs. Between a quarter and a third of the delinquent

*Some states have antifornication laws for adults, but these laws are rarely enforced. However, juvenile statutes that merely *imply* antifornication sanctions are used vigorously against female juveniles.

children in correctional institutions are there for juvenile-status offenses. More than half of the girls and about a fifth of the boys in detention programs are JSOs. Thus, by conservative estimate, JSOs constitute one-third of the overall delinquent population and the majority of female delinquents.

If we expected juveniles who commit only juvenile-status offenses to be treated more leniently by the courts, we would be wrong again. According to Lerman, juvenile-status offenders are more likely to be sent to an institution than juveniles who are found guilty of committing a crime for which an adult would be arrested.[1] Of those juveniles who were convicted of Part I crimes, which include robbery, rape, burglary, and grand theft, 23 percent were placed in some controlled setting. Only 18 percent of the juveniles convicted of the less serious Part II crimes, such as petty theft and malicious mischief, were sentenced. However, 26 percent of the juvenile-status offenders, who had committed neither Part I nor Part II crimes, were sent away. There appears to be no logic to these figures. If Part II crimes are less serious than Part I crimes, and if juveniles who are convicted of Part II crimes are less likely to be incarcerated than those who commit Part I crimes, it would seem to follow that juveniles who have committed *no* crime for which an adult could receive punishment would be the least likely to be placed in or committed to a detention facility. However, they are the most likely to be committed.

Similarly, if we examine the length of incarceration, we find that JSOs receive more severe treatment than delinquents who have committed an adult-status crime.[2] For the latter, the length of institutional stay ranged from 2 to 28 months, but for JSOs it was from 4 to 48 months. Those who were sentenced for a Part I or Part II crime were incarcerated for a median of 9 months and a mean of 10.7 months; the JSOs institutional stay was for a median of 13 months and mean of 16.3 months. No matter how we look at it, juvenile-status offenders end up in a detention setting for a longer period than juveniles who commit adult crimes.

The number of juvenile-status offenders officially judged to be delinquent and the severity of punishment for these youths seem to indicate that society is more concerned about juveniles' willingness to go to school, obey their parents, and refrain from experimenting with alcohol or sex than about their tendencies to commit rape, robbery, or assault. However, there is evidence that juvenile-status offenses are believed by the general public to be less serious than almost all other types of crime. In a study by Rossi and others, respondents ranked repeated runaways as 137th in seriousness out of 140 crimes, repeated truancy 136th, repeated refusal to obey parents 130th.[3] Compared to these typical juvenile-status offenses, all ranked near the bottom of the list, almost all crimes for which an adult could be arrested were ranked as more serious. Why is it that the juvenile justice system uses so many resources to punish children for acts that society as a whole sees as relatively inconsequential?

THE CHANGING POSITION OF STATUS OFFENSES

In several states recent changes in the laws have been designed to remove the delinquent stigma from juvenile-status offenses. Most laws stipulate that JSOs are to be treated as other than delinquents and to be separated from delinquents. The separation of JSOs from delinquents will be discussed in detail in Chapter 12; for now suffice it to say that many states now have laws on the books that divert JSOs from delinquents.

The new laws vary from state to state. In Florida, the laws regulating "children in need of supervision" (juvenile-status offenders) stipulate the following:

(1) (a) When any child shall be adjudicated for the first time by the court to be a child in need of supervision, the court having jurisdiction of the child shall have power by order to make any disposition authorized for a delinquent child except commitment to the Division of Youth Services.[4]

In practice, what this law means is that JSOs are diverted from detention centers for first offenses. Instead of being taken to detention, runaway children for example, are brought to volunteer homes where they stay until their parents come to get them or send them the fare to return home.

The Florida law also stipulates that a child who repeats a status offense can be treated like a delinquent. The following subsections are relevant:

(b) For any subsequent adjudications as a child in need of supervision, the court shall have power, by order, to make any disposition authorized for a delinquent child.

(c) The jurisdiction of the court and any commitment made pursuant to this subsection shall be continued until terminated by the court or until the child is discharged by the division or reaches the age of 18.[5]

Laws like those in Florida do two things. First, they give the first-time offender an official break. Second, and more important, they recognize the differences between "children in need of supervision" and delinquents. Of course, the laws always differentiated between JSOs and juveniles who broke adult laws, but since the treatment of JSOs and other offenders was essentially the same, the new laws point out that the treatment of JSOs should be different.

Other states, such as California, have much more lenient laws regarding JSOs. Runaways, truants, incorrigibles, and other JSOs cannot be placed in "secure detention" under the California law. Instead, they are placed in a Youth Service Bureau or some other facility that does not constitute lock-up. A youth who runs away from home repeatedly may be placed in a foster home, from which he or she might also run away, but such juveniles cannot be locked up.

These new laws have been hailed as steps to decriminalize much youthful behavior, and labeling theorists point to the benefits of not designating a whole class of juveniles as delinquent. Likewise, differential association theorists applaud the fact that JSOs will not be locked up with delinquents and have the opportunity to learn how to become part of a delinquent behavior system.

Yet, events may not take the path intended by legislators. In discussions with the police and with personnel working in juvenile probation and corrections in Florida and California, I learned that an informal understanding is emerging with respect to the arrest of JSOs. The police were told by juvenile probation officers to charge JSOs with something other than juvenile-status offenses when they made arrests. For example, if a runaway is picked up, the police should consider whether the juvenile could be charged with trespassing or some other offense so that he or she could be placed in secure detention. As its reason for this treatment the probation department notes that there are an insufficient number of volunteer homes or other nonsecure facilities, so that there is no place to put a child arrested solely for a juvenile-status offense. From my own observations, it was clear that there were insufficient volunteer homes, and the probation department was making every effort to find places for the JSOs. Moreover, the delinquent charges were later dropped, and there was every indication that the police and probation officers were sincere in their concern to overcome the problem of where to put JSOs and not interested in "getting" kids on more serious charges. Here is what appears to be, in part at least, a matter of legislation having been passed without sufficient means to implement it.

In later chapters we will explore the full range of treatment received by the youths brought into the juvenile justice system and the demands and constraints placed on all of the parties involved. A few observations should be made here, however, regarding the practice of "overcharging" JSOs. First, police officers could let JSOs go free if they cannot find a place for them to stay until they return to their parents or a suitable home is found. This solution would probably be adopted by the police and probation officers as well were it not for the fact that the police would be violating the law by not bringing in known status offenders. Moreover, if the police had knowledge of a JSO, especially a runaway, and did nothing about it and something happened to the child, they could be held liable. In Houston several years ago the police came under severe criticism when a number of runaway boys were drugged, raped, and murdered by homosexuals. If it could have been shown that any of the murdered boys had been "given a break" by the police and released, the police department could have been sued by the parents. From the police point of view, it is better to be on the safe side and avoid the trouble that can arise from being found to have broken a rule.[6] As a result, police cover themselves by overcharging juveniles who are picked up for status offenses, making sure that if nonsecure detention is not available, juveniles can still be put somewhere.

A second consideration having to do with overcharging JSOs involves the law that forbids JSOs from being placed in secure detention. Given the dilemma that it has caused, many people believe that the law is a poor one. Again, however, the problem is not having available the resources necessary for implementing the law. As we have seen, it is probably a good thing to minimize the delinquent label, and it also makes sense to keep JSOs separate from delinquents to minimize associations that may lead to further delinquency. As the laws are now written, however, the police and probation personnel are placed in a double bind. The way out of the bind can take two directions. First, further facilities for JSOs could be provided by additional funding, or as some states are now doing, more volunteers making their homes available as temporary shelters. Obviously, permanently funded facilities would be preferable because they would constitute a stable group of units where juveniles could be sheltered until some disposition were made. However, this would be an added government expense and would create a whole new sub-bureaucracy. Volunteer homes involve the community in juvenile justice, but there are surprisingly few committed volunteers, even among those who fervently believe in the worth of the new juvenile-status laws. The second way out of the bind is to rewrite the laws so that the police and probation personnel will have some other option than to overcharge JSOs.

We can see that in many cases the present structure of the laws governing JSOs create conditions in which both the spirit and the intent of the laws are broken. Perhaps it is time to rethink the value of juvenile-status laws altogether or to consider seriously taking the enforcement of the laws out of the hands of the juvenile justice system.

THE JUVENILE AND SEX OFFENSES

One of the most ambiguous types of juvenile-status offenses is the sexual offense. First, heterosexual intercourse between consenting juvenile couples, like most sexual liaisons, is usually private and undetected. Therefore, unlike the number of runaways and other noticeable juvenile offenses, the extent of sexual offenses is unknown. Second, when the juvenile court adjudicates a sexual offense, it often masks the transgression under the category of "ungovernability," "loitering," "immoral or indecent conduct," or even "runaway" in order to protect the youthful defendants. We can only guess at the number of juveniles incarcerated for having sexual relations and must rely on self-report surveys to determine how many juveniles engage in sexual behavior of some sort. Short and Nye found that 95.1 percent of the girls committed to training schools and 14.1 percent of the high school girls (in West High) admitted to having had sexual intercourse.[7] Since the Short and Nye study, sexual morality has undergone a significant change, and the incidence of adolescent sexual activity is probably higher today.[8] In 1970 Gibbons found in a self-report study that 33.2 percent of the females and 36.6 percent of the males had had heterosexual relations.[9]

These statistics tell us very little beyond the fact that sexual chastity does not seem to be valued as much as it used to be. It is more important to understand sexual activity in the context of society and, more specifically, in the context of the juvenile justice system.

A dominant theme in American sexual relations is the "double standard" —the belief that sexual relations are a good thing for men and a bad thing for women. Among adolescent males, there is peer pressure to have sex with as many girls as possible, and there is pressure for girls to remain virgins until marriage. If the boys meet their goals, then at least some girls will fail to meet theirs, and vice versa. It is true that this double standard is now widely regarded by youth as stupid and hypocritical, but premarital sex is still frowned upon by most parents, and many juveniles still believe that on the whole they should go along with their parents' views.[10] Of course, the parental frown on premarital sex is directed toward daughters, not sons; a father may be distraught over his daughter's loss of virginity but secretly applaud the same transition for his son.

Albert Reiss explains the double standard in terms of role expectations.[11] Boys are taught to treat sexual intercourse as an *end.* By promising love, affection, dates, or even marriage, boys attempt to convince girls to have sex. Girls, on the other hand, are expected to use sex as a means to entrap some boy and not as an end. Implicit in this arrangement is the Victorian dictum that for women sex is something to be tolerated but that for men it represents conquest and, almost incidentally, enjoyment. Thus, a girl who has sex with a boy she loves is seen to be using sex as a means of keeping him, while a boy who has sex with just about any girl is behaving in terms of role expectations, since sex to him is merely an end.

According to Reiss, problems occur for juveniles when these role expectations are upset.

> An extremely important element determining public reaction to acts of sexual deviation is the *degree to which the status and role of the participants in the sexual act depart from the status and role expectations for these persons apart from the sexual act itself.*[12]

In sexual matters aggressive females and passive males are reversals of role expectations. Females who treat sex as an end and actively seek out sexual partners simply because they enjoy sexual intercourse are considered promiscuous. Males who do not act aggressively toward females sexually are suspected of being "sissies" or effeminate. Thus, it is not sexual activity per se that is likely to bring a juvenile's status into question but also the role expectations. It is unlikely that a girl who had sex with a boy "because she was in love" would be treated in the same way as a girl who had sex "because she was horny." The former has treated sex as a means and the latter as an end, and it is the latter girl who is more likely to be considered delinquent.

The consequences of role expectations for young men and women can be seen in the differential treatment they receive in the juvenile justice system. Chesney-Lind pointed out that the police were more likely to arrest girls than boys for a sexual offense, although obviously in most cases there is an equal number of boys and girls engaged in a single heterosexual act (other than "gang bangs," in which several boys have intercourse with one girl).[13] However, since boys are fulfilling role expectations in having premarital relations, they are not seen to be deviant. In terms of the double standard of sexual morality, it is not surprising that more girls are arrested for sex offenses.[14]

Interest in young women's sexual activity by the juvenile justice system does not stop with those girls who are arrested specifically for sexual offenses. In New York, when a girl is brought before the juvenile court for any reason, a vaginal smear is taken to determine whether she has venereal disease.[15] Originally, vaginal smears were taken to determine whether girls had had intercourse, but now officialdom justifies them in terms of the rise in venereal disease among young people. A girl arrested for offenses other than sexual is subject to a vaginal smear in the name of preventive medicine; one arrested for shoplifting, say, is as likely to be examined as is a girl picked up for sexual promiscuity. Skolnick and Woodworth noted in their study of statutory rape the following:

> When a teen-age girl runs away from home, her parents usually file a missing-person report with the police. When she is located, one of the first questions asked of her by the officers, whether police or probation is, "Which boys were you with?" A signed statement is taken from the girl including the names of the boys she had sexual relations with, if any. These names are then reported to the police department, where a crime report is made.[16]

Hence, we can see that the juvenile justice system takes an extraordinary amount of interest in young girls' sexual behavior. Were these steps taken merely in the name of sexual hygiene, then boys would be given the same examination. Only rarely, however, are boys questioned about their sexual activity or examined for venereal disease, while girls routinely suffer the indignity and degradation of a compulsory vaginal examination. The wish to reduce venereal disease among the young is understandable, but the right of the juvenile justice system to usurp public health functions is questionable, and the exclusive focus on girls is indefensible.

Cavan characterizes the sexual activity of young females in terms of socioeconomic status, differential values, and problem solving.[17] Lower-class girls, she says, have the same aspirations for marriage as middle-class girls, but they do not engage in the same temporal planning or sexual restraint. Sexual activity is more likely to be viewed as fun by these girls, and even though they are interested in maintaining a respectable reputation, they are not willing to postpone sexual activity until marriage. By having sexual liasions with boys who are not from their town or neighborhood, they are able to preserve their reputations and at the same time enjoy sexual activity. These sexual contacts are not intimate, nor do they involve obligations; they are treated as ends. When the lower-class girls reach their middle and late teens, they enter more serious relationships with boys from their community, which eventually result in marriage.

Not all lower-class communities have the same patterns of sexual activity, however. Among Italian and Spanish groups, virginity is highly valued, and the community is organized to protect unmarried girls through such mechanisms as chaperones. In these communities, young men go elsewhere for sexual activity before marriage and return to the neighborhoods when they wish to settle down and marry. Black communities, on the other hand, view sexual activity as natural for unmarried males and females, and there are no negative sanctions applied to unmarried girls for sexual activity.[18] Thus, sexual activity for girls varies depending on differential community and ethnic values in the lower class. While some of the values might be considered much looser than middle-class values, others are much stricter.

Cavan also assessed the sexual activity of juvenile females in terms of problem solving. Young lower-class girls who run away from home have few survival resources, but they can survive by picking up men, as well as by petty larceny. Girls who find themselves in this situation are likely to be apprehended by juvenile authorities since they must actively seek partners. Therefore, girls who come into contact with the juvenile authorities are likely to have engaged in other crimes besides sexual offenses. It is understandable, then, that the juvenile authorities come to suspect that girls who are picked up for delinquent activity unrelated to sex are guilty of sexual offenses as well.

Illicit Sex and Boys

In discussing relations between older men, called "chickenhawks," and young boys, MacNamara and Sagarin describe the relationship as noncoercive, and for the most part, a form of business.[19] The following characterizes the sexual encounters:

> It appears that the offenders in these cases were homosexuals interested in "chicken," or very young boys, and that those men who were apprehended had explored slightly lower age levels. Seldom was force or threat used, and some of

the youths were apparently willing partners if not actually the "aggressors." Some, even at the tender age of eight or nine, were active boy prostitutes, selling their favors for money, meals, or entertainment denied them in their economically deprived homes, . . .[20]

The boys did not consider themselves to be hustlers but instead saw their homosexual activity as merely one of many things they did in what was often a pattern of delinquency. "Getting a queer" was a way to make money; theft and burglary were other illegal means to the same end. In their collective definition of their activities, the boys did not see themselves as engaging in homosexual activity, and "getting a queer" did not imply anything other than that the boy earned some money, not unlike a waiter getting a tip. As one boy explained,

No matter how many queers a guy goes with, if he goes for money, that don't make him queer. You're still straight. It's when you start going for free with other young guys, that you start growing wings.[21]

Furthermore, boys who use homosexual adult males to earn money typically do not enter the gay life, but instead, when they are able to hold a job or decide to settle down, they give up "getting queers," enter into conventional adult roles, and raise families.[22] No stigma is attached to them for their activity with homosexuals when they were juveniles.

However, even though the boys do not define their activities as homosexual, the juvenile authorities do. Moreover, the authorities are likely to see their intervention in a boy's life as "saving" him from the advances of adult homosexuals instead of denying the boy his freedom. Heterosexual relations for boys, as we noted above, are considered a sign of normal adolescent development, but homosexual activity is viewed as damaging. It is of little interest to the juvenile authorities that the boys do not define their activities as homosexual and consider "queers" as a world apart.

Perhaps the best way to understand the relationship between lower-class boys and adult homosexuals is to view it as part-time or occasional male prostitution. From the boys' point of view it is clearly not homosexual activity on their part, and if the juvenile justice system is interested in protecting boys from becoming homosexuals, they are not doing so by incarcerating boys who hustle adult male homosexuals. Ironically, the juvenile justice system is more likely to encourage homosexuality by putting boys together in detention centers. In these so-called training schools, boys may form homosexual relationships with boys their own age without any financial exchange, and that's when they "start growing wings." It would seem that the juvenile justice system could better meet its goal by providing lower-class boys with legitimate opportunities to earn money rather than incarcerating them. However, since the juvenile authorities see the boys as homosexuals and the problem as sexual rather than as an illegitimate means employed by certain cohorts of lower-class boys to earn money, it is unlikely that the system will contribute to meaningful change.

Changing Sexual Norms

Changing morals and values among the young and their parents, especially in the middle class, point to less concern with sexual chastity, and the more this "new morality" permeates society, the more likely it is that adolescents will engage in sexual activity. As this occurs, more boys and girls will come to the attention of the juvenile courts; but at the same time, we suspect that sexual offenses will not be officially adjudicated—not so much because the juvenile justice system will become less interested in "protecting" the young as because many of the girls who come to their attention will be middle class and will be more likely to question the system's right to be the guardian of their private activities. Boys will probably be left alone for sexual offenses except for homosexual activities, including those of self-defined non-homosexuals who hustle. The homosexual laws in several states are changing, and homosexual activity may soon no longer be considered a crime: this may lead to less interest in adult and juvenile homosexual activity. If "hustling" —that is, making money from "suckers"—is redefined as male prostitution, it is likely that different approaches to the problem will be initiated. Thus, we can expect to see fewer boys incarcerated for sexual offenses and more programs developed to offset the need to raise money by hustling.

Statutory Rape

A final matter involving juveniles and sex is statutory rape. Essentially, statutory rape involves sex between an adult and a youth under the age of consent.[23] The age of consent varies, of course, and married girls under the age can legally have sex with an adult husband. Moreover, statutory rape implies that the victim (the juvenile) engages in sex voluntarily.

In examining the frequency of statutory rape and the criminal justice system, MacNamara and Sagarin quote Slovenko in demonstrating that most rape convictions are for statutory rape.* Slovenko found that

approximately 80 percent of so-called rape convictions are of the statutory rape variety. In one ten-year period in New York City, 82 percent of all rape convictions were for statutory rape. For the same period, 59 percent of all convicted sex offenders were charged with statutory rape. A five- to ten-year maximum sentence is a typical provision of laws proscribing such behavior.[24]

*It should be noted that the relatively high proportion of statutory rapes was due to the antiquated and restrictive laws regarding forcible rape. These data reflect elements of the criminal justice process more than the incidence of rapes.

It may appear that statutory rape and juvenile delinquency are only re-motely connected since it is the adult who is charged with the crime. How-ever, when we examine the outcome of cases involving statutory rape, or offenses that are related to statutory rape (for example, child molesting, contributing to the delinquency of a minor), we find that the child is often charged as well. Of course, the juvenile who is involved in a statutory rape case is not charged with rape but with a juvenile-status offense. In their study of a police morals detail, Skolnick and Woodworth found that in almost a quarter of the cases (23 percent) in which an adult male was accused of a sex-related morals charge, the juvenile was turned over to the juvenile au-thorities.[25] Considering that 80 percent of all rape convictions are for statu-tory rape, it is clear that merely by examining the statistics on rape convictions we can establish that a good proportion—roughly 15 to 20 per-cent—involves the arrest of a juvenile for a status offense.

Since statutory rape is considered "rape" because it is done without the legal consent of the child (that is, the child is below the age of legal consent even though there may have been actual consent on his or her part), it would seem to follow that the young boy or girl is innocent of any offense. After all, the rationale for prosecuting adults in such cases rests on the assumption that a child is too young and inexperienced to give informed consent to a sex act. Nevertheless, we find that the charge of statutory rape masks a large proportion of juvenile-status arrests involving children who legally "didn't know any better."

In Chapters 11 and 12 we will see that the intent of juvenile justice is not to punish juveniles but to "help" them. Juveniles who are arrested for in-volvement in statutory rape are not officially seen to be punished, but instead are viewed as coming under the "protection" of the juvenile court. The reality of the situation for the juvenile is that he or—more often—she is being punished for having sex. For now, it is enough to point out that the juvenile justice system gives great attention to looking after the sexual morals of youths, especially girls, and even when it charges adult offenders for taking advantage of the young, it charges the young people as well.

THE RUNAWAYS

One of the most common forms of juvenile-status offenses is running away from home, but unfortunately this has been one of the most neglected areas in the study of juvenile delinquency. Those included in the runaway statistics range from the Huckleberry Finns who leave home for a few days to the young who have been placed in foster homes and are attempting to escape "home" permanently. Some are attracted to the freedom once promised in youthful hangouts such as San Francisco's Haight Ashbury district and New York's East Village; others are squeezed out by family problems; still others simply want to exercise their autonomy. Like other juvenile-status offenses, running away from home is not a crime for which an adult would be committed, but since it is typically reported by parents to the police, it is the most visible juvenile-status offense.

For the police, runaway juveniles present both problems and opportunities. On the one hand, juvenile detectives can establish a relatively high "clearance rate" (the proportion of cases solved to those reported) because runaway juveniles typically frequent certain specific locations and the police generally have descriptions and photographs of such juveniles. On the other hand, police would rather concentrate on more serious crimes and not have to bother with runaways.[26] The dilemma for the police is how to handle the runaway problem without devoting too much time to it. In the first eight months of 1973, the Los Angeles police received 4,360 runaway reports; the previous year the total was 7,601, representing a great deal of investigative time.[27] A single juvenile investigator in Los Angeles during a single day in 1973 had 71 runaways to locate, and this caseload left him no time for any other work.

The significance of the runaway in the context of juvenile delinquency and the juvenile justice system is that parents typically initiate the characterization of the act as a problem to be handled officially by the police. Although many parents do not report their children for other juvenile-status offenses, the parents of runaway children usually do, regarding the children as in need of protection. This was dramatically illustrated in 1973 when 27 young boys in Houston, Texas, were found to have been sexually assaulted and murdered.[28] It was later learned that a number of the dead boys had been reported as runaways, and the police were blamed for not having done anything to find them before the wholesale slaughter. This led to a greater concern to locate runaways not only by the police but also by parents. Those who had reported their children missing began to apply increased pressure on the police to find them, and parents who normally would not report their children missing started calling the police and demanding that the children be found. However, the panic caused by the Houston murders was transitory; although such spectacular cases may result in policy changes in police departments, they do not linger long in the public's mind as new dramas draw attention elsewhere. Nevertheless, the police will use the killings to justify their work, including policies that reward them for seeking out juveniles who are not in the control of their parents.

As the juvenile justice system ponders new policies to "protect" runaway juveniles, parents need not initiate the process whereby a juvenile comes to be arrested as a runaway. Originally, the police waited until a worried parent called to report that a child had left home. When the pressure increased to locate missing youths, police departments initiated the policy of arresting any juvenile who was not in his or her parents' control, using as the criterion the fact that the youth was in a city or county where the parents did not reside.

Many young people who were not considered runaways by their parents came to be defined as such by the police. Thus, we have come full circle from the parents' being the initiators of runaway reports to the police's taking an increasingly active role in defining which juveniles are within the sanctioned control of parents. Considering the scope of the problem, there are relatively few studies of juvenile runaways. However, by looking at what findings there are, we can begin to get a picture of why youths leave home.

Why Youths Leave Home

According to Homer, most people believe that all runaways have experienced conflict at home and that by intervening in the home social workers can solve the runaway problem.[29] It is true that a number of youths leave home because of family conflict, but many leave to seek adventure, and many of those who leave home because of conflict do so only long enough for things to cool off. Moreover, it has not been shown that the problem can be resolved by intervening in the home situation. Another myth explains runaways as a "cry for help" on the part of juveniles. The explanation that runaways "want attention" is unfounded, and even though some youths may want to *call attention to a family crisis,* it is not true that they leave home so that attention will be heaped on them. Finally, it is believed that runaways are children of the wealthy who are repudiating middle- and upper-middle-class values. Homer found in her study of runaway girls that they were from predominantly lower- and lower-middle-class backgrounds, with 70 percent from families on welfare.[30]

Most of these girls were either "pushed" or "pulled" out of the house. Some 35 percent who left home were running *from* an unpleasant family situation, but most were running *to* something. Many girls were attracted by sex, drugs, liquor, and other "pleasures" forbidden in the home. Additionally, there was peer-group support for running away and engaging in numerous adventuresome activities, usually including crime.

The runaway girls' explanations of their own activities fell into four categories: (1) could not tolerate home situation; (2) don't know; (3) want to be with boy friend; and (4) like running, as well as what happens on the run. The last two were the most frequently offered explanations. As we noted in discussing Goffman's explanation of juvenile delinquency, some juveniles are structurally denied character-building situations and therefore create their own. By running away from home, a youth is not only able to show that he or she has the strength of character to make it without parental support but can also locate and manufacture "action." Moreover, since many runaways leave home in a group of two or more, differential association theory is applicable here as well; by thinking of runaways as a peer-oriented, action-seeking group, we can better understand why juveniles leave home. Instead of placing all the emphasis on the runaway's home life, we should look to his or her other associations and the possible adventures in self-realization available outside home *and* school.

In further examining the reasons youths run away from home we can see that running away is situational and a form of adventure. In a study by Shellow it was found that the runaway episode was poorly planned.[31] In only a third of the cases did the runaways have more than one dollar. Unlike the Homer study cited above, it was found that only 28 percent were from low-income families, with 15 percent from the upper middle class and the remainder from middle- and working-class homes.[32] Moreover, most of the runaway episodes were short-lived, and the children returned on their own. Were it the case that there were serious home problems, it is doubtful that the children would have returned voluntarily or as quickly as they were found to have.

Shellow and his associates reported another important finding concerning the "push" factor in homes. While it is commonly assumed by families of runaways and the runaways themselves that home problems are the cause of much of the runaway problem, this entire issue has in general been ignored. More than 75 percent of the parents of runaways thought there was conflict in the family, but at the same time 80 percent of the children in the Shellow study thought there were problems in the home, *whether they were runaways or not.*[33] In other words, since the vast majority of the juveniles believe that there are problems in their families, yet only a relatively small proportion of them run away, something other than the "push" of family conflict is likely to be involved.

Even though a large proportion of juveniles who run away are from broken families, Wedemeyer reports that most runaways come from intact families.[34] More girls run away from home than boys by a slight margin (roughly 52 percent of runaways are girls), and running away is not only an American problem. In a report from *Trud,* a Soviet trade union paper quoted by Trimborn, it is clear that the Russians have a similar problem for similar reasons.

> There is a very big category of wanderers who cause much trouble to the militia and their parents. There are teenagers, boys most of all, who start their search for adventure without warning their parents. The militia finds them in trains, railway stations and elsewhere and sends them first to a receiving station before they are sent home.[35]

The problem is to discover what juveniles from different social classes, sexes, and cultures have in common that causes them to run away from the security of their homes.

To begin this examination of the conflicting social conditions related to runaways, we can look at the distribution of runaways by age and sex to see if any patterns exist that may provide clues to the causes. Table 6–1 gives the distribution of runaways in 1971 from Montgomery County, Maryland.

TABLE 6-1.   Sex and Age of Runaways[a]

Age	Males	Females	Total
Under 11	24 (86%)	4 (14%)	28 (2%)
11–12	65 (71%)	27 (29%)	92 (6%)
13–14	265 (50%)	269 (50%)	534 (34%)
15	158 (42%)	221 (58%)	379 (24%)
16	150 (45%)	182 (55%)	332 (21%)
17	75 (38%)	122 (62%)	197 (13%)
	737 (47%)	825 (53%)	1562 (100%)

[a] J. A. Bechtel, "Statement Before the Senate Subcommittee to Investigate Juvenile Delinquency" (Washington, D.C., January 14, 1973).

A number of interesting patterns can be seen from the distribution of sex and age of runaways in the table. First, until the ages of 13–14 the bulk of runaways are boys, but since runaways under the age of 13 account for only 8 percent of all runaways, this age group does not constitute a significant cohort. As a way of characterizing them, though, we might see them as the Huckleberry Finn runaways, and even though some of them may be "chickens" out hustling homosexuals, most of these boys are probably nothing more than the short-term runaways who return home shortly.

Beginning at age 13, we see a dramatic change in both the number and distribution of runaways. Girls and boys are equal in the percentage of runaways for the 13–14-year-old group, but at 15 girls begin outnumbering boys. At age 17, the figures for boy runaways drop dramatically in both number and proportion, while there is a drop in the number of girl runaways but an increase in their proportion.

In order to understand these patterns, we will turn to Goffman's theory of "action" discussed in Chapter 5. We can account not only for the distribution of boy and girl runaways, but also for the drop in runaways as youths approach the legal age of adulthood.

As Homer found, most of the youths who ran away from home were being "pulled" by an attraction outside the home rather than being "pushed" by problems in the home. One report of runaways found that "Objectives were to acquire a place to sleep and then look for adventure—get a crash pad and some kicks."[36] Therefore, we can examine runaways as "looking for action" instead of as "running *away* from home." However, we must remember that the goal does not account for the act, because the same objective may be met in nondelinquent ways. What we must do is to explain why leaving home is a *means* for accomplishing the goal.

The Huckleberry Finns can be seen as junior adventurers who are out seeking some action in terms of images of "Injun Joes" and homemade rafts drifting down the Mississippi. The older children, though, need to be understood as little people who are attempting to establish themselves as adults before they are deemed to be so by the law. The constraints of home and school do not allow for all of the juveniles to "make it" academically or athletically, and to the extent to which they think they can "prove themselves" by taking on the adventure and freedom of the streets, they will leave home. The fact that they are looking for adventure is documented by the places they go. During the late 1960s and early 1970s the centers for youthful action were such places as Los Angeles' Sunset Strip, San Francisco's Haight-Ashbury, and New York's East Village. In the late 1970s these youthful hangouts lost their glamour, and runaways were likely to be found in nearby cities.[37]

Since girls are more restricted than boys in seeking adventure, especially sexual encounters, they are more likely to believe that the only way to "have some fun" is by running away from home.[38] The conflict with the family is not so much a cause of running away from home as it is a symptom of young people's attempts to find action. Especially among girls, their attempts cause conflict, so that after finding it difficult, if not impossible, to "have some fun" and live at home, they leave. As their children approach adulthood parents are more likely to loosen up their restrictions, explaining why there is a drop in the number of runaways at age 17, especially among boys. Simultaneously, at age 17 both boys and girls are preparing to graduate from high school and either enter college or take on the adult responsibilities of jobs and families. Therefore, they reason it is not worth leaving home because in a year they will be free anyway.

Harsh Realities of the Streets

If runaways are looking for action, what are they seeking to find? The data are somewhat contradictory on this point, and depending on how we interpret them and which data we examine, we come up with slightly different conclusions. One study found that 70 percent of the runaways merely ran to a friend's or relative's house, while only 13 percent went "on the road."[39] A more recent study based on a nationwide survey found that 2 percent of all children between the ages of 10 and 17 ran away from home.[40] Of these, the study characterized 92 percent as *serious runners* on the bases that they stayed away from home for more than 48 hours, that they were reported missing by their parents, that they had no idea of where they would go, and that they traveled 10 miles or more away from home. Youths who run to friends' or relatives' homes would not appear to be serious about running away permanently, and it is difficult to say that they are looking for action. On the other hand, if we take the data from the latter study, which shows youths going further away from home and having no idea where they would go for shelter, we can surmise that the runaways were seeking adventure.

The other end of the runaway's trip is not the end of the rainbow. In testimony before a Senate committee on the problem of runaways, a minister in New York City's Greenwich Village, a once-favored area for runaways, stated that youths flocked to the area in order to be part of the action.[41] When they arrived they found something very different. "Crash pads" (places to sleep) generally exploited them. The crash pad boss would take the juveniles' money and then tell them that if they wanted to stay they would have to come up with more money. Typically, the girls would be exploited sexually, and the cost of a night's stay was to sleep with whomever ran the crash pad.

Prostitution. For many youths the experiences of living "off the streets" through hustles of various sorts was an adventure, but for many others it was enough to drive them home again. Those who did not return home found that they had to do something to make a living, and the hustles became more permanent than panhandling or having sex for a night's shelter. Many turned to prostitution. The extent to which this mode of earning money became popular among runaway girls can be seen in the average age of prostitutes arrested by the police during the period when teenage juveniles were flocking to the "fun" cities. In New York, the figure for prostitute arrests involving girls under 25 rose from 24 to 74 percent; in Boston, the average age of prostitutes dropped to 20, and in Miami, the average age of prostitutes was only 18, while three years before the influx of runaways the average age was 23.[42]

A more recent report on runaway prostitutes found that young girls were taken by pimps from Minneapolis to New York, where they were forced into prostitution.[43] Two examples illustrate the not-so-adventuresome aspects of life on the streets.

Karen, 14, met a pimp in downtown Minneapolis one day at 9 A.M. He bought her breakfast and took her to his apartment and bedded her. Next day she quarreled with her parents over having stayed out most of the night, so she ran off to see her new friend. He said she would have to work the street to stay with him and steal money from her customers so she could get the bus fare to Chicago. Once there, she earned another $800 in three weeks. The two moved to Manhattan, where she picked up men around luxury hotels, robbing them when she could. Sick of the life after six weeks, she tried to leave her pimp, but he broke her jaw. After hospitalization, she was forced back on the streets by him with her jaw wired shut. When an attempt to kill herself failed, she phoned her parents and fled New York. In ten weeks she had provided her pimp with some $4,000.

Clare, 16, having run away from home met a pimp along Minneapolis' Hennepin Avenue and moved in with him. He persuaded her to hit the streets. "He wouldn't let me come into the house unless I brought him $150 a day," she recalled. After she was arrested for prostitution, she and her pimp flew to New York, where she collected at least $100,000, of which she saved only $800. She was arrested 42 times for prostitution and once for grand larceny ("It was a trick who wanted his money back"), but never served a day in jail. When she tried to return home the pimp beat her so badly that she was hospitalized.

These cases constitute somewhat dramatic examples, employed for making journalistic copy rather than sociological understanding; however, they serve to illustrate a number of important points. First, pimps are rough on their girls if they do not produce, and girls cannot simply walk away and leave their pimps.[44] Second, these illustrations indicate the alternatives available to runaway girls and how many girls end up if they choose to stay on the streets. At the same time, however, there does not appear to be widespread white slavery (involuntary prostitution), but rather, as MacNamara and Sagarin point out,

> Many women (and a few males) are held in prostitution by ties to others, by dependence on drugs, by lack of other opportunities, by feelings of worthlessness, by unresolved emotional problems, even by threats from pimps, usurers and madams; still their activities are sufficiently voluntary to distinguish these individuals from sex slaves who are held captive. That some instances of white slavery exist is undisputed. However, most prostitution can be better understood as not involving sex slavery, and most involuntary servitude can best be understood as not involving prostitution.[45]

Freda Adler points to a more complex relationship that binds young girls to pimps. While most older prostitutes have stopped using pimps, younger girls depend on them. In discussing the pimp's attitude toward getting young girls into a "stable," Adler makes the following observations:

> A highly successful urban pimp who apparently prided himself on keeping abreast of scientific progress boasted that turning a young girl out is "a brainwashing process. The whole thing is creativity," he said. "When you turn a chick out you take away every set of values and morality she previously had and create a different environment." His approach, while successful, is not nearly so impressive as he believes, because his subjects are as different from those of the Chinese interrogators as fish in a barrel are from fish in the open sea. He is not, as he boasts, cutting their previous ties, for if the ties were at all viable he would have few attractive inducements to tempt them into his stable. It is the very absence of those ties and the vulnerability inherent to the nonadapted state that ensures his success.[46]

Thus, the runaway girl who starts off looking for adventure is soon faced with the necessity of keeping herself alive and finding emotional support. The pimp exploits this condition, and as a result many young girls end up hooking. The difference between having sex with men for adventure and having sex for money is not so different in the context of the runaways' milieu. Young runaway girls are exploited sexually by men almost as soon as they hit the streets. Wherever a girl stays, she is expected to "pay" for her room by having sex with the person whose room she is sharing. Initially, this may appear to be an adventure, even love, but the excitement lies in the newness of the experience. As bedding men for a night's room becomes routine, runaway girls may come to see the arrangement as a strictly economic one offering little or no emotional support. Since the economics of the arrangement are fairly unrewarding, both emotionally and financially, the pimp is seen as a source of improvement.

The use of prostitution by runaways to finance their independence is not solely a female enterprise. For example:

> In San Francisco last week, a convicted child molester was arrested on a charge of running a child prostitution ring that may have involved 30 boys. Police Sergeant George Huegle, who made the arrest, said that the kids were brought to customers in various parts of the city and were "exhibited like livestock, naked."[47]

Such pimp-run outfits are probably rarer for boys than for girls, since the emotional attachment for boys involved in hustling centers around their group.

Surviving on the Streets.   Aside from prostitution, how do runaways—both boys and girls—survive on the streets? Most do not have much money when they leave home, and they must pay their way like everyone else. Some may find jobs, but given the age of most runaways, it is doubtful that many are hired either because of child labor laws prohibiting their employment or because employers view them as inexperienced and unreliable. We could conclude, as many police officers do, that runaways inevitably end up in some kind of crime to support themselves, but there is little evidence of this. One study showed that most runaways are not delinquent,[48] and other figures indicate that relative to the number of juveniles arrested for juvenile-status offenses, the proportion of runaways picked up for other crimes is relatively low. For example, the Children's Bureau reported that less than 4 percent of jailed children were arrested for offenses against persons, including such fund-raising crimes as mugging and armed robbery. The same report, however, showed that 41 percent of the juveniles arrested were picked up solely for juvenile-status offenses.[49] A high proportion of thefts and burglaries is committed by juveniles, of course, but, there is no evidence that the bulk of these crimes are committed by runaways. In fact, in Chapter 7 we will see that an extremely high proportion of juveniles commits such crimes—far more than the 2 percent who run away from home.

In order to get a clearer idea of how runaways survive, it is necessary to understand that there are different types of runaways. How long a juvenile meets survival requirements depends on the reason the youth is on the run. In a study by English, four types of runaways were distinguished based on commitment to stay away from home and the initiating circumstances of the departure.[50] By examining these types we can get a better view of how runaways manage.

Floaters.   These are children who leave home in order to relieve tensions caused by the home-school milieu. They have no intention of staying away permanently but only until "things cool off." A call to parents or a little prodding from just about anyone is enough to send them home. However, if they receive no encouragement to return home, and if they find shelter along with someone to teach them how to exist on the streets, floaters may become full-fledged runaways.

Runaways.   The difference between floaters and runaways is in the length of time they stay away from home. While floaters stay away for only a few days, runaways will be away from home for weeks or even months. The reasons for leaving vary. Unlike Homer, English found that the initial home leaving was more a case of running *from* something than *to* something. One common reason was to get out of a destructive family situation. Another, more complex reason was to call attention to the problems that existed at home. One runaway girl explained:

> My old man's got a girlfriend and my mother refuses to believe it. Instead she's starting to hit the bottle real hard and all kinds of bad stuff is coming down so I split.
>   I don't want to go back unless things are going to get better. Like, I figured if I split they might see how bad things are. . . . I think I better stay away for a few days so that they really get worried—that way they may be ready to talk.[51]

The girl did not want attention for herself but left home so that her parents would realize the state the family was in. She hoped her absence would bring her parents to the realization that they should try to resolve family problems.
    A third reason juveniles leave home is the presence of a difficult and unsharable problem.[52] They believe that if their problem became known others would be hurt as well as themselves. The following interview by English with a 15-year-old boy and his 14-year-old girl friend illustrates one kind of secret unsharable problem:

ERIC: Hey, can we talk to you? Like we are really hung up.
ENGLISH: Sure, what's wrong?
ERIC: Like me and Mary have been on the run for a couple of months.
ENGLISH: Yeah, I knew that and I've wondered how you been makin' it.
ERIC: Well, that's our problem 'cause Mary's knocked up and that's why we split in the first place.
ENGLISH: How far is she?
ERIC: A little over four months.
ENGLISH: Well, that's a little late for an abortion. Is that what you want to do?
ERIC: Well, man, it's a little more complicated than that. Like someone told us that if she did some speed she would drop the kid.
ENGLISH: So you tried some speed. What happened?
MARY: I ran some speed a few times and I think I got hepatitis.

ENGLISH: Have you seen a doctor?

ERIC: Not yet, and that's not all. You see when we first hit town we didn't know anyone and didn't have a place to crash so we stayed with Tim and those dudes for a while.

ENGLISH: So what happened?

ERIC: Well, they threatened to throw us out unless Mary put out for them all and well, like we were real up tight and it was really cold out and well, she screwed for them a couple of times.

ENGLISH: That's pretty bad.

ERIC: I know, but now it looks like Mary has the syph.[53]

Not only did these young people feel that they had no one they could trust for help in the adult world, but when they sought help on the streets, they were hurt and exploited. It was learned later that Mary did have syphilis, and she eventually aborted the baby and was placed in a detention home. Had the couple turned to the adult authorities in the beginning, Mary would probably have been sent to a detention home anyway and judged to be delinquent. Had the juvenile authorities provided some real help, it would have been unnecessary for Mary and Eric to resort to the course of action they took. Thus, in a very real sense, because of the structure of the juvenile justice apparatus, they were left with running away as the only solution for their problem.

Splitters.   The splitters, a third type of runaway, are very similar to the pleasure-seekers described by Homer. Having run away from home and returned, the runaway juvenile acquires a new status. The youth's peers see the runaway as a "bad boy" or "bad girl," and depending on the milieu, this is a high-or a low-status ranking. Additionally, the parents may begin asking themselves, "What did we do wrong?" and the runaway will be made to feel significantly more important than before. Moreover, a juvenile probation officer will fuss over the youngster in an attempt to find out why he or she ran away from home. In short, much is made of the returning runaway.

However, as is true in all homecomings, the fanfare soon dies down, although by the time it does, the runaway has firmly established a new self-conception as an adventurer. He or she begins to find home and school boring compared with the exciting and independent life among friends on the streets. As things "get old" at home, the appeal of the adventures on the run lures the youth away from home again and he or she packs up and leaves.

Returning to the streets, the runaway is greeted by his or her "old friends," and this time the splitter is street-wise. The initial trauma of being alone away from home is not present, and soon the splitter is back in the swing of things. As the street life "gets old," the youth again returns home to relax and recuperate until that "gets old," when he or she returns to the streets. This cycle represents a continual search for something new and exciting. By alternating between home and the streets, youths attempt to keep their life fresh until they are prepared to leave both home and the streets as they enter adulthood.

Hard-Road Freaks.   The final type of runaway has left home for good, having rejected the straight world for life in the streets. Hard-road freaks are older, generally between 17 and 20, and many would not be considered juveniles. They make up the stable (if that word can be used) core of the transient young. Being completely independent, they make a living by various legal and illegal means. They generally have at least one legitimate skill, such as carpentry or painting, and also have extensive hustling experience. They have the highest status among the transient youth population, and the younger runaways and splitters look to them for guidance. In turn, the hard-road freaks exploit their young admirers in the guise of providing street experience.

A high percentage of hard-road freaks are from working-class backgrounds and, unlike middle-class runaways, do not rely on verbal skills but instead tend to aggressive physical action. This feature gives them a considerable edge over the middle-class runaway, for they are likely to use physical aggressiveness to exploit and intimidate middle-class juveniles.

It is unlikely that a floater will become a hard-road freak. In fact, relatively few floaters become runaways. Similarly, few runaways become splitters, and even fewer splitters become hard-road freaks. What is important for our analysis is the existence of these various delinquent patterns and the possibility that juveniles will be exposed to them. The extent to which the juvenile's home and school milieu lacks opportunities for youthful fulfillment provides a structural "push" into the street life of the runaway. Additionally, the lack of support by the juvenile justice structure and process limits the avenues available to youths for resolving their problems legitimately. The "pull" is provided by the adventure of life on the run; while the "fun" may be greatly exaggerated, it is seen as better than life at home and in school. Furthermore, the returning runaway is labeled as somehow deviant, whether or not this is a hero's label. This serves to separate the juvenile from the standard life-style expected of youth. Thus the process intended to correct runaways operates to push them out and away from the desired path.

TRUANCY

Truancy is the final juvenile-status offense that we will discuss. Essentially, truancy consists of not going to school during the age of compulsory education. However, like all other forms of delinquency, what is seen as truancy and what is not depends on the actors and the definers. "Doing truancy" has a defiance about it that appears to be lacking in some of the more elaborate forms of skipping school. In comparing two different groups, Chambliss found that "nice" middle- and upper-middle-class boys employed elaborate ruses to skip school and were not seen as truants, while working-class boys who did the same thing without the schemes were considered truants.[54] The following is an illustration how the "good boys" got away with skipping school:

> The Saints' principal daily concern was with getting out of school as early as possible. The boys managed to get out of school with minimum danger that they would be accused of playing hookey through an elaborate procedure for obtaining "legitimate" release from class. The most common procedure was for one boy to obtain the release of another by fabricating a meeting of some committee, program or recognized club. Charles might raise his hand in his 9:00 chemistry class and ask to be excused—a euphemism for going to the bathroom. Charles would go to Ed's math class and inform the teacher that Ed was needed for a 9:30 rehearsal of the drama club play. The math teacher would recognize Ed and Charles as "good students" involved in numerous school activities and would permit Ed to leave at 9:30. Charles would return to his class and Ed would go to Tom's English class to obtain his release. Tom would engineer Charles' escape. The strategy would continue until as many of the Saints as possible were freed. After a stealthy trip to the car (which had been parked in a strategic spot), the boys were off for a day of fun.
>
> Over the two years I observed the Saints, this pattern was repeated nearly every day. There were variations on the theme, but in one form or another the boys used this procedure for getting out of class and then off the school grounds. Rarely did all eight of the Saints manage to leave school at the same time. The average number avoiding school on the days I observed them was five.[55]

This group of boys who regularly avoided school were not considered truants because they were able to engineer logical accounts for their absences and as a result their absences were not questioned. Those students who did not manufacture accounts to be absent from school were considered truant, and since only the well-placed students were in a position to construct convincing accounts, most of those who were considered truant were those with lower social standings in the school and community.

In examining other aspects of truancy and school-related problems we can see that truancy and suspensions tend to discriminate against lower-class and minority groups. First, from one study of truancy and suspensions we can see that truancy is one of the main reasons students are suspended from school. Table 6–2 shows this relationship.

As can be seen, truancy is the fourth most common reason for school suspension. The relative amount of truancy is higher than indicated, however, because the high school in which this study was conducted did not suspend students over 16 for truancy.

TABLE 6–2.   Reasons for School Suspensions[a]

Reasons	Number and Percent of Suspensions	
	N	*Percent*
Disobeying teacher or staff	70	27
Disruptive behavior	56	21
Fighting	48	18
Truancy	35	13
Other	27	10
Skipping classes	26	10
	262	99*

[a] *Community Compact in Youth Development, 1* (9) (Gainesville, Fla., June 1977), p. 5.
* Less than 100 percent due to rounding.

In examining the sex and ethnic distribution of students who were suspended, we can see that the actual number of black students suspended was twice as high as that for whites, but the proportion was about three times as high. We can also see that boys were far more likely to be suspended than girls. Table 6–3 shows this distribution.

The only activity that resulted in suspension which is a clear violation of the criminal law is fighting. All of the other reasons, except "other," which included some criminal violations (for example, possession of drugs), were forms of juvenile-status offenses. If we combine skipping classes with truancy, we see that being absent from classes accounts for 23 percent of the suspensions—the second most likely reason for suspensions. It is ironic that suspensions were used to punish students for not attending school, since the suspension provided the "legal" basis for truancy.

TABLE 6–3.   High School Suspensions[a]

Race and Sex	School A	School B	School C	Total
Percent blacks in total population, 1975–76	28%	25%	34%	
Blacks suspended	144 (61%)	90 (81%)	18 (85%)	253 (67%)
Whites suspended	91 (39%)	22 (19%)	3 (15%)	116 (33%)
Total	235	112	21	368
Girls	74 (32%)	38 (34%)	10 (45%)	122 (34%)
Boys	161 (68%)	74 (66%)	11 (55%)	246 (66%)

[a] *Community Compact in Youth Development, 1* (9) (Gainesville, Fla., June 1977), p. 6.

Delinquency and School Performance

At this time it is appropriate to discuss the relationship between school and delinquency on a more general level. The issues involved concern school performance, intelligence as measured by IQ tests, and school attendance. Central to such a discussion is the relation between intelligence as measured by IQ tests and the incidence of delinquency. One recent study in this area found that there is a relationship between delinquency and IQ.[56] Since criminologists have generally discounted any relationship between measured intelligence and delinquency on the grounds that IQ tests are a reflection of middle-class values and knowledge, and since any relationship that does appear between IQ and delinquency is ascribed to social-class differences, this study by Hirschi and Hindelang is important to examine.

The researchers, using self-report surveys to determine the extent of delinquent involvement among 3,600 boys, found that there was a stronger relationship between IQ and delinquency than (1) between social class and delinquency and (2) between race and delinquency.[57] Since the data were gathered on the basis of self-report surveys, it was not the case that there were more delinquent boys in the sample with low IQ's because the "smart ones" were better able to avoid detection. Moreover, since there was a stronger relationship between IQ and delinquency than between delinquency and either race or social class, the argument that the relationship is a spurious one reflecting ethnic and social backgrounds is unfounded.

Whether IQ measures native intelligence or something else is really not at issue here. Whatever is measured by IQ tests appears to have some kind of strong relationship to delinquency. Moreover, several other studies have found a similar relationship. The argument of sociologists is not that the relationship does not exist but that these studies attempt to explain away the effect of intelligence on delinquency by pointing to social factors that are more significant.[58]

Hirschi and Hindelang explain the relationship between delinquency and IQ in terms of the effect of low IQ on school performance.[59] Students with low IQ's do poorly in school and make adjustments through delinquent activities. The less students liked school, the more likely they were to engage in delinquency, and liking school correlated highly with nondelinquency.[60] Social rewards in school were sufficient to dissuade students from committing delinquent acts and constituted one degree of measurement of the extent to which students were committed to conformity. Losses for delinquent acts were not only the sanctions imposed by the juvenile justice system but also the losses incurred by the social stigma attached to the delinquent label. Those with a great deal invested in the conventional system represented by the schools stood to lose a good deal more than those who did not.

Other studies have found similar relationships between school performance and attendance and delinquency. In summarizing the findings between delinquency and school, Glaser has made the following points:

1. Rebelliousness towards school, including truancy, was strongly related to delinquency.
2. Students who had been having trouble in school had less delinquency after they dropped out, especially if they got married and took a job.
3. The compulsory school year ages constitute the ages leading in arrests for property felonies, and arrests for such felonies fell off sharply for the ages after the compulsory school age.[61]

These findings do not confirm the validity of the IQ tests, especially certain biases built into the tests, but they tend to explain what IQ tests measure—namely, the ability of persons to cope with institutionalized social expectations, in this case school performance. As people who are having trouble in school are released from the expectations and rewards in the school system, they are released from the accompanying problems and adjustments to these problems. Relative to the school situation, their situation in life improves, and they can realize rewards through nondelinquent means.

SUMMARY

In order to commit a delinquent act there must be a rule to break that can be formulated in terms of the delinquency laws. Since juvenile-status offenses are a whole set of regulations that do not constrain adults, juveniles literally have more opportunities to violate the law. At the same time, there are few immediate status awards available for juveniles or legitimate avenues for pursuing such goals. The situation of the juvenile created by the constraints results in what we referred to in Chapter 4 as a subculture of juvenility. Young people in the juvenile situation come to share certain common world views in terms of their common situation. The understandings of delinquent acts, especially ones that happen to be especially popular at a given time (for example, drag racing in the 1950s and the current marijuana fad), are not so much an aspect of a subculture of delinquency, as Matza contends, but part of a subculture of juvenility.[62] The acts involving violations of either the criminal laws or juvenile-status offenses are too much a part of all juvenile groups to be considered centered in lower-class milieus where there is a high incidence of visible delinquency (gang fights, killings). And since there is substantial evidence that virtually all juveniles are involved in at least some delinquent acts, any subculture we speak of must include more than just lower-class boys.

Juvenile-status offenses are important because they define the juvenile status, setting juveniles apart and creating the subculture of juvenility. We see crimes of all types drop dramatically as juveniles leave the age and status of juveniles. Not only do delinquent acts involving status offenses completely disappear, for by legal definition and application they no longer apply, but other crimes are sharply curtailed as well.

Commitments to the adult world are permitted, for juveniles can take jobs without interference by parents or school authorities, they can get married, and in general they can "become somebody" in the social sense that they have defined their role in life. Juvenile-status offenses prevent young people from doing this by keeping them in school, setting the time they have to be home, and tying them to their parents. The laws regulating juveniles obviously are not designed to constrain them in such a way as to encourage delinquency, but they are intended to "protect" juveniles so that they can make the necessary preparations for adulthood. However, we are not concerned so much with the intent of the laws, even to the extent of criticizing certain Victorian standards of morality that appear to dominate them. The point is, instead, that the laws create, sustain, and define the status of the juvenile in such a way that at least some delinquency can be expected from virtually all juveniles and that the bulk of many types of crimes is committed by juveniles. The subculture of juvenility encourages certain forms of delinquency and does little to contain or dissuade others. On the other side of the coin, the reward structure of the greater society offers little to the juvenile in terms of immediate payoffs, and so there is little to lose from the point of view of the juvenile. The result is the high rate of violations among juveniles.

NOTES

1. Paul Lerman, "Delinquents without Crimes," in Abraham S. Blumberg (ed.), *Law and Order: The Scales of Justice* (New Brunswick, N.J.: Transaction Books, 1973), pp. 241–269.
2. *Ibid.*, pp. 250–251.
3. Peter Rossi, Emily Waite, Christine E. Bose, and Richard E. Berk, "The Seriousness of Crimes: Normative Structure and Individual Differences," *American Sociological Review, 39:*224–237 (April 1974).
4. *Florida Juvenile Laws: 1974–1975,* Chapter 39–Chapter 959. (State of Florida, Department of Health and Rehabilitative Services, Division of Youth Services), p. 17.
5. *Ibid.*
6. William B. Sanders, *Detective Work: A Study of Criminal Investigations* (New York: Free Press, 1977), p. 42.
7. James F. Short, Jr., and Ivan F. Nye, "Extent of Unrecorded Juvenile Delinquency: Tentative Conclusions," *Journal of Criminal Law, Criminology, and Police Science, 49:*296–302 (November–December 1958).
8. Daniel Yankelovich, *The New Morality: A Profile of American Youth in the 70's* (New York: McGraw-Hill, 1974), p. 91.
9. Don C. Gibbons, *Delinquent Behavior* (Englewood Cliffs, N.J.: Prentice-Hall, 1970).
10. Ira L. Reiss, "Premarital Sex as Deviant Behavior: An Application to Current Deviance," *American Sociological Review, 35:*78–87 (February 1970).
11. Albert J. Reiss, Jr., "Sex Offenses: The Marginal Status of the Adolescent," *Law and Contemporary Problems, 25* (Spring 1960).
12. *Ibid.*
13. Meda Chesney-Lind, "Juvenile Delinquency: The Sexualization of Female Crime," *Psychology Today* (July 1974), pp. 43–66.
14. Freda Adler, *Sisters in Crime* (New York: McGraw-Hill, 1975), pp. 90–91.

15. Chesney-Lind, pp. 45–46.
16. Jerome Skolnick and J. Richard Woodworth, "Bureaucracy, Information and Social Controls: A Study of a Morals Detail," in David Botdua (ed.), *The Police: Six Sociological Essays* (New York: Wiley, 1967), p. 106.
17. Ruth Shonle Cavan, *Juvenile Delinquency* (Philadelphia: Lippincott, 1962), pp. 105–107.
18. *Ibid.*, p. 107.
19. Donald E. J. MacNamara and Edward Sagarin, *Sex Crime and the Law* (New York: Free Press, 1977), p. 85.
20. *Ibid.*
21. John Rechy, "A Quarter Ahead," *Evergreen Review, 5:*118 (July–August 1961).
22. Albert Reiss, Jr., "The Social Integration of Queers and Peers," *Social Problems, 9:*102–120 (Fall 1961).
23. MacNamara and Sagarin, p. 80.
24. Ralph Slovenko, "Statutory Rape," *Medical Aspects of Human Sexuality* (March 1971), pp. 155–167.
25. Skolnick and Woodworth, p. 113.
26. Sanders, *Detective Work,* p. 132.
27. Bella Stumbo, "Spector of Houston Haunts Parents," *Los Angeles Times* (September 16, 1973).
28. *Ibid.*
29. Louise Homer, "Community-based Resource for Runaway Girls," *Social Casework* (October 1973).
30. *Ibid.*, p. 474.
31. Robert Shellow, "Suburban Runaways of the 1960's," *Monographs of the Society for Research in Child Development, 32* (1967).
32. *Ibid.*, p. 17.
33. *Ibid.*, p. 18.
34. John Wedemeyer, "Statement Before Senate Subcommittee on Juvenile Delinquency," (Washington, D.C., January 14, 1972).
35. Harry Trimborn, "Russia Has a Runaway Problem," *Gainesville Sun* (September 1, 1971).
36. "Prostitutes: The New Breed," *Newsweek* (July 12, 1971), p. 78.
37. "Why Children Are Running Away in Record Numbers," *U. S. News and World Report* (January 17, 1977), p. 62.
38. M. C. Howell, E. B. Emmons, and D. A. Frank, "Reminiscenses of Runaway Adolescents," *American Journal of Orthopsychiatry, 43:*840–853 (October 1973).
39. Institute for Social Research, *Newsletter* (Spring 1974), p. 7.
40. Opinion Research Corporation, "Summary: National Statistical Study on Runaway Youth" (Princeton, N.J.: The Corporation, 1977).
41. Fred Eckhardt, "Operation Eye-Opener," Statement Before Senate Subcommittee on Juvenile Delinquency, (Washington, D.C., January 14, 1972).
42. *Newsweek* (July 12, 1971), p. 78.
43. "Youth for Sale on the Streets," *Time* (November 28, 1977), p. 23.
44. MacNamara and Sagarin, p. 117.
45. *Ibid.*, pp. 117–118.
46. Adler, p. 72.
47. *Time* (November 28, 1977), p. 23.
48. Opinion Research Corporation, p. 1.
49. John Downey, "Why Children Are in Jail and How To Keep Them Out," *Congressional Record* (August 6, 1971), p. S13417.
50. C. J. English, "Leaving Home: A Typology of Runaways," *Society, 10:*22–24 (July–August 1973).
51. *Ibid.*, p. 23.

52. Donald R. Cressey, *Other People's Money: A Study in the Social Psychology of Embezzlement* (Belmont, Calif.: Wadsworth, 1971).
53. English, pp. 23–24.
54. William Chambliss, "The Saints and the Roughnecks," *Society,* *11:*24–31 (November–December 1973).
55. *Ibid.,* pp. 24–25.
56. Travis Hirschi and Michael J. Hindelang, "Intelligence and Delinquency: A Revisionist Review," *American Sociological Review, 42:*571–586 (August 1977).
57. *Ibid.,* p. 574.
58. Edwin H. Sutherland and Donald R. Cressey, *Criminology,* 10th ed. (Philadelphia: Lippincott, 1978), pp. 156–158.
59. Hirschi and Hindelang, p. 584.
60. Travis Hirschi, *Causes of Delinquency* (Berkeley: University of California Press, 1969), p. 156.
61. Daniel Glaser, *Crime in Our Changing Society* (New York: Holt, Rinehart and Winston, 1978).
62. David Matza, *Delinquency and Drift* (New York: Wiley, 1964).

7 Juvenile Property Crimes

INTRODUCTION

For most people property crimes include petty offenses such as theft, burglary, and vandalism. Since juveniles commit a high proportion of these types
of crimes, it is assumed that youths are responsible for the major part of the
property crime problem. Yet embezzlement, security thefts, land frauds,
check frauds and forgery, wholesale hijackings, corporate frauds, illegal car-
tels, consumer frauds, and similar white-collar crimes cost the public far more
in property losses than juvenile property crimes.

At the same time that the public is illegally relieved of billions of dollars
in money and property by adult criminals, there is little outcry over or
knowledge of these costly crimes.[1] Why, for example, are such crimes not
listed in the FBI's crime index? On the other hand, people are very concerned
about the petty crimes committed by juveniles. The amount of property taken
in such crimes is typically very little, while losses in most adult property
crimes is staggering. The reason for this discrepancy lies in the knowledge
that the public has about crime and criminals. Much of it is the fault of the
media for playing up stories about juvenile crime, often either ignoring up-
perworld crimes or hiding them in the business news.[2] Likewise, criminologists have been doing little to investigate the whole area of white-collar crime,
although much attention has been given to juvenile misconduct.

Although we are dealing with juvenile delinquency in this book and not
adult property crimes, in order to understand the patterns of juvenile property crime we must look at the larger context, which includes all property
crimes. We see that it is not so much the case that juveniles commit the
majority of property crimes but that they are responsible for a certain type
of property crime. Moreover, juvenile property crimes occur in the context
of a subculture of juvenility. Youths are forbidden by their status from being
in positions to commit adult white-collar crimes. Were juveniles able to work
as stockbrokers, real estate developers, or corporate executives, we might see
very little in the way of shoplifting, burglary, car theft, and other typical
juvenile property crimes. Not only are such crimes as land fraud far more
profitable than shoplifting, they are less likely to result in detection or prosecution. However, not only are youths not in positions to commit white-collar
crimes, but such offenses would probably not provide them with the same
"kicks" as the kinds of property crimes they typically engage in. Thus it is
important to put crime in its proper perspective and move away from the idea
that property crime is predominantly a juvenile area.

Here we will investigate the ways in which young people engage in various
offenses against property. First, we will examine the types and frequency of
juvenile property crimes to provide an overview. Then we will discuss the

major forms of crimes in this category—shoplifting, auto theft, and vandalism. We will contrast them with adult versions of the same crimes in order to show that juvenile property crime has a nature all its own.

TYPES AND FREQUENCY OF JUVENILE PROPERTY CRIMES

Over a decade ago the President's Commission on Law Enforcement and Administration of Justice reported that in 1965 the 11- to 17-year-old group, representing 13.2 percent of the American population, accounted for over 50 percent of the arrests for property offenses involving burglary, larceny, or motor vehicle theft.[3] More than 60 percent of the motor vehicle thefts were committed by juveniles, and even though most cars were stolen merely for joy rides and then abandoned, felony theft is involved. Since the 1967 report these patterns have changed little. The fact that a relatively small proportion of the population is held responsible for so large a percentage of certain kinds of property crimes suggests that these offenses have a uniquely juvenile character. To understand why this is true, even though adults contribute to the commission of these crimes to no small extent (mostly adults under 25 years of age, however), we have to examine exactly what happens when juveniles are the offenders.

One characteristic of juvenile property offenses is that they tend to be committed by groups.[4] The group tradition among juveniles has frequently been noted. Clifford Shaw pointed out several examples in his pioneering works on delinquency.[5] Irving Spergel found that juveniles belonging to "theft subcultures" typically engage in group stealing.[6] Moreover, he found that groups of juveniles who engage in property crimes are likely to "specialize" in stealing as opposed to drug use or fighting, and that where there are strong subcultures centered around stealing, proportionately more larceny takes place than where such subcultures do not exist.

Furthermore, juvenile thievery is not always utilitarian in terms of the value of the property taken, but is often seen as an occasion for juveniles to show one another that they have the courage and composure to steal or as a kick, undertaken for the thrill of flirting with danger. Adults, on the other hand, are more likely to steal property for money. However, stealing for fun by juveniles is often regarded in retrospect as training for those who later become adult thieves and burglars. This pattern was explained by an older thief as follows:

> Pete said that when he was a kid the guys used to go around from car to car and see if they could break into glove compartments. They did this mainly to see who was the best "stealer." Pete recalled that he was "busted" when he was fifteen years old for stealing hubcaps. Actually, he didn't get much money out of it.

Much of it was a matter of who could steal the most hubcaps. Richie said that you couldn't help learning while you were doing these things . . . and when you got older you didn't rob for "kicks" but for money. That's what most of the guys who were in trouble did now.[7]

Thus, even though these juveniles did not steal for profit, the skills they developed in stealing for kicks could be and were utilized later in stealing for money.

Rosenberg and Silverstein report that most youths begin tapering off their group-stealing activities at around 16 years old.[8] Group support for shoplifting and other forms of stealing lessens, and instead of being defined as a kick or a demonstration of character, these pursuits come to be seen as "kid stuff." The same group pressures that lead juveniles to go along with stealing also lead them away from stealing a few years later.

The exception to this pattern are the alienated hard-drug addicts who operate on their own.[9] They steal only to supply their drug habits, and they get their kicks from the use of heroin, not from the stealing. Drug addicts will steal anything they think will bring them money to buy drugs, and they will steal from anyone. It is not at all unusual for youthful addicts to steal from their parents, for example, although most other juvenile thieves and burglars have some limits, perhaps parents or blind people or church collection boxes.

Shoplifting

Although it is probably inaccurate to say that all juveniles steal, it is true that a good deal of stealing is committed by juveniles. Juveniles themselves have been heard to say that "everyone" steals, meaning "everyone our age" or "everyone in our group."[10] In a study by Short and Nye, more than 60 percent of the high school boys and more than 90 percent of the training school boys admitted to having taken things that didn't belong to them.[11] Similarly, more than 30 percent of the high school girls and almost 80 percent of the training school girls reported that they had stolen something. Most of these confessions probably involved some form of shoplifting—stealing from stores during regular operating hours.

In considering shoplifting, we must first consider the opportunity structure for taking things from stores—how simple it is, or appears to be, for someone to take something without paying for it. Most stores display merchandise so that shoppers can pick it up and examine it or take it to a cashier and pay for it. Providing easy access to the merchandise for shoppers minimizes the number of clerks necessary and permits the shoppers to get a close look at the articles they are considering purchasing. But this arrangement provides not only legitimate shoppers but also shoplifters access to merchandise. Small items can be placed in a pocket or purse or held in the hand, concealed from the clerks. It is very simple to pick up a lipstick case, for example, and leave the store without paying for it. In large stores this appears to be even easier, for there are more places in the store where one can carry on illicit activities unobserved.

At the same time that shoplifters are aware of the opportunities for shoplifting, so too are store owners and managers. In small stores, clerks are alerted to watch for shoplifters, and in larger establishments, special security teams are hired to apprehend them. However, the stores must be careful in accusing people of shoplifting, for they don't want to offend their customers or be charged with false arrest. Therefore, they usually wait until the suspected shoplifter is outside the store before stopping him or her. (It is commonly believed that a person must leave a store with the merchandise in order to be stopped, but that requirement exists in only a few states.) Even if the merchandise is in the subject's possession, he or she may claim that failure to pay for it was a case of forgetfulness. Often a store manager will accept such an account, especially from a regular customer.

With juveniles, on the other hand, store owners are less concerned about the possibility of giving offense, the status of juveniles is such that they are often offended by adults. If there is the slightest suspicion of juvenile involvement in shoplifting, store detectives will take the subject "to the office." Even if the youth is innocent, it is less consequential to stop him or her than to pick up an innocent adult.[12] Juveniles can almost always be accused of "disorderly conduct" or some similar disturbance; if an adult is falsely accused, there is more likely to be a lawsuit or, at the very least, an offended adult shopper who may boycott the store.

In a study in Philadelphia, Gerald Robin found that the majority of those caught shoplifting were juveniles.[13] In part this was because juveniles are more likely to be accused than adults, but this fact alone does not explain the overrepresentation of persons under 18 among those apprehended for shoplifting.

Like other forms of juvenile stealing, shoplifting is a group activity. In 75.3 percent of the cases Robin studied, juveniles apprehended for shoplifting were in the company of other juveniles at the time. This compares with only 23.3 percent of the adult shoplifters caught in groups. Typically, juvenile shoplifters divide the labor, with one acting as the lifter and the other as the lookout or distractor.[14] However, it is questionable that this division of labor is employed as an efficiency measure; most juvenile shoplifters like to have someone along to "keep them company" and fortify their nerve. As one girl who reluctantly went along on shoplifting activities explained, "I was always invited. I never went on my own. I didn't care for it. I never stole anything. I just used to be the lookout. I'm too nervous."

Or, more directly, one boy admitted: "When I go stealing, I got to be with somebody because I get scared being by myself."[15] Thus, juveniles who shoplift in a group are able to "go along" with the others, and supply peer support for the activity.

Once apprehended for shoplifting, it is unlikely that a juvenile will be prosecuted, even if he or she is caught red-handed. Store detectives have three options in handling juveniles. They can (1) release them, (2) turn them over to the juvenile authorities for court action (that is, arrest), or (3) turn them over to the juvenile authorities for remedial (unofficial) action.[16] With adult shoplifters, the detectives can either release them or have them arrested.

It would appear at first that juveniles have a marked advantage, since there is the option of informal handling by the juvenile authorities. For example, in one of the stores Robin studied, all juveniles apprehended for shoplifting were turned over to the juvenile authorities, and in only 5.5 percent of the cases did the official recommend prosecution. Of the adults who were apprehended, 25.8 percent were turned over to the police for arrest. But *all* of the juveniles received some kind of official record of law violation, even though only a small percentage were prosecuted; by contrast, only about a quarter of all adult shoplifters apprehended received a criminal record. The fact that most juveniles were not prosecuted does not mean that they received no record, for it has been found that some official record is maintained for all juvenile arrests, whether or not there is any prosecution.[17] Thus, we find that juveniles apprehended for breaking the law are four times more likely than adults to have an official record.

It should be noted here that unlike juvenile-status offenses, in which no victim is involved, shoplifting does have a "victim"—the store detective or manager who reports the crime. Many stores have a policy of leniency toward first-time offenders, reflecting the management's desire not to be seen as harsh. Since store owners generally believe that handing juvenile offenders over to the juvenile authorities is an "informal" process that may not involve official sanctions or prosecution, they think this is being lenient. They do not understand the impact of a juvenile record, whether "informal" or "formal." This is not to criticize store owners or even to say that juvenile shoplifters should not have records, but merely to point out that if store owners desire leniency for juvenile shoplifters, they should not expect to achieve it through the juvenile justice system. A previous record of shoplifting will be used in interpreting a juvenile's subsequent behavior even if that behavior has nothing to do with shoplifting. For example, suppose a boy is found to be drinking beer with some friends and is picked up. If he has a record of shoplifting, his biography will be interpreted as that of a delinquent. The record, no matter how informal, will be used to document his "delinquent" character.[18] In deciding how to handle cases involving juveniles, judges and probation officers are more likely to be harsh with youths who have records than with those who do not. Thus, any official handling of shoplifting, whether or not prosecution is involved, leads to some form of sanctioning.

The implications of shoplifting, then, go far beyond a single occasion when a juvenile is caught and "warned." It is known by those in the juvenile justice system and by security people in department stores that a delinquent record has detrimental consequences. Otherwise the system would not go to such great lengths to keep the records secret from the public, nor would store managers insist on lenient treatment of juvenile shoplifters. However, *within* the juvenile justice system a juvenile's record is no more secret than the time of day. Even though the record-keeping activities are designed to protect them, the juveniles are not protected from the "protectors."

The dilemma for the juvenile justice authorities is to keep track of shoplifters but at the same time not to criminalize juveniles for a single offense. To meet this goal they issue a warning for a first offense. However, they must keep some record of those whom they have warned so that if the same juvenile is apprehended on subsequent occasions, his or her recidivism will be known to them. If no records were kept, they would have no way of differentiating first-time offenders and recidivists. Nevertheless, the records do serve as "criminalizing" devices since the juvenile's moral character is evaluated in terms of his or her record. No matter how lenient the juvenile authorities are with first-time offenders, the record remains as a stigma.

An important feature of shoplifting is the number of females who appear to be involved in the crime. Robin found that 60 percent of the suspected shoplifters in one sample were women.[19] More recently, in a shoplifting study of a major department store it was found that 86 percent of all apprehended shoplifters were female. Table 7-1 shows the breakdown of shoplifters according to age and sex.

From the data it is clear that not only is shoplifting very much a female crime (in department stores, at least), but it is also a juvenile female crime. The connection between juveniles and theft is nothing new, as we saw in our discussion above. However, massive female involvement in any type of crime is a recent development. As is the case with most such patterns that go against standard criminological notions, there is usually a rush to explain away such anomalies. Robin, for example, attempted to explain the unusually large number of female shoplifters arrested by pointing out that most of the security people were women, and these female store detectives were more likely

TABLE 7-1.   Sex and Age of Department Store Shoplifters[a]

Age	Sex		Total
	Female	Male	
17 and Under	220 (62%)	30 (8%)	250 (70%)
18 and Over	87 (24%)	19 (6%)	106 (30%)
Total	307 (86%)	49 (14%)	356 (100%)

[a]Steve Bounton, San Diego State University, 1977.

than male detectives to be suspicious of women.[20] Such an argument has merit conceptually, and a number of sociologists have argued that reactions to possible deviance has favored females because people are less likely to assume that females may be involved in crimes.[21] However, females are less likely to seem as "innocent" among their own gender than they are among males. Therefore, females in control roles are more likely to arrest females than are males. In an experiment testing the extent to which females are less likely to be reported for shoplifting, however, this situation did not hold true. Females were as likely to be reported for shoplifting as were males by both male and female observers.[22]

Another "explanation" of why females may be more involved in shoplifting, but not thievery in general, than males is that "shopping" is a female role, and therefore women would be more likely to shoplift, especially in department stores that carry more female-oriented items. This explanation is all right as far as it goes, but the implications of linking the female role with certain forms of crimes would demand far more female involvement in other types of crimes. For example, since women are more likely to be at home during the day than are men, they might be expected to be involved in more daytime residential burglaries than men. However, it is men, usually under 25 years of age, who commit the vast majority of such burglaries.[23]

A more plausible explanation has to do with the assumption, by criminologists and many others, that little girls are made of sugar and spice and wouldn't do such things. Most shoplifting involves petty larceny, and since not until recently has the FBI's uniform crime report included this category, such crimes were not even counted. Moreover, in an incredible omission, Law Enforcement Assistance Administration-(LEAA) sponsored victimization surveys which did not include questions about commercial larceny! Instead they asked only about burglary and robbery of commercial establishments, two crimes that, combined, account for less financial and property loss than shoplifting

The frequency and ubiquity of shoplifting is such that it constitutes the single most common form of larceny against commercial establishments, and perhaps of all larcenies. Given the high proportion of females involved in shoplifting and its high frequency, there may not be that much difference between the actual amount of crime committed by males and females. The form and severity of the crime may differ with sex, and there is little doubt that men commit certain violent crimes more than women. By the same token, though, boys probably do not shoplift as much as girls do, no matter how the figures are counted. Department stores cater more to women than to men, but they carry ample lines of men's items to draw most males and females. To be sure, we would find more shoplifting in hobby shops by juvenile boys, but we would find even more by girls in a dress shop or other women's store. Thus, as has been the case in other spheres of life, we see that women have largely not been counted.

A further examination of the findings from the department store data

TABLE 7–2.   Sex, Age, and Shoplifting[a]

Age	Sex		Total in Percent
	Female	Male	
10–11	5 (1.4%)	2 (0.6%)	2.0
12–13	33 (9.2%)	1 (0.3%)	9.5
14–15	87 (24.3%)	14 (3.9%)	28.2
16–17	96 (26.9%)	13 (3.6%)	30.4
18–19	32 (8.9%)	7 (2.0%)	10.9
20 and over	54 (15%)	12 (3.4%)	18.4
			99.4[*]

[a]Steve Bounton, San Diego State University, 1977.
[*]Less than 100 percent due to rounding.

reveals a similar pattern to that noted in the discussion of general delinquency: As girls reach adulthood their participation in larceny drops markedly. Table 7–2 shows the drop in shoplifting at the end of the juvenile years.

There is a clear increase in the frequency of larceny among both boys and girls until 16–17 years of age, with a marked decline at age 18. (Actually, the decline begins at age 17 after a peak at age 16.) The decline among 20-year-olds and over in frequency of shoplifting is even further accelerated (Table 7–3).

The data compiled for department store shoplifting covered ages all the way up to 68; those over 20 accounted for only 18.4 percent, with about half of these persons being between ages 20 and 25. Looking at shoplifting crimes in this manner, we see that the fact that females commit most of them is not as interesting as the fact that, like other forms of juvenile crime, shoplifting stops as youths approach adulthood. This puts the emphasis on age differences rather than sex differences, and as a result, we can account for the patterns of shoplifting in terms of the subculture of juvenility and the situations of delinquency.

TABLE 7–3.   Shoplifting from Age 20 to 25[a]

Age	Frequency	Percent
20	5	1.4
21	10	2.8
22	7	2.0
23	6	1.7
24	3	0.8
25	1	0.3

[a]Steve Bounton, San Diego State University, 1977.

First, as a person leaves the age and subculture of juvenility, shoplifting is reduced. Not only does the support for such activities fall off as the juvenile enters into the responsibilities and opportunities afforded by adult status, but so does the need. For one thing, a person with adult status enjoys more economic independence. This is not to say that juveniles who shoplift cannot afford to buy what they steal, for often they have the money or credit cards with which to purchase the items they lift. Typically, however, their money and credit cards come from their parents, so that juveniles are economically dependent. Thus by stealing they assert their economic independence. It should be noted that this thesis is only partially true, because there is no evidence that juveniles who have part time jobs and thus are economically independent as far as nonessentials are concerned engage in any less shoplifting than other youths.

A more important consideration is what juveniles have to lose if they are caught. The loss of status and face may be involved, but these can be minimized because the status at stake is not very high to begin with. With little to lose, and with the support of their peers, shoplifting for juveniles is much easier socially than it is for adults. At the same time, a juvenile can raise his or her status by showing off his or her ability to beat the system.

In a study of middle-class delinquency, Norman Weiner found that a number of adolescent girls who engaged in shoplifting regularly did so with some amount of sophistication.[24] They would choose a downtown department store rather than a suburban one because they believed that store detectives in downtown stores would be more likely to keep an eye on lower-class juveniles who shop than on well-dressed middle- and upper-middle-class youths. Likewise, they reasoned, the store detectives would be less likely to offend a middle-class youth than a lower-class one. Therefore, even if a detective suspected a middle-class youth of shoplifting, he or she would be unlikely to stop such a suspect.

The actual shoplifting activity also demonstrated some forethought and method. For example, one girl described by Weiner took along a stapler and a staple-remover as tools of the trade. She would buy something that would be bagged and stapled with the sales slip on the outside of the bag. Then she would take a number of dresses into the dressing room along with the bag of goods she had purchased. Inside the dressing room she would unstaple the bag, put one of the dresses inside, then restaple the bag and leave without paying for the dress. Thus, rather than being haphazard, shoplifting among middle-class adolescent girls is systematic and, if we can generalize from Weiner's findings, sanctioned by associates.

Shoplifting among middle-class youth does not appear to bring on pangs of guilt or self-condemnation. Instead they "neutralize" their delinquency by establishing and maintaining a vocabulary of motives that justifies their activities.[25] Weiner explains how they viewed their own shoplifting activities:

Karen is not unusual. Her whole crowd steals. The same reasons are always heard. "I needed it; I only take from big stores." They only take what they "need," or, more precisely, what they claim they need. They never use the word "steal." It is always "get." They set up a vast web of rationalizations and excuses: "The large stores are impersonal and coldly efficient; they can stand the loss." This is merely an extension of the attitude that most people feel toward vending machines. To whom does one complain when a soda machine proffers a cup but no Coke? Thus, when a person gets back too much change from such a machine, he believes he is justified in keeping it. When these middle-class adolescents steal, they feel the same elation that most of us feel when we get something for nothing, especially if they think they have beaten the system.[26]

As Weiner notes, the juveniles develop a vocabulary of motives embedded in the subculture of juvenility that provides the rationale and the "fun" of shoplifting. At the same time the subculture of juvenility that is socially bounded by the Establishment, the adult world, or merely a subjectively restrictive "them" creates the limitations that generate the sensibility of youths to their patterns of activities. That is, any juvenile who subjectively experiences his or her status in terms of the restrictions placed on youths can understand the rationales used by juvenile shoplifters. The reason is that the subculture of juvenility shapes the juveniles' collective experience and world view. The facts that shoplifters are predominantly juveniles, that they are not restricted to ethnic, economic, or ecological categories, and that shoplifting drops off as juveniles reach adult status are evidence that the juvenile status is linked to patterns of shoplifting. The overrepresentation of girls in the data suggests that shoplifting is the female form of property crimes and serves to support further the notion that a subculture of juvenility is pervasive among youths and not, as is widely believed, particularly associated with male delinquency.

Auto Theft

More than half the cars stolen annually in the United States are taken by persons under the age of 18.[27] Most juvenile car thieves have no intention of keeping the cars or selling them.[28] The cars are not used as getaway vehicles, nor do juveniles typically belong to car theft rings. Instead, they take the cars for a "joy ride," and the thrill of riding in a stolen car serves as the end. The stolen cars are driven a few blocks and then abandoned. This is why the police are relatively successful in recovering stolen automobiles.

The laws pertaining to auto theft usually do not differentiate between "joy riding" and "grand theft auto." Stealing a car is a felony. However, juveniles are not subject to adult penalties, and most law-enforcement agencies and the courts make *de facto* distinctions between "joy riding" and "auto theft."[29] Nevertheless, taking someone's automobile without permission is considered a serious offense, and, unlike a number of juvenile-status offenses and shop-lifting, it is not something "everybody does."[30]

Although adults also commit car theft, juvenile car theft has certain "juvenile characteristics." Like a number of other forms of delinquency, it usually involves groups rather than individuals.[31] Further, as we have noted, juveniles take cars for the thrill of the joy ride whereas adults are more likely to steal cars for use in the commission of a crime or for the money.[32] When adults choose to steal cars in groups, it is in order to make the car theft more efficient by dividing the labor. One felon will act as lookout and the other will break into and start the car. Juveniles accompany one another in car thefts for the shared thrill of stealing the car and taking it for a joy ride.

Given these differences between juvenile and adult car theft, what we see are actually two different events, although the law (on the books at least) makes no distinction. Since the law forbids stealing cars by anyone, juvenile or adult, we are dealing in both cases with criminal activities. Nevertheless, there are enough qualitative differences in the ways in which the crimes are committed and the goals of the activity to warrant regarding the typical juvenile car theft as a phenomenon of juvenile crime. Those juveniles who steal cars to use in a holdup or for sale can be treated analytically as "acting like adults": conversely, adults who take cars for a joy ride are exhibiting "juvenile characteristics" in their crime. In this context we can see that "stealing cars" is an inappropriate classification by itself. We need to examine the occasion of a car theft in order to form an accurate picture of the event. Merely pointing out that stealing cars is against the law does not help us to understand delinquency.

In examining who steals cars, there have been conflicting findings. In some studies it was found that juvenile car theft was largely committed by white, middle-class youths, suggesting the greater car orientation of suburban youths over urban youths, especially lower-class juveniles.[33] In other studies, however, there was clear evidence that it was the lower-class black youths in urban centers who were responsible for the majority of juvenile car thefts, suggesting that limited access to legitimate means to obtain an automobile was the cause of youthful car theft.[34] The most recent study on juvenile auto theft found that there were no significant differences between lower-class and middle-class rates of car theft.[35] Thus, as with many of the other forms of delinquency examined, we find that this kind of property offense can be viewed in the context of the subculture of juvenility and not as a characteristic of social class.

In conclusion, automobile theft is generally committed by youths in groups of two or more, largely for "kicks." Analytically, we might refer to juvenile car theft as a "group action," using Goffman's specific meaning of "action," discussed in Chapter 5.[36] This is because the juvenile car thief typically does not steal a car to keep or strip and sell for parts. Were it the case that youths stole cars for the economic gain, we would find that a far lower proportion of stolen cars are recovered.

Vandalism

Juvenile vandalism is a much talked about but little studied area of property delinquency. Clinard and Wade define vandalism as the deliberate defacement, mutilation, or destruction of private or public property by a juvenile or group of juveniles not having immediate or direct ownership in the property so abused.[37] This definition ties vandalism to juveniles to property destruction, and we would probably be better advised to use a broader definition, such as the one provided by Martin that simply defines vandalism as the destruction of property.[38] We could modify the definition by noting that if one destroys one's own property vandalism is not involved, but then we would prejudice our definition against juveniles because they legally cannot own property. However, since this prejudice exists, we would not be altering reality by adding this proviso to our definition. Moreover, we want to retain the words "defacement" and "mutilation" in the definition since technically many forms of property can be vandalized without being destroyed.

We need first to put juvenile vandalism in proper perspective by noting that adults, especially adult organizations, engage in a good deal of vandalism, but it is usually couched under another name, such as "pollution" or "environmental damage." Strip mining in Montana, for example, has ruined acreage the size of the state of New Jersey. Even the most malicious juvenile vandal could not reap such destruction. Furthermore, the damage to property by water and air pollution is far more dangerous and destructive than the kinds of vandalism engaged in by juveniles. In the 1960s, surfers were accused of massive vandalism along the beaches, and while they did damage beach property, their crimes were minor in comparison to the 1969 oil spill in the Santa Barbara, California, channel that killed sea life and totally devastated beaches. These points are made not to justify vandalism but to point out that vandalism and juveniles are not inextricably linked.

Explanations of juvenile vandalism have been sketchy and general. Moreover, the explanations often tend to stereotype vandalism in terms of traditional assumptions made about crime and delinquency. For example, Clinard and Wade assume that most vandalism is practiced by boys and explain male vandalism in terms of the male role in American society:

> Since, American culture does not place the same inhibitions on the boy's outward expression of his feelings, positive or negative, as it does on that of girls, the male youth, as one author has suggested, often appears to feel it essential to be self-destructive in order to be considered masculine and acceptable to his peers. Participation in vandalism is one way of meeting these needs for autonomy and peer group acceptance.[39]

This implies that girls are culturally inhibited from such "outward" expression of feelings, and further, that their expressions would not be realized in the form of vandalism.

The problem with this analysis is that it overkills the phenomenon. First, boys' roles may be clearly different than female roles, but there is a strong prohibition against senselessly destroying property. The entire male role in American society is centered around acquiring and developing property, not destroying it. Furthermore, when we examine the data, only a small percentage of juveniles engage in malicious vandalism, and there is no significant difference between vandalism by girls and boys. The assumption that boys "naturally" engage in more vandalism than girls is grounded in the same stereotypes that overlook other forms of juvenile crimes by girls, and the male role stereotype is characterized in such a way to "explain" the differences while overlooking other role expectations that are contrary to underlying assumptions.

A preliminary report by Pamela Richards, Richard Berk, and Brenda Forster found that among elementary, junior high, and high school students sex was not a general determining factor in predicting vandalism. This was found to be especially true when vandalism was divided between "defacement" vandalism and "damaging" vandalism. The authors point out that

> the division of vandalism into two types (defacement and damaging) is useful in countering the assumption that vandalism is an exclusively male activity. 5th and 6th grade girls participate about equally in damaging and may even deface slightly more often than boys. However, the overall incidence of vandalism is small with only about 3% of these students reporting any kind of damaging more than once or twice in the last six months.[40]

In addition, after an overall rise in vandalism among the junior high age group, vandalism drops as students approach adulthood in high school.[41] This pattern is similar to the one we noted in discussing shoplifting and is consistent with the idea that while in the subculture of juvenility, young people commit certain forms of delinquent acts that are linked with their status as juveniles. During the peak ages of self-reported vandalism, at least 50 percent of the sample had committed vandalism in the six months prior to the study. This suggests a good possibility that most of the rest of the students had committed some form of vandalism, whether it was defacement or damage, during their juvenile years. Thus, instead of a small group of juveniles engaging in delinquent vandalism, we find instead a general involvement, at least to some extent, by people passing through the age of juvenility.

Why is it that virtually all juveniles have probably engaged in some form of vandalism? Clinard and Wade offer some valid points: "Much teen-age vandalism . . . is extemporaneous behavior, adventitious and fortuitous in character . . . ," and they note that the self-image of the juvenile vandal is that of a prankster.[42] Put simply, it's fun to watch a window break, and it's exciting to pop out a street light and run like crazy. This is not, however, the "angry young man," as suggested by Clinard and Wade in the same article. There is a difference between being "frustrated" and "having kicks," according to Goffman (see Chapter 5). The image of the frustrated, angry young man is not consistent with the general juvenile self-image and the way others see the juvenile role. Juveniles are not taken seriously, they are seen as irresponsible and they are treated as children. When they act irresponsibly they are behaving completely consistently with their position in the subculture of juvenility. In those situations where they are taken seriously, for example, when they drop out of school and take a job and family, they stop committing delinquent acts. As we have seen with vandalism and shoplifting, as juveniles approach adulthood, delinquency drops dramatically.

Types of Vandalism

Vandalism takes different forms, and as we will see, the different types constitute very different acts and not just variations of the same behavior.

Residual Vandalism.   When vandalism is the result of some criminal activity, the "residue" is property destruction, known as *residual vandalism.* For example, if a house is torn apart so that the copper wiring can be taken out and sold, the damage to the house is residual vandalism. The economic payoff, rather than the destruction, is the objective of the act. John Martin, who refers to this activity as "predatory vandalism," points out the utilitarian nature of the activity, whereas most theorists assume that vandalism is nonutilitarian in nature.[43] Residual vandalism is a consequence of another crime, which is itself utilitarian in the conventional sense.

A number of types of residual vandalism are typically committed by juveniles. Old houses contain much material that can be sold to junk dealers— for example, lead from pipes, copper wiring, and other fixtures. The money this material yields can be worth the effort to remove it, but the damage caused to the structure is extensive and expensive. For example, Thrasher reports that two boys got three dollars from a junk dealer for some lead pipe they tore out of a house, but they did two hundred dollars' worth of damage to the house.[44] Rubinstein says that in Philadelphia abandoned houses are commonly vandalized by young boys who tear out anything they think they can sell, but the police rarely consider this vandalism serious enough to write a report about, even if the house is not intended for demolition.[45] Residents of neighborhoods where this kind of vandalism is common report it, usually as burglary, but since they know that the police rarely do anything about vandalism reports, they attempt to keep houses occupied until new residents move in, for once a house is believed to be unoccupied, the kids destroy it.

Residual vandalism is also committed on cars by juveniles in search of parts they can sell. This may be done on an "orders taken" basis or simply in terms of opportunity. One juvenile who stole car parts explained how he took specific orders:

> You go around and hear them talking that they need a wheel, they need a battery, and they only got so much money to give you. So you take a guy aside and tell him you could get it. If you don't know the guy you tell him, "Give me the dough, and I'll bring you the wheel." You keep the dough and don't bring him no wheel. . . . If I know you and you need a wheel, you tell me the size and stuff, I go around walking normal like, and I look at all the wheels and I figure out which one you need. Then I go get the rest of the guys, and they haul up the car while I pick up the wheel, and we take that one wheel.[46]

Juveniles also take car parts for use on their own cars or for some other purpose of their own. Car radio antennae, for example, are often broken off for use as weapons in gang fights or for making more sophisticated weapons. In describing how to make a zip gun, one boy explained:

> Ya get a car antenna and a piece of wood and a can opener. Ya cut out a piece of wood in the design of a gun. Then ya drill a hole [lengthwise] right through the middle on the top and stick ya antenna in there and then ya take ya can opener and take the top off—what ya turn with—then ya file a point on it. Then ya have a hole in the gun and ya stick the can opener in it. Then ya tie rubber bands on it and pull it back ta fire ya gun.

When asked why the boys never considered buying an antenna he explained: "Why should ya buy one when they're out on the street to take? They cost a coupla dollars."[47]

Parking meters, vending machines, public telephones, and any other device that yields money when destroyed are also targets of residual vandalism. For example, store windows are broken not merely for the fun of it but to permit "smash-and-grab" thefts by juveniles and others. A bottle of liquor, a piece of jewelry or clothing, or anything else displayed through a window, not the window itself, accounts for the shattered glass.

It appears, then, that residual vandalism, is "done for the money," since the vandalism is a means and not an end. However, the correct question to ask in studying this type of vandalism is, Why did the culprit choose this particular means? Residual vandalism is certainly not a "nonutilitarian" reaction, as Cohen would have us believe, but instead involves learning an available pattern of delinquent behavior.[48] In his study of vandalism, Martin found that residual vandalism was a form of delinquent activity that was passed on as a community tradition. Referred to as "junking," the vandalism was seen to be merely one of many forms of delinquent activity.[49] It was learned in association with other delinquents, and it was usually committed with other delinquents.

We can account for the patterns of residual vandalism in terms of differential association. For example, consider the formula for making a zip gun. The formula is relatively complex, and it is unlikely that anyone who had not learned that technique of making a zip gun would consider using a car antenna for doing so. In a similar way, the boys learned that it was "stupid" to pay money for a car antenna. It was best to rip it off someone's car. In other words, residual vandalism is a delinquent technique that is learned as anything else is learned.

Vandalism for Kicks.   A second form of vandalism identified in the studies of juvenile property destruction has been labeled "wanton vandalism," but we will refer to it as "vandalism for kicks" because, from the point of view of those who commit it, they were "just having fun." There is a wide range of activities that constitute this type of vandalism, from breaking windows to destroying whole towns. For example, a boy described some of his activities:

> We did all kinds of dirty tricks for fun. We'd see a sign, "Please keep the street clean," but we'd tear it down and say, "We don't feel like keeping it clean." One day we put a can of glue in the engine of a man's car. We would tear things down. That would make us laugh and feel good, to have so many jokes.

Easter-week school vacations often result in large-scale destruction in such places as Fort Lauderdale, Florida, and Balboa, California. Once a town called Zap, North Dakota, decided to try to attract vacationing students; by the end of the first night the National Guard had to be called in to save the town from total destruction. As it turned out, Zap lost more in property damage from the rampaging students than it received in revenues. Every store in town suffered serious damage.[50]

Numerous additional examples could be provided. Many readers can probably remember their own juvenile high jinks that resulted in some form of property damage. The problem, however, is to explain why this activity occurs. At first we might dismiss differential association as an explanation, since most people learn at an early age that property has value, and since this form of vandalism is not a residue of some other activity; therefore we cannot explain it in terms of learning illegitimate means for obtaining learned and desired ends.

However, there are a number of actions people learn that might lead them to see property destruction as "fun." For example, consider Halloween. The kids in the neighborhood extort "treats" from people by the threat of pulling some "trick," like breaking a window or burning the house down. Of course the literal sense of "trick or treat" is probably employed only rarely, and the people in the neighborhood who don't come up with something for their nocturnal visitors are rarely vandalized on Halloween. But the point is that we do have institutions that teach the fun of vandalism even while they are apparently designed to contain it. Similarly, children hear stories from their parents of stunts they pulled in college, or the father returning from a convention in some distant city relates as a joke the petty vandalism he and his pals pulled.

Just about everyone learns that some fun can be had from vandalism. He or she also learns that a large part of the fun derives from the victim's reaction of helpless rage and frustration. The adventure of being chased by a vandalism victim is a thrill, a kick.[51] In Goffman's term, it provides "action," something out of the mundane, routine life juveniles must lead at home and at school.[52] In that this form of vandalism provides action, it fits into Goffman's framework of activities that provide adventure for the young.

Here we should note that pointing out the motives underlying any form of vandalism is not meant to provide a justification for the activity; nor does it matter in terms of the consequences whether the vandalism was caused by thieves or pranksters. What is important is that the acts resulting in vandalized property may differ from the point of view of the actor and also in terms of the judgment others make regarding whether these acts are delinquent or not. The qualitative results may be identical, but since the understandings of the acts as well as the ends of the acts are qualitatively dissimilar, we need to understand the various forms. In fact, we should treat different types of vandalism as distinct types of activities, just as we differentiate burglary and running away from home. The legal pronouncement may be the same for the record—"malicious mischief"—but the police, courts, and probation officers understand the culprits not merely in terms of the consequences but also in terms of what they consider to be the motives.[53]

Malevolent Vandalism.   Malevolent vandalism, also called "angry vandalism" and "vindictive vandalism," is activity in which property is destroyed out of malevolent motives on the part of the perpetrators.[54] Schools, the most common target of juvenile vandalism, are often wrecked because of youths' distaste for these institutions. For example, Cavan describes the extent of damage committed by juvenile vandals on schools:

> Over the Memorial Day weekend, 1960, 25 Chicago schools received an estimated $50,000 worth of damage. Classrooms and offices were ransacked, a fire was set in the principal's office, windows were broken and ink was splashed on walls and used to make crude drawings or write obscene phrases; in one school a radio, phonograph and records were damaged. In some schools lunchroom iceboxes were broken into and food was thrown against walls and ceilings. Many schools not entered had windows broken from the outside.[55]

A more troubling and equally prevalent form of malevolent vandalism expresses the deep-seated racial and ethnic divisions of the general population. Children pick up the stereotypes and hatreds of their parents. For example, synagogues are often the target of anti-Semitic acts of vandalism.

During World War II, when the United States fought the Nazis and a popular distaste for anti-Semitism was widely expressed, the following episode occurred:

> Temple Ohabed Zedek, 954 ———— Avenue, is part of a two-family house. The rabbi and his family lived upstairs. Windows were broken in the synagogue on the nights of March 9, 10, 11 and 16, 1943. Vandalism stopped when a policeman was stationed outside. Five members of a gang were arrested. . . .
>
> [One of them,] K.D., eighteen, testified that he had broken windows "to try to get the Jews off the block." In 1941 he had broken into a store owned by Jews and stolen money, cigarettes and shoes. Caught and held delinquent, he blames Jews because the store was "Jewish." He said his gang believed Jews were no good in the war, they were "yellow." K.D. had transferred to high school from parochial school. He left school at sixteen. . . .[56]

Like residual vandalism, vindictive vandalism is probably learned in association with others. However, instead of being a phenomenon of peer relationships, it is more likely to be passed on to youth by adults.

A Little at a Time: Erosive Vandalism.   When vandalism is the result of a long procession of "little vandalisms," it is called "erosive vandalism."[57] The most common example can be seen on the nation's highways and in public parks, which have been turned into junkyards by litterbugs whose collective carelessness results in damage that no single rampage could produce. However, even though erosive vandalism is certainly as destructive as any other type, it usually is not seen as an instance of malicious mischief or as a peculiarly juvenile activity.

One form of erosive vandalism that *is* peculiarly juvenile has emerged recently and is worth consideration. This is the use of aerosol spray paint to deface public and private property. In New York City it is difficult to find a subway car or station that is not liberally covered with spray paint. In addition to the names and street numbers of the perpetrators, such as "Taki 168," abstract designs are to be found as well. Gangs in various other parts of the country paint their gang names and slogans on walls and fences. For example, in the Watts district of Los Angeles one can find "Denver Lanes" and "Bounty Hunters" sprayed on fences, while in the Hyde Park area of Chicago one finds "Black P. Stone Nation" or "Stone Rules."

One group of youths in New York City who were especially active with spray paint redefined their activities as "art" and organized themselves into the "Graffiti Artists United." They were commissioned to paint a mural at one of New York City's public colleges in their unique style and received others' recognition for it. A spokesman for the graffiti artists explained: "A lot of people don't like it, man, but like it or not, we've made the biggest art movement ever to hit New York City."[58]

Apparently the state of New York sees the activity in the traditional frame of reference and has passed laws stipulating $1,000 fines and a year in jail for convicted graffiti writers. The New York City Transit Authority estimates the costs of removing graffiti at 1.3 million dollars per year, and it is unlikely that it will ever consider selling a transit car as a work of art.[59]

Numerous explanations have been offered for this activity. Some writers have pointed out that the impersonal character of public buildings offends the spray paint vandals, who make these alien monoliths the targets of violence.[60] When Columbia University in New York City instituted a program to open its facilities to neighborhood youth, the incidents of vandalism diminished as the youths came to define the university as part of their community. However, since many of the spray paint vandals decorate their own communities with their names and slogans, it is not necessarily true that a feeling of community reduces this form of vandalism. It may well be that the spray painting is regarded as a decoration or even as a celebration of their identity with the community. Or it could be a way of "claiming" territory or immortality. All we know for certain is that the introduction of aerosol spray paint was a prerequisite for the activity and that its use is widespread. The last feature suggests that this is not an idiosyncratic form of vandalism but one that is probably picked up by kids from one another. That is, like so many other forms of delinquency, spraying the walls with anything from obscenities to name and street number is learned in association with other spray paint vandals.

Social Characteristics of Vandals

What are the characteristics of juveniles who commit acts of vandalism? In answering this question we will be somewhat cautious, for as we have seen, according to the study by Richards *et al,* some form of vandalism is committed by virtually all juveniles. The present discussion is based largely on Martin's study conducted in 1961, which is instructive because it compares labeled delinquents.

Martin found that more boys were involved in vandalism among the labeled vandal-delinquent group than among boys in the general delinquent population. Of the vandal-delinquent population, 96.9 percent were male as compared to 87.6 percent of the general labeled delinquent population. Similarly, Martin found that the average age of labeled general delinquents was slightly higher than that of the juvenile vandals. The average labeled vandal was 13 years old, while the average labeled delinquent was 14.5 years old. There seemed to be no other differences between vandals and delinquents in general except that there was a slightly (but insignificantly) higher proportion of whites and Puerto Ricans in the vandal population and the vandals were generally from a lower socioeconomic stratum.

Martin identified three types of vandals: (1) disturbed, (2) essentially lawabiding, and (3) subcultural.[61] The "disturbed" group included those who committed vandalism because of some psychological disturbance; the "essentially law-abiding" youths had somehow been talked into or had stumbled into the opportunity to commit vandalism; and the "subcultural" group committed vandalism as one of several delinquent activities. Two-thirds of the labeled juvenile vandals belonged to the subcultural group. Generally, the vandalism committed by the subcultural group was the residual type, where the boys would steal something of value and tear up property while doing so. It appears that this type of vandal comes into contact with patterns of vandalism, and those who commit vandalism thereby learn the patterns. For example, one boy explained that

> he and his brother were never "in trouble" before moving to Third Avenue, although there had been ample opportunity for breaking into places where they had previously lived. Frankie continued by saying, "But when ya live here ya see a lotta guys—big guys—doin' that and doin' this and then ya get the habit of it."[62]

The boy who made the statement had been involved in vandalism, but not until he began associating with the subcultural vandals. In this type of instance we can clearly see the application of differential association theory, and we can explain most of what Martin calls subcultural vandalism by differential association. However, we must recognize that this group consists of *those most likely to be labeled and incarcerated* for vandalism and not most vandals *per se*.

The group of vandals identified as essentially law-abiding probably includes the greatest number of actual vandals because it draws from the largest population of juveniles. This group is not part of a subculture of delinquency in Matza's sense of the term. Rather, these youths are part of a subculture of juvenility that does not constrain certain limited forms of delinquency and that in certain defined situations allows a good deal of delinquency.[63] However, because the "essentially law-abiding" juvenile is just what the term "law-abiding" implies in the context of the juvenile world, his or her delinquency goes largely unnoticed, denied, or forgiven and, therefore, not counted. The patterns of association with others in the same boat, namely, other juveniles who are all part of the subculture of juvenility, follow the principles of differential association. Instead of being predominantly delinquent, however, the learning follows a secondary emphasis on delinquency, including vandalism in certain situations, and a primary emphasis on being a juvenile in society.

SUMMARY

In reviewing juvenile property crimes we find that three features stand out. First, virtually every juvenile engages in some form of property crime during the juvenile years. Clearly some engage in more property crimes than others, but significantly as youths approach the end of their tenure as juveniles their crimes against property drop dramatically. Therefore we have argued that many property crimes are linked to the status of being a juvenile and not, as labeling theory and delinquent subculture suggest, the status of a delinquent.

Second, when we look at the intended ends of these activities, we find that a good deal of it is done for "fun" or "kicks." Many of the shoplifters can afford to buy what they steal, and most juvenile car thieves have no intention of keeping the automobile. The excitement generated by the activity, not the money to be realized from the stolen or destroyed property, is the prime motivating element. The performance, moreover, is done not merely for themselves but also for the others who go along on these escapades. They find intrinsic excitement in breaking the law and also the opportunity to show others that they have the strength of character to carry it off.

Third, juvenile property crimes are typically committed in groups. The group interaction provides a generating force not available from any single member. Methods, justifications, challenges, and solidarity are all made available through group interaction; only the methods exist for the lone delinquent. The structure of the interaction makes delinquent property offenses possible and even, in some instances, obligatory in the same way that different interaction structures make other people feel obliged to mow their yards, wash their cars, and generally "keep up with the Joneses."

NOTES

1. Gilbert Geis and Robert F. Meier (eds.), *White-Collar Crime* (New York: Free Press, 1977), pp. 23–27.
2. *Ibid.,* pp. 6–8.
3. President's Commission on Law Enforcement and Administration of Justice, *The Challenge of Crime in a Free Society* (Washington, D.C.: Government Printing Office, 1967), p. 56.
4. James F. Short, Jr., *Gang Delinquency and Delinquent Subcultures* (New York: Harper & Row, 1968), p. 79.
5. Clifford Shaw, "Juvenile Delinquency: A Group Tradition," Bulletin of the State University of Iowa, No. 23, N.S. No. 700, 1933.
6. Irving Spergel, *Racketville, Slumtown and Haulburg* (Chicago: University of Chicago Press, 1964).
7. *Ibid.,* p. 51.
8. Bernard Rosenberg and Harry Silverstein, *The Varieties of Delinquent Experience* (Waltham, Mass.: Blaisdell, 1969).
9. *Ibid.,* p. 103.
10. *Ibid.,* p. 97.
11. James F. Short, Jr., and Ivan F. Nye, "Extent of Unrecorded Juvenile Delinquency: Tentative Conclusions," *Journal of Criminal Law, Criminology, and Police Science, 49*:296–302 (November–December 1958).
12. Gerald Robin, "Patterns of Department Store Shoplifting," *Crime and Delinquency, 9:*163–172 (April 1963).
13. *Ibid.,* p. 167.

14. Donald R. Cressey, *Criminal Organization: Its Elementary Forms* (London: Heinemann, 1972).
15. Rosenberg and Silverstein, p. 104.
16. Robin, p. 167.
17. William B. Sanders, *Detective Work: A Study of Criminal Investigation* (New York: Free Press, 1977), pp. 130–149.
18. Aaron Cicourel, *The Social Organization of Juvenile Justice* (New York: Wiley, 1968); Harold Garfinkel, *Studies in Ethnomethodology* (Englewood Cliffs, N.J.: Prentice-Hall, 1967).
19. Robin, p. 167.
20. *Ibid.,* p. 168.
21. Darrell J. Steffensmeier and Robert M. Terry, "Deviance and Respectability: An Observational Study of Reactions to Shoplifting," *Social Forces, 51:*417–426 (June 1973).
22. *Ibid.,* p. 425.
23. Harry Scarr, *Patterns of Burglary* (Washington, D.C.: Department of Justice, 1972).
24. Norman Weiner, "The Teen-age Shoplifter: A Microcosmic View of Middle Class Delinquency," in Jack Douglas (ed.), *Observations of Deviance* (New York: Random House, 1970).
25. Gresham Sykes and David Matza, "Techniques of Neutralization: A Theory of Delinquency," *American Sociological Review, 22:*664–670 (December 1957).
26. Weiner, p. 113.
27. Helen MacGill Hughes, *Delinquents and Criminals: Their Social World* (Boston: Holbrook Press, 1970).
28. Ervin Schepses, "Boys Who Steal Cars," *Federal Probation,* pp. 56–62 (March 1961).
29. Howard C. Daudistel and William B. Sanders, "Police Discretion in Application of the Law," *Et Al, 3:*26–40 (1974).
30. William Wattenberg and James Balistrieri, "Automobile Theft: A 'Favored Group' Delinquency," *American Journal of Sociology, 57:*575–579 (May 1952).
31. Schepses.
32. John E. Conklin, *Robbery and the Criminal Justice System* (Philadelphia: Lippincott, 1972); Ruth Shonle Cavan, *Juvenile Delinquency* (Philadelphia: Lippincott, 1962), p. 145.
33. Schepses, pp. 59–60; Wattenberg and Balistrieri, p. 576.
34. Charles H. McCaghy, Peggy C. Giordano and Trudy K. Henson, "Auto Theft: Offender and Offense Characteristics," *Criminology 15:*367–385 (1977). Marvin E. Wolfgang, Robert Figlio and Thorsten Sellin, *Delinquency in a Birth Cohort* (Chicago: University of Chicago Press, 1972).
35. Paul C. Higgins and Gary L. Albrecht, "Cars and Kids: A Self-Report Study of Juvenile Auto Theft and Traffic Violations," unpublished research paper, University of South Carolina and University of Illinois, 1980.
36. Erving Goffman, *Interaction Ritual* (New York: Doubleday, 1967).
37. Marshall B. Clinard and Andrew L. Wade, "Toward the Delineation of Vandalism as a Sub-Type in Juvenile Delinquency," *Journal of Criminal Law, Criminology and Police Science, 48* (1958).
38. John M. Martin, *Juvenile Vandalism: A Study of Its Nature and Prevention* (Springfield, Ill.: Charles C Thomas, 1961).
39. Clinard and Wade.
40. Pamela J. Richards, Richard A. Berk, and Brenda Forster, "Age and Gender Trends in Self-Reported Vandalism: A Preliminary Report," mimeographed (December 10, 1975), p. 12.
41. *Ibid.,* p. 17.
42. Clinard and Wade.
43. Martin; Albert Cohen, *Delinquent Boys* (New York: Free Press, 1955).
44. F. M. Thrasher, *The Gang* (Chicago: University of Chicago Press, 1936).
45. Jonathan Rubinstein, *City Police* (New York: Farrar, Straus & Giroux, 1973).
46. Rosenberg and Silverstein, p. 106.

47. Martin, p. 51.
48. Cohen.
49. Martin, p. 48.
50. *Time,* "Zapping Zap" (May 16, 1969).
51. Arnold Madison, *Vandalism: The Not-So-Senseless Crime* (New York: Seabury Press, 1970), p. 38.
52. Goffman, p. 185.
53. Cicourel, p. 22.
54. Madison; Martin.
55. Cavan, p. 147.
56. S. Tenenbaum, *Why Men Hate* (New York: Beechhurst Press, 1947), p. 104.
57. Madison, p. 25.
58. David L. Shirey, "Semi-Retired Graffiti Scrawlers Paint Mural at C.C.N.Y. 133," *New York Times* (December 8, 1972).
59. *Ibid.,* p. 49.
60. Martin R. Haskell and Lewis Yablonsky, *Juvenile Delinquency* (Chicago: Rand McNally, 1974), p. 274.
61. Martin, pp. 28–71.
62. *Ibid.*
63. David Matza, *Delinquency and Drift* (New York: Wiley, 1964).

8 Juveniles, Drugs, and Alcohol

INTRODUCTION

In this chapter we will explore the delinquent use of drugs and alcohol. Since so much has been written on the adverse physiological and psychological effects of juvenile drug and alcohol abuse, it would seem at first blush that we too should enter the debate. However, to enter such a debate is to miss the *crucial* sociological point in the study of drugs and alcohol, because we would be assuming that there is a relatively uniform physiological effect that may or may not cause the problems being debated. Thus, such a debate assumes the very thing to be explored; namely, the effect of the intoxicant.

In order to understand drug and alcohol use, it is crucial to analyze the social meanings of these substances and the social reality of their use. Medical understandings are one type of social interpretation, and what physicians have to say about the impact of drugs and alcohol on the body are important. However, medical understandings deal with only a single dimension, the physiological one. In order to understand the social dimension of drug use, we will examine the social understandings and realities of drug use as constructed by juvenile users.

Having an idea of how meanings of drugs and alcohol are constructed socially, we will begin to examine how the trend in drug use, especially among middle- and upper-middle-class youth, began and developed. Our focus will be on marijuana since it is the commonest and most widespread illegal drug used by juveniles. Likewise, we will touch on other drugs, such as LSD and heroin, to show different patterns of drug use, although the purpose of this chapter is not to survey all of the drugs used by juveniles. Our objective, rather, is to develop an understanding of the sociological dimension of drug use among youths. Juveniles who use PCP, barbiturates, amphetamines, model airplane glue, or any of a variety of other intoxicants can be understood in terms of the same sociological concepts we will discuss in dealing with marijuana.

Alcohol use among juveniles will be treated separately since it is a distinct social category. Unlike intoxicants called drugs, alcohol is a socially acceptable drug in our society, and while forbidden to juveniles, it is legally available to adults. For this reason the social patterns of juvenile alcohol use are different from those that are associated with drug use.

SOCIAL UNDERSTANDINGS OF DRUGS

Folk wisdom tells us that "Beauty is in the eye of the beholder," but it does not tell us that the eye of the beholder is socially determined. For years medical research findings have been the "eyes" of conventional understandings of drugs and have determined the official position in the debate on drugs. Yet this single viewpoint is quite different from the views of youthful drug users. For example, in describing the effects of marijuana, one physician said:

> Physiologically, dilation of the pupils frequently occurs. . . . Presumably, increased secretion of adrenalin produces a rise and then a sudden fall in blood sugar, which calls forth an increased appetite, especially for sweets. Hunger is observed more often in the beginner than in the chronic user. . . . Another difference is the drowsiness that many mention toward the end of a marijuana session, whereas wakefulness is the rule with strong psychedelics. . . . It is when [the marijuana user] is under stress that difficulties in judgment and coordination may arise.[1]

Compared to this physiological description of the effects of drugs, users have an entirely different conception. They do not speak of using drugs to "dilate their pupils" (for example, "Let's go smoke some grass and get our pupils dilated"). Instead, drugs are used to "get high" or "stoned" or some similar subjectively meaningful condition. To understand juveniles and drug use, therefore, it is necessary to understand the meaning of various drugs in the context of their use, in addition to their physiological effects.

Exactly what constitutes a drug is confusing, for drugs are as much a social understanding of certain substances as they are combinations of chemical elements. Eric Goode points out that an adequate definition of drugs should "(1) unambiguously group together all elements sharing a given characteristic, and (2) unambiguously exclude all elements not sharing that characteristic."[2] However, pharmacology textbooks define drugs vaguely and broadly as being any chemical agent that affects living processes—a definition that could include anything from heroin to the chemicals in organically grown stringbeans. Given the criteria for an adequate definition of "drugs," and the importance of understanding drugs as they are used in society, both in terms of ingestion and meaning, Goode offers the following insight:

> In actuality, the term "drug" is a social fabrication. The fact is that no formal, objective pharmacological characteristic of chemical agents will satisfy both criteria of an adequate definition simultaneously. *There is no effect common to all drugs* that, at the same time, is not shared by substances not considered drugs. Some agents called drugs are psychoactive, while some are not. Some affect the central nervous system, and some do not. Some drugs are physically dependency-producing—are "addictive"—while some are not. Some drugs are extremely toxic, while many, in the doses typically taken, are comparatively innocuous. This does not mean that drug effects are not "real." Drugs, of course, have chemical and pharmacological properties; they do act on human tissue. But the way they act has relatively little to do with how they are viewed and defined. Society's attitudes toward a given substance have very little to do with its laboratory-identified properties—and a great deal to do with sentiment and emotion. Society, or rather certain segments of society, define what a drug is, and the social

definition, the linguistic device, largely determines our attitudes. The statement "He uses drugs" calls to mind only certain specific *kinds* of drugs. If what is meant by that statement is "He smokes cigarettes and drinks beer," we are disappointed; cigarettes and beer are not part of our stereotype of what a drug is, even though we will find a description of the effects of nicotine and alcohol in any pharmacology textbook.[3]

In other words, what constitutes a "social drug"—that is, one defined by society as a "drug"—differs from other things that get people "high." If a newspaper headline said, "President's Brother Is Heavy Drug User," we would be shocked, but if we learned that it meant he liked to drink beer and smoke cigarettes, there would be some confusion since we do not normally think of nicotine and alcohol as drugs. However, these "not so bad" socially acceptable drugs are no less real or, in many instances, damaging than the substances we consider to be "real" drugs.

What we consider to be real drugs (illicit ones, at least) to no small extent is influenced by pronouncements on the part of the bureaucracies responsible for controlling illegal substances. Becker has documented efforts by the Federal Narcotics Bureau to define marijuana as an evil and dangerous drug in the same category as opium.[4] The Bureau went so far that later, when the public had a clearer understanding of marijuana and its effects, its credibility suffered, as noted by Polsky.

> Although the better-educated segment of the public is now aware of the myths for what they are—knows, for example, that the myriad college students who currently smoke marijuana are not thereby "led to" heroin addiction—this has in no wise lessened the efforts of the Federal Narcotics Bureau to perpetuate the myths and otherwise suppress the scientific evidence of marijuana's harmlessness. The Bureau's undiminished efforts have led a number of sociologists, including myself, to come round to the view long maintained in heroic isolation by Alfred Lindesmith of Indiana University that some Bureau officials are not dedicated truth-seekers having honest differences of opinion with the academic investigators but, on the contrary, dedicate themselves first and last to extending the power of the Federal Narcotics Bureau—to the extent of deliberate falsification of evidence.[5]

Ironically, this mythology, some investigators believe, is responsible for some of the drug experimentation by juveniles. When a youth tries the "killer weed" and finds that he does *not* turn into a heroin addict, he is likely to dismiss as a lie *anything* he hears from the officials. A 19-year-old user of and dealer in narcotics explained:

> A person . . . can't have helped but hear that grass is, you know, when you're growing up that grass is, you know—marijuana and juvenile delinquency and all that. And . . . I think a person who tries it, having had all this knowledge about it before, suddenly he realizes something he has been told is all wrong, that this can't help but lead him to think the same way about other things.[6]

The idea that alcohol and nicotine can be placed in the same category as such "heavy" drugs as heroin and marijuana from the standpoint of physical effects is still foreign to many people. However, simply by comparing the physically addictive aspects of acceptable and unacceptable drugs, we find that the very criteria used to argue that such drugs as heroin should be illegal —namely, they are addictive—also apply to favored substances such as alcohol and barbiturates. Again quoting from Goode, we find the following:

> All [depressants] are physically addicting, or produce a physical dependency.[7] This means that withdrawal symptoms appear upon discontinuation of heavy, relatively long-term use. The delirium tremens of the alcoholic is an example of these withdrawal symptoms. The "cold turkey" symptoms (so called because of the appearance of gooseflesh upon withdrawal) of the "kicking" heroin addict are well known. Nausea, convulsions, muscular spasms—hence the term "kicking"—diarrhea, extreme irritability and nervousness, insomnia, and bodily aches and pains are typical withdrawal symptoms after physical dependency on any of the depressants. There is some evidence that the severity of these symptoms is greatest with the barbiturates. It must be emphasized that the alcoholic and the barbiturate-dependent are addicts—"junkies"—in every physical sense, and in this respect do not differ from the heroin addict; it is only because of our society's partial tolerance of the first two, and its complete rejection of the third, that addiction is thought to involve only the narcotics. In fact, in sheer numbers, addiction to alcohol and barbiturates is a problem of far greater magnitude than addiction to heroin.[8]

If we think of drugs as including such widely used substances as alcohol and barbiturates (especially in the form of diet-control pills), we can see that drug use to a large extent is socially approved. The point here, however, is not to show that drinking alcohol and taking barbiturates are "just as bad" as taking heroin. Rather, our purpose is to demonstrate that the *social definitions* of "real" drugs are based on social understandings and meanings rather than on strict pharmacological criteria or physiological effects.

TRENDS IN DRUG USE BY JUVENILES

Officially, we can see that there has been an increase in juvenile drug use by examining the FBI's *Uniform Crime Reports.*[9] In 1960 there were only 1,583 drug arrests of urban youth aged 18 years and under. In 1972 there were 79,449 arrests. Thus, in only twelve years, there was a 5,000-percent increase in drug-related juvenile arrests. The police did beef up their narcotics squads during this period, and in part this may account for the increase in the number of arrests, but data from self-report surveys also show massive increases in juvenile drug use. In a study in 1958, Short and Nye found that fewer than 2 percent of their high school subjects had used narcotics of any kind; in a study of suburban high school students in the Midwest twelve years later, this author found that about 20 percent had used some narcotic—a 1,000-percent increase.[10] Since the 1970 study was conducted in an area where there was generally less crime than in the urban centers, the overall increase in juvenile narcotic use was probably even greater. These figures show that something happened between the late 1950s and the early 1970s that led to a surge in juvenile narcotic use.

Lumping all drugs in a single category results in inaccurate medical and social understandings, and later we will examine patterns of drug use in terms of different drugs. However, because the surge in overall drug use occurred in a relatively short span of time and because drugs are legally grouped together, we can discuss the recent trend in illegal narcotic use by juveniles in general terms.

The Beat Movement.   During the late fifties and early sixties, there was relatively little drug use. This period in the United States saw the short-lived but well-publicized "beat movement." The mass media churned out articles on the beats, usually emphasizing their bizarre and "exhibitionist" activities, but according to Polsky the beats preferred solitude to publicity. Many of them were runaway teenagers, but the majority were in their twenties and thirties. Most were middle class. The beat activities included drug use, but, significantly, the mass media generally did not pick up on this ubiquitous feature of beat life. Although some articles written about beats did note that drug use occurred, it was never widely publicized, either by the beats or by the press. According to Ned Polsky, there were few beats who did not use some drug, usually marijuana but also heroin, peyote, hashish, and synthetic mescaline. However, unlike their spiritual descendants, the hippies, the beats kept their drug use as private as possible.

There are two significant consequences of the beats' furtive drug use. First, it did not draw the attention of the police, even though there were a few undercover agents spying on various beat groups. Second, imitators who adopted the outward appearance and expressed the generally known sentiments of the beats but were not full-fledged members of the beat movement did not know their drug-use patterns. These factors explain why the beat movement never initiated a widespread drug culture, as did the hippie movement later in the sixties.

The Hippies.   The connection between the beats and the hippies is indirect, but they did to some extent share the same life-style and world view. Unlike the beats, however, the hippies emerged at a time when youth was becoming increasingly vocal in its demands for change. The beats were antipolitical, whereas the hippies were at first apolitical and then, later, as yippies, were actively political. Both groups were anti-establishment, rejecting the existing social institutions and life-styles. The hippies, though, were far less secretive about their activities, including drug use. For example, Timothy Leary, a one-time university professor, publicly urged others to use drugs and drop out of the establishment. His slogan, "Turn on, tune in, and drop out," had all the pithy eloquence of a television commercial, but it served to summarize much of the hippie philosophy and it was easily communicated. This was in 1965.

When the mass media began examining the hippie phenomenon, it was impossible for them to overlook the use of drugs. Hippies smoked marijuana openly, discussed psychedelic drugs in terms of their "magical" properties, and attacked the drug laws as unjust and stupid. The large number of nonhippies who sympathized with the hippie attitude toward drugs and who smoked marijuana with no ill effects made it difficult for the Federal Bureau of Narcotics to continue to portray every drug from marijuana to heroin as addictive and damaging, and discredited the old myths generated by the Bureau. At first, LSD was looked upon as another drug the Bureau had lied about, but after a number of disconcerting experiences the hippies developed their own sense of caution about its use. Similarly, Methedrine ("speed") was at first used widely but proved to be dangerous and even fatal to many users. Marijuana, however, remained a staple drug in the hippie scene, and its use became commonplace.

The hippie phenomenon did not spread independent of the larger social context. There was general disillusionment among the nation's youth, especially with the Vietnam war. A series of lies regarding the war and national policy in general were uncovered, and the credibility of the entire authority structure was crumbling on several fronts. It was discovered that marijuana was not the killer weed it had been described to be. Material wealth did not bring happiness as had been promised, and many other things youth had been told were found to be doubtful or simply untrue. The distrust of adults—"anyone over 30"—became a rationale for experimentation with activities that the young had been warned not to try. The number of youths actively involved in the hippie life-style was relatively small, but the ideas and images faithfully carried by the mass media provided rapid dissemination of their message. Part of that message was that drugs were a necessary component of being "hip."

The Impact of Advertising.   For years television had been plugging various drugs as essential for the "good life." A "bad mother" was shown yelling at her children and husband; then she took a tablet or pill and was transformed into a loving, caring person. However, these were "good drugs," "wonder drugs," "miracle drugs," and the stuff sold on the streets was "dope," the road to perdition and damnation. According to the ads put out by the drug companies, wonder drugs made you happy, popular, and healthy; dope made you dependent, nauseous, and wicked. But since there had been a tendency for the lawmaking bodies to group drugs, it was only a small step to collapse the "good drug" category with the "bad drug" category. Indeed, some of the "good drugs," such as a number of legally produced barbiturates, found their way into "bad hands" and became part of the street market for drugs.

The impact of pharmaceutical advertising on the American view of drugs cannot be precisely determined, but clearly the sponsors, at least, believe that advertising does something to promote the use of products. Four of the five top spenders for television commercials are drug companies. One researcher points out:

Drug advertising is not the *only* cause of drug abuse, but I do believe it is an important contributory cause. Advertising, in general, has a great deal of power to affect behavior. The over-the-counter drug industry is absolutely convinced of the ability of advertising to sell drugs. Advertising agencies argue that they can affect behavior. This means that advertising has social consequences, for if large numbers of people do something—whether it be purchasing a car or a cold remedy—that is a social consequence, with implications as far as social actions are concerned.[11]

Clearly drug advertising has only an indirect affect on drug abuse, but it provides a model for coping with problems of living. Berger has characterized this model as the "Pain-Pill-Pleasure" sequence.[12] Some kind of discomfort is presented, a drug is taken, and the person is free of pain and feels pleasure. A specific drug is claimed to have the best results for a certain type of ill—whether nervous tension or a condition invented by the drug companies, such as "the blahs." However, there are so many drug companies saying the same thing and presenting the same model that not only do the specific drugs become glossed into drugs-in-general but the ills are meshed into problems-in-general. The result is the general belief that "drugs can make you happy."

Turning to illegal drugs, we see that the same model can be applied. If aspirin can reduce pain and bring pleasure, so can marijuana, LSD, and heroin. Simon and Gagnon found that children whose parents had tolerant views regarding the ingestion of drugs as a general problem solver were more likely to use drugs, especially marijuana, than those whose parents relied less on drugs, whether "good or bad."[13] Simply by substituting marijuana for, say, Vanquish, juveniles engage in the same patterns of drug taking for pleasure as do their parents. The widespread use of alcohol, which is, of course, a drug, also points to parental patterns picked up by children.

In view of the conditions that existed in the mid-sixties we can understand how the dam broke on juvenile drug abuse. First, there was a general movement of youth dissatisfied with the establishment; second, there was a drug-oriented society fed by the mass media and drug companies; third, there was an articulate group, the hippies, that proselytized the use of drugs. In the late fifties and early sixties, the televised drug commercials were well established, but there was no general youth movement, and the beats were not openly advocating the use of drugs. There was a clear differentiation between "good drugs" and "bad drugs" at that time. How did the definition of drug use come to change so that there was a massive increase in the use of drugs in the mid-sixties? To understand this phenomenon, we must appreciate how the hippies were able to redefine narcotic drugs.

We must remember that such a "redefinition" of what drugs are and what they do must be in terms of some established definition. The definition of drugs fostered by the Federal Bureau of Narcotics was a "redefinition" of what the general understanding of narcotics was before the Bureau's campaign to warn the public of the dangers of narcotics. Similarly, the drug companies not only define and redefine the therapeutic value of their products but formulate an ever-increasing number of situations in which their products may be properly used. In the context of their subculture, the hippies did nothing more or less than what these so-called legitimate definers do in the context of the media subculture.

Becker points out that the drug-using cultures are continually defining the effects of drugs for novices.[14] If novice users are uncertain of how to evaluate their experiences, they are assured by other users that the effects must be properly interpreted for pleasure or that the unpleasantness is only transitory and a pleasant sensation will follow. There is a culturally shared definition of the situation of drug use in that the drug's effects come to be verbalized in patterned formulations. As Becker notes:

> They [experienced users] redefine the experience he [the novice] is having as desirable rather than frightening, as the end for which the drug is taken. What they tell him carries conviction, because he can see that it is not some idiosyncratic belief but is instead culturally shared. It is what "everyone" who uses the drug knows. In all these ways, experienced users prevent the episode from having lasting effects and reassure the novice that whatever he feels will come to a timely and harmless end.[15]

This implies, of course, that the effects of drugs are not solely, or even predominantly, physiological. Lower-class blacks and Puerto Ricans used marijuana before engaging in gang fights, and if it was defined as making them better fighters, it probably had that effect. And some couples use marijuana before making love, expecting and perhaps experiencing similar improvements. However, it is doubtful that the subjective experiences of the gang youths and lovers were similar even though the marijuana may have had similar physiological effects on both groups. That is, the definition of the situation, which depends on expectations and the occasioned activities (that is, what takes place in the context of a given occasion), is of more actual consequence than whatever physiological rearrangement may occur.

We have just seen how the sense of a drug experience is dependent on linguistic formulations. Similarly, there are verbalizations that induce juveniles to attempt drugs in the first place. As we pointed out, the slogans and jingles used by drug manufacturers are believed to be effective in attracting consumers to try one kind of drug or another. Those advertisements promote the use of so-called legitimate drugs and constitute a vocabulary of motives for drug use. We also noted that the official position against the use of illegal drugs provides slogans for *not* taking drugs. For example, in one television antidrug commercial the audience is asked, "Why do you think they call it dope?" This is part of a vocabulary of motives for not taking illegal drugs. What we must now determine is how the argument for *not* taking illegal drugs was replaced by the rationalizations *for* taking illegal drugs.

First we must understand the group context of drug use. Typically, juveniles with no drug-using associates do not take up drugs. One study found that 99 percent of those juveniles who took drugs had at least one friend who used drugs.[16] Experienced drug users provided the novice with a vocabulary of motives for trying the drugs and also, as noted above, with the definition of the situation.

The structure of the drug-using occasion also creates pressure on nonusers to try various drugs. For example, when marijuana is smoked, the smokers typically hand the cigarette from one person to the next. Each person in the group draws on the "joint" and passes it on. This pattern forces some amount of conformity, and nonusers are obliged to "at least try it." During these initial experiences, novices are provided with the necessary vocabulary of motives and learn how to use dope.[17]

In explaining the belief system that fosters drug use, Sherri Cavan likened the "hippie ethic" and the "spirit of drug use" to Max Weber's classic formulation of the Protestant ethic and the spirit of capitalism. Like the early Calvinists, the hippies had a vision of life—a transcendental vision. Drugs, especially LSD and other psychedelics, helped them to realize this vision, and in this way drug use had a central place in their belief system and life-style in the same way that work has a predominant position in the Protestant ethic and capitalist production.

The "pure" vision of the hippies, like the "pure" vision of the Protestants, is not a necessary condition for drug use, and the large numbers of drug users who imitated the actions of the hippies probably did not hold this "pure vision." The Protestant work ethic took on a life of its own. While it had its historic taproots in Calvinistic visions, it was subject to changes in interpretation and to the materialistic demands of capitalist production. Similarly, the imitators of the hippies learned enough to establish a vocabulary of motives allowing drug use, but instead of being immersed in the substance of the hippies' belief, they could only mouth the slogans.

The hippie beliefs constituted the beginning of a new type of drug-using culture in America, which at the time was acceptable to and received by a large number of youth from many areas of society. As the drug-use pattern grew, drug use became more and more a social activity, without the visionary ends sought by the hippies. Like the work ethic, which lingers in American society, residues of the hippie ethic linger in the drug-using groups. However, as the once pure Protestant vision of Calvin became diluted, the transcendental vision of the hippies survives as only a vague remnant of an articulate past.

Marijuana

Of all the illicit drugs used by adolescents, marijuana is the most typical and widespread. The use of marijuana, mainly a staple of lower-class youths, skyrocketed among the middle-class juveniles in the late 1960s in the vanguard of drugs introduced by the hippie movement. In describing the introduction of drugs to his high school, one student wrote:

SUBJECT: Well, like it started really weird last year in the fall, hearing about people turning on, and then like pretty soon it seemed like everybody was turning on. And then right about Christmas time it was really getting heavy, and last spring, wow, there was so much dope around everywhere, ya know, and like last year it was a big thing if once a week somebody smoked a joint in the bathroom, and I figured this was as great as it ever was going to get. And then I came to school this year, just spending a relatively dry summer, considering, and on the first day of school I met this chick who I thought was "straight" and ya know, she wants to run off and get stoned during lunch and it's becoming like a regular habit. There are more stoned people running around in the halls right now than you would believe.[19]

A 1968 study of the county in which the reporting high school student lived showed that 36 percent of the boys and 30 percent of the girls had used marijuana, LSD, or amphetamines at least once.[20] Since most students who had used LSD and amphetamines had also used marijuana, we can say that about a third of the high schoolers had tried marijuana. There is no way of knowing for sure exactly when the jump in marijuana use occurred, because before 1968 there was so little concern about its use in middle-class high schools that no surveys were taken to measure the incidence of marijuana use. Nevertheless, if we take the student's description of the sudden rise in marijuana use as an accurate qualitative indicator, there was a sudden (instead of gradual) introduction of drugs around 1967 that spread rapidly to at least a third of the student body.

The study just mentioned was conducted in a middle-class high school near San Francisco where the hippie movement had its roots. But what about the rest of the country? Could we find similar patterns among middle-class high school students in suburbs far away from Haight-Ashbury in San Francisco and the East Village in New York City? In a 1970 study of two suburban midwestern high schools, the author found that 20 percent of the students

TABLE 8-1. Student Estimates of Marijuana Use among Peers

Less than 5 percent	16 percent
Between 5 percent and 20 percent	41 percent
Between 20 percent and 50 percent	33 percent
Over 50 percent	10 percent

admitted having used marijuana at least once, but about 50 percent admitted to having a *close friend* who smoked marijuana. When asked to estimate the percentage of the student body who used drugs, the students replied as shown in Table 8-1.

The modal estimate (between 5 and 20 percent) was an accurate guess of the amount of marijuana use, according to self-reports. However, 43 percent of the students estimated a good deal more marijuana use than was reported. This perception of the popularity of marijuana use strengthened the notion that a "drug culture" exists among the student population in general.

When we examine the groups of students involved in marijuana use, we find the reverse of what is normally found in studies of juvenile delinquency: those from the *highest* socioeconomic class are the most likely to use marijuana (Table 8-2).

These data suggest that by 1970 marijuana was no longer merely the drug of the hippies on the East and West coasts but had filtered down to the suburbs of the Midwest. Compared to one third of the student body who had tried marijuana in the San Francisco suburb in 1968, only one fifth of the students in the suburban midwestern high school had tried marijuana. However, when we look at the distribution of marijuana use among different socioeconomic classes, we see that it is centered in the upper-middle class. Since the midwestern sample contained fewer children of the professional socioeconomic status than the suburban San Francisco sample, it is quite possible that we are not looking at a general trend of marijuana use that spread throughout the country, but instead spread rapidly through the

TABLE 8-2. Marijuana Use and Socioeconomic Status

SES*	Percent Who Had Tried Marijuana
Professional	43
Semiprofessional and Business	20
Clerical and Sales	11
Farmer	0[†]
Factory and Other Blue-collar Worker	18

*Socioeconomic status of student's father, or mother in father's absence.
[†]Only 3 cases out of 583 sample total; cannot be considered significant.

adolescents of the upper-middle class, and to a lesser or more gradual extent to the children of the middle and working classes.

The "Drug Culture".   In order to examine the use of drugs by certain cohorts of juveniles, we will have to examine their drug use conceptually. On the one hand we can talk about these groups as making up a "drug culture" or "drug scene" and at the same time participating in that culture or scene. If a marijuana culture did exist, it was located predominantly in the upper socioeconomic strata and not, as is typical with other forms of delinquent behavior, in the lower classes.[21] Since members of the same socioeconomic group share one another's company, those in the upper strata of the group studied are more likely to come into intimate contact with marijuana users than are those in other classes. We now need to examine the nature of the marijuana-smoking group and culture and to explain why relatively few juveniles from the higher social classes get in trouble with the police.

First, when we discuss a "culture" we imply that a distinctive way of life and world view exist. The extent to which a whole way of life revolves around the use of marijuana and other drugs points to a distinct culture, and the hippie way of life and beliefs, as described by Cavan, would certainly stand as a distinct culture.[22] However, if a group of students use marijuana while not significantly altering their other behaviors and beliefs from those of the dominant culture, we are discussing a partial culture or part-time culture. The beliefs and values that foster the use of marijuana may be the only vestiges of the full-blown hippie culture of the late 1960s. Marijuana use has been added onto otherwise normal juvenile activities for some users, while for others it is an ongoing part of life. For example, a college freshman explained his use of marijuana:

I have been smoking in the evening a lot, but usually I am straight during the day. On the weekend, if it is sunny, it is really nice to smoke in the morning and just spend a completely stoned day.

So when you smoke dope* what happens, what does it do to you?
Well, it depends largely on the dope.

There's different kinds of dope? Different potencies?
Definitely, but more than different potencies, I have been getting into a thing lately where I think of dope as being wired dope or good dope.

How is "good" different from "wired"?
Well, when I smoke, if I smoke a joint after dinner of supposedly good dope, ah, I get physically tight sometimes and I get speedy. And I am getting to the point where I can control that now by consciously saying, you know, relax, take

*"Dope" in this context refers to marijuana, although the term is often used for all illegal drugs.

it easy. But I still have a feeling, like I know that my heart speeds up when I smoke dope, period, but, ah, cause, like I have been lying in bed sometimes after I have smoked and I just feel my heart beating. So there is the wired thing and then there is good dope, which is, I can relax my body without a hassle and, ah, it is a head thing, you know?

No, tell me.

All right, with good dope I can either concentrate very heavily on one thing, such as playing guitar, and just be completely into the music; all my senses are listening and feeling the music. I find in a conversation I can be really in depth into one thing and just carry it, carry the conversation to its ultimate conclusion you know, or, ah, if not its ultimate conclusion, really, it's whatever happens to it, it just goes on and on, like I could take just one thing and continue about it. Or take a starter, talking about my school thing and getting into friends of mine, just getting completely off the thing, but not hassling about it. It's fun, things don't have to be connected. On the other hand I find, well, now I might be getting off the beaten track.

I am interested in knowing what you think the effects of smoking are, and you have been covering that. Can you think of anything else to say about that?

I get more divorced from that, ah, as I smoke more, ah, I can just sit and get into something I haven't gotten into before, like silence maybe, like something visual, like looking at a picture in a different way, ah, yeah. It is in a different way cause I am, my perception is changed, and I can talk fairly easily about music, like when I am playing guitar, the more loaded I get, I'll be more willing to try something completely experimental on the guitar, like if I am playing a lead, to hit a bunch of notes I don't know, you know, are going to come out in a specified pattern that I have played lots of times before.[23]

Some sense of "cultural" belonging can be inferred from this articulation of what smoking marijuana has to do with the speaker's life, and more might be inferred about the youth's world view. Whatever the inferences, it is clear that smoking marijuana is a significant part of his life.

As compared to this heavily involved young man, other juveniles use marijuana instead of some other form of "high," such as beer or whiskey. It may be conceived of as a fad that has become popular among a certain set of youth. Such youth may employ the jargon and even affect some of the styles of the group that initiated the popularity of marijuana, whether it be the hippies or any other group, but since the use of marijuana is not a central feature of their life-style, they cannot be considered to be a "drug culture." In the 1950s "hot rods" were the fad, and many of those who were part of the era but not "into" what might be called the "car culture" nonetheless paid attention to their automobiles in terms of certain aspects of the car culture. Similarly, when surfing was popular on the West Coast in the early sixties, many juveniles took it up, along with the language and general surfing style, but were never dominated by it in the same way a hard-core few were.

Compared to the college freshman quoted above, for whom marijuana use was a daily affair, there is a substantial group which is in no way an integral part of a "drug culture." Even though these youths use marijuana, they have only a "piece of the culture" around which drug use revolves. They may experiment with marijuana a few times or use it occasionally, but they do not smoke pot all the time. Only 25 percent of the college-aged smokers used marijuana more than once a week, and only 22 percent of the high school students who smoked marijuana used it regularly.

We can see from these data that juveniles who use marijuana need not adopt a "drug culture." The existence of a drug culture, along with beliefs, attitudes, and language revolving around drug use, appears to be a prerequisite for large-scale change in the patterns of use, but the total adoption of that culture is unnecessary for the use of marijuana. One can adopt a piece of the culture with no great alteration in other patterns. That marijuana smoking or other drug use necessarily leads to a change in basic behavior patterns appears to be true only of youth who adopt the entire culture: when only the activity of marijuana smoking is adopted, a small part of the culture is integrated into otherwise normal juvenile activities.

We might compare the majority of marijuana smoking with the majority of liquor consumption. While the skid row inhabitant's life may revolve around the bottle, one need not adopt the entire life-style of skid row to become either an alcoholic or a social drinker.[25] Most drinking is situational; unless an occasion arises when alcohol is appropriate, most people do not drink. Similarly, among most juvenile marijuana users, the use of marijuana appears to be not ubiquitous or constant but situational—in preparation for a rock concert, at a party, and on similar occasions when marijuana smoking is sanctioned. For those who are caught up in the drug culture, almost any time is appropriate, just as for skid row bottle gangs any time is appropriate for drinking. For the typical marijuana smoker, there are only a limited number of specified occasions on which marijuana is used.

The importance of the fact that most juveniles who smoke marijuana are not involved in a drug culture is that those who are "into" drugs and a way of life revolving around drugs are not likely to limit their drug use to marijuana. The available data indicate that there is a rapid falloff in the percentage of juvenile marijuana smokers who admit the use of stronger drugs. We infer that those who use all sorts of drugs are truly "into" drugs and a drug culture, and those who only smoke marijuana are not. It might be noted, further, that the erroneous belief that smoking marijuana leads to the use of other drugs is typical of the kind of distorted logic that so often characterizes officialdom. Getting into a drug culture may lead someone to use all kinds of drugs, and the first illegal drug used is likely to be marijuana. However, if one does go on to use other drugs, it is not because of some inherent property of marijuana that "leads" to the use of other drugs but because of involvement in a drug culture.

DRUGS AND JUVENILE GROUPS

As we have seen, one need not be in a drug culture to come to use marijuana even though certain ideologies from what might be called a drug culture constitute rationales for using drugs. It is more accurate to say that drug use is a part of the subculture of juvenility, and as such drug use is common knowledge among juveniles. This is not to say that juveniles are forced or even greatly pressured into taking drugs, but there are opportunities, rationales, and connections for those who want to.

The study by Joseph Weis of a high school in "Beachtown" (a suburb of San Francisco) found that while drug use was widespread, only certain groups of students took drugs, and the drug-using groups differed in their style of drugs use.[26] Three "crowds" were identified as using drugs, and depending on the crowd, the style of drug use varied.

Nonchalant "Doper" Crowd

The "doper" group takes drugs something like one takes a drink at a party. It is done as part of a social function or for social purposes like a beer at a beach party. Weis found this group to be the largest of adolescent drug users, and it is largely limited to marijuana users. The social nature of the drug use is stressed, and in no way is use a form of protest or dissent.[27] In describing this group, one informant explained:

> It's really weird the way the drug scene up here is set up. Like there's a whole bunch of social people, ya know, and all these people do really weird things; well not really weird, in fact they are really normal things and that's why they're really weird. They do these really *normal type games* and stuff, but they just *throw in drugs instead of beer*. Maybe they talk every so often about some sort of ideas, which is revolutionary for them. They are the kind of person who likes to be stoned like that. That's all; but *doesn't want to make any changes.*[28]

As marijuana smoking has become increasingly common among both juveniles and adults, it appears that the social "doper" will dominate even more, for not only is the "newness" of marijuana wearing off, but the social and legal stigmas attached to its use are no longer sufficient to make the users concoct special meanings for the activity. In other words, its use is routinized into otherwise conventional patterns of social interaction.

Ego "Doper" Crowd

The second type of drug-using group identified by Weis is linked to a social type in the high school he investigated. This type was identified by other students as "hard guys," otherwise known as "hoods," and similar titles denoting expressive toughness.[29] This group was also involved in social drug taking, but used other drugs besides marijuana, with the exception of heroin. Sometimes these youths were identified as "speedfreaks" or "dopefreaks," indicating that their use of drugs was more frequent and involved heavier drugs.

Their use of drugs did not, however, alter their life-style. The roughness and rowdiness characteristic of the hard guys did not take on the "mellow" styles popular among the social users and the general doper styles of the times. Instead, like the nonchalant doper crowd, all the hard guys did was to replace one substance with another (drugs for alcohol), and nothing significant changed otherwise. In describing the hard guys, one subject related:

> Well, like they [hard guys] *turn on now.* Last year when this big drug thing started happening I started thinking, "Wow, if everybody turns on it's going to be really groovy because all the *hard guys aren't gonna be hard guys* anymore." But, I've discovered after observing what has happened this year that the *people who were,* if you'll pardon the expression, *pricks before they started turning on are still pricks.* [30]

It was the same show with different props; and instead of the drug molding the scene, the scene molded how the drug would be used and what "effect" it would have.

Serious Drug Takers

By "serious" Weis refers not to serious physiological damage or heavy use but instead to the fact that the users took their drug experiences seriously.[31] Those who took drugs seriously tied their use to various ideologies—social, political, religious, or mystical. Theirs was a search for a transcendental experience that would allow them to break out of what they saw as a confining mold. Marijuana, LSD, and other psychedelics were the drugs of choice, and the serious drug takers did not merely get stoned as a social amenity but instead to "expand consciousness" or to achieve similar philosophically accountable experience.

Perhaps what is most interesting about the serious drugs users is that they were a minority among the juvenile drug-using groups while their style of drug use became the stereotype of all drug use among the young. The "drug culture" was nothing more than a stereotype based on what became the most popular *image* of drug use. As a result, there were many mistaken beliefs about drugs and the "counterculture" that grew up around them. What in fact took place was an exaggeration of certain social types that were around anyway, and even though there was a new respectability—a "hipness"—to certain intellectual and religious pursuits, few of these pursuits were serious. Drug use merely added a new ritual.

In concluding this section, it is important to understand the central point made by Weis in delineating different styles of juvenile drug use:

> The different styles of drug use and associated emergent types of users cannot be understood or explained unless one recognizes the effect of the different social-type life styles and cultures on all facets of adolescent life, including drug use. Neither the cultural milieus nor the structure of social relationships can be disregarded; the etiological factors are not the same for all types of adolescents or all types of adolescent drug users, and explanations must take this into account.[32]

The extent to which the life-style of one social type held sway over that of another depended on its position in the adolescent social scene; besides the new style introduced by the hippies, other changes that occurred with the development of drug use among adolescents was more cosmetic than substantive. By paying attention to the effect of the drug, we miss the real causes that determine the social patterns. An old principle in performing magic tricks is to distract with one hand while manipulating with the other; and unfortunately, we've paid too much attention to the magic and not enough to the manipulation.

THE SOCIAL CONSTRUCTION OF THE ACID TRIP

The single drug most popularized by the hippie movement was LSD (lysergic acid diethylamide), commonly called acid. Regardless of its medical and pharmacological properties, LSD came to be defined by the hippies as having "mind-expanding" or "mind-blowing" properties. It served as an initiation into the hippie world. LSD was provided to the novice in a setting controlled by users. The music, lights, and other props used by the initiators were arranged to provide a specific definition of the drug experience, and herein lie the important social conditions that lead to the unique acid trip.

At the time of the initial acid trip, the novice is introduced not only to the physiological effects of the drug but also to the culture. Various backstage activities are brought to the fore to be seen in the light of the altered perception brought on by the drug.[33] The user may confuse the actions of the initiators with the effects of the drug, and he or she is unable to distinguish between what is happening and the drug's effects. If the user is unprepared and unaware of what to expect, he or she may react violently or with terror, or may accept and adopt the activities and world view of drug users. The more the novice knows about what to expect, the better equipped he or she is to choose whether or not to try the drug and the accompanying experience. Like the backstage behavior of most groups, however, the activities on a drug trip are kept secret until the novice's acceptance of the action or his or her discretion is assured. Persons who have self-administered LSD are hardly in a position to call the cops or anyone else for help. By accepting the activities and the culture, they become co-conspirators; if they reject them, they become informed, but silent, outsiders.

From the literature on drug use, it appears that many writers are unaware of the initiation ritual, but some have noted the significance of the social situation in which people are introduced to LSD. Simmons and Winograd noted that some initiates to the underlife of the drug scene are shocked by what these researchers describe as a "cultural" phenomenon.[34] The initiate may be revolted or fascinated by the explosive confrontation with what he or she sees at first as an alien culture. If one has any idea of what to expect, one is more likely to accept it, but the uninformed may have what psychiatrists call a psychotic reaction. What is important, as Simmons and Winograd make clear, is that the physiological effect of the drug is not the only, or even the most significant, aspect of the acid trip. Further, the initiation to LSD is often an initiation into a world view.

As we pointed out in the general discussion of drugs and drug cultures, the language of a group provides a unique reality. The medical community has a language with which to discuss drugs, and the drug-using subcultures also have a language. The medical talk is no more objective or accurate than the talk employed by the drug users; it is merely another way of formulating a sense of what happens when people use drugs. In fact, if everyone talked about drugs the way medical experts do, it is unlikely that many people would take them. For example, Sidney Cohen, a physician, describes the effects of LSD as follows:

> The single most notable physical sign of LSD action is dilated pupils which do not contract completely when illuminated. Nausea, more rarely vomiting, and chilliness and tremulousness are sometimes seen. Aside from a rare convulsion, the serious physical side effects are minimal.[35]

If LSD users described the experience in this way to a nonuser, the person would wonder what is appealing about an activity that produces dilated pupils, nausea, vomiting, and chilliness. However, LSD users speak about "insight," "mind expansion," and other effects attributed to the drug. This kind of talk provides an interpretive scheme for enjoyment and excitement, and the LSD user elaborates any LSD experience in terms of such schemes and talk.[36]

Thus physicians and users have competing interpretive frameworks for LSD use, and each group believes its position is the more valid. As one LSD user explained:

> Just taking LSD doesn't insure that you get any insight out of it. There are a lot of people whom I have met who have taken LSD who are just as nutty as they can be. I have seen people blow their minds from LSD. People whom I was very

close to and living with. The experience of stepping out of the social structure is a very liberating experience, especially if the structure has been oppressive and has made them distrustful of their own inner nature or uncomfortable with their own inner nature. To step out of that is a pleasant experience. For some people getting out is an end in itself. That's all they are interested in doing. They keep stepping out, and stepping out, and stepping out.

Each time they do, they give up their personality, or ego, or whatever you want to call it. They see shedding their ego as a virtue because it feels good. They have set up a structureless personality for themselves. That leads them to become relatively passive people, who don't have the perimeters of a personality. They have what might be referred to as "blown minds."

They have to restructure themselves if they want to come out of this. Most of them convince themselves that there is nothing they can do. They don't believe in anything. I met a guy who had taken two hundred acid trips and he didn't believe anything. That's what he told me, but actually, what he did believe in was that there is nothing to believe in. Do you follow me? And that was something that he had imposed upon himself and then conditioned into himself.

Now he was on a closed circuit where there was nothing to believe in. "There is nothing to believe in." And he just keeps taking acid and believing in nothing. And he tends to be cynical and unhappy.

On the other hand, if you take acid with the proper preparation and in the proper setting, in order to go inward and with specific goals to accomplish, it's fantastically effective. It can assist you in making any changes that you want to make. If your body is not well, it can place you in harmony with your body, so that your body can heal itself. If you are locked in very heavy ego games you don't understand, you can step out of those games and look at them and see what's happening, and then step back into them and act in a different way.

What's your opinion of Dr. Sidney Cohen's opinion on hippie patterns of LSD use?

Cohen is on a Sidney Cohen trip. He is out to be *the* expert on LSD. He's going to be the Establishmentarian expert. No matter what happens or what is determined, he is able to channel it into the Establishment's viewpoint on LSD.

The mass society would like to hear that LSD is the answer to all their dreams, which it is. But there are a lot of people in political power who want people to keep coming to work every day at nine o'clock and stay there until six. Then they can go home and watch TV until they fall asleep. And then come back the next morning at nine and work there the whole day. They should also wear white shirts and neckties. If these people started taking acid, they wouldn't do that any more. LSD could liberate these people but they won't let it happen. Many professionals are rewarded by the Establishment with grants, professorships, and awards to say what they want to hear, that LSD is not good and it will kill you. LSD could liberate many more people than hippies, but the Establishment won't let it happen.*

As can be seen from this description, LSD users have a linguistic reality that differs from that of the medical experts. They do not describe the experience

*From *The Hippie Trip* by Lewis Yablonsky, copyright © 1968 by Western Publishing Company, Inc., reprinted by permission of the publisher, The Bobbs-Merrill Company, Inc.

in terms of possible physiological damage. This is not to say that the hippies are "right" and the medical experts "wrong," or vice versa. Rather, each group is operating in terms of its own linguistic reality. It is something like a debate between a Chinese and an Italian, each speaking in his or her own language.

As the LSD advocate claims, the purpose of the drug use was to "get out of ego games," "find oneself," and the like. In general, there is support for these ends in the larger society. Thus, the values of the hippies have at least something in common with the larger culture. The *means* by which these ends are achieved are the point of difference. The Girl Scouts and the Army, for example, advertise that members have a chance to "find themselves" by joining the group; in a sense, the hippies are doing the same thing. They backed up their claim by pointing out that the Establishment had failed to provide opportunities for self-discovery and that drug use is a much faster route than the conventional modes.

TRANSFORMING REALITIES

Other illegal drugs that became part of the drug scene also came to be interpreted in terms of the drug culture's linguistic format and interpretive schemes. Amphetamines, such as Methedrine, were ingested or injected for a "high" or "trip," and the influence of "speed" was discussed in terms of its special assumed properties. When certain devastating effects of amphetamine use came to light, the hippies developed negative linguistic terms to interpret the dangers (for example, "bummer") and warn others ("speed kills"). This and other drugs that were found to produce physical deterioration came to be used less frequently.[37]

The acknowledgment of the existence of a drug culture undermined the myth that drug use is "antisocial." While the call to "drop out" of society appeared to some as antisocial, it was actually an invitation to join another social group and partake in a different life-style. In addition to a new language, initiates to drug use learned new types of relationships with one another and with the rest of society. Drug users had their own norms and sanctions. For example, it was a cardinal norm among drug users not to "fink" on their supplier or on fellow drug users. To say that such behavior is antisocial not only is inaccurate but it puts the focus of drug studies in the wrong place. If we recognize the very social nature of drug use, we are in a better position to come to terms with it and understand what causes juveniles to turn to drugs.

What followed the early drug movement was what we might call the "war of glosses." The antinarcotic forces put all illegal drugs in the same boat and claimed that all were dangerous or at least led to the use of dangerous drugs. On the other hand, members of the new drug-using culture developed glosses for "getting high" on almost anything, and it was not until later that they particularized their talk and actions concerning drug use. Research from the scientific community did little to confirm or refute the allegations regarding drug use. However, a dialogue of sorts did develop between those who preferred formal terminology in their talk about drugs and the hippies, who spoke their own language. In an effort to communicate with youthful drug users, some physicians began to explain drug-related problems in the terminology of the young. "Getting high" and "coming under the influence" mean pretty much the same thing even though the connotations are different. Being "strung out" is close to being "addicted." More important, some physicians honestly began to differentiate among types of illegal drugs and came to learn how to relate to someone on a "bad trip." Marijuana was less and less seen to be a "bad drug" that inevitably led to heroin use, and became something kids "experimented" with. One police department, which screened recruits with a lie detector test, was unable to find a single applicant who had not smoked marijuana; so it began asking potential recruits whether they had used marijuana in the previous six months.* After all, "a little pot" was not seen to be harmful.

The transformation in the talk about drugs, especially marijuana, led to a reconsideration of what was delinquent. Since for the police and others the term "getting high" did not carry the same connotations as "killer weed," young people who used marijuana were not seen to be necessarily "hard-core" delinquents. This is not to say that the police did not arrest them for breaking the law, but, for the most part the police did not believe that a juvenile who smoked a little pot was necessarily bad. As one juvenile detective put it in discussing the moral character of a girl involved in one of his cases, "Yeah, sure she smokes grass, but basically she's a good kid."[38] Moreover, a number of states reduced the penalties for possession of marijuana, and Alaska completely decriminalized its cultivation and private use in the home. Such penalty reductions were possible only in the context of having specific linguistic devices for understanding the drug in a radically different way than the formulations that were used to justify the drug's criminalization.

THE ROUTINIZATION OF JUVENILE DRUG USE

What began as a split in generational habits and understandings concerning drug use has become a routine among youths. The mysticism surrounding drug use during the initial stages of the hippie phenomenon has become a "normal trouble" in society for users and authorities alike, especially for marijuana. What's more, there is a second generation emerging in the 1980s

*This practice was related to me by a member of the department, in the southeastern United States. The officer and the police department will remain anonymous for obvious reasons.

whose parents smoked marijuana in their youth, so that there is not the same pressure exerted by parents to restrict drugs either through law enforcement or rehabilitation programs.

In a study of "deviant socialization" Adler and Adler found that certain parents whose life-styles include the use of drugs, especially marijuana, are rearing their children to use drugs.[39] The group studied were called the "tinydopers," young children between the ages of infancy to 8 years old whose parents were between 21 and 32 years of age. These children will enter their teens in the 1980s, and so instead of having learned to avoid drugs, this group will enter adolescence with an established pattern of drug use. To be sure, these youths will not be typical of juvenile-aged children in the 1980s, but it is important to examine their socialization because they will no doubt have an impact on other juveniles with whom they will associate.

To begin with, these children's parents see smoking marijuana as beneficial to their children's development. One set of parents, for example, explained the benefits they saw in giving their children marijuana:

A "hyper" child, they claim that it calms him down to a more normal speed and often permits him to engage in activities which would be too difficult for his powers of concentration. He also appears to become more sedate and less prone to temper tantrums, sleeping deeper and longer.[40]

One may argue to what extent these "benefits" really exist, but as long as the parents act upon these beliefs, they constitute a social reality. This social reality, in turn, is incorporated into the child's socialization. At the same time, we can see certain conventional cultural aspects to the use of drugs to solve problems adults see in children. Schools have used drugs for "hyperactive" children who disrupt the classroom, and even though the use of tranquilizers is usually concentrated in classes with misbehaving lower-class children, the idea of drug control for behavior problems is not deviant in American society. Thus, instead of a fully deviant socialization, as Adler and Adler suggest, parents who give their children marijuana are engaged in certain conventional socialization practices with only the prop being deviant.

As a final note on transgenerational drug use, the explanation that is offered for giving marijuana to children is different from the typical rationale offered for marijuana use by users of the drug.[41] As we saw earlier in this chapter, drug use is typically explained in terms of "getting high," or some similar fun or sociable end. In other words, marijuana is discussed as a "toy"—something to have fun with. For parents who give their children marijuana as a means of correcting behavior problems, the drug is a "tool," not a "toy." This reconceptualization may be nothing more than what the parents believe to be an acceptable account for a deviant pattern, but the fact that it is used is bound to have an impact on how the children will come to see marijuana. The exact direction such understandings will take and the patterns that will develop are unknown, but research in the future should address this most interesting issue.

HEROIN AND JUVENILE ADDICTS

Heroin use has often been "traced" to experimentation with marijuana, and many heroin users will say that they began their drug habit with marijuana. In one sense it is accurate to say that one got into drugs through marijuana, but only if we mean that marijuana was the first illegal drug used. Marijuana can lead to heroin only in the sense that one's contacts with marijuana use and distribution are more likely to result in contacts with heroin. There are, however, several reasons that the use of marijuana does not predict heroin use. First, most marijuana users do not go on to heroin or, in fact, any other drug.[42] Conversely, although almost all heroin users did use marijuana before starting with heroin, they also did a lot of other things before using heroin, such as drink alcohol. However, most drinkers do not go on to use marijuana (or to become alcoholics); in the same way, most marijuana smokers do not go on to heroin.

Heroin use is a serious problem because it may be physically addictive, as may alcohol use. Once a person starts using heroin, he or she is likely, but not certain, to become physically dependent on the drug and the life surrounding its use. If we can identify the social situation in which one begins to use heroin, we can account for the initial cause of heroin use. Once started, the heroin user is pulled along not only by his or her physical dependency on the drug but also by the life-style that goes along with it.

To see how juveniles begin taking heroin, consider the following two cases:[43]

Sheera is 14, red-haired and wholesome-looking, the teenage girl next door. Her father manages a restaurant in New York City; her mother works in the records department of a city hospital.

I didn't start using heroin until I was 13. I guess I started using drugs to be like everyone else. There were older kids that I looked up to, but there were kids my age, they were also using drugs. I wanted to try it too. I messed around with pills and pot. Then I went to Israel for a summer and came back, and all my friends were on heroin. I snorted [ingested through the nose] a couple of times, skinned [injected in the skin] a lot, and after that I mained [injected in vein] it. I was sent to a school for emotionally disturbed children. Getting drugs there was easier for me than on the streets. Except for heroin. There wasn't much of that.

I don't know if I would have been accepted by my friends if I hadn't used drugs. My feelings are that I wouldn't have been. I wanted to be like them. They were all using drugs because they got bored with things. My parents never spoke to me once about drugs before I got involved. After I got involved, I used to see my father, but my father wouldn't say anything. My mother used to lay down a few rules. I talked to them about it. I used to go and tell my mother, kind of hoping that she'd say to me, "Stop and that's final." But she never did.

Bill is 16, and a bit withdrawn; his father is a New York City librarian.

There were no big problems with my family. The main thing is that the friends I was with—there was so much drugs that everybody was using them. My friends would say let's get high. I didn't want to say no, so I got high with them. I'd just say all right. I got started through drinking and then smoking reefers. I started heroin when I was 14. I wasn't really strung out. I wouldn't get sick and upset. I used to take money from my father's drawer and ask for money on the street, some change sometimes. I used to get heroin from anywhere. I'd get it in my building, the next building, on the street corners. I got arrested with my friends. We were shooting up in the hallway, and a cop came along and busted us.*

From these two accounts it can be seen that involvement with heroin had its roots in the association with friends who used heroin, not with some shadowy figure who hung around the school grounds and lured juveniles into the habit; nor was it the case that these juveniles were reacting to intolerable home situations or conditions of poverty. Quite simply, their friends were users and got them involved.

Heroin is a killer, but this medical fact has a sociolegal context. In 1969 in New York City 224 teenagers died from heroin overdoses or heroin-related infections. Overdoses are due to the user's inability to determine the strength and purity of the drug that is available on the street, and most infections are due to the filthy conditions under which heroin users shoot the drug into their veins. Because the use of heroin is illegal, users are forced to take a chance on the unregulated heroin available on the street; because unprescribed possession of hypodermic needles and syringes is also illegal, they often share a set of works or fashion makeshift outfits to inject the drugs. Infection, especially hepatitis, is caused by using unsterilized paraphernalia.

Not all heroin addicts, however, are subject to the dangers of poor quality and uncontrolled doses of heroin or unsafe needles. In a study of physicians who were narcotic addicts, Winick rarely found an overdose problem or infection from the use of heroin or morphine.[45] Since the physicians had access to controlled dosages of drugs and also to sterilized needles for injecting drugs, they rarely overdosed or contracted diseases associated with drug abuse. However, most juvenile users have neither the knowledge nor the equipment available to physicians.

In Great Britain, heroin use is illegal as in the United States, but heroin addicts are registered and can get the drug legally if necessary, without turning to illegal outlets. For a very small sum of money, a registered addict in Britain can buy enough heroin to prevent withdrawal symptoms, but not enough to get "high." In this way, the British have been able to regulate the

*Reprinted by permission from *Time,* The Weekly Newsmagazine; copyright Time Inc.

flow of heroin without legalizing it. Moreover, registered addicts rarely die from overdose, impurities in the heroin, or diseases contracted from the paraphernalia.[46]

Under the British system we would expect heroin use to be widespread since the drug is cheap and does not involve the stigma attached to drug use here. However, we find the opposite to be true. The rate of addiction in Great Britain was 5.1 per 100,000 in 1968 and 4.7 in 1970. In the United States the rate was 157 per 100,000 in 1969 and 335 in 1971. Assuming that the 1970 rate in Britain remained the same for 1971, we see that the United States has 70 times the amount of heroin addiction as Great Britain—and, as we have mentioned, the dangers of heroin, to both the user and society, are a great deal more severe here than in Britain, where it is regulated.

The use of heroin, like the use of other drugs and other kicks, will be seen as "something to do" as long as there is some group sponsorship and support for it. Juveniles who get into heroin use do so in much the same way as they come to use other drugs. If they conceived of their drug use as dangerous, they probably would not begin in the first place or encourage others to use drugs. Massive warnings of drug dangers have been distributed through every media by the government, and these warnings may have had some effect, but until there are changes in the drug groups that provide the justifications and vocabulary of motives that make it "all right" to use drugs, it is unlikely that juvenile drug use will decline. When juveniles are no longer supported by an intimate group of fellow drug users, not only will numerous users drop the habit but fewer juveniles will take up with drugs.

PATTERNS OF DRINKING AMONG JUVENILES

Drinking among juveniles is widespread, and few juveniles wait until the legal age before having a drink. In a 1978 survey of college students, the author found that almost all of those surveyed (92 percent) had tried alcohol before they reached 18 years of age. Some of this drinking was nothing more than having an occasional glass of wine at home with their families, while other drinking included drunken parties with friends. Very few seemed surprised that so many had tried alcohol, since it was "culturally acceptable."

As we saw earlier in this chapter, alcohol has a special absolution from the "bad"-drug category, but it is not the case that alcohol is free from the same debilitating effects of many of the "bad" drugs. If we thought of "hangovers" as mild and short-lived withdrawal symptoms—which is exactly what they are—we would not be so apt to laugh or tease people about "morning-after" blues.[47] Imagine how callous we would think someone was who laughed at a heroin user going through withdrawal.

Just as we minimize the direct physical dangers of alcohol in comparison with other depressants, we also tend to minimize the indirect dangers.[48] For example, a teen-aged girl was driving home from a friend's house where she had been drinking. She crashed into another car, and although the girl was unhurt, four people in the other car were killed in the accident. In such cases involving alcohol and juvenile auto accidents, the accidents are attributed to the *irresponsibility of the juvenile* and not the alcohol, since it is assumed that the youth should have known better than to drink and drive. Had the girl been using LSD or some other illegal drug, the emphasis would have been on the *drug* more than on the person. Thus, by absolving the drug (alcohol) in cases of auto accidents or similar catastrophes, society minimizes the dangers of the drug. Likewise, if a juvenile commits suicide under the influence of LSD, the LSD is blamed, but if a juvenile who has been drinking commits suicide, we do not hear about the possible link between the alcohol and the suicide. Socially unacceptable and illegal drugs have always been directly linked with accidents, suicides, and delinquency, and only because of its special social status has alcohol not been.

Frequency and Distribution of Juvenile Drinking

Juvenile alcoholism is not a new trend. A national study of adolescent drinking patterns found that there were serious exaggerations of problem drinking among juveniles.[49] The assertions that there has been a recent increase in juvenile alcoholism are probably attributable to the subsiding concern over marijuana and the drug culture that shocked the public in the 1960s and early 1970s. Since substance abuse for the last two decades has almost exclusively meant "dope," juvenile alcoholism has been ignored, and the "rediscovery" of juvenile drinking patterns has led to the misfounded conclusions that there has been a sudden wave of juvenile alcoholism. To be sure, there are adolescents with severe drinking problems, but there is no evidence to even suggest that juvenile alcoholism is greater than or even as great as adult alcoholism.

In the Short and Nye study published in 1958 (see Chapter 1), about 62 percent of the boys and about 54 percent of the girls from the high school groups had tried alcohol in their homes. A later study found that about 75 percent of the boys and girls in two suburban Midwest high schools had tried alcohol.[50] In the 1978 survey mentioned above, 92 percent of college students had tried alcohol when they were juveniles in the mid-1970s. At first, it would seem that indeed there has been an increase in alcohol use among juveniles, but the data are a little misleading. First, there is an increased frequency of juveniles who have tried drinking as the age nears 18, and since the 1978 study dealt with a cohort that had all passed the juvenile age, the report covered all ages of juvenility. The 1970 study dealt with juveniles from 15 through 18, and so included a large number of students who would probably try alcohol before they reached 18. Similarly, the Short and Nye study dealt with juveniles of differing ages, and thus it is not the case that drinking has jumped from about 58 percent to over 90 percent. Instead, the increase has been only from about 58 percent to 75 percent. Moreover, in the 1970 study, only about 64 percent of the juveniles who had tried drinking did so without parental knowledge.

Involvement in drinking and delinquency simultaneously have been noted in studies of delinquent groups, and as was found in the Short and Nye study, the training school boys and girls were far more likely to have tried alcohol than the comparison groups. More recently, Cockerham found that institutionalized youths were more likely to engage in drinking and to drink more heavily than noninstitutionalized youths.[51] However, both groups held norms that approved of drinking, and so it is not true that drinking is due to "delinquent attitudes." Furthermore, there appears to be little difference between boys and girls in patterns of drinking,[52] and girls coming from alcoholic homes were no more nor no less likely to become alcoholics themselves.[53] Since sex differences in delinquency are often believed to be significant, these findings are noteworthy, and coupled with the findings concerning shoplifting discussed in Chapter 7, we have further evidence that delinquent or delinquent-related activities are not the sole domain of boys.

Drinking among juveniles, both delinquent and nondelinquent, is situational and is governed by understandings of appropriate behavior for situations in which alcohol may or may not be used.[54] The amount of involvement and the situations deemed appropriate, though, is greater among labeled delinquents. The "delinquency," then, is not so much the drinking but the amount of and the situations defined as appropriate for drinking. Thus, in examining norms that support alcohol use among juveniles, it is important to consider the situations that give normative support to drinking and the amount of drinking that is considered to be appropriate in different situations.

The relationship between committing delinquent acts (other than drinking —a delinquent act itself) and drinking does not appear to be causal. That is, drinking does not appear to cause delinquency. Rather, drinking is a part of involvement in delinquency, or the "action"[55] that generates activities which come to be characterized as delinquent. We saw that both labeled delinquent and nondelinquent groups drink, and most studies show that drinking—at least experimenting—is part of growing up.[56] What is more important in adolescent drinking is the intra- and interpersonal dynamics of getting into drinking.[57] If a juvenile gets into a group that engages in a variety of acts that are defined as really delinquent as opposed to "sowing wild oats" or some similar nondelinquent formulation, that juvenile is more likely to take on the drinking patterns of that group, including other delinquent activities, than if his or her main interaction were with nondelinquents. This is because the delinquent group defines more situations as appropriate for drinking and allows heavier drinking than the nondelinquent group. The nondelinquent group keeps drinking at a level and in situations that are not as likely to be noticed and/or defined as delinquent. Moreover, they limit their activities in such a way as to prevent drinking from becoming delinquently defined. Thus, it is the association with and investment in delinquent groups that leads to heavy drinking and not the reverse. We conclude, therefore, that delinquency can lead to heavy and noticeable drinking.

DRUG AND ALCOHOL USE AS A SOCIAL, MEDICAL, AND LEGAL PROBLEM

As the use of drugs increased among the young, especially in the middle- and upper-middle class, new methods other than incarceration came to be employed to "cure" the problem. The legal sanctions seemed to have little effect, and many people began to see drug use as a medical and/or social problem. Free clinics were established to help youths who were having frightening drug experiences and to treat diseases related to drug use. Methadone programs were introduced to get users off their heroin habit, and various self-help groups were established. "Detoxification" centers have replaced the "drunk tank," and even though the label alcoholic at an early age has certain dangers, it is perhaps a more accurate one than that of delinquent. Several states, including Alaska, California, Mississippi, and Oregon, have changed their laws regulating the possession of marijuana, reducing it from a felony to a misdemeanor.

The success of these programs has been mixed, and some, such as halfway houses, were outright failures.[58] Others, such as Synanon, showed a great deal of early success, even in the face of opposition,[59] but more recently it has taken on many aspects of a fanatic cult and no longer enjoys the public support it once had. However, with the influx of drugs into the middle class, there came to be more acceptance of alternatives to incarceration, for drug abuse was no longer a problem only of the poor. As middle- and upper-class communities came to see the problem as their problem, attitudes changed. Providing help for these juveniles gained increasing respect and came to be viewed as the right thing to do.

The reaction of law-enforcement agencies also changed. Instead of concentrating on the kids who were using drugs, they began to go after the "pushers" or "dealers." Police task forces were organized; governmental pressure was put on countries in which opium was legally grown, especially Turkey, to curtail production; and users came to be seen as victims rather than offenders. This reaction, of course, solved the problem of how to handle the drug-using children of the affluent while at the same time continuing to condemn the traffic in illegal drugs. Now juveniles who used dope could be sent to some kind of treatment center, and the real villains, the dealers, could be sent to jail.

A final development in the drug scene that should be noted is the establishment of an illicit market structure.[60] Many youths who got into the drug scene also got into the drug business. The profits to be realized from selling marijuana and other drugs were considerable, and a youth who began dealing generally found them too attractive to give up. A former student of the author's who came from an upper-middle-class background explained the operation of dealing cocaine. There was no feeling on his part that the activity was wrong; his only concern was to avoid being caught. Moreover, as a dealer, he enjoyed high status in the youthful community. When he became involved in dealing, he found that the money to be derived from selling cocaine on the wholesale level was astronomical. Like any other going economic concern, such a market structure, once established, is difficult to shut down, and because there is always someone to profit from the high "criminal tariff" imposed on illegal goods and services, it is unusually lucrative.[61]

In the meantime, drinking among juveniles had been largely ignored. The deaths from alcohol-related incidents, notably traffic accidents, far exceeded deaths from drug overdoses, but drinking has been culturally accepted, and the alcohol deaths were not connected with alcohol in the same way as deaths from LSD (accidents or suicides), barbiturates, or heroin were linked to these substances. In the last several decades no pressure groups lobbied for the death penalty for alcohol pushers, no right-thinking citizens group formed task forces to stamp out booze, and in some cases adults were downright relieved to find their offspring drinking instead of smoking marijuana. Only recently has there been renewed concern about juvenile drinking.

SUMMARY

In this chapter we examined why juveniles use drugs and drink alcohol. Much has been written about the horrors and the glories of drugs and liquor from the medical, psychological, and sociological points of view, but the effects of drugs and alcohol and the causes of their use often become blurred. We have concentrated on the processes whereby juveniles come to be attracted to various illicit drugs and alcohol and how meanings associated with drugs have developed and been transformed.

Since drugs have been around for quite a while, we cannot simply say that the greater availability of drugs is the cause of increased use any more than we can say that more juveniles have tried alcohol in recent years because of its increased availability. With drugs, the supply increased to meet the increased demand. Therefore, we have sought to explain why the demand became so great, especially since the middle of the 1960s. We found that the "hippie ethic" provided a new way to look at and mold the drug experience. Additionally, we saw that the mass media have encouraged Americans to take drugs as problem solvers. The main difference between the illegal and legal drugs, besides the interpretation of the effects, is that it is against the law to use the former but not the latter.

By redefining illegal drugs, it was possible for juveniles and others to establish a general drug-using subculture. As "bad drugs" were reformulated as "good dope" and backed by a drug-using subculture to provide new understandings, juvenile use of illicit drugs multiplied. This new conception of drugs has permeated many other segments of society as well; in some states, for example, certain formerly illegal drugs have been decriminalized. Thus, we see the power of interpretation, not only to explain why juveniles changed their ideas about drug use but to account for changes in the rest of society as well.

NOTES

1. Sidney Cohen, *The Drug Dilemma* (New York: McGraw-Hill, 1969), p. 52.
2. Eric Goode, "The Criminology of Drugs and Drug Use," in Abraham S. Blumberg (ed.), *Current Perspectives on Criminal Behavior* (New York: Knopf, 1974), p. 165.
3. *Ibid.*, p. 165.
4. Howard S. Becker, *Outsiders: Studies in the Sociology of Deviance* (New York: Free Press, 1963), pp. 135–138.
5. Ned Polsky, *Hustlers, Beats and Others* (New York: Doubleday, 1969).
6. James Carey, *The College Drug Scene* (Englewood Cliffs, N.J.: Prentice-Hall, 1968).
7. N. B. Eddy, *et al.*, "Drug Dependence: Its Significance and Characteristics," *Bulletin of the World Health Organization, 32*:721–733 (1965).
8. Goode, p. 167.
9. Federal Bureau of Investigation, *Uniform Crime Reports: Crime in the United States* (Washington, D.C.: Government Printing Office, 1972).
10. William B. Sanders, "Drug Use among Suburban Midwest High School Students," unpublished consultant paper prepared for Palos Township Youth Council, 1970.
11. Arthur Berger, "Drug Advertising and the 'Pain, Pill, Pleasure' Model," *Journal of Drug Issues, 4*:208–212 (Summer 1974).
12. *Ibid.*, p. 209.
13. William Simon and John H. Gagnon, "Children of the Drug Age," *Saturday Review, 51*:60–78 (September 21, 1968).
14. Howard S. Becker, "History, Culture and Subjective Experience: An Exploration of the Social Bases of Drug-induced Experiences," *Journal of Health and Social Behavior, 8*:163–176 (September 1967).
15. *Ibid.*, p. 168.
16. Sanders, "Drug Use among Suburban Midwest High School Students."
17. Becker, *Outsiders*.
18. Sherri Cavan, "The Hippie Ethic and the Spirit of Drug Use," in Jack Douglas (ed.), *Observations of Deviance* (New York: Random House, 1970), pp. 314–326.
19. Joseph G. Weis, "Styles of Middle-Class Adolescent Drug Use," *Pacific Sociological Review, 17*:251–286 (July 1974).
20. *Ibid.*, p. 266.

21. Christine Carol Schub, "A Comparison of Social and Personality Characteristics of Incarcerated Drug Users and Non-Users," master's thesis, University of Florida (1973); Richard H. Blum, *et al., Students and Drugs* (San Francisco: Jossey-Bass, 1970).
22. Cavan.
23. Thomas Wallace, "Culture and Social Being," Unpublished master's paper, University of California, Santa Barbara (1972).
24. Peter Andrew Knocke, "The Economics of Marijuana: Current Estimates of Supply and Demand in an Illicit Market," master's thesis, university of Florida (1973); Sanders, "Drug Use among Suburban Midwest High School Students," p. 13.
25. James Spradley, *You Owe Yourself a Drunk* (Boston: Little, Brown, 1970); Jacqueline Wiseman, *Stations of the Lost* (Englewood Cliffs, N.J.: Prentice-Hall, 1970).
26. Weis, p. 269.
27. *Ibid.,* p. 270
28. *Ibid.,* p. 270.
29. *Ibid.,* pp. 258–259.
30. *Ibid.,* p. 271.
31. *Ibid.,* p. 272.
32. *Ibid.,* p. 274.
33. Erving Goffman, *The Presentation of Self in Everyday Life* (New York: Doubleday, 1959).
34. Jerry Simmons and Barry Winograd, *It's Happening* (Santa Barbara, Calif.: Marc-Laird, 1966).
35. Cohen, p. 14.
36. Harold Garfinkel, *Studies in Ethnomethodology* (Englewood Cliffs, N.J.: Prentice-Hall, 1967).
37. Martin R. Haskell and Lewis Yablonsky, *Juvenile Delinquency,* 2d ed. (Chicago: Rand McNally, 1978), p. 320.
38. William B. Sanders, *Detective Work: A Study of Criminal Investigations* (New York: Free Press, 1977).
39. Peter Adler and Patricia Adler, "The Tinydopers," unpublished research paper, University of California, San Diego, 1977).
40. *Ibid.*
41. Marvin B. Scott and Stanford Lyman, "Accounts." *American Sociological Review 33:*46–62.
42. Sanders, "Drug Use among Suburban Midwest High School Students."
43. *Time,* "Kids and Heroin: The Adolescent Epidemic" (March 16, 1970).
44. *Ibid.*
45. Charles Winick, "Physician Narcotic Addicts," *Social Problems, 9:*174–186 (Fall 1961).
46. Philip Whitten and Ian Robertson, "A Way to Control Heroin," *Boston Globe Magazine* (May 21, 1972).
47. Goode, p. 167.
48. *Ibid.,* p. 168.
49. P. Marden and R. Zylman, "Comment on 'A National Study of Adolescent Drinking Behavior, Attitudes and Correlates,'" *Journal of Studies on Alcohol, 37:*1346–1358 (September 1976).
50. Sanders, "Drug Use among Suburban Midwest High School Students."
51. W. Cockerham, "Drinking Patterns of Institutionalized and Noninstitutionalized Wyoming Youth," *Journal of Studies on Alcohol, 36:*993–995.
52. H. Wechsler and M. McFadden, "Sex Differences in Adolescent Alcohol and Drug Use," *Journal of Studies on Alcohol, 37:*1291–1301 (September 1976).
53. H. Hoffmann and A. A. Noem, "Alcoholism among Parents of Male and Female Alcoholics," *Psychological Reports, 36:*322–326 (February 1975).
54. J. D. Orcutt, "Deviance as a Situated Phenomenon: Variations in the Social Interpretation of Marijuana and Alcohol Use," *Social Problems, 33:*346–356 (February 1975).
55. Erving Goffman, *Interaction Ritual* (New York: Doubleday, 1967).

56. R. Jessor and S. L. Jessor, "Adolescent Development and the Onset of Drinking," *Journal of Studies on Alcohol, 36:*27–51 (January 1975).
57. R. Z. Margulies, R. C. Kessler, and D. B. Kandel, "A Longitudinal Study of Onset of Drinking among High School Students," *Journal of Studies on Alcohol, 38:*897–912 (May 1977).
58. D. Lawrence Wieder, *Language and Social Reality: The Case of Telling the Convict Code* (The Hague: Mouton, 1974).
59. Lewis Yablonsky, *The Tunnel Back: Synanon* (New York: Macmillan, 1965).
60. Knocke, p. 37.
61. Herbert L. Packer, *The Limits of the Criminal Sanction* (Stanford, Calif.: Stanford University Press, 1968).

9 Delinquent Gangs

INTRODUCTION

Not long ago movies depicting gang warfare were blamed for encouraging gang violence. The films *The Warriors* and *Boulevard Nights* showed violent but romanticized versions of gang activities in urban areas. It is doubtful that movies cause intergang violence, because if opposing gangs show up to see virtually any film at the same theater the chances for violent conflict are high. What is important, though, is to understand why gangs fight at all and the nature of delinquent gangs.

In this chapter we will look at the phenomenon of gangs. First, we will see what a gang is, differentiating gangs from street groups and cliques. The characteristics of gangs must be clearly identified in order to estimate the frequency and distribution of gangs in the United States. Second, we will differentiate between types of gangs based on the dominant forms of delinquency they engage in. Ironically, the gangs that turn to heavy drug use cease to be gangs, but we will, nevertheless, look at the relationship between gangs and dope to understand why gangs attempt to keep narcotics away from their members.

Finally, we will examine gang violence. Since gang violence is the most visible aspect of gangs in the public mind and the most troublesome type of gang delinquency, this subject will be explored in detail. We will begin by showing the relationship between maintaining a reputation and the necessity for fighting other gangs. Then we will look at the escalation of violence in the use of weapons, especially guns, by contemporary gangs. The weapons are used in "rumbles" (fights between entire gangs) and "hits" (isolated attacks) resulting in injury and death of gang members. Last, we will discuss the role of territory in gang violence and honor and see how public places come to be defined as boundaries in gang fiefdoms.

A brief history of juvenile gangs will help put them in the proper context. First, gangs did not begin in the 1950s in the United States complete with ducktail haircuts and switchblade knives. From the time there have been urban centers in America there have been groups of juvenile boys who have engaged in ganglike activities. For example, an observer in Brooklyn in 1856 wrote:

> At any and all hours there are multitudes of boys . . . congregated on the corners of the streets, idle in their habits, dissolute in their conduct, profane and obscene in their conversation, gross and vulgar in their manners. If a female passes one of the groups she is shocked by what she sees and hears.[1]

Urban development after the Civil War saw the increase of delinquent gangs, and by the early 1920s when Thrasher conducted his classic study on gangs, there were 1,313 gangs in Chicago alone.[2] There was only sketchy information on the development, frequency, and distribution of delinquent gangs until Thrasher's work, but given the number of gangs he found, plus the little information available on ganglike delinquency from the American Revolution until the turn of the century, we can conclude that gangs have been with us since the country's founding.

The longevity of gangs is as remarkable as are their conflicts. A gang called the "Red Raiders" has hung out on the same corner in Boston since at least the 1930s, and a war between two gangs, the "Tops" and the "Bottoms," began in the 1930s in West Philadelphia and was still going on in the mid-1960s.[3] Conflict between certain gangs has been going on so long that no one knows why the gangs fight. In an interview in the late 1970s, one East Los Angeles gang member, when asked why his gang was fighting another, said he honestly did not know, but for as long as he could remember, including before he joined the gang, his gang had been at war with the other gang.

From the mid-1960s until recently there has been waning attention given to delinquent gangs by both the popular press and academic researchers. In part this has been due to the increased interest in the middle-class youth drug phenomenon and the hippies of the sixties. A renewed interest in gangs today has revealed that gangs are more violent than ever and still very much with us.

GANG CHARACTERISTICS

The first step in our examination of gangs is to specify what kind of grouping constitutes a gang. Walter B. Miller developed the following definition based on a national survey of people working with gangs:

> A gang is a group of recurrently associating individuals with identifiable leadership and internal organization, identifying with or claiming control over territory in the community, and engaging either individually or collectively in violent or other forms of illegal behavior.[4]

Broken down, this definition points to five key elements of gangs.[5]
1. Violent or criminal behavior as a major activity of group members.
2. Group organization with functional role-division, chain-of-command.
3. Identifiable leadership.
4. Group members in continuing recurrent interaction.
5. Group identification with, claiming control over identifiable community territory.

It is significant that in defining delinquent gangs Miller has revised an earlier definition of gangs which specified that the youths be from "urban" areas.[6] This changed definition not only reflects changes in U.S. population characteristics but also provides a broader view of delinquent gangs. However, since territoriality—the defense of territory—is part of the definition, there is an implicit exclusion of certain groups of youths who engage in a good deal of delinquency, namely, middle- and upper-middle-class youths. It is true that gangs are typically viewed as a lower- and working-class phenomenon,[7] but the implicit characterization of the activities of lower-class youth as "ganglike" and those of middle-class youth as "clublike" may express nothing more than class bias. In a comparison of a middle-class group and a working-class group of boys both of which engaged in numerous delinquent acts, it was found that only the lower-class group was considered delinquent by the community.[8] The middle-class boys routinely indulged in truancy, drinking, wild driving, petty theft, and vandalism, but instead of being defined by the authorities as a delinquent gang, they were characterized as young men "sowing wild oats." On the other hand, the working-class boys who engaged in delinquent activities were seen by the community, the school, and the police as young hoodlums and criminals. The middle-class gang actually committed *more* delinquent acts than the working-class gang, but they were accorded the status of good, upstanding youths with promising futures. The working-class gang's style of delinquency probably accounted for their being labeled delinquents since they were less likely to act contrite when apprehended and more likely to fight; however, since under the law a delinquent act is a delinquent act, demeanor and social class should have nothing to do with whether a group is accorded the status of a delinquent gang.

If we keep in mind that the social definitions of delinquency are the ones that matter, it would be socially accurate to deal with working-class gangs and other groups defined by the community, schools, and police as delinquent gangs. This does not mean that middle-class youth do not engage in ganglike delinquent activities, but since their activities are treated by the community as mere youthful high jinks, the consequences of their actions are not *in fact* delinquent. That is, if the agencies that label youths delinquent do not define middle- and upper-middle-class youths as delinquent, *socially* they are not delinquent. Even though it is possible to demonstrate class bias in the social labeling practices, a redefinition of delinquent gangs would not change these practices. We are dealing with delinquent gangs as defined by the community and not in terms of what can be shown to be their involvement in ganglike delinquency.

A second important feature of Miller's definition and the assessment of the criteria evaluated by the respondents is the relatively low consensus that violence and criminal behavior are major activities of gang members. Since the most common image of gangs centers around gang violence and crime, it is an interesting point to note. Miller found that the reason most respondents did not include violence and crime as necessary criterion for a gang was the belief that gang formation is a natural tendency of youths of similar ages to form themselves into groups for a variety of purposes and that illegal behavior is only incidental to the formation of the group and not a necessary part.[9]

Perhaps the best way to differentiate gangs from what Miller referred to as "hanging groups" or "street groups" is on the basis of the extent of violence and serious crime and degree of formal organization. "Hanging" or "street" groups congregate around parks, housing projects, and stores; engage in noisy disturbances; and commit minor offenses such as petty shoplifting, marijuana use, drunkenness, and vandalism.[10] Such street groups commit crimes, but they lack the structure and commitment to serious criminal behavior, especially violence. The respondents in Miller's study *did* differentiate between such groups and gangs, and therefore the issue of whether violent or criminal behavior is in fact a necessary criterion for a gang looms large. This is because without the criterion of serious and violent crime, a "gang" of juveniles could be little more than a structured street group.

To better understand the characteristics of gangs, we will examine one gang that operated in a Washington, D.C., ghetto during the early 1960s. First, we will look at the gang organization and leadership as described by a former gang member.

> When I got out of Junior Village [a juvenile detention center] the second time I was almost fourteen, and the streets had really changed. Everyone had joined a gang, and the most important thing that was going on was gang fights. Now, a lot of these guys in the gangs were pretty big and pretty tough. I have been president or boss of several gangs, but only that once where I shot that guy was it through a takeover. Most of the crowds I hung with had a whole lot of experience, and until I had that experience I didn't make my move. When I did make my move, I made it through becoming a warlord—I just handled all the weapons. When the dudes called a meeting, they thought about me knowing how to do everything. I know the right place to hit somebody with a rock and a sock—that was one of the main gang-fight weapons—or I knew how to make a zip gun real well or I knew how to handle an ice pick and a straight razor or a stiletto or a switchblade. I even knew how to handle small rifles and pistols.[11]

As can be seen in the description of the gang organization, there was identifiable leadership (president or boss), and there was functional role division (warlord with the duty of organizing for fights). Other roles in the gang might have included treasurer, thieves (members who added to the gang's treasury through theft and burglary), "hit-men" (often younger members who were assigned to kill rivals but because of their age were unlikely to receive stiff penalties), and various other roles depending on the size and activities of the gang. Frequently the specialized roles were vague, and a member would become recognized as an incumbent in a particular role merely by carrying out a function without any formal appointment.

Next, the gang violence and territory can be seen in a further description of gang life.

When my gang challenged another gang, then I would always try to find some kind of way of going into the other gang's section. We only had a one-to-two-to-three-block radius, that was our territory.

I was in the Keystones in S.E. Then we changed our name from the Keystones to the Tagalongs. There were other gangs like the Southwest Stompers—we fought them—Peach and Honey, Tophat, the Mau-Maus. One of the most powerful gangs that ever came out of the district was the Mau-Maus, but *the* most powerful gang in Washington, D.C., in them gang-fighting days was Le-Broit Park. LeBroit Park was said to have seven hundred members. They had branches everywhere—S.E., S.W., N.W.—but their main branch was in the N.W., up around the ball park. Because of their large numbers, they easily moved over quite a few gangs. There was a time when I was up on their turf in N.W., visiting a girl I had met. At the time, I had on my Tagalong sweater and a little cap, letting them know that I was one of the Tagalongs. About six LeBroit Park members chased me clean out of N.W.

. . .There was usually a few guys that did get seriously hurt. When you get hit with a bat, then you seriously hurt. Or when you get hit with a chain or if somebody stab you with an ice pick or a straight razor or shoot you with a zip gun. I was just lucky, 'cause I was into this for about three years, from fourteen to seventeen, and none of them things ever happened to me. I mean, I've been beat up on—that kind of hurt—punched in the face, black eye. But real hurt like shot or stabbed or beat real bad with a bat, that never happened to me. A lot of my friends wasn't so fortunate. A lot of them still carry scars from old gang-fight days.[12]

The territory of the gangs varied from a few blocks to several sections of the city, and there was a definite sovereignty over the territories. Later, we will examine the relationship among territory, honor, and violence, but for now it is enough to understand that gangs do define and defend territory and that they do so with violence.

ESTIMATING GANG FREQUENCY

There is considerable variation in the estimated number of gangs based on Miller's definition. Table 9–1 shows various estimates by the police and other agencies that deal with juvenile gangs.

These variations in the number of gangs estimated by different agencies reflect different understandings of gangs, and the high estimates probably include several groups that do not meet the gang criteria.[13] At the same time, they shed light on different gang groupings. For example, note that there is little variation in the estimated numbers of gang members in Los Angeles, while there is a considerable difference in the estimated numbers of gangs in that city—a high of 1000+ and a low of only 160. The higher figure is probably more accurate given what we know about gangs. Los Angeles is spread out over hundreds of square miles, and so gang territories would tend

TABLE 9-1.   Numbers of Gangs and Gang Members in Six Gang-Problem Cities, 1973–1975[a]

City	Estimated Number of Gangs		Estimated Number of Members
New York	High	473	40,000
	Low	315	8,000–19,500
Chicago	High	700	10,000
	Low	150–220	3,000–5,000
Los Angeles	High	1,000+	15,000
	Low	160	12,000
Philadelphia	High	400	15,000
	Low	88	4,700
Detroit	High	110	1,250
	Low	30	500
San Francisco	General	20	250
Six Cities	High	2,700	81,500
	Low	760	28,450

[a]Walter Miller, "Violence by Youth Gangs and Youth Groups as a Crime Problem in Major American Cities" (Washington, D.C.: U.S. Department of Justice, December 1975). National Institute for Juvenile Justice and Delinquency Prevention; Office of Juvenile Justice and Delinquency Prevention; Law Enforcement Assistance Administration; U.S. Department of Justice (Washington, D.C.: Government Printing Office).

to be either spread out further or chopped up into a larger number of "turfs" (gang territories). The latter interpretation, that the territory is chopped up into several smaller turfs suggests that there are more gangs. I found from my own observation, that a number of gangs existed in relatively small areas, separated by streets and block boundaries. While observing police patrol with the Los Angeles Police Department's 77th Street Division in the Watts section of the city, I learned that a gang named "The Denver Lanes" had their territory claims on the same wall as did the "Baby Bounty Hunters" (a subgroup of a larger gang) in an area no larger than a few blocks. This would further suggest that Los Angeles has more gangs spread out over the vast area that encompasses the city, as opposed to a few gangs with large territorial claims.

Another way of estimating the number of actual gangs as opposed to street groups and hanging groups is to examine the number of violent crimes committed by gangs. The most serious violent crime a gang can commit is murder, and so by looking at the numbers and rates of gang homicides, we can estimate the amount of gang violence in a city. Tables 9–2 and 9–3 show the number and rates of gang killings and a comparison of juvenile homicides and gang-related killings.

The tables show the relative proportion of gangs in the cities studied in a different light. Philadelphia had the highest homicide rate by juvenile gang

TABLE 9–2.   Rates of Gang-Related Killings: Five Cities, 1972–1974[a]

City	Three Year Totals	Rate[*]
Philadelphia	126	7.4
Los Angeles	141	6.0
Chicago	102	3.5
New York	128	2.1
San Francisco	28	0.6
Five Cities	525	3.9

[a]Walter Miller, "Violence by Youth Gangs and Youth Groups as a Crime Problem in Major American Cities" (Washington, D.C.: U.S. Department of Justice, December 1975), p. 31.
[*]Per 10,000 males 10–19, U.S. Census, 1970.

members, while estimates by respondents showed it to be fourth in number of gangs and gang membership. New York City, which had the highest estimates of gangs and gang membership, had the second lowest gang-related killings. At the same time, these figures show the relative impact on the juvenile homicide rate. In San Francisco, with the lowest estimates of gangs and gang membership along with the lowest number and rate of gang-related killings, gang-related killings made up almost three-fourths of all juvenile homicides. Thus, the impact of gangs in San Francisco is far greater in terms of its effect on the juvenile murder rate. If gangs were eradicated in San Francisco, 7 juvenile homicides would have occurred instead of 25, since 72 percent of the homicides were gang related. In Chicago, on the other hand,

TABLE 9–3.   Juvenile Homicides and Gang-Related Killings[a]

City: Year	Murder/Homicide Arrests, Persons 17 and Under Number	Gang-Related Killings as Percentage of Juvenile Homicides Percent
San Francisco: 1974	18	72
Los Angeles: 1973	92	42
Philadelphia: 1972	127	30
New York: 1973	268[*]	15
Chicago: 1973	188	10
Five Cities	693	24

[a]Walter Miller, "Violence by Youth Gangs and Youth Groups as a Crime Problem in Major American Cities" (Washington, D.C.: U.S. Department of Justice, December 1975), p. 31.
[*]Years 16 and 17 via extrapolation.

10 percent of juvenile homicides were gang related, so that gangs have relatively less impact on the violent crime rate of juveniles.

Before examining the structure of juvenile gangs, to provide a broader view we will examine gang membership from another point of view and along different dimensions. In a study by Savitz, Lalli, and Rosen, cohorts of black and white boys in Philadelphia were studied to determine, among other things to be discussed later, gang membership.[14] The researchers differentiated between "structural" gangs and "functional" gangs. A structural gang was identified as having acknowledged leadership, a common gang meeting place, and a territory or turf within which the group feels safe and where entry by others can provoke the group to violence.[15] A functional gang member was described as "someone whose group of friends fought with other groups, who was expected to participate in any group or gang fight, and who felt that failure to comply with the group requirement to fight would result in his being disaffiliated from the group."[16] The researchers had expected that a high percentage of all of the subjects would have belonged to one or the other or both types of gangs, but found that only 12 percent of the black boys and 14 percent of the white boys belonged to structural gangs, while 44 percent of the blacks and 65 percent of the whites belonged to functional gangs. In general terms we can estimate that about 50 percent of the youths in the sample were affiliated with *some type* of gang activity.

JUVENILE GANG STRUCTURE

A youngster's identification with a juvenile gang depends to a large extent on the makeup of the gang and the gang activity. If a gang is loosely structured and membership is casual, then members' identification with the gang is likely to be casual and weak. Also, we can differentiate between a core membership, whose identity is tied up in the gang, and peripheral members, who have little of their identity tied into the gang.

Gangs can be divided along sex and age dimensions, and even though there is an identity with the entire gang, each member sees his or her place in the gang in terms of these subdivisions. For example, Miller identified six subdivisions in a gang he referred to as the Bandits.[17] There were four male groups: (1) the Brigands, aged 18 to 21; (2) the Senior Bandits, 16 to 18; (3) the Junior Bandits, 14 to 16; and (4) the Midget Bandits, 12 to 14. The two female subdivisions were the Bandettes, aged 14 to 16, and the Little Bandettes, aged 12 to 14.

Yablonsky characterized gangs as having "diffuse role definitions, limited cohesion, impermanence, minimal consensus on norms, shifting membership, disturbed leadership, and limited definitions of membership expectations."[18] This characterization, in contrast to most popular notions of fierce gang loyalty and cohesion, was confirmed by Short.[19] However, other observers have found a good deal of loyalty and cohesion among gang members over time. For example, in a study of female gang members, Quicker notes: "Perhaps the most impressive quality of these groups is the overwhelming emphasis on group loyalty. Its closest analogue on this dimension is the family."[20] Quicker quotes the following assertions by female gang members attesting to this loyalty:

> To us, we're like one big family, if they do wrong to my homegirl or homeboy [fellow gang member], it's like they're doing wrong to me and it hurts me.
> . . . They are like our sisters, you know, and how would you feel about them if they came home and told you somebody did this and this to you or one of your relatives, someone you're really close to? You'd get mad.

Similarly, Miller summarized his findings about juvenile gangs in terms of strong ties and gang structure:

> The experiences of Midcity gang members show that the gang serves the lower-class adolescent as a flexible and adaptable training instrument imparting vital knowledge concerning the value of individual competence, the appropriate limits of law-violating behavior, the uses and abuses of authority, and the skills of interpersonal relations. From this perspective, the street gang appears not as a casual or transient manifestation that emerges intermittently in response to unique and passing social conditions but rather as a stable associational form, coordinate with and complementary to the family, and as an intrinsic part of the way of life of the urban low-status community.[21]

The disagreement among sociologists as to the makeup of and identification with juvenile gangs indicates a need for more information. However, since Yablonsky and many other sociologists spent most of their time studying fighting gangs whereas Miller, Quicker, Cloward and Ohlin, Cohen, and others studied less violent gangs,[22] it may be that different types of gangs vary in the group identification and loyalty of members. Gangs differ not only in the types of their activities but also in the structures and types of their community relationships. Thus, the strength of gang loyalty may vary with the makeup of the gang.

The differences among the findings on gang loyalty may also be rooted in different understandings of gang structure and leadership. Haskell and Yablonsky characterize the gang as a "pseudocommunity" which develops out of defective socialization, alienation, dissociation, and paranoid reactions.[23] In this view, the gang members are seen as sociopathic personalities, and the highly unstable structure of the violent gang constitutes a pseudocommunity. This same structure, however, can have an entirely different interpretation. Miller contends, as we have noted, that the structure of gang membership and leadership is highly flexible, and this loose, flexible structure may be misinterpreted as "unstable."[24] Instead of having a single, well-defined leader, gangs have several leaders, but this is far from being a sign of weak structure; on the contrary, it is a highly resilient form of leadership. If one leader is arrested, another leader can hold the gang together. Thus, the gang's leadership structure provides for the contingency of a gang leader's absence. Furthermore, in that the gang members are willing to follow more than a single leader, those studied by Miller show a great deal more identity with the gang as a whole than with a single charismatic leader. This attests to very strong group identification and loyalty.

Determining the members' identification with the loyalty to a gang has more than merely academic importance. The extent to which members identify with a gang determines the extent to which they will participate in the gang's activities. If there is strong identification and loyalty, there is greater likelihood that members will engage in the activities, delinquent and nondelinquent, that are typical of the gang. For example, if a gang is involved in stealing and the gang members are going out on some caper, a member who strongly identifies with the gang is more likely to go with them than one who does not. Conversely, if the gang is one with little member identification, none of the members feels pressured or obliged to do what the other gang members do.

Furthermore, if a gang member has strong identity ties with the gang, it is less likely that he or she will be exposed to nondelinquent behavior patterns and belief systems. A member can become somewhat isolated from delinquent patterns if there is only a casual identification with the gang, but in delinquent gangs in which there is total identity and association, it would be very difficult for gang members to have the intimate association with nondelinquent others that is necessary if they are to take on nondelinquent values. In questioning members of a Chicana (female Mexican-American) gang, Quicker found that there was little association outside the gang.

> All the girls that go down to my house are from M [name of gang]. All the guys that I know that I am close to are from M.
> *Don't you have any friends that aren't from M?* Ya, from school, you know, there are always people who aren't from the gang. But they are the ones that are my friends, my real friends, the ones I consider my friends, they are all from M.[25]

The isolation from others is not a physical matter, for, as this gang member indicated, there were girls in school she knew. However, they were not considered "real" friends. In further questioning, Quicker found why this gang member drew all her friends from the gang.

> I don't trust anybody else, that's why. They're the only ones I can depend on, cause I know if I get into hassles they'll help me, and the other girls like one time we went to B—, we used to go to hang around there, and some girls were going to jump me, and all the girls I was with took off and they left me there alone. . . . That's when I said I was only going to hang around with my homegirls.[26]

This finding is consistent with the findings of Haskell and Yablonsky, who point out that a violent gang has its origins in part in paranoid reactions to the social milieu.[27] According to Haskell and Yablonsky, members develop "delusions of persecution," the feeling that others are out to get them, and they seek out the gang's protection. However, it is questionable whether the fear of others is always a delusion. The Chicana gang member we have quoted was attacked by girls from another gang, and such beating by other gang members is not uncommon. Fear of others, then, may not be a delusion of persecution; there is actual danger in the slums, barrios, and ghettos, where violent gangs are most common. While it may be the case, as Haskell and Yablonsky argue, that gang members greatly exaggerate the danger of their situation, it is nevertheless true that they define it as very dangerous and act in terms of that definition.

To test whether or not juveniles who belong to gangs are delusional in their perception of danger and what impact this has on their activities, we will examine data describing the incidence of gang-member victimization and the kinds of actions, places, and events that give rise to fear among gang members. To the extent that the fear is not delusional and actions are taken to avoid danger, we can indirectly show solidarity within a gang.

Tables 9–4 and 9–5 show victimization by membership in gangs and altered behavior by juveniles to avoid danger based on gang membership.

As can be seen from Table 9–4, gang members experience victimization more than do nonmembers with the exception of black nonmembers who are slightly more likely to be victims of extortion and white nonfunctional gang

TABLE 9–4. Victimization of Juveniles by Membership in Structural and Functional Gangs, Black and White, Time Two*[a]

Victimization of Juveniles	Black Structural Gang Member		Black Functional Gang Member	
	Yes	No	Yes	No
Robbed	44%	28%	30%	30%
Assaulted	27%	17%	22%	15%
Extortion	6%	8%	7%	8%
	White Structural Gang Member		White Functional Gang Member	
	Yes	No	Yes	No
Robbed	33%	24%	24%	26%
Assaulted	33%	22%	24%	21%
Extortion	6%	6%	6%	6%

*Time Two refers to the second of two observations in the study being cited.
[a] Leonard D. Savitz, Michael Lalli, and Lawrence Rosen, "City Life and Delinquency—Victimization, Fear of Crime and Gang Membership" (Washington, D.C.: U.S. Department of Justice, April 1977), p. 55.

TABLE 9-5. Juvenile Altered Behavior by Membership in Structural and Functional Gangs, Black and White, Time Two[a]

Altered Behavior by Juveniles	Black Structural Gang Member		Black Functional Gang Member		White Structural Gang Member		White Functional Gang Member	
	Yes	No	Yes	No	Yes	No	Yes	No
Avoidances								
Try not to go a block or two at night when alone	28 (54%)	214 (54%)	100 (51%)	142 (56%)	22 (32%)	90 (21%)	64 (20%)	48 (27%)
Try not to go more than block or two at night, alone	29 (56%)	275 (56%)	102 (60%)	151 (60%)	23 (33%)	117 (27%)	86 (27%)	54 (31%)
Try not to go more than block or two at night with friends	26 (50%)	221 (55%)	89 (45%)	158 (62%)	39 (57%)	219 (51%)	156 (48%)	102 (58%)
Avoid talking to strangers	35 (67%)	294 (74%)	0	0	14 (20%)	78 (18%)	43 (13%)	49 (28%)
Cross street as a group of strangers approaches	31 (60%)	241 (61%)	117 (59%)	155 (61%)	36 (52%)	198 (46%)	149 (46%)	85 (48%)
Avoid some gang's turf in daytime	27 (52%)	250 (62%)	126 (64%)	151 (59%)	31 (45%)	143 (33%)	104 (32%)	70 (40%)
Avoid some gang's turf at night	30 (58%)	292 (73%)	144 (73%)	178 (70%)	47 (68%)	215 (50%)*	166 (51%)	36 (49%)
Weapon Reactions								
Carry gun or knife for protection	5 (10%)	32 (8%)	17 (9%)	20 (8%)	14 (20%)	40 (9%)*	35 (11%)	19 (11%)
Carry something else for protection	17 (33%)	87 (22%)	49 (25%)	55 (22%)	21 (30%)	50 (11%)*	43 (13%)	28 (16%)
Total	52	400	198	254	69	433	325	177

[a] Leonard D. Savitz, Michael Lalli, and Lawrence Rosen, "City Life and Delinquency—Victimization, Fear of Crime and Gang Membership" (Washington, D.C.: U.S. Department of Justice, April 1977), p. 57.
* Relationship is a statistically significant one.

members who are slightly more likely to be robbed (neither significantly so). This suggests that the fears of victimization are *not* delusional, as suggested by Yablonsky, and therefore the boys cannot be said to be paranoid. From a comfortable and relatively safe middle-class perspective, we tend to assume that any estimates that do not conform to our own experiences are exaggerated. However, if we stop to consider that middle-class parents warn their children to stay out of particular parts of town and give their children special precautionary measures to take when visiting urban areas, we can see that fear of gangs (among other assorted urban bedevilments) is really not considered to be delusional even by the middle class. Therefore, we will treat the beliefs about the dangers of gangs and one's own identity with a gang as *experientially* based in the social milieu of gang members. No doubt that many a gang clash is exaggerated, but the fact remains that such clashes exist to be exaggerated.

In examining altered behavior due to crime (Table 9–5), we see that black juveniles altered their behavior more so than white juveniles, but both groups showed they feared treading on alien gang territory during day or night. However, white boys were more likely to carry guns or knives than were blacks, but the vast majority (72 percent) of the boys who were not members of black structural gangs and made up the largest cohort of black youths in the study ($N = 400$) carried some kind of weapon for protection. From this evidence, we can infer that those who belonged to gangs probably did identify with them fairly closely. This is because the greater the threat outside a gang (or any group), the greater the internal solidarity of the group.[28]

In conclusion, while not all gang members have the fierce loyalty described by Quicker, it does *not* appear that gangs are so transient in their makeup as to have the minimal loyalty and identification described by Yablonsky. Rather, it seems that gang members do identify with their gangs to the extent that a great deal of their delinquent activity can be explained in terms of going along with gang expectations. Later, when we discuss gang violence, we will explain the structure of identity involvement that leads to delinquency. Here we merely wish to note that gang members define themselves to a significant extent in terms of their gang membership.

TYPES OF GANGS

Delinquent gangs have been characterized on a continuum from essentially social to essentially delinquent and in terms of various types of modal delinquency. Our discussion will center on modes of delinquent activity and will exclude the "social gang" and the "hanging group." These groups are involved in delinquent activities, but their delinquent behaviors are not uniquely different from nongang delinquency. Rather, following Short's typology, we will look at conflict, criminal, and drug-using gangs.[29]

Conflict Gangs

Gang conflict is not restricted to conflict gangs. Other types of gangs also engage in violence, including some "social gangs," which engage in very little delinquency. By "conflict gangs" we mean gangs whose major reason for existence is to fight and maintain a reputation for toughness. Haskell and Yablonsky describe these gangs as follows:

> In contrast with the other gang types, the violent gang is primarily organized for emotional gratification, and violence is the theme around which all activities center. Sports, social, even delinquent activities are side issues to its primary assaultive pattern. The violent gang's organization and membership are constantly shifting in accord with the emotional needs of its members. Membership size is exaggerated as a psychological weapon for influencing other gangs and for self-aggrandizement. Small arsenals of weapons are discussed and whenever possible accumulated. These caches include switchblades and hunting knives, homemade zip guns, standard guns, pipes, blackjacks, and discarded World War II bayonets and machetes. The violent gang is thus essentially organized around gang-war activities, although occasionally certain youths will form delinquent cliques or subgroups within the overall violent gang.[30]

The structure of conflict gangs reflects their focus on battle activity. For example, such positions as "war counselor" and "armorer" exist in conflict gangs but not in other types of gangs.[31] These roles are high in status, and the incumbents jealously guard their positions. The war counselor serves to identify enemy gangs and prepare for fights with other gangs or assaults on isolated enemy gang members, and the armorer sees that the necessary arsenal is maintained. The very existence of these roles in the gang structure makes it probable that the gangs will engage in some form of conflict.

The number of actual gang fights is relatively small; most gang conflict is a combination of "cold" and "guerilla" warfare rather than major battles. Generally violence is visited on single members of a gang by members of another gang. However, sometimes the beating of a lone gang member will lead to a full-scale war between gangs. For example, a journalist reports a telephone call from a street gang worker:

> "I thought you might be interested," he said. "The Cherubs are rumbling. They just put Jerry Larkin, from the Stompers, in the hospital. Caught him out of his neighborhood and left him for dead. He'll be all right, but they beat him up pretty bad. I think they worked him over with one of those iron tire chains." He said that there was now a full-scale war between the Cherubs and the Stompers, and that he had been talking with members of both groups, trying to get them to call it off.[32]

Spergel contends that different types of subcultures spawn different forms of delinquent activity.[33] In comparing neighborhoods with high delinquency

TABLE 9–6. Major Gang Fights, Actual and Threatened, in Two Communities*[a]

Neighborhood and Group	Threats of Gang Fights	Gang Fights	Total
Racketville			
Vultures	2	4	6
Stompers	3	5	8
Slumtown			
Regals	10	17	27
Noble Lords	8	19	27

*Calculated from answering-service messages and street club worker estimates, Big City Youth Board, for a twelve-month period, with age of group members and size of groups held approximately constant. A major gang fight threat was any threat important enough to be telephoned in to the answering service.

Differences between Racketville and Slumtown groups are statistically significant, using a t test, $p(s)$ .05.

[a] Irving Spergel, *Racketville, Slumtown, and Haulburg* (Chicago: University of Chicago Press, 1964).

rates, he found four times as many gang fights in Slumtown, an essentially conflict-oriented subculture, as in Racketville, a neighborhood characterized by a highly organized criminal subculture. Table 9–6 shows the differences between the two neighborhoods in this respect.

As can be seen from this table, there is a greater trend toward violence observable in Slumtown as compared to Racketville. A major gang fight took place or was threatened on the average of every two weeks for each gang in Slumtown, while in Racketville there was a threat or fight on the average of every two months for each gang. Spergel explains this difference on the basis of the different subculture and neighborhood which gave rise to the gangs.

Criminal Gangs

Haskell and Yablonsky, using the term "delinquent gang," describe the kind of group generally called "criminal gang":

The delinquent gang is primarily organized to carry out various illegal acts. The social interaction of the members is a secondary factor. Prominent among the delinquent gang's activities are burglary, petty thievery, mugging, assault for profit—not simply kicks—and other illegal acts directed at "raising bread." It is generally a tight clique, a small, mobile gang that can steal and escape with minimum risk. It would lose its cohesive quality and the intimate cooperation required for success in illegal ventures if it became too large. Membership is not easily achieved and must generally be approved by all gang members.[34]

This definition points to the utilitarian nature of delinquent activities; however, a good deal of delinquency in the criminal gang is performed for "kicks"—for example, stealing cars—or for building a "rep" as a competent thief or burglar.[35] The gang's expectation that its members are worthy of gang membership is realized through daring thefts, burglaries, and robberies. Although many of these crimes are certainly profitable, many are committed primarily to build a reputation. Members of criminal gangs strive for recognition through their crimes and collect any newspaper items that recount their exploits. Miller notes:

> Newspaper citations functioned for the Senior Bandits somewhat as do press notices for actors; gang members who made the papers were elated and granted prestige; those who did not were often disappointed; participants and nonparticipants who failed to see the stories felt cheated.[36]

Because the crimes committed by criminal gangs are so frequent, arrests are numerous. Because of the high frequency of arrests for law violation among criminal gangs, flexible leadership is a necessity for the gang's survival. At any one time a gang is likely to have several members in the reformatory. Miller documents the trouble one gang had with authorities:

> The frequency of the Senior Bandits' crimes, along with the relative seriousness of their offenses, resulted in a high rate of arrest and confinement. During the contact period somewhat over 40 percent of the gang members were confined to correctional institutions, with terms averaging 11 months per boy. The average Senior Bandit spends approximately one month out of four in a correctional facility. This circumstance prompted one of the Bandettes to remark, "Ya know, them guys got a new place to hang—the reformatory. That bunch is never together—one halfa them don't even know the other half."[37]

Like the conflict gang, the criminal gang is more likely to be found in a certain type of community and neighborhood than in another. Spergel differentiated between the Racketville and Slumtown gangs not only in their patterns of violence but also in the types of criminal gangs they represented. In Racketville, criminal activities were highly organized, involving a large number of people in a bureaucratic structure.[38] The gang boys hoped to "get a piece of the action" when they grew up, and they acted in apprenticeship roles in the rackets during their youth. Their orientation was in terms of gaining access to the illegitimate opportunity structure, which was best accomplished through connections with those in the rackets. However, in the theft subculture of Haulburg, where no organized rackets existed, the delinquent boys were oriented to more conventional beliefs about getting ahead in life, even though they engaged in a great many delinquent activities. Boys from Racketville were more likely to be involved in the policy racket ("numbers") or loan sharking, while the Haulburg boys were more likely to commit car thefts, apartment burglaries, and other types of stealing. For example. Spergel provides the following illustrations of Haulburg thefts:

Patrolman K. showed me a list of names of boys from——Street who constituted a serious problem during the last three years. These boys, seven or eight
of them, were repeatedly picked up for breaking into the coin boxes of public
washing and drying machines in the building basements. They also broke into
parking meters. They were constantly appearing in court but the judges were
reluctant to send them to the training school at so early an age. Patrolman K. said
that he had been able to persuade the local settlement house to assign a street-
club worker, half-time, to this group.[39]

Thus, even though the boys from both Racketville and Haulburg formed
criminal gangs, the gangs differed because the communities in which they
lived differed. Whereas conflict gangs typically formed in disorganized communities, criminal gangs were more commonly found in more organized
neighborhoods.

Drug Use and Gangs

The drug-using gang today would probably be characterized as a group of
young dopers who hang around together. If the group was using marijuana,
it would likely be upper-middle class; if it was using amphetamines, it would
probably be lower class.

The problem in characterizing a cohort that used drugs as a "gang" is that
the members' identification with the cohort does not have ganglike qualities.
A drug-using group and another kind of gang may have similar grouping
qualities and even a similar territory pattern (e.g., hanging around certain
corners); however, the members of the former may see one another as a bunch
of guys or a clique instead of as a gang that will persist over time with a
different set of members. Modern drug-using groups appear to lack the dura-
bility of the gangs we have described.

Members of other types of gangs often view drug users as unreliable, and
drug-using members of either violent gangs or criminal gangs have low status
or are ostracized. For example, in talking about other gang members who used
drugs, one respondent said:

"Man, that Jo-Jo!" Benny said. "He's stoned *all* the time."
"What's he on—horse?" Ricco asked, meaning heroin.
"Who knows with that creep?" Benny said.
I asked Benny if any special kind of boy went in for dope.
"The creeps," he said. "You know, the goofballs." He searched for a word.
"The *weak* kinds. Like Jo-Jo. There ain't nothing the guys can't do to him. Last
week, we took his pants off and make him run right in the middle of the street
without them."
"You wouldn't do that to Dutch," Ricco said.
"Man, Dutch *kicked* the habit," Benny said. "We told the guy he didn't kick
the habit, he was out of the crew. We were *through* with him. So he kicked it.
Cold turkey."[40]

This exchange occurred in the 1950s. Since then there may have been some alteration in attitudes toward drugs, especially marijuana, but there is still a good deal of negative feeling about drugs among gang members. Discussing "new gangs," a *Newsweek* reporter found:

> Their rules on drugs are notably strict. Most gang members have no aversion to dropping acid or blowing grass, but sticking a needle in their arms is seldom tolerated. In the Javelins, for instance, the penalty for messing with heroin is twenty lashes if you're a girl and a thrashing if you're a boy. Like the gangs of old, however, the chief object is still achieving a "bad rep."[41]

Thus, while some gang members use drugs, there has been little change in gang attitudes toward addictive drugs, which threaten a gang's reputation. For the gang members, there is a simple rationale for their stand on drugs. If they are attempting to achieve a reputation as a tough gang, they have to fight. Members who are junkies or strung out on an addictive drug cannot be relied on in a fight. Therefore, the gangs use their own means to control drug use among members. It is not moralism but practicality that guides their attitudes.

In terms of Merton's subcultural scheme, drug use is seen to be a retreatist adaption.[42] That is, those who turn to drugs have given up not only legitimate means to achieve success goals but also the culturally prescribed goals themselves. In more contemporary parlance, they have "dropped out."

It was found that many drug users had been engaged in other forms of delinquency before they turned to drugs; it appears, therefore, that instead of drug use leading to delinquency, it may be the failure to achieve success through delinquent means that leads to drug use. Cloward and Ohlin sum up their position on drug use and retreatist adaptations as follows:

> Generally speaking, it has been found that most drug addicts have a history of delinquent activity prior to becoming addicted. In Korbin's research, conducted in Chicago, "Persons who became heroin users were found to have engaged in delinquency *in a group-supported and habitual form* either prior to their use of drugs or simultaneously with their developing interest in drugs." And from a study of drug addicts in California, "A very significant tentative conclusion [was reached]: namely, that the use of drugs follows criminal activity and criminal association rather than the other way around, which is often thought to be the case." In other words, adolescents who are engaged in group-supported delinquency of the criminal or conflict type may eventually turn to drug use. Indeed, entire gangs sometimes shift from either criminal or conflict to retreatist adaptations.[43]

Individuals who take on the retreatist mode include boys who have low status in criminal or conflict gangs, which indicates failure through illegitimate means. As we saw, the gang's treatment of retreatist drug users lowers their status in the gang even further. Group adaptations of retreatism through drug use point to gangs that have lost their reputations and are no longer considered "reputable" by other gangs. Moreover, when a gang loses its standing, it also loses its ability to attract new members, and this spells the end of the gang. Thus, when the gang turns to hard, addictive drugs, it begins its disintegration.

GANG VIOLENCE

Violence is a major identifying characteristic of gangs, and we will now examine the nature of violence as it pertains to gangs. Horowitz and Schwartz conceptualize gang violence as follows:

> As we define it, a clash between peers must satisfy three conditions to be classified as an instance of gang violence. First, at least one party to a face-to-face encounter must feel that the presence of the other party in this setting on his behavior on this occasion endangers his safety or impugns his dignity. In light of the actor's definition of the situation as threatening and provocative, he must make a decision on the spot. If he does not assume the role of an aggressor, he may play the part of a victim.
>
> Second, the actor must respond to this emotionally charged situation in a way that visibly reveals his resolve (i.e., he feels his words, gestures, or actions express a definite intention) to inflict physical injury on his antagonist or by actually doing so.
>
> Third, the actor must account for his conduct on this occasion in terms of his status as a member of a gang.[44]

According to this definition, for gang violence to occur there must be (1) perceived danger and/or an attack of one's honor and (2) physical assault or a commitment to it, and (3) all this must be in terms of one's gang membership.

We have already discussed the aspect of real or imagined danger among lower-class gang members. If there is some actual danger, then there is likely to be a good deal of imagined danger in a gang milieu. However, it is probable that far fewer gang fights arise from threats to safety than from the desire to build or protect the gang's honor and reputation.

"Rep"

To many, it may seem quaint in this day and age to fight over "honor." However, not many years ago during the Vietnam war the President of the United States declared that this country would not pull American troops out of Vietnam until there was "peace with honor." Delinquent gangs are also willing to fight, maim, and even kill over honor. Since a gang's reputation is the measure of its standing in the community, gang members feel compelled to fight if their honor is challenged. Failure to respond with action to any slight to their reputation lowers a gang's status, and when a gang's status falls, much of the point in having a gang at all is lost.

In describing how a gang gained status, a former gang member described not only how a "rep" was built but also explained the etiquette of gang fights in terms of challenges and battlefields:

We got a lot of challenges, which gave us some headway, 'cause that meant a lot of fights was on our own ground. Now, a rival gang when they just outright challenged you always wanted to use you as a stepping stone, just like boxers do. They figure if they could chalk up a lot of wins in gang fights, then they'd be in a better position to fight somebody big. Now, the advantages of having a gang challenge your gang and fighting in your territory is who knows your territory better than you and your gang? Who knew all the little alleys and back alleys and the old houses to climb on top or to go in or what bushes to hide behind, or what old cars to hide behind, or how we would spring out and trap them, how we would close them in in a particular block?[45]

Even in situations where discretion was the better part of valor, it was still important for a gang to "do something" to maintain its reputation. In describing a battle with the biggest gang in Washington, D.C., a former gang member explained how his outnumbered gang managed to salvage some of their honor even in defeat.

We also had occasion to get in a semi-big rumble with them. What it was all about I don't really remember. But when they came, they came. They must have stole every truck and car in seeing view. There was so many of them that it really wasn't even a fight. Seeing all the trucks and all them niggers piling off, then we knew we didn't have a chance. . . . So we scattered. But we had to save face, 'cause when we scattered that didn't look too good. So we did a lot of picking, a lot of dummy attacks. We met on this playground field where we were supposed to fight. Twenty-five or thirty guys would rush the field, pop off some zip guns, throw some bricks and bottles, maybe get into a few tangles, and then back off. Hit them and run, hit them and run, until finally they just got tired of it. They didn't know where we was going to come from next, what we was going to do next, so finally they got off our turf. But when it go down in the books, they was the victors of that particular fight because of all of us scattering in the beginning.[46]

To understand the place of honor among lower-class boys and the relationship between honor and violence, we need to understand what resources for obtaining status are available to males in the lower-class community. Lower-class boys have little opportunity to accumulate material wealth legitimately, and athletic honors are limited to a highly skilled few. At the same time that legitimate status resources are limited, illegitimate resources abound. One such resource is violence, and it is used to maintain self-respect. However, in no way does this imply that the boys see violence as legitimate or good.

Miller paraphrases what he considers to be the typical gang boy's attitude toward violence:

"We know perfectly well that what we are doing is regarded as wrong, legally and morally; we also know that it violates the wishes and standards of many whose good opinion we value; yet, if we are to sustain our self-respect and our honor as males, we *must*, at this stage of our lives, engage in criminal behavior."[47]

In our earlier discussion of Erving Goffman's theory, we noted that character was built around risk. Since engaging in violence involves both the risk of one's physical well-being and the possibility of an encounter with the law, it has a double capacity to show the world that one is to be treated, if not honorably, at least seriously. A new gang trying to establish a "bad rep" is forced to commit some kind of violence to show everyone that it "means business." Once having established its reputation, a gang can ease off, for it has an established record that it is to be taken seriously.[48] However, to maintain a reputation, both within the community or neighborhood as a gang and within the gang as a member in good standing, one must deal forcefully with any threat to one's individual or collective honor. Otherwise, the gang or the gang member will lose status.

At the same time that one attempts to raise his own status and that of his gang, he also shows, or attempts to show, that other gangs have less status. To do this involves making statements to the effect that the other gang or its members somehow lack character. These insults in turn provoke the other gang to retaliate, and the result is further violence. Thus, we can see a cycle of defending one's honor and attacking another's. The cycle ends only when one gang becomes so strong so as to be able to coerce others to its ranks. Given the territorial parochialism of gangs and their lack of large-scale organizational skills, this is unlikely.

Middle-class youth, whose status is built on their parents' ability to provide them with material symbols, rarely display physical violence. In middle-class adolescent groups, a show of coercive force demonstrates a lack of control as well as of the intelligence to manipulate the situation to advantage without resorting to violence. Thus, lower-class youths in a middle-class setting find themselves in much the same situation as police in lower-class settings. They can bully the population into grudging compliance, but they cannot gain the respect and honor they seek. Therefore, since there is little payoff for being tough and engaging in violence (other than the organized fights on the gridiron), we find relatively little violence among middle-class youth or in suburban settings as compared to the slums, ghettos, and barrios.

Given the system of provocation and defense of honor, it would seem that there should always be a rash of violence, but according to Miller, violence is usually a matter of simple assault (a fistfight), and the severity is low.[49] There is evidence, however, that the severity of violence has increased.

Weapons

Horowitz and Schwartz attribute the increased violence to the use of guns by gang members.[50] Exactly how much gun use by delinquent gangs has increased has been the subject of much speculation and discussion. However, Miller points out that we should not jump to the conclusion that guns are a recent innovation among gangs.[51] Miller cites the following newspaper item from October 27, 1919, that was mentioned in Frederick M. Thrasher's classic work *The Gang:*

> "(The Elston gang member) was killed by a bullet from a .22-caliber rifle. In the last two years, when the two gangs realized the impotency of using bare knuckles and ragged stones, each turned to firearms."[52]

This is not to say that more guns are not being used today than previously. When conducting research on diversion in San Francisco, I found that a Youth Service Bureau director who was to be interviewed had been shot and killed the day before by gang members in the area where he was attempting to bring peace between gang members; and Horowitz and Schwartz cite the following instance to document the increased violence:

> In June 1973 the initiator of a partly successful area-wide peace movement was shot while standing in the corner in the park on the western section of the community, talking about peace to a group who was having problems with another gang. At a memorial ceremony, it was estimated that fifty gang members had been killed in gang conflicts over the past five years. This did not stop the shooting even though all the gangs in the area, except the gang that shot him, were present for the service.[53]

Thus, while we must use caution in stating that the gun is a "new" gang weapon, Miller points out that

> The prevalence, use, quality, and sophistication of weaponry in the gangs of the 1970's far surpasses anything known in the past, and is probably the single most significant characteristic distinguishing today's gangs from their predecessors.[54]

There is no evidence that the gangs in the 1980s will de-escalate gun use, for like the international arms race, in which each country attempts to outarm the others, once a gang begins using guns to maintain or establish its reputation, other gangs follow suit. Given the state of very real fear that gang members have of opposing gangs, we can expect increasing gun use and the deadly consequences until the gangs are forcefully disarmed, or out of self-preservation decide to disarm themselves.

Rumbles and Hits

What constitutes the dominant form of gang violence is problematic. The most popularized form of gang violence is the "rumble," in which two opposing gangs meet in full strength to do battle. This image of gang violence is especially relevant to the study of a gang's honor maintenance, but rumbles constitute only part of the overall picture of gang violence. To show the distribution of gang violence and the forms it takes on, Table 9-7 gives both the forms of violence and the victims.

From these data, which were gathered from newspaper accounts and therefore constitute only a partial representation of the incidents from an unknown sample, it is clear that the majority of gang violence is against other gang members, and the most common form is through the rumble (31.9 percent of all incidents). In number for all of the cities studied, this constitutes only about 96 gang fights in a period of two years. This is not very many rumbles, and, in fact, such rumbles are infrequent. Miller, in an observational study of gangs, found only one fight involving two gangs, but there were several threats of gang fights that never reached the stage of full-scale battle.[55] A fully developed gang fight was conceptualized by Miller as involving four stages: initial provocation; the initial attack; strategy, planning, and mobilization; and finally counterattack. The provocation was typically a question of honor, and the initial attack was an isolated fight. To defend its honor against further assault, the gang would then prepare for full-scale battle, and subsequently, unless there was some interference, the gangs would clash.

However, Miller found that even though the beginning stages of the gang fight were not uncommon, it was rare that the gangs would let it go to a

TABLE 9-7.   Victims of Gang Violence: Four Cities, 1973-1975[a]

	City				
Type of Victim	NYC N = 80	Chicago N = 58	Los Angeles N = 108	Philadelphia N = 55	Four Cities N = 301
Gang Member	51.2	56.9	66.7	65.5	60.5
Via rumble, warfare	36.2	22.4	35.2	28.2	31.9
Via band, individual assault	15.0	34.5	31.5	36.2	28.6
Nongang member	48.8	43.1	33.3	34.6	39.5
Peers	11.5	8.6	11.1	18.2	11.9
Children, adults	37.5	34.5	22.2	16.4	27.6
	100	100	100	100	100

[a]Miller, "Violence by Youth Gangs and Youth Groups as a Crime Problem in Major American Cities" (Washington, D.C.: U.S. Department of Justice, December 1975), p. 39.

full-scale battle. Sometimes each gang would send a representative to engage in a "fair one"—that is, to fight each other. Sometimes they would call the police and have them break up the fight before it could occur, or they would allow themselves to be "convinced" by a street worker to mediate their differences.

By preparing for an all-out fight, the gangs were able to maintain the impression of toughness and keep an honorable posture. At the same time, they were able to avoid the very real dangers of the fight. In this way, they could have their cake and eat it too. They would fight like devils if they were the subject of humiliation or if provoked, but the situation of provocation rarely resulted in anything more than an isolated beating, for during the time between the provocation and scheduled fight, they could usually rely on a face- and limb-saving solution.

The full-scale gang battle, while the kind of incident that makes headlines in the newspapers, and therefore the data in Table 9–7, is not the most deadly type of intergang violence. A planned gang fight can be prevented in face-saving ways, and if it does begin, it can be stopped by the police (who are usually alerted to its time and place). Ironically, what appears to be the most violent is, in fact, the least violent. Far more deadly—and apparently becoming the dominant form of intergang violence—is the "foray," where small groups make raids on rival gangs. The "foray" combined with the "hit" resembles the "search and destroy" missions and the guerilla raids of the Vietnam war. Miller describes them as follows:

> This pattern (the "foray"), locally called "guerilla warfare," and by other terms, involves relatively small (five to 10) raiding parties, frequently motorized, reconnoitering in search of rivals, and engaging in combat if contact is made. Forays are seldom announced, and count on surprise for their success. Raiding parties are almost always armed, and tactics are mobile, fluid, and often intricate. Since the raiding parties almost always carry firearms, such engagements frequently involve serious injuries and sometimes death. The "hit" resembles the foray in that it involves a small band of gang members generally in automobiles scouting out individual members of rival gangs, finding one or two, and blasting away at them with shotguns, rifles, or other firearms. In a variant of a hit, members of the marauding band leave the auto once a rival is located and engage him on foot.
>
> One pattern of engagement which combines several of the forms just cited was reported, with high consensus as to details, by a majority of Chicago respondents. A carful of gang members cruises the area of a rival gang, looking for rival gang members. If one is found, he will be attacked in one of several ways; gang members will remain in the car and shoot the victim, or will leave the car and beat and/or stab him. If the victim is wearing a gang sweater, this will be taken as a trophy, and in fact this kind of coup-counting is often given as the reason for the "hit" expedition. This type of initiatory incident (called a "preemptive strike" by one respondent) is followed by a retaliatory attack in numbers by the gangmates of the "strike" victim, generally in the form of an unannounced excursion into rival gang territory, although in some instances retaliation may

take the form of a planned rumble. The latter form was stated to be more common for conflict occurring in school environments, and among Latino gangs.

One respondent stated that while motorized forays and/or hits are common in Chicago, its consequences are less lethal than in Philadelphia, since the major type of weapons used, .22 pistols or rifles, are less likely to produce death or serious injury than the sawed-off shotguns characteristically employed in the latter city. A Philadelphia respondent reported that local gang members often conduct an initial reconnoitering excursion on bicycles, and return with cars once gang rivals have been located.[56]

To what extent these tactics of intergang violence are a reflection of larger conflicts in society is not known. However, in comparison to the rumble where the gangs were faced off to do battle, reminiscent of World War II and the Korean War in which great massed land battles occurred between opposing armies, the newer form of gang fighting (called "japping" after World War II) is very close to the style of warfare in Vietnam.

TURF

Gang territory, or "turf" or "dirt," is especially important in understanding gangs. On the one hand, turf defines the gang and the perimeters of gang activity; on the other hand, it serves as a boundary between gangs and therefore as a possible point of honor and conflict.

As a general sociological concept, we can take Lyman and Scott's definition of "home territories" as "areas where the regular participants have relative freedom of behavior and a sense of intimacy and control over the area."[57] These authors paraphrase Zorbaugh[58] and Jacobs[59] as follows:

> Among the most interesting examples of colonizing on the public lands are attempts by youths to stake out streets as home territories open only to members of their own clique and defended against invasion by rival groups. Subject always to official harassment by police and interference by other adults who claim the streets as public territories, youths resolve the dilemma by redefining adults as non-persons whose seemingly violative presence on the youths' "turf" does not challenge the latters' proprietorship.
>
> Streets are the most vulnerable to colonizing in this manner and indeed, as the early studies of the Chicago sociologists illustrated so well, streets and knots of juxtaposed streets become unofficial home areas to all those groups who require relatively secluded yet open space in which to pursue their interests or maintain their identities.[60]

The transformation of a public thoroughfare into a home territory is accomplished in part with the cooperation of those who live in or near the place where the gang hangs out. In his discussion of white gangs, Miller describes how a store owner watched over a gang of boys who hung around the corner where his store was located:

Ben was a bachelor, and while he had adopted the whole of the Bandit neighborhood as his extended family, he had taken on the 200 adolescents who hung out on the Bandit corner as his most immediate sons and daughters. Ben knew the background and present circumstances of every Bandit and followed their lives with intense interest and concern. Ben's corner-gang progeny were a fast-moving and mercurial lot, and he watched over their adventures and misadventures with a curious mixture of indignation, solicitude, disgust and sympathy.[61]

There was some reciprocity in the gang's recognition of home territory. Gang members would not allow members to shoplift in "their" corner store, nor would they allow boys from other neighborhoods or gangs to steal or cause trouble on their corner. Miller goes on to describe how members of the Bandits protected their corner store:

At least three times during the observation period corner boys from outside neighborhoods entered the store obviously bent on stealing or creating a disturbance. On each occasion these outsiders were efficiently and forcefully removed by nearby Bandits, who then waxed indignant at the temerity of "outside" kids daring to consider Ben's a target of illegal activity. One consequence, then, of Ben's seigneurial relationship to the Bandits was that his store was unusually well protected against theft, armed and otherwise, which presented a constant hazard to the small-store owner in Midcity.[62]

The extent to which gang members consider their corner to be home territory was documented by Werthman and Piliavin in their study of a West Coast gang:

Since all routine life functions are at one time or another performed on the streets, the conventional standards of public decorum are considerably relaxed. Entrance into the private space or hangout occasions a noticeable relaxation of physical posture. Shoulders slump, shirttails appear, and greetings are exchanged with an abandon that is only achieved by people who usually receive houseguests in the kitchen. A good deal of time is also spent combing hair in front of store windows and dancing to rock and roll (often without a partner and without music) as if completely absorbed in the privacy of a bedroom.

Yet as soon as the boys leave the street corner, they become self-consciously absorbed in the demands of a public role. They pay careful attention to uniform —either casually immaculate ("looking sharp") or meticulously disheveled ("looking bad")—and cover the territory in the characteristic hiking style ("walking pimp"). Most of the boys would no sooner start a poker game two blocks away from the privacy of the hangout than more respectable citizens would think of making love in their front yards. Of couse there are many notable exceptions to this rule, and on an irregular basis most boys do both.[63]

The patterns of carving out home territories in public places can be understood, in part at least, in terms of the limited availability of private space to most gang members. Private space can be defined in terms of *continuous discretionary* control over who crosses one's boundaries.[64] By this definition, the home territories of the gangs are to them at least private places. However, the police, among others, do not recognize the gang's right of possession of their territory even though they may well understand that a certain gang considers a certain corner to be its own. Since the police have restricted access to private places, homeowners, apartment renters, and the like are relatively free from police intervention. Middle-class youths typically have access to large yards or their own rooms as well as other places, such as rooms in their schools, where they can congregate without fear of disturbance or invasion. Lower-class youths, on the other hand, have limited access to private space, and the space that has been made available to them by public agencies is either uncongenial to their desired activities (that is, subject to restrictions as to time and form of activity) or in short supply (for example, school playgrounds). Therefore, the youths make private space out of public space, and therein lies their conflict with the law. And as Stinchecombe has noted, the less access one has to private space, the more likely one is to come to the attention of the police.

SUMMARY

Gangs constitute a stable pattern of delinquency in American society, spanning generations. A substantial amount of juvenile delinquency is linked to gangs, and even though it is impossible to blame gangs for the majority or even a plurality of delinquent activities, delinquent gangs loom large in contributing to the more violent forms of delinquency.

It is tempting to point at urban slums, poverty, racism, ignorance, and the dilemmas of postindustrial society to explain gangs, because it is clear that children of the urban poor, especially ethnic minorities, make up the bulk of gang membership. However, to make such an assertion deflects from the delinquent activities of middle-class "cliques," who though not as violent as the lower-class "gangs," nevertheless engage in a good deal of group delinquency. Moreover, the violence of the typical gang is not necessarily linked to poverty but rather to gaining "respect." One might argue that the lack of status among the lower class in general generates the gangs as a status-developing group, but when we consider the meager status resources for juveniles as a whole, we may reach another conclusion: namely, that ganglike behavior can be found in all social strata. And, indeed, we do find delinquent group activities among all youths, the variation being in the types of delinquency and structures of the groups. The lower-class groups identified as gangs tend to be more violent and more structured than their middle-class counterparts, who tend to commit property and consensual crimes (for example, drug use) and exhibit little or no structure.

To be in a gang appears to do two important things. First, it is a means for establishing character—a "reputation," "to be somebody"—not available in the juvenile role. A boy can be a "man" among his peers and someone who is "taken seriously," aspects of identity for juveniles that are denied in larger society. Second, gangs constitute "action," the thrills of taking chances with others with whom to share the experience. Each youthful generation passes on to the next the gang formula for this combined group-supported self and activity. While we might wish for something less violent and destructive, at least gangs can be understood to be something other than a wholly mindless rabble that society wishes would go away.

NOTES

1. Walter Miller, "White Gangs," *Trans-action* (September 1969), pp. 11–26.
2. Gilbert Geis, "Juvenile Gangs," from *Report of the President's Committee on Juvenile Delinquency and Youth Crime* (Washington, D.C.: Government Printing Office, 1967), pp. 1–16.
3. Miller, "White Gangs," pp. 11–12.
4. Walter Miller, "Violence by Youth Gangs and Youth Groups as a Crime Problem in Major American Cities" (Washington, D.C.: U.S. Department of Justice, December 1975).
5. *Ibid.*
6. Miller, "White Gangs," p. 25.
7. Don C. Gibbons, *Delinquent Behavior* (Englewood Cliffs, N.J.: Prentice-Hall, 1970), pp. 126–141.
8. William Chambliss, "The Saints and the Roughnecks," *Society* 11:24–31 (November–December 1973).
9. Miller, "Violence by Youth Gangs . . . ," p. 9.
10. *Ibid.*
11. John Allen, *Assault with a Deadly Weapon* (New York: McGraw-Hill, 1977), p. 45.
12. *Ibid.*, pp. 47–49.
13. *Ibid.*, p. 17.
14. Leonard D. Savitz, Michael Lalli, and Lawrence Rosen, "City Life and Delinquency—Victimization, Fear of Crime and Gang Membership" (Washington, D.C.: U.S. Department of Justice, April 1977).
15. *Ibid.*, p. 49.
16. *Ibid.*, p. 51.
17. Miller, "White Gangs."
18. Lewis Yablonsky, *The Violent Gang* (Baltimore: Penguin Books, 1962).
19. James Short, Jr., *Gang Delinquency and Delinquent Subcultures* (New York: Harper & Row, 1968).
20. John Quicker, "The Chicana Gang: A Preliminary Description," paper presented at the annual meetings of the Pacific Sociological Association, San Jose, Calif. (1974, mimeographed).
21. Miller, "White Gangs," p. 25.
22. Miller, "White Gangs"; Quicker; Richard A. Cloward and Lloyd E. Ohlin, *Delinquency and Opportunity: A Theory of Delinquent Gangs* (New York: Free Press, 1960); Albert Cohen, *Delinquent Boys* (New York: Free Press, 1955).
23. Martin R. Haskell and Lewis Yablonsky, *Juvenile Delinquency* (Chicago: Rand-McNally, 1974).
24. Miller, "White Gangs."
25. Quicker, p. 10.

26. *Ibid.*
27. Haskell and Yablonsky, pp. 179–180.
28. Lewis A. Coser, *The Functions of Social Conflict* (New York: Free Press, 1956).
29. Short.
30. Haskell and Yablonsky, p. 175.
31. Short, p. 20.
32. Walter Bernstein, "The Cherubs Are Rumbling," *The New Yorker* (September 21, 1957).
33. Irving Spergel, *Racketville, Slumtown, and Haulburg* (Chicago: University of Chicago Press, 1964).
34. Haskell and Yablonsky, p. 174.
35. Short, p. 81.
36. Miller, "White Gangs," p. 17.
37. *Ibid.*
38. Spergel, p. 30.
39. *Ibid.*, p. 51.
40. Bernstein, p. 28.
41. "The New Gangs," *Newsweek* (May 8, 1970).
42. Robert K. Merton, *Social Theory and Social Structure* (New York: Free Press, 1957).
43. Cloward and Ohlin, p. 177.
44. Ruth Horowitz and Gary Schwartz, "Honor, Normative Ambiguity and Gang Violence," *American Sociological Review, 39:*238–251 (1974).
45. Allen, p. 46.
46. *Ibid.*, pp. 48–49.
47. Miller, "White Gangs," p. 23.
48. Erving Goffman, *Interaction Ritual* (New York: Doubleday, 1967), p. 235.
49. Walter Miller, "Violent Crimes in City Gangs," *Annals of the Academy of Political and Social Sciences* (March 1966), pp. 97–112.
50. Horowitz and Schwartz.
51. Miller, "Violence by Youth Gangs and Youth Groups . . . ," p. 41.
52. Frederick M. Thrasher, *The Gang* (Chicago: University of Chicago Press, 1936).
53. Horowitz and Schwartz, pp. 239–240.
54. Miller, "Violence by Youth Gangs and Youth Groups . . . ," p. 41.
55. Miller, "Violent Crimes in City Gangs."
56. Miller, "Violence by Youth Gangs and Youth Groups . . . ," pp. 36–38.
57. Stanford Lyman and Marvin B. Scott, *A Sociology of the Absurd* (New York: Appleton, 1970).
58. Harvey W. Zorbaugh, *The Gold Coast and the Slum* (Chicago: University of Chicago Press, 1929).
59. Jane Jacobs, *The Death and Life of Great American Cities* (New York: Vintage Books, 1961).
60. Lyman and Scott, pp. 58–59.
61. Miller, "White Gangs," p. 15.
62. *Ibid.*
63. Irving Piliavin and Scott Briar, "Police Encounters with Juveniles," *American Journal of Sociology, 70:*206–214 (September 1964).
64. Arthur L. Stinchecombe, "Institutions of Privacy in the Determination of Police Administrative Practice," *American Journal of Sociology, 69:*150–160 (September 1963).

10 Police-Juvenile Encounters

INTRODUCTION

The police represent the link between the community and the official processing system, and as such they constitute the first encounter juveniles typically
have with the legal system. The significance of police–juvenile encounters lies
in the fact that what the police do when they make judgments concerning the
fate of juveniles for delinquent acts can be important in determining the
youth's status as a delinquent. For the most part the police reflect the community and its assessment of juveniles as being delinquent or not.[1] At the same
time, though, the police take specific actions resulting in general social assessments—labels—of juveniles that have far more influence than any single
informal judgment by the community. As a result, the police have the power
to transform informal community understandings into official records, and so
the study of the situations in which the police must make official decisions
is central to understanding delinquency.

The police have far more discretion with juveniles than with adults in arrest
situations. The following alternatives are used by police when they encounter
juveniles who have broken the criminal law or committed juvenile-status
offenses:

1. Arrest and placement in detention (for example, juvenile hall).
2. Issue citation (traffic; petty theft) requiring court appearance and/or
   official record.
3. Arrest and placement in diversion unit (mainly for juvenile-status
   offenses), but no court appearance or delinquent record.
4. Take juvenile home to parents with reprimand but no further action by
   juvenile justice system.
5. Warn and release.

Depending on the course of action the police take, the juvenile will either
be cast further into the official processing system or away from it. The question we will address in this chapter involves the elements that go into police
decisions and the nature of the situations in which these decisions are made.
To the extent to which the police choose the official processing system, the
juvenile is likely to be labeled a real delinquent, while the more informal
choices result in less labeling or no label at all. The two basic elements in the
police decision we will examine in order to assess the influences of discretion
are the situations in which the police make contact with the juveniles and the
structure of the police department. First, in examining the encounters between the police and juveniles, we will look at the seriousness of the crime,
the juvenile's previous record, what the citizen complainant wants done, and
other variables that go into the police officer's decision. Second, we will look
at the structural variables that determine the options police officers have and

the pressures placed on them by the department and the community for taking various courses of action in their work with juveniles.

ENCOUNTERS WITH THE POLICE

In a classic study of police-juvenile encounters, Piliavin and Briar[2] examined the nature of juveniles' demeanor and the likelihood of arrest. With cases involving serious crimes, such as robbery, homicide, or rape, the police exercised very little discretion with juveniles or adults; however, in about 90 percent of the cases studied by Piliavin and Briar, the actual violation played only a minor role in the police decision to be lenient or harsh in dealing with the juvenile actor. The researchers found that some juveniles were released and others were arrested for similar offenses, and the question they posed was, "What is it in the discretion situation that leads the police to choose a more lenient or a harsher disposition?"

Next to the seriousness of the offense, they found that the juvenile's prior record was the most important influence. If the police knew that the juvenile had a delinquent record, they were more likely to make an arrest than if the juvenile had no record, but police in the field rarely have access to records. However, sometimes an officer would know the juvenile personally and whether or not there was a police record, and in such situations this information could be used as a resource in making a decision.

Since the police usually had no knowledge of a juvenile's record, Piliavin and Briar sought to learn whether or not a juvenile's demeanor in the discretion situation had any effect on the officer's decision. They found that the more cooperative a youth was with the police, the more likely he was to receive a mild disposition. Those juveniles who were polite and appeared to be apologetic for their actions were most often given an informal reprimand or "admonished and released."* On the other hand, juveniles who were uncooperative and generally showed lack of respect for the police were most likely to be arrested or given a citation or official reprimand.

Table 10–1 shows the disposition of 66 cases observed by Piliavin and Briar. As the table clearly indicates, juveniles who were uncooperative were far more likely to be arrested than those who were cooperative. Those who were cooperative were far more likely to receive the least severe disposition (24:1). In fact, it was extremely unlikely that uncooperative youths would receive a lenient disposition. We can conclude that, given the same crime, a youth's demeanor, not his delinquent involvement, is the chief determinant of his being arrested.

*When there is an "informal reprimand," the police write up a "field interrogation report" describing their contact with the juvenile. No record of any sort is made when they merely "admonish and release" a juvenile.

TABLE 10–1.   Severity of Police Disposition by Youth's Demeanor[a]

Severity of Police Disposition	Youth's Demeanor		Total
	Cooperative	Uncooperative	
Arrest (most severe)	2	14	16
Citation or official reprimand	4	5	9
Informal reprimand	15	1	16
Admonish and release (least severe)	24	1	25
Total	45	21	66

[a] Irving Piliavin and Scott Briar, "Police Encounters with Juveniles," *American Journal of Sociology, 70:* 210 (September 1964).

In the Piliavin and Briar study, cues in the interaction situation were used to determine whether or not the youth under suspicion was a "good kid." Included in these cues were the "youth's group affiliations, age, race, grooming, dress, and demeanor." Those who were most likely *not* to present the necessary cues to be considered a "good" or "decent" boy were

older juveniles, members of known delinquent gangs, Negroes, youths with well-oiled hair, black jackets, and soiled denims or jeans (the presumed uniform of "tough boys"), and boys who in their interactions with officers did not manifest what were considered to be appropriate signs of respect.[3]

The fact that the chief criterion for arrest was a lack of manifest respect toward the police and the situation did not escape the notice of the boys who most frequently encountered the police. When asked how best to avoid arrest, one gang member responded:

If you kiss their ass and say, "Yes Sir, No Sir," and all that jazz, then they'll let you go. If you don't say that, then they gonna take you in. And if you say it funny they gonna take you in. Like, "Yes *Sir,* No *Sir!*" But if you stand up and say it straight, like "Yes Sir" and "No Sir" and all that, you're cool.[4]

Since the boys were aware of what the police expected of them, one might wonder why they did not always display this demeanor. That is, why did some of the boys act in a way that they knew would anger the police in a situation where the police were deciding whether or not to send them to jail?

Among the gang boys, the reason was bound up in their notion of honor and respect. "Kissing ass" would enable them to maintain their freedom. However, it would cost them the respect of their peers and themselves. Through artful displays of insolence, the boys can maintain their dignity while not giving the police enough rope to hang them on demeanor; however, if the police demand more than civility, the boys will often respond with acts of blatant disrespect. Thus, by demanding more respect than they expect to receive, the police can set up situations in which both their own authority and the honor of those they confront are at stake. As long as the situation is framed in such a manner, there can be no winners. Similarly, if the gang boys refuse to give the police the minimal respect they accord to others, they set up threats to the policeman's authority, and the same cycle is started all over again.

Except for serious crimes, it would seem that police prejudice and character cues play more important roles in an arrest situation than does the nature of the law violation. We certainly cannot deny the importance of prejudice; however, in an extensive study of policy encounters with juveniles, Black and Reiss found that the most important factor in the police disposition decision was the complainant's desire that an arrest be made. In no case where the complainant lobbied for leniency did the police arrest a juvenile; and in cases where the complainant demanded an arrest, the police were more likely to arrest the suspect than in any other type of situation. In the cases studied, 21 percent of the black victims and 15 percent of the whites demanded that an arrest be made. Moreover, white complainants were more likely to request an informal disposition (58 percent of the cases), while only 31 percent of the blacks showed a preference for an informal disposition.[5]

Given the relative preference for leniency in situations with white complainants, we could expect more white offenders to receive informal dispositions instead of an arrest. In encounters with blacks, we find that there is a 21-percent arrest rate, and in police encounters with whites there is only an 8-percent arrest rate.[6] That is, the arrest rate for blacks is well over twice that for whites. In situations where *only* the police and the suspect are present (that is, no complainant is present), a white youth is only slightly less likely to be arrested than a black youth—10 percent versus 14 percent, respectively. Thus, even though black youths in general are more likely to be arrested than whites, it appears that the police act to minimize the inequity in arrests. The citizens who make the calls and are present when police must decide whether or not to make an arrest play an extremely important role in the determination of the disposition. The racial difference in arrests can be attributed largely to citizen preferences and not solely or even necessarily to police prejudice.

Black and Reiss also examined suspects' demeanor. Unlike Piliavin and Briar, they did not find a direct relationship between demeanor and the likelihood of arrest. Black and Reiss distinguished degrees of deference from "very deferential" to "civil" to "antagonistic." We would expect the most arrests in situations where juveniles behaved antagonistically and the least where juveniles acted in a very deferential manner. However, this was not the case. Those who were antagonistic were the most likely to be arrested, those who were very deferential were next most likely to be arrested, and those who were merely civil were the least likely to be arrested.[7]

In accounting for this pattern, Black and Reiss suggest that juveniles who know that they are liable to arrest and serious sanctions may attempt to behave in an especially deferential way in an effort to stave off going to jail. Realizing that those who are overly polite may be hiding something, the police may be more likely to arrest them than youths who are simply civil in their manner. In the cases examined by Black and Reiss, the majority of juveniles (57 percent) were civil in encounters with police. Juveniles were antagonistic in 16 percent of the cases and very deferential in 11 percent. The relationship between the juvenile suspect's degree of deference and the likelihood of his being arrested suggests that most juveniles took the course of action that was least likely to draw suspicion to themselves.

Perhaps the most important thing to note in the Black and Reiss study is the overall leniency of the police. In fully 76 percent of the situations where the police encountered antagonistic black juveniles, no arrests were made, and this group had the highest likelihood of arrest. In only 12 percent of their encounters with juveniles where the police either suspected or were certain that a crime had been committed did they make an arrest. In part this low percentage is due to the need for situational evidence. It is rare for the police to make an arrest without strong evidence that a crime has been committed by the person who is taken into custody. Even though arrests can be made on the basis of "suspicion" of almost anything, the police do not appear to be abusing their power to make arrests.

The exact extent to which the police make judgments mainly on the basis of demeanor is uncertain, however. There is clear evidence that the *police believe* that they make decisions on the basis of how the juvenile behaves when questioned. Stark reported that the police said they used the "attitude test" to determine whether or not to make arrests.[8] From observations of the police on the West Coast and in the Southeast I found that the police also mentioned the "attitude test."[9] However, when examining the data from these studies, it was found that there was no overall relationship between citizens' demeanor and patterns of arrests. In part the problem lies in complainant intervention, for as we have shown, the police base their decisions largely on the basis of what the citizen wants. If the suspect in an encounter behaves antagonistically toward the police officer but the complainant refuses to supply the cooperation necessary to establish probable cause for arrest, then there is little the police can do, even though they might want to arrest the person.

In situations in which only the police and the suspect are present, demeanor appears to play a much greater role. In a study of drunks, Lundman found that those who show a "high level of impoliteness" were far more likely to be arrested than those with a low level of impoliteness.[10] Of those who show a low level of impoliteness in encounters with the police, only 26 percent were arrested, while 44 percent of those who displayed a high level were arrested.

A further consideration the police were observed to make revolved around the nature of the occasions in which they encountered citizens. In a study in the Southeast I found that much of the antagonism observed was already in the situation when the police arrived, and the hostility was not directed solely at the police but instead was part of a preexisting situation.[11] For example, in a situation in which juveniles had been in a fight, all of the combatants were angry when the police arrived, and the police appeared to understand that the antagonism which was directed toward them was in fact merely part of the situation. The observers recorded the juveniles' antagonism, but they did not specify its direction. Therefore, it is likely that in the Black and Reiss study the same phenomenon existed—namely, there was a generalized situational antagonism instead of specific hostility toward the police. Typically, the police were able to separate the combatants and send them home, and even though this action was not met with cordiality by the juveniles involved, the situation was restored to the satisfaction of the police.

What the police do appear to be doing is following an informal processing or harassment model of controlling juveniles instead of the formal processing model.[12] That is, instead of sending juveniles into the formal mechanisms of the juvenile justice system by invoking the law, they tend to "keep them in line" by harassing them. The police view the juvenile justice system as at once too harsh and too lenient. For those whom they consider "hard-core" delinquents, the police see the juvenile justice system as too soft; for those who merely need a "good spanking" or a firm hand, they see the imposition of a delinquent record as far too harsh a punishment. Using their own informal techniques, they can mete out the appropriate amount of sanctioning to juveniles and at the same time maintain some semblance of law and order.

This kind of "curbside justice," as it is often called by the police, is for the most part a breach of police duty, if not actually against the law. However, informal handling of juveniles is by no means necessarily a bad or corrupt practice. Of course, it can lead to excesses and brutality. Typically, though, the police see their activities in terms of their mandate of enforcing the law and maintaining order. By harassing juveniles, they are able to maintain order and enforce the law, yet at the same time control all aspects of the situation. If they merely make arrests, they lose control of the fate of the juveniles. A juvenile who is freed without sanction by the juvenile authorities for what the police regard as serious misconduct no longer sees the police as a threat, and the police feel that they have lost respect and authority in his eyes. More importantly, though, the police believe they are better able than the juvenile authorities to individualize sanctions and work through complex situations. In their view, they can differentiate between kids who are "really bad" and those who are not, since they are the only ones in the criminal justice system who see the kids in the streets.

Discretion and Departmental Structure

In a study comparing two cities, Wilson attempted to determine whether police professionalism had any effect on police handling of delinquents.[13] The "Western City" police department was characterized as a modern department with a high degree of professionalism; "Eastern City" was one with low professionalism. The police officers of Eastern City had a punitive and restrictive attitude toward juveniles and interpreted problems in terms of personal and familial morality. In contrast, Western City police were more likely to interpret problems in terms of psychosocial complexities and saw the solution in terms of rehabilitation instead of punishment.

It was expected that the officers of Western City would be less likely to make arrests or engage in actions that would lead to formal legal sanction. However, the opposite results were found. The department in Western City, which was considered more likely to restrict the freedom of juveniles, processed a larger proportion of suspected offenders and arrested a larger proportion of those processed. This finding can be accounted for in part by the stricter regulations in a "professionalized" police department. Officers are more likely to "go by the book" in such a department, and, instead of giving a juvenile a "second chance," are more likely to arrest him, sincerely believing that the rehabilitation promised by the correctional facility will in fact come about.

The far less professionalized Eastern City police operated with what would appear to be much greater leniency. They had a "pass system" whereby a juvenile would be given a reprimand the first few times he was caught. Even though this is clearly "unprofessional," it cannot be considered inhumane. One officer explained it as follows:

Most of the kids around here get two or three chances. Let me give you an example. There was this fellow around here who is not vicious, not, I think, what you'd call bad; he's really sort of a good kid. He just can't move without getting into trouble. I don't know what there is about him. . . . I'll read you his record. 1958—he's picked up for shoplifting, given a warning. 1958—again a few months later was picked up for illegal possession [of dangerous weapons]. He had some dynamite caps and railroad flares. Gave him another warning. 1959—he stole a bike. Got a warning. 1960—he broke into some freight cars. [He was taken to court and] continued without a finding [that is, no court action] on the understanding that he would pay restitution. Later the same year he was a runaway from home. No complaint was brought against him. Then in 1960 he started getting into serious stuff. There was larceny and committing an unnatural act with a retarded boy. So he went up on that one and was committed to [the reformatory] for nine months. Got out. In 1962 he was shot while attempting a larceny in a junkyard at night. . . . Went to court, continued without a finding. Now that's typical of a kid who just sort of can't stay out of trouble. He only went up once out of, let me see . . . eight offenses. I wouldn't call him a bad kid despite the record. . . . The bad kids: we don't have a lot of those.[14]

As can be seen from this account, the boy was given a number of chances before the police took any action, and after his arrest he was given several breaks by the courts. Most interesting, however, is the officer's conception of the boy. One would think, given his extensive delinquent record, that the police would characterize someone like this as "bad"; however, as we noted when discussing the Piliavin and Briar study, a juvenile's being seen as basically good or bad depends not so much on what he does in terms of breaking the law but on whether the juvenile shows the proper deference to the police officer. Furthermore, although the police will arrest some of those who do show the proper demeanor, this does not mean that the police consider them "bad." When they "have to" arrest someone they consider to be a "basically good" kid, they tend to think of the juvenile as "falling into" or being "unable to avoid" trouble instead of as one who *causes* the trouble. The "bad" kids create trouble and the "good" kids somehow stumble into it. By focusing most of their attention on the "bad" kids (that is, those who do not show the proper respect for police authority), the police believe they are making efforts in the right direction.

Social Class and Discretion

Given this conception of delinquency by the police, we find that lower-class and upper-middle-class groups of boys who come to the attention of the police receive different treatment by the police. In a study by William Chambliss, the "Saints," who consisted of upper-middle-class boys, were seen as "basically good" boys by the police, and the "Roughnecks," a lower-class group, were seen as "basically bad." Chambliss describes the differential treatment of the boys as follows:

> The local police saw the Saints as good boys who were among leaders of the youth in the community. Rarely, the boys might be stopped in town for speeding or for running a stop sign. When this happened the boys were always polite, contrite and pleaded for mercy. They received the mercy they asked for. None ever received a ticket or was taken into the precinct by the local police; [however,] over the period that the [Roughnecks were] under observation, each member was arrested a number of times and spent at least one night in jail. While most were never taken to court, two of the boys were sentenced to six months' incarceration in boys' schools.[15]

As can be seen, one group presented themselves to the community and the police as "good boys" and were accepted as such, but their activities belied this image, for even though the Saints did what was necessary when confronted by authority, they were by no means nondelinquent. In fact, Chambliss points out,

In sheer number of illegal acts, the Saints were the more delinquent. They were truant from school for at least part of the day almost every day of the week. In addition, their drinking and vandalism occurred with surprising regularity. The Roughnecks, in contrast, engaged sporadically in delinquent episodes. While these episodes were frequent, they certainly did not occur on a daily or even a weekly basis.[16]

Why were the Saints treated with leniency while the Roughnecks were not? First, the Saints were not so likely to fight. In fact, they never fought either among themselves or with others outside their group. This is not to say that they did not endanger others' physical well-being, for their driving was at best risky and at worst nearly fatal. The Roughnecks, on the other hand, did engage in physical conflict, and this behavior was viewed as indicative of delinquency. It was not difficult for the police and others to formulate activities such as drinking and truancy as "high jinks" or "youthful pranks," but fighting was more difficult for them to regard as anything other than outright delinquency.

The Roughnecks were also more visible than the Saints in their delinquent activities. As Chambliss explains:

> This differential visibility was a direct function of the economic standing of the families. The Saints had access to automobiles and were able to remove themselves from the sight of the community. In as routine a decision as where to go to have a milkshake after school, the Saints stayed away from the mainstream of community life. Lacking transportation, the Roughnecks could not make it to the edge of town. The center of town was the only practical place for them to meet since their homes were scattered throughout the town and any noncentral meeting place put an undue hardship on some members. Through necessity the Roughnecks congregated in a crowded area where everyone in the community passed frequently, including teachers and law-enforcement officers. They could easily see the Roughnecks hanging around the drugstore.[17]

As we noted earlier, the Saints were more likely to act contrite when approached by the police. The Roughnecks sometimes tried to act pleasant, but their general disdain for the police and other authorities usually showed through any facade of deference. In part the nature of the interaction between each group and the authorities reflected the reciprocal expectations of the boys and the police. The Saints were virtually certain to receive leniency in response to their deferential demeanor, and they were generally approached by the police, teachers, and other authorities in a civil manner. Being treated politely, it was easier for them to reciprocate in kind. The Roughnecks, who were assumed to be "bad," were approached with less civility and reacted with less civility.

A final consideration is how the police and the community came to see one group as "good" and the other as "bad," although both committed delinquent acts. As we have noted, the Saints' activities were characterized as "sowing wild oats" or by some similarly disarming idiom. Delinquent activities that are discussed and regarded as nondelinquent are for all intents and purposes nondelinquent. When an interpretive scheme is provided for particular acts, the acts are *made to be* whatever the scheme elaborates them to be. An underlying pattern is assumed to go with a given linguistic formulation, and the particulars are elaborated in terms of the formulation.[18] More simply, there is a reflexive relationship between talk about the activities and the activities themselves. The talk elaborates the specific sense of the action, and the action warrants the particular talk. Thus, when people talked about the Saints' vandalism as "pranks," the authorities were dealing with mere pranks instead of with vandalism. Conversely, when the Roughnecks' "goofing off" was formulated as "delinquency" by the authorities, then the social reality of the situation was delinquency. What is important is not the content of the act, for the content of acts is always subject to an infinite number of linguistic formulations given an unlimited number of possible underlying assumptions. Rather, it is the interpretive practices that lead to one sense or another that must be understood. Delinquency is inexorably tied to the interaction between events and the formulations that interpret the events in one sense or another.

JUVENILE OFFICERS

Juvenile Detail

Urban police departments and sheriffs' offices typically have special assignments and positions for handling juveniles and offenses related to juveniles. Included in the duties of juvenile officers are all juvenile-status offenses, crimes committed by juveniles that are petty, and certain crimes committed against juveniles by adults, mainly child abuse and child molesting. For the most part, working in the juvenile detail is not considered a choice position. Juvenile officers are called "kiddie kops" by other police officers, and much of the work they do involves minor crimes which go unheralded in the department. Youthful offenders are characterized as typically "nonserious" and "minor" in nature, and even though they account for a high proportion of serious crimes, such as robbery, burglary, and sexual assault, juvenile investigators usually deal only with the petty offenses. Juveniles involved in more serious crimes are handled by the investigative units that deal with serious crimes (for example, the robbery detail investigates all robberies, including those involving juveniles). This arrangement belies the difficulty of the work in the juvenile detail, because even though the investigators do not get the "celebrity crimes," they have a wider variety of problems to deal with than any other investigative unit in police departments. Not only must they deal with numerous general crimes, they also must cope with all of the juvenile-status offenses.[19]

In a study of juvenile detectives I found a relationship between the policy of the juvenile detail and the official labeling of certain juveniles.[20] In all police departments crimes are ranked on a hierarchy, from those that will receive the most investigative attention to those that will receive the least. In the juvenile detail reports of runaway juveniles received the highest priority and therefore the most investigative efforts, while more common cases, such as petty theft, received less investigative time. Table 10–2, a log of the reports received over a three-month period by two juvenile detectives, provides an idea of the frequency with which various different types of crime are reported in the juvenile detail.[21]

The table is a typical representation of the kinds of activities that lead to contact between juveniles and the police. However, the detectives, as we have noted, spend most of their time on cases involving runaways, and it is this group of juveniles who had the greatest probability of coming into contact with law officers.

In a study of the distribution of serious crimes, however, runaways were ranked 137th out of 140,[22] while petty theft and malicious mischief, the two most commonly reported juvenile offenses, were ranked higher in seriousness. Since the police usually devote most investigative resources to those crimes considered socially and legally the most serious, it is worth noting that

TABLE 10–2.   Reports Received by Juvenile Detectives

Crime	Number of Reports	Percent of Total Cases
Theft	81	47.4
Malicious mischief	40	23.4
Runaway	17	10.0
Mailbox tampering	12	7.0
Burglary*	4	2.3
Wife/child beating	3	1.8
Assault	3	1.8
Possession of stolen property	4	2.3
Loitering around schoolyard	1	0.6
Mental case	1	0.6
Child stealing	1	0.6
Forgery	1	0.6
Oral copulation	1	0.6
Annoying children	1	0.6
Prowler	1	0.6
Total	171	

*Since in most burglary cases it was unknown whether the suspect was juvenile or adult, these cases were typically worked by burglary detectives.

much police time is spent hunting down juveniles who ran away from home. In order to understand the intensity of police efforts to find runaways, it is necessary to understand the interaction between parents of runaways and the police.

Those who report that their children have run away from home are generally very concerned and distraught. They demand action. In contrast, those who report thefts rarely expect to see their missing goods again. Moreover, detectives often tell victims of theft that there is little chance of recovering their goods, since typically there are no leads in such cases. Failure to recover missing juveniles, however, is cause for alarm among parents, who put increased pressure on the department. Even though the act of running away is in itself not considered to be socially serious, it is extremely serious to the parents; juvenile detectives therefore give these cases the highest priority.

The result is that juveniles are more likely to be labeled delinquent for running away from home than for any other delinquent acts. This is not because the juvenile officers believe that runaways are the most dangerous delinquents; they do not consider them to be delinquents at all. Rather, the department gives highest priority to runaway cases as a result of parental pressure, and it is for this reason that runaways are the most likely to be officially judged and recorded as delinquents.

Because juvenile detectives in most cases, work mainly if not exclusively with juveniles, they have greater discretion than other detectives. With runaways, of course, there is virtually no discretion; if a juvenile detective finds a runaway, he has no choice but to take the youth into custody. In cases where the detectives do have discretion, they assess the juvenile's character in terms of appearance, demeanor, and past record. Unlike most other officers, who are regular patrol officers or detectives in other details, the juvenile detective who contacts a runaway usually has an accurate idea of the youth's previous record. Juveniles with a record are assessed not merely in terms of what the record reports but also in terms of how those detectives who were involved in the case characterize the record. If a juvenile has been in trouble before, the record reflects just those items which could be officially put down on paper. Subjective assessments of the juvenile's moral character are not in the police records, and in order to find out what the juvenile is "really" like, the detectives often ask the officers who were actually involved in the case. Thus, a long record of contact with the authorities is not automatically taken to be indicative of a juvenile's moral decline by the detectives. Conversely, a short record of apparently trivial offenses does not necessarily indicate a "good kid." Sometimes a detective who has been involved in a case dealing with a juvenile explains that the juvenile is not so bad but got into trouble because of circumstances beyond his control.

If a juvenile has no record at all or an equivocal record, the juvenile detectives rely on their encounter with the juvenile to make an assessment. In one observed case, a juvenile detective was sent to investigate a theft by a boy who had a record involving a minor incident in the past. The detective explained before the visit that he had no intention of arresting the boy, especially if he admitted the crime and returned the money that he was reported to have taken. When the detective went to the boy's house, he was not at home, and the mother asked him to return later. When the detective returned, he found that the house had been cleaned by the boy's mother and a Bible placed in full view, along with the boy's athletic trophies. The boy appeared in athletic shorts, explaining that he had been practicing track at the high school when the detective came by earlier. In the observer's opinion, the boy was arrogant, uncooperative, and unwilling to accept responsibility. Nothing the detective could do elicited a confession from the boy, and he finally decided to drop the case. Later, he told the observer that he was unsure of the boy's guilt. He explained that the youth's interest in athletics indicated that he was a "basically good kid," and the detective saw no reason to disbelieve him. The boy's demeanor in the encounter was of the kind typically taken to indicate questionable character; however, his athletic activities were taken to be a stronger clue to his true identity. Therefore, demeanor in the encounter was not sufficient by itself to be taken as indicative of "badness" in the boy.

Often detectives make a tentative decision as to their disposition of a case before encountering the suspect. In these cases, an exemplary performance by the suspect, for better or worse, sometimes changes the detective's mind. In one case, for example, a group of boys had knocked another boy off his bicycle and sprayed him with paint. When the detective interviewed the boys, they reported that their victim had been defacing a wall with the spray paint when he was caught and attacked by the group. Since all the boys eventually admitted their participation in the attack and the boy who was attacked had been committing a delinquent act himself, the detective decided only to give them a warning and make them pay for the boy's clothes that were ruined by the paint. Before the interview, the detective had decided to refer the boys to probation, a relatively severe disposition.

The important aspect of this case is that the disposition did not relate to the seriousness of the delinquent act. One of the boys involved had chased the victim down the street after the attack but had not participated in the attack. However, the detective almost referred this boy to probation because he insisted that the attack had never occurred. By not cooperating, the boy presented himself to the detective as a delinquent and to the other boys as a "tough guy"; and even though this boy's participation in the attack was minimal, in the encounter with the detective he came across as the "bad one."

Informal dispositions by detectives are of two distinct types. In the first type, the detectives issue a friendly, even parental warning to juveniles who have been in some kind of trouble, not so much in an effort to scare them into compliance with the law as to offer simple guidance on how to stay out of trouble. The following transcript illustrates an informal warning given to a boy accused of trespassing:

DETECTIVE: "Now also, ah legally, there is a law about trespass which is in the Penal Code, it is an offense. Before you go to one of these places, what were you guys doing? Collecting bottles or something like that?"

JUVENILE: "Yeah, old bottles."

DETECTIVE: "You are? Yeah, as a matter of fact one of my ex-sergeants I used to work for, he's a bottle collector himself, I can understand that. . . .

"The thing to do when you go up to one of these places is to go up to the house and explain what you're doing and get permission to do it. Okay?"

JUVENILE: (Nod)

DETECTIVE: "And that's the main thing."[23]

The second kind of informal disposition is intended to threaten the juveniles with invocation of juvenile statutes, arrest, or referral to probation. If a juvenile is being especially troublesome but the detective does not want to make an arrest or refer the juvenile to probation, the warning can be given the necessary emphasis by calling the juvenile's parents. This is the most severe informal warning, and it is reserved for juveniles who are seen to be salvable but uncooperative. The following exchange between a detective and a juvenile's father illustrates this most severe informal disposition:

DETECTIVE: "Mr. Jones?"

FATHER: (Nod)

DETECTIVE: "I'm Detective Knight of the Sheriff's Department. Sorry to meet you under these circumstances. Wonder if you could come over here and talk to me a minute. Ah, this afternoon at approximately 3:15 we had a fight occur in this vicinity. We rolled units into the area. There were 50 to 60 juveniles gathered here who wouldn't break up. . . .

"There was a small group who were harassing the officers. We asked them on several occasions to leave the area. This they failed to comply with. Your daughter, Alice, was standing out here. She, ah, was talking back, to put in a blunt term, 'hassling' the officers around here. I asked her to move on several occasions. She said I didn't have any authority to tell her to, I couldn't tell her what to do. I asked her name several times. She refused to give me her name. I said, 'What about your folks, what are they going to say about this?' And she said, 'I don't have any parents.' I said, 'Well, where's your home?' 'I don't have a home. You can't do this to me. My father's going to take care of you.'

"Ah, we had to fight tooth and nail to get any information out of her at all. . . . Ah, generally, she just tried to create a disturbance for the officers, and so it finally got to the point where she failed to obey our commands, and she was interfering with an officer in the performance of his duty and contributing to, ah, the fact, ah, what we call a public disturbance, a 415. So I just finally took her name and placed her in the car and decided to call you, rather than lock her up. So I'm going to release her in your custody. I thought you'd better hear about it."

FATHER: "Well, I'll take care of that."[24]

As can be seen from this account, the detective called the girl's father because she did not honor his authority and refused to cooperate. In other studies of police discretion it has been found that such disrespect frequently leads to arrest or even police brutality.[25] However, in dealing with juveniles, police officers have a greater choice of action. They can even take informal action, which, from the youth's subjective view, may be quite serious. In the case described above, the girl was extremely upset by the officer's call to her father. However, the detective chose this course rather than "making" the girl an official delinquent by invoking the law.

SUMMARY

What distinguishes a delinquent from a nondelinquent is not necessarily that the former engages in delinquent activities while the latter does not. Not all actions that could be construed as delinquent are in fact defined as delinquent by observers. Of those actions that are considered delinquent, not all are reported to the police or observed by the police. Finally, not all actions that are considered to be delinquent and come to the attention of the police lead to the invocation of official sanctions. Only among those cases that entail the official use of the law do we find the great bulk of juvenile delinquents. To be sure, there are a number of juveniles who are seen to be "getting away with" delinquent acts, and some of these youths are no doubt considered to be juvenile delinquents by the community. But, as we have seen, to be a delinquent typically involves an *official* police record of delinquent actions.

It may seem at first that the police have enormous power in picking out the delinquents, but upon close analysis we find that community and parental definitions of delinquency have an equally great impact on what is and is not to be treated with official police action. The case of runaways, for example, shows that parental pressure on the police, not police discretion alone, is the primary factor leading to the delinquent label. Although the police certainly have power in deciding the fate of juveniles, their power is often no more than a reflection of community values, beliefs, and prejudices.

NOTES

1. Clayton A. Hartjen, *Crime and Criminalization* (New York: Holt, Rinehart and Winston, 1974).
2. Irving Piliavin and Scott Briar, "Police Encounters with Juveniles," *American Journal of Sociology,* 70:206–214 (September 1964).
3. *Ibid.,* p. 210.
4. Carl Werthman and Irving Piliavin, "Gang Members and the Police," in David J. Bordua (ed.), *The Police: Six Sociologial Essays* (New York: Wiley, 1967).
5. Donald J. Black and Albert J. Reiss, Jr., "Police Control of Juveniles," *American Sociological Review,* 35:63–67 (February 1970).
6. *Ibid.,* p. 68.
7. *Ibid.,* p. 75.
8. Rodney Stark, *Police Riots* (Belmont, Calif.: Focus Books, 1972), p. 61.
9. William B. Sanders, "Police Occasions," *Criminal Justice Review* (Spring 1979). See also, Sanders, *Detective Work: A Study of Criminal Investigations* (New York: Free Press, 1977).
10. Robert Lundman, *Police and Policing: An Introduction* (New York: Holt, Rinehart and Winston, 1980).
11. Sanders, "Police Occasions."
12. Black and Reiss, p. 74.
13. James Q. Wilson, "The Police and the Delinquent in Two Cities," in Stanton Wheeler (ed.), *Controlling Delinquents* (New York: Wiley, 1968), pp. 9–30.
14. *Ibid.,* p. 10.
15. William Chambliss, "The Saints and the Roughnecks," *Society,.* 11:24–31 (November–December 1973).
16. *Ibid.,* p. 28.
17. *Ibid.,* p. 29.
18. Harold Garfinkel, *Studies in Ethnomethodology* (Englewood Cliffs, N.J.: Prentice-Hall, 1967).
19. Sanders, *Detective Work,* p. 131.
20. *Ibid.,* pp. 130–149.
21. *Ibid.,* pp. 133–134.
22. Peter H. Rossi, *et al,* "The Seriousness of Crimes: Normative Structure and Individual Differences," *American Sociological Review,* 39:224–237 (April 1974).
23. Sanders, *Detective Work,* p. 145.
24. *Ibid.,* p. 146.
25. William A. Westley, "Violence and the Police," *American Journal of Sociology,* 49:34–41 (July 1953).

THROUGH THE GUIDING LIGHT OF WISDOM AND
UNDERSTANDING SHALL THE FAMILY ENDURE
AND CHILDREN GROW STRONG IN THE SECURITY OF
THE HOME, FOR THEY ARE THE HOPE OF THE FUTURE

11 Juvenile Justice

INTRODUCTION

Once a juvenile is arrested, he or she is turned over to what we can generally call the juvenile authorities. For the most part juvenile authorities consist of personnel in the probation department, before, during, and after any official disposition. Relatively few juveniles actually go to court, and the dispositions tend to be handled by the probation intake officer. Unlike adults, juveniles who do go to court are not actually charged with criminal violations. Instead, a juvenile court petition is brought to compel the juvenile and his or her parents to appear before the court.[1] What happens to the juvenile from the time of arrest until the final disposition is the topic of this chapter. In certain respects juvenile justice operates like the adult court in that both systems of justice use an abundance of informal measures to cope with defendants.[2] In other respects, however, the two systems and their courts are entirely different in both function and atmosphere. In order to appreciate the unique character of the juvenile justice system, we will first examine the history of the court and its development. Next we will investigate the assumptions that underlie court proceedings, comparing them with the actual proceedings. Throughout the chapter the key role of the probation officer will be discussed. Even though the juvenile court judge is the official who is ultimately responsible for court outcomes, we will see that in relation to the probation officer, the judge plays a minor role in juvenile justice.

THE DEVELOPMENT OF JUVENILE JUSTICE

In the late nineteenth century, certain philanthrophic groups, backed by the general reform movement, came to see the problems of American society as largely the result of rapid urbanization.[3] The reformers decided that something must be done to save the children who lived in the slums and labored in sweatshops, mines, and factories, where plentiful cheap unskilled labor was required. The reformers regarded the appalling conditions in the slums and work places as largely responsible for the increase in juvenile crime and the generally "immoral" behavior of lower-class children. To offset these debasing conditions, supporters of the child-saving movement began to look at the treatment of juvenile offenders. At the time, juvenile offenders were given the same treatment as adults by the criminal justice system. Young boys and girls were imprisoned together with adult criminals; there were no special accommodations for them.

A number of cities, notably Chicago, began developing special courts and procedures for juveniles around the turn of the century, although many felt that such benevolence would only spoil juveniles. In fact, under the zeal of reform, although the courts were supposed to protect them, juveniles were stripped of the constitutional right to due process in criminal matters enjoyed by adults, and several offenses that had previously been ignored or handled informally were brought under the jurisdiction of the newly formed juvenile courts.[4] Not only did these courts handle all acts that would be criminal if committed by an adult and acts that violated city and county ordinances; they also became responsible for a residual category of juvenile conduct defined as "vicious or immoral behavior, incorrigibility, and truancy." As we noted in Chapter 5, juvenile-status offenses make up a large proportion of what is considered juvenile delinquency, and these offenses were the product of the reform-minded juvenile court.

The "help" that was supposed to be provided by the juvenile court was forced like castor oil down the collective throats of the juveniles who came to the attention of the authorities. Those who were in control of the juvenile court system became increasingly authoritarian in deciding what the children needed, and the spirit of helping the juveniles was replaced by the spirit of "straightening them out." To do this, the child-savers sometimes engaged in procedures that denied children their civil rights. Since these actions were defined as "clinical treatment" and "moral development," they were not questioned.[5] Moreover, since the juvenile court was defined as civil rather than criminal, the civil rights of juveniles were not protected. Just as medicine is seen to be only helpful, never harmful, so the juvenile court was not conceived of as an instrument of oppression, and the officialdom of the court did not see the due-process problems created by the "solutions" they offered.

To distinguish the proceedings of the juvenile court from those of the criminal court, much of the language was changed, but the consequences remained the same. Instead of a criminal complaint, a juvenile court petition was given, but the juvenile still had to appear in court. Similarly, arraignments came to be called "initial hearings," convictions were renamed "findings of involvement," and sentences were replaced by "dispositions."[6] All these changes in nomenclature were supposed to restructure the proceedings along the lines of the new clinical ideal and to further the goal of investigation, diagnosis, and prescription of treatment rather than to adjudicate guilt or fix blame.[7] The hearings were held in private, theoretically to protect the juvenile from the stigma of criminal involvement; the privacy of these hearings, however, allowed the judges to do what they wanted to do without being held accountable to the public.

The courts also went into business for themselves by identifying a group they called "predelinquents" or "PINS" (Persons in Need of Supervision)—children who had done nothing illegal but were believed to be on the path to becoming delinquent.

The unique character of the child-saving movement was its concern for predelinquent offenders—"children who occupy the debatable ground between criminality and innocence"—and its claim that it could transform potential criminals into respectable citizens by training them in "habits of industry, self-control and obedience to law." This policy justified the diminishing of traditional procedures and allowed police, judges, probation officers, and truant officers to work together without legal hindrance. If children were to be rescued, it was important that the rescuers be free to pursue their mission without the interference of defense lawyers and due process. Delinquents had to be saved, transformed, and reconstituted.[8]

Thus, not only did the juvenile courts suspend the rights of juveniles who were brought before them for criminal activities; they also established a whole new group subject to the meddling attention of the courts, and this group too had none of the rights enjoyed by adult criminals. Had the members of this group been adults, they could not legally have even been brought before the courts.

Behind the movement to save the children were powerful forces in society. Instead of the stereotype of a moralistic "do-gooder" who is imagined meddling out of a genuine concern for the fate of wayward children, there is another factor behind the reform movement, according to one group of researchers. According to the neo-Marxists, the power elite were behind the movement to "save" children so that they could gain control of the youths. In analyzing the development of the juvenile reformers, Platt concluded that the movement resulted from the attempt by corporate powers to bureaucratize and streamline social control.[9] In the squalid slums of urban areas, such as Chicago, there were a large number of "wayward youths." Since these youths were seen to be out of control, and the cause was seen to lie in the environment, the reform movement sought to take these children out of their setting and place them in institutions that would make them useful in a capitalist society. According to Platt, even though most active and visible supporters were from the middle class and the professions, the power, in terms of economic and political support, came from the elite.[10] Without the support of the elite, and without having it be in the interests of the elite to control and channel lower-class youths, the movement would not have succeeded.

In documenting the control of the movement by the elite in other cities, Shelden has shown how the reform effort developed in Memphis, Tennessee.[11] Behind the movement was a powerful group known as the Friends of the Needy Circle, which was one of the committees of another group known as King's Daughters. King's Daughters consisted of a group of women married to upper-class business and professional men in Memphis.[12] This group enlisted the backing of a local paper, the *Commercial Appeal,* to gain community support for their effort. Essentially, the Friends of the Needy Circle wanted to establish a training school for both predelinquent and delinquent children, and the manifest justification for it was summarized in a *Commercial Appeal* editorial as follows:

So far as punishment is concerned, the sending of . . . a boy to a reformatory is all that is needed in the average case. Here he is given some moral instruction, he receives some education, and he is taught some useful trades.

Morality must be inculcated in children, who, either from heredity or environment, have been drifting down toward the black pools of crime. Furthermore, as the mere detention of these children would accomplish nothing for them, it is considered imperative that they should be sent to school for several hours every day, and that they should receive some industrial training which will enable them to be self-supporting when they are thrown upon the world again.[13]

The school that was eventually built along the ideals expressed in the editorial was backed by local elites. Of those directly responsible for its establishment, 80 percent were upper class.[14]

The extent to which such institutions would generate "productive citizens who would be able to fit into the corporate order of work," as Shelden states, is equivocal.[15] The training envisioned by the founders of the school, according to Shelden's own account, was something less than preparation to enter the corporation's factory. In describing the purpose of the school, the president of the Friends of the Needy Circle described the school as

a place where we could educate the youths confined there in the practice, as well as the science, of agriculture; a place where they could be taught to get the best results from the cow in the way of milk, butter and beef; a place where they could not only raise cotton, but could learn to make it into cloth; a place where they could acquire a knowledge of carpentry, blacksmithing, shoemaking, broom-making, designing, horticulture, floriculture, etc.; in fact, a place where from whence they could go with a technical knowledge which would enable them to take a position in the world as useful citizens; to do all this requires a room—requires land. . . . Properly managed, the sale of dairy products, hay, fruit, vegetables, poultry and other products of the farm should add greatly to its income.[16]

There is nothing obvious in the remarks of the group's president that suggests a conspiracy to enslave the young by harnessing them to an assembly line. Indeed, the types of skills suggested could be used fairly independent of the "corporate order of work," if we mean a given position in a corporate organization. Moreover, we must remember that the same child-savers that organized the founding of the juvenile justice system also sponsored laws forbidding child labor. It would be contradictory to do away with the highly profitable exploitation of children in factories and mines and at the same time contribute money to provide a children's training school. Surely the programs proposed in the child-saving movement were every bit the "bureaucratized forms of control" described by the critical criminologists, but to jump from that observation to the assumption that this was then profit exploitation is a weak argument.

It must be understood that the establishment of the juvenile courts was not intended to be a backward move in criminal justice, and, indeed, the reform movement accomplished a number of improvements in the handling of juveniles. Juvenile records were kept secret, far more so than were adult records. Children were no longer thrown in with adult criminal suspects, and the dispositions were by and large more lenient than were criminal sentences. But the reformers' juvenile court system was characterized by a lack of due process and the belief that what the court decided was necessarily good. Sending a child to a reformatory in the judges' view was not a punishment but a treatment, intended to help the child. However, since this disposition involved deprivation of freedom, there was not a great deal of difference to the child between being sent to a reformatory and to a penitentiary. In fact, being sent to a juvenile correctional facility has come to be regarded as a "more serious" disposition than probation, and a number of those who work in juvenile courts now see sending juveniles to state reformatories as equivalent to consigning them to prison. Moreover, a court disposition to a reformatory carries an open-ended term; the juvenile who is sent to such a facility thus has no idea how long he or she must remain in confinement. The adult prisoner at least knows the maximum period he or she must serve.

THE ASSUMPTION OF GUILT AND ABSENCE OF DUE PROCESS

Perhaps the greatest problem with juvenile courts is the assumption of guilt in cases involving juveniles. Since juvenile courts are officially viewed as noncriminal, the issue of criminal or delinquent culpability is not relevant. The court's function is not structured around the adversary system, with innocence or guilt to be hammered out between the prosecutor and defense counsel, as in the criminal courts. Instead, under the philosophy of *parens patriae,* the court is supposed to act like a parent and attempt to help the children who come to its attention, whether or not they are guilty of a crime.

This is not to say that the juvenile courts put every juvenile who comes before them on probation or in a reformatory. In fact, the modal disposition in juvenile courts is dismissal. A juvenile's account means something in the court hearings, but since he or she is defined as "in need of assistance" in the first place, what the child has to say about the conduct in question carries very little weight. Instead, as we have stressed, the juvenile's rights are suspended. If the courts frequently dismiss cases, it is difficult to rationalize the suspension of rights on the ground that the courts are in existence to guide and assist juveniles.[17] How can juveniles be helped if their cases are dismissed?

Furthermore, when we look at the actual hearings in juvenile court, we find that juvenile cases are not handled in a wise and considered manner but rather are shuffled in and out as expeditiously as possible. In a study in Los Angeles in 1957, it was found that the larger juvenile courts spent an average of three minutes on each case. To some extent, this rapid handling is possible because the judge tends to rely on probation officers' reports. However, judges are not supposed to see these so-called social history reports until *after* there is an adjudicatory decision. It would seem, therefore, that more than a few minutes would be necessary to hear each case.[18]

In some states there are split hearings. During the first hearing the judge is supposed to determine jurisdiction; in the second hearing he or she is to decide what disposition is to be made, in part on the basis of the social history report. However, in a study of split hearings in New York and California, Lemert found that two-thirds of the judges used social history reports during the first hearing.[19] Since these reports indicate a youth's previous delinquent involvement, those with a juvenile record were more likely to be seen as in need of the court's "guidance." In an adult court, a defendant's previous record cannot be entered during adjudication, and a judge and jury cannot use a criminal record as a resource in conviction. But since the determination of jurisdiction (that is, the decision that the court should do something about a juvenile) is essentially the same as a conviction, juveniles with records suffer the same stigma the juvenile courts had been set up to abolish.

A further problem with the *parens patriae* philosophy of the juvenile courts is that it tempts the court to reach out ever further to involve itself in the lives of children who normally would not come to its attention. If the court sees itself as a "parent," and if parents are good for children, then the more children the court can reach the better. One judge went so far as to suggest:

> It seems to have been demonstrated that the broad powers of the juvenile court can be helpfully invoked on behalf of children whose maladjustment has been brought to light through juvenile traffic violations. A girl companion of a youthful speeder may be protected from further sexual experimentation. Boys whose only amusement seems to be joyriding in family cars can be directed to other, more suitable forms of entertainment before they reach the stage of "borrowing" cars when the family car is unavailable.[20]

There seems to be no question in this judge's mind about what juvenile traffic violators are likely to be up to, even though such an assumption would appear absurd were it applied to adult drivers.

To refer to a traffic violation as an indicator of "maladjustment" stretches the limits of delinquency theory beyond both scientific and commonsense boundaries. Note also the judge's smug assumption that the juvenile court can be helpful in such cases. To date there is no evidence whatsoever that the juvenile court has helped juveniles who get into trouble. It has punished some and in this way may have frightened them and others into compliance with juvenile statutes and criminal law, but there is no evidence even for this. If anything, the evidence shows that the juvenile justice process sets up a delinquent identity and leads to secondary deviance (see Chapter 4). The notion that one can be "killed with kindness" applies in the case of the juvenile courts. They believe that only good can come from their procedures and that therefore the greater their involvement the better. Certainly it is the intention of the juvenile courts to benefit children, but intentions and consequences do not always correspond.

Juvenile court judges, like just about everyone else in the criminal justice system, complain of an excessive volume of work. Because of the increasing number of cases they receive, they explain, there is not enough time to give each one the consideration necessary for a wise disposition. For some judges, it is undoubtedly true that the number of cases they receive precludes careful examination of each one. Table 11-1 provides a breakdown in caseloads of juvenile court judges.

As can be seen from the table, more than half the full-time judges and more than three-fourths of the part-time judges hear 250 or fewer cases per year. These judges certainly appear to have sufficient time to make the necessary decisions in line with the intent of the juvenile courts. Perhaps it is true that judges who work in large urban areas and must deal with thousands of cases a year do not have enough time to handle all their cases properly. However, the majority of full-time judges and the greater majority of part-time judges in the juvenile court cannot use this excuse. Importantly, this situation raises a question as to the effectiveness with which the juvenile justice system *can* help juveniles. There is no evidence that the judges with few cases are making wiser decisions than the judges with overloads. That is, even if the judges had all the time they believe they need to make decisions in juvenile cases, there is no reason to think there would be a marked improvement in the dispositions made.

TABLE 11-1.   Number of Juvenile Cases Handled per Year[a]

| | Full-time Judges | | Part-time Judges | |
Caseload	Number	Percent	Number	Percent
100 or less	287	32.1	38	56.9
101–250	201	22.4	21	25.9
251–500	126	14.1	9	11.1
501–1,000	85	9.5	9	4.9
1,001–2,000	73	8.2	3	3.7
2,001–3,000	37	4.1	5	6.2
3,001–4,000	23	2.6	0	0
4,001–5,000	20	2.2	1	1.2
Over 5,000	37	4.1	1	1.2
Total	889	100.0	87	100.0

[a] Kenneth Cruce Smith, "A Profile of Juvenile Court Judges in the United States," *Juvenile Justice, 25:* 34 (August 1974).

Furthermore, since the judges' decisions are based largely on the social history reports submitted by probation officers, there is not much for the judges to do. And because judges are typically trained in law schools and have little background in such fields as social work, psychology, or sociology, they may not be the best qualified people to determine dispositions. It appears that judges serve as rubber stamps for decisions made by others in the juvenile justice process, and the fact that some judges handle more than 5,000 cases annually suggests that their work can be done without a great deal of deliberation. If the judges' role is to be a viable one, they must make decisions on the basis of the law, not merely the probation officer's evaluation.

In the late 1960s a number of Supreme Court decisions held that *some* of the rights granted adults should also be granted to juveniles. In the landmark *Gault* decision, the Court ruled that juveniles must be given a number of protections enjoyed by adults and previously denied to youths, including the right to counsel, the right against self-incrimination, notice of charges, confrontation, and the right of cross-examination. Several rights enjoyed by adults, including the right to a jury trial, are still denied to juveniles, but the *Gault* decision, along with the decision in *Kent* v. *United States* a year earlier, pointed to general dissatisfaction with the operation of the juvenile justice system. As Handler said, "There may be grounds for concern that the child receives the worst of both worlds: that he gets neither the protections accorded to adults nor the solicitous care and regenerative treatment postulated for children."[21]

At the same time that these decisions established broader rights to be afforded to juveniles, they did not abolish the informality of the juvenile courts, which had always been seen as helpful to juveniles. The decisions did, however, provide a more compelling role for the judge, and as the spirit of these decisions was incorporated into state statutes governing juvenile procedures, the judge became a decision maker on legal requirements—a role that he was better equipped to perform than that of an expert on juvenile needs. Nevertheless, the juvenile court was not completely revamped by the *Gault* decision; juvenile-status offenses and other noncriminal activities are still handled by the court, caseloads are increasing, and dispositions are typically predetermined by probation officers.

JUVENILE COURT PROCESS

In discussing the process of the juvenile court we need to keep in mind the philosophy and the informal character of the juvenile court. Furthermore, because of various state, regional, and district differences, the description here may not represent all juvenile courts in America. Some courts are more fully developed than others, and what will be described in this section represents a typical fully developed urban juvenile court.[22] Less fully developed courts contend with similar processes, but they tend to have less specialized roles for operations.

Typically, a juvenile is brought to the attention of the juvenile justice system by a member of the community.[23] The police are called, and they bring the child to the probation department; sometimes the parents of a child bring their child in themselves. The first real contact a juvenile has with the courts is with the intake officer, who decides whether or not the youth should be referred to the court and, if so, what should be done with him or her. At this point we come to a critical juncture, for the intake officer is the key decision-making person in the juvenile court system. Cressey and McDermott point out:

The design of the buildings and the rooms used for giving justice to juveniles hides the fact that the intake officer is the most important person in the juvenile justice system. This man's workroom is smaller and barer than the "chambers" of juvenile court judges, the suites used by Chief Probation Officers, and the offices of the probation department section chiefs called supervisors. In his little cubicle there are no flags, no polished wood furniture, no paneled walls, no carpet, and no statue of the blindfolded lady. The cubicle is equipped with a cheap metal desk and a couple of straightbacked chairs. A few unframed prints and a diploma or two are temporarily taped on the walls. The intake officer doesn't wear a robe or a wig. He sits at his bare desk, often wearing an open-collared shirt, and does justice.[24]

In the context of the juvenile justice system, including the police, the intake officer is in a key position between the community (represented by the police who bring in juveniles typically referred to them by the citizenry) and the mechanisms that officially designate a youth to be delinquent or not. The decision by the intake officer has ramifications all the way up the line to the disposition of the case, for it is he or she who sets the tone and theme for the rest of the system's treatment of the juvenile. As can be seen in Figure 11–1, the "court-intake screening" occupies a strategic position in the key decision point in the juvenile justice system.

The importance of the intake officer's decision can be appreciated when we consider the wide range of discretion afforded him or her. Cressey and McDermott identified the following six options available to the intake officer (listed from most frequently to least frequently employed).

Counsel, warn, and release is the most commonly utilized option. This disposition is an almost automatic response to cases brought in via citations. The child is usually discharged after a warning, a lecture, or a short conference with him and his parents. The case is not carried in the official records as "dismissed," even though CWR (counsel, warn, release) is sometimes called "dismissed" rather than a disposition.

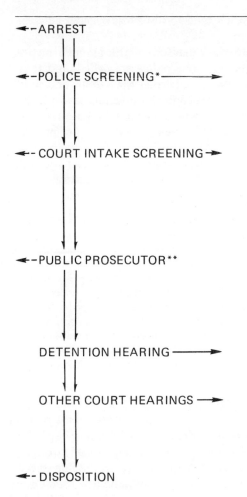

◄─ARREST

A patrol officer decides whether or not to make a formal arrest, but has no authority to detain.

◄─POLICE SCREENING*─────►

A youth officer decides whether or not the youth should be referred to court and if so, whether or not the youth should be detained pending the initial court hearing.

◄─ COURT INTAKE SCREENING ─►

A court worker—and in some cases a prosecutor or judge—decides whether or not a petition should be filed and if so, whether or not the youth should be detained pending final disposition. Most status offense complaints are initiated here.

◄─PUBLIC PROSECUTOR**

A prosecuting attorney decides, after reviewing the court worker's decision, whether to file a petition. The prosecuting attorney, however, has no role in determining whether to detain the youth.

DETENTION HEARING ─────►

The judge, usually based on the recommendation of a case worker, decides whether to detain the youth.

OTHER COURT HEARINGS ─►

The judge, after review of previous decisions, decides whether to continue detention of the youth based on new information presented by a defense attorney.

◄─ DISPOSITION

The judge decides the kind of care or treatment the youth will receive.

CODE:

╎╎ Prosecution with Detention

──► Prosecution without Detention

◄─ ─ Dismissal or Diversion

*This stage is omitted in some jurisdictions; particularly in small communities which cannot afford a special youth officer. It may be handled by a social service employee rather than a police employee.

**The prosecutor has authority to override decisions to dismiss or to prosecute based on social reasons. The authority only exists in two states.

Figure 11–1. Decision Points Within the Juvenile Justice System

Informal probation is the option whereby, under Mountain State law, a juvenile might be placed on a maximum of six months' informal probation if he and his parents agree to it. In practice the term of probation is rarely less than six months.

Probation diversion units may be used for the particular types of cases they have been established to receive. The intake officer may be required to refer certain cases (usually predelinquents or minor lawbreakers) to such a unit. In addition, or in some locations, he may opt to send other cases there. When a child is sent to a diversion unit, his case is officially logged as "dismissed." However, the child is strongly urged to participate in the special unit's program.

Referral to another agency (or to a person) is a common disposition of walk-in and phone contact cases. Such referral is an attempt to handle the case "unofficially" by sending the juvenile to someone that "is better able (qualified) to handle this case." This disposition is sometimes used for other than "walk-ins" by intake officers on night duty. These officers tend to be viewed by detention center staff members and the police as "troubleshooters." Intake officers receive cases from them that have not "officially" come to the attention of the juvenile justice system, and they dispose of them officially. It is questionable, then, whether such referrals are "dispositions," "diversions," "dismissals," or something else.

Petition for an official hearing before a juvenile court referee or judge is the "classic" disposition used in "serious" and "last resort" cases. It is something like the filing of charges in criminal cases. The papers on the case are simultaneously filed with the court and with a regular probation officer (as indicated above) who makes an investigation and reports back to the court, which then conducts a hearing.

Dismissal is the least-used option. It occurs most frequently when the intake officer decides there is not enough evidence to justify further action, or when he believes the technicalities of the arrest were improper.[25]

Given these dispositions, we find that the juvenile court judge is not the major decision-maker in the juvenile justice system. Retrospectively, when we look at Table 11–1, we can see that the judges' caseloads represent only a small proportion of the cases coming to the attention of the juvenile justice system. Alternatively, if the judges are counting *every* case that comes to the attention of the intake officer, then their caseloads are far lower than the statistics lead us to believe.

Because the official philosophy of juvenile justice revolves around the individual needs of its clients, or the individualization of cases, we would expect this to lead to occasions similar to those of police-juvenile interaction in which intake officers make decisions on the basis of encounters between themselves and the juveniles. However, we find instead an even more perfunctory handling of cases. The general formula works something like this: First offenders are counseled, warned, and released; second offenders are given informal probation; and third offenders are petitioned to court. Talking with the child and his or her parents is not essential to the decision-making process, and as one intake officer explained, "You know what you are going to do or recommend after reading the report and records. You don't have to see the kid."[26] This bureaucratically efficient method contrasts with the individualized ideal that is officially espoused. Therefore, the decision about what option is to be taken is determined more by a routine formula than a method of evaluating the needs of the individual juvenile.

If the intake officer options to counsel, warn, and release the child, then the juvenile is finished with the juvenile justice system. However, if a juvenile receives informal probation, then he or she is placed in a situation in which the juvenile justice system exerts control without the formal proceedings of a hearing. This is done without any of the legal procedures seen either in a criminal case or in a juvenile hearing. Informal probation is "voluntary" in that the intake officer cannot place a child on informal probation without parental permission. However, if the option is between informal probation and going to court, with the possibility of receiving formal probation or even detention, the parents and child are typically willing to take informal probation. The "informality" of the probation, however, is not quite what the term implies. Youths on informal probation cannot choose to show up for their meetings with the probation officer at their own convenience. Instead, the informality comes to mean not going to court and not being placed on formal probation. The juvenile and his or her parents are told that the child is going to be placed on informal probation, and their agreement is more ore less automatic. A typical and generic conversation between the intake officer and a youth and his or her parents is illustrated by Cressey and McDermott on the basis of studies of several such hearings:

INTAKE OFFICER: I'm going to put you on informal probation for six months; what do you think?
YOUTH: Okay.
PARENT: Okay.
INTAKE OFFICER: You'll have to sign this form agreeing to the probation department rules, okay?
YOUTH: Okay.
PARENT: Okay.

This type of interchange would not occur in a vacuum, but after the intake officer has spelled out the alternatives, especially the serious consequences that could occur if the parent and youth are uncooperative. In many respects the probation department is offering the youth a "break," and the fact that it follows a formula does suggest equity in the treatment of juveniles. However, in contrast to the ideal of individualized justice, something even probation officers feel is an overstatement of what they have the resources to do, such routinization of cases belies anything other than mass processing. Finally, there is virtually no due process in the determination of "involvement" (guilt) of the youth, and even though the juvenile court is not much more meticulous in routinely determining involvement, it does afford the protections afforded in the *Gault* decision.

The compelling force behind informal probation lies not in the good intentions of the juvenile or his or her parents; rather, it derives from the fact that the probation officer can refile on the original charges if the youth refuses to cooperate after agreeing to the informal probation. The charges against the juvenile are *not* dropped as soon as informal probation begins, but instead are suspended until the juvenile has completed the term of probation. If the youth does not commit another offense, does not violate the conditions of probation, and successfully completes the period of informal probation, then the suspended charges are dropped. It is the dropping of these charges that is the "break" given by informal probation mentioned above. If, on the other hand, the youth gets into trouble, the original charges can be refiled and he or she can be sent to court.

The "diversion" alternative is available in some states, especially for juvenile-status offenders, mainly runaways; under certain circumstances, the intake officer *must* refer a juvenile to a diversion alternative. Essentially, the purpose of diversion is to go around the official mechanisms of the juvenile justice system, or, as some put it, to "minimize penetration" into the system if there are limited or inadequate diversion alternatives. Since diversion is an especially important and relatively new approach to handling juveniles in trouble, it will be discussed in detail in Chapter 13. For now, it is enough to know that diversion is a means of avoiding the formal proceedings of a juvenile court hearing.

If a court hearing has been deemed the proper course of action in the case, charges against the juvenile are served to him or her and the parents. At this time both the child and the parents are advised of the right to counsel and other rights available to juveniles. A hearing is then held in which delinquent involvement is determined. Since the *Gault* and *Kent* decisions, such hearings supposedly resemble criminal court hearings, and a "conviction" is to be had only if the evidence shows delinquent involvement "beyond a reasonable doubt."[28] However, the cases involving juvenile-status offenses require only a "preponderance of evidence" for an adjudication of delinquency (that is, conviction). Since juvenile-status offenses make up the great bulk of the cases, especially the cases involving girls, there is no necessity of proving guilt beyond a reasonable doubt as is required in adult criminal court. Therefore, even though some claim that the *Gault* decision has transformed the juvenile court into a criminal court in terms of the requirements of proof, it is unlikely that the treatment of most of those brought before the court for juvenile-status offenses has changed significantly since *Gault*.

After the adjudicatory hearing, a probation officer makes up the social history report used by the judge as a resource for making a dispositional (and often an adjudicatory) decision. The social history report is based on investigation of the child's background and such artifacts as his school records, prior delinquent record, family relations, and mental and physical health history.[29]

Later we will consider how probation officers establish a particular juvenile's "social history." Here we wish to point out that the social history is not merely an objective set of facts but an organizationally produced document based on other organizationally produced documents. The reality of what a juvenile is or is not may not correspond to what he has done or is likely to do in the future. However, the reality of a juvenile as presented to the judge in a social history report is contingent on the organization of "facts" about the juvenile and those organizations which produce such facts. Once the judge decides what disposition should be made, the probation office or some other agency takes over, and the "court" aspect of juvenile justice is concluded.

Before examining the role of the probation officer, let us consider briefly the significance of what has been said thus far about the juvenile justice process. It has been shown that the juvenile justice system is not the benign institution envisaged at its inception. It is important to realize that the juvenile justice process is a socially organized phenomenon that serves *officially* to create delinquents. This is not to say that the system *causes* delinquency; in fact, it may even help to prevent delinquency, although we have no evidence to that effect. However, a great deal of activity that could be characterized as delinquency goes unnoticed by the juvenile justice system or, if noticed, unattended, and only those who go through the juvenile justice process are socially and legally considered to be delinquents. Moreover, this process can best be understood in terms of its organizational routines rather than its intentions and ideals. We have examined the juvenile justice process not so much in an attempt to condemn it as to point out what it actually is and does in terms of the phenomenon of juvenile delinquency. A reformed juvenile justice process might conceivably be more equitable or effective, but it would still operate to create official delinquents. Since some social agency and process will operate to create delinquents socially and legally, we need to understand the dynamics of such processes and structures.

PROBATION DECISIONS

Probation was created by the juvenile court system, and except for dismissals, it is the most common juvenile court disposition.[30] Officially, probation is a guidance program to help juveniles overcome problems that may lead to delinquency and to keep an eye on juveniles who have been found to be in need of official supervision. However, the police regard probation as something juveniles "get off with," and many juveniles who receive probation instead of incarceration view it in the same way. On the other hand, it can also be seen as an infringement on the rights of juveniles to do what they want to do, and very few see it as any "guidance" at all. The dilemma between "guidance" and "control" is nicely summed up by Emerson:

The formal goal of probation is to improve the delinquent's behavior—in short, to "rehabilitate" him. This goal is short-circuited, however, by a pervading preoccupation with *control*. Reflecting insistent demands that the court "do something" about recurrent misconduct, probation is organized to keep the delinquent "in line," to prevent any further disturbing and inconveniencing "trouble." The ultimate goal of permanently "reforming" the delinquent's personality and conduct becomes subordinated to the exigencies of maintaining immediate control. Probationary supervision consequently takes on a decidedly short-term and negative character; probation becomes an essentially disciplinary regime directed toward deterring and inhibiting troublesome conduct.[31]

From the point of view of the probation officer, something must be done to stop a juvenile from persisting in delinquent activities. Often by the time a juvenile is placed on probation, he or she has a record of previous run-ins with the juvenile justice system, usually the police. The courts attribute the juvenile's previous troubles to something wrong with the youth or with his social milieu. It is inconceivable to them that the juvenile's problem may be due to the court's program for guidance and control. They see the juvenile's record in terms of trouble that he has caused or gotten into instead of as a formulation assembled by various people in the juvenile justice process. That is, they treat a juvenile's record as a set of relevant facts instead of as a social production created by an organization.

In a study of the juvenile justice system, Cicourel found that probation officers, like others in the system, constructed images of the juveniles they dealt with in terms of background expectancies for various particulars in a juvenile's past.[32] Out of a vast array of previous activities, probation officers built up an account to explain the juvenile as someone who either was or was not in need of their attention. This was all accomplished in terms of some departmental rule or policy for handling juveniles.[33] The probation officers saw themselves as merely employing a set of facts, but actually they elaborated the "facts" in terms of commonsense notions of what was "known" to accompany a "set of facts." In this way, they accomplished an orderly sense of what a juvenile had done and what he or she was. They were then in a position to use this "order" as a resource in decision making, following some policy for "offenders like this one." Instead of having an orderly prodecure, either for evaluating juveniles or for administering policy, they established the order in an ongoing ad hoc process. Sometimes there was ambiguity as to what a juvenile "in fact" was and what was the proper course of action to take. However, by constructing an image of a juvenile in terms of rules and policies, they could define any juvenile who came before them in terms of whether he or she was "in need" of the probation officer's attention. This is not to say that the work accomplished by probation officers was slipshod or arbitrary. Instead, Cicourel points out that reality as seen by the probation officer is an ongoing social production, not a reaction to an objective set of facts somehow emanating from the juvenile's behavior.

In order to understand better the process a youth undergoes when in contact with a probation officer and the resources employed by the probation officer in the juvenile justice system, we will look at some of the reports, interviews, recommendations, and other resources employed by probation officers. These will provide insight into the production of an official delinquent. Our account is not intended as a criticism of what probation officers do but as a realistic picture of this aspect of juvenile justice.

Probation officers give a great deal of credence to the police record, which is used to determine whether a juvenile has been in trouble before. Actually, however, these "delinquent histories" reflect only those times when a juvenile has been judged officially to have been in trouble. Cicourel quotes the following police record of a middle-income youth who came to a probation officer's attention:

	Act	*Disposition*
4/27/60	Juvenile bothering	Warned & released by patrol
12/6/61	Shot BB gun in city	Witness only
1/6/63	Petty theft—shoplifting	Warned & released to parents
1/21/63	Petty theft (purse and money)	Restitution—released to dad, pet. filed
2/14/63	Prob. office—informal prob. till 3/14/63	
5/28/63	Juvenile fight	Contacted & released by patrol
6/1/63	Petty theft—stepping stones (susp. only)	Not contacted
7/22/63	Burglary	Released to parents, pet. filed
8/9/63	Burglary (susp.)	Cleared
9/1/63	Burglary	Ref. on above
9/21/63	Burglary	Released to parents, pet. filed to include above
10/6/63	Burglary	Included on above
10/13/63	Suspicion juvenile	Talked to—warn. & rel.
12/26/63		Juv. court order: Declar. ward; rel. to parents; curfew: 8:00 P.M. weekdays; 10:00 weekends; restitution; am't. decided by P.O.
4/24/64	Petty theft—purse burglary (suspect only)	Dad will check out
10/6/64	Petty theft—purse from vehicle	Application for pet. filed
10/8/64	Prob. Dept. above not filed yet pending psycho. evaluation	
11/23/64	Battery (Teacher at Jr. Hi); loiter at school	Pet. filed cont. ward: Rel. to parents.
12/28/64	Juv. ct. order	Curfew: 8 P.M. (10 P.M. Weekends)[34]

Such a report is taken as a set of facts about the juvenile and used as a resource in determining what the youth "really" is. It should be noted that after the record began to develop this youth became a suspect in a number of thefts and burglaries. Such suspicions may be based on the youth's record, but at the same time they *add* to his record. On the one hand, they may be seen by police and probation officers as instances when the boy "got away with" something. On the other hand, they can be viewed as a result of his previous record. That is, since the boy had a record, he was more likely to be a suspect than a boy without a record, regardless of involvement.

The particulars of any given delinquent act categorized in the police record are provided in the individual police reports. These reports provide the context of what youth "really" is.[35] A burglary, for example, is seen as serious or trivial depending on the context provided in the report. The following report might be used by a probation officer to "show" that the juvenile described was in need of psychiatric care:

Subject admitted that he entered to use female clothing to excite his sexual desires and while in the house took 2 one-dollar bills. The victim later contacted and she stated that they were missing the 2 dollars but thought that it was on a later date. It appears possible that either the same boy was in the house twice or the money wasn't missed until later. . . . The subject later contacted and reported that he was in this house on three separate occasions.[36]

The reference to the use of "female clothing to excite his sexual desires" is the type of detail that typically leads a probation officer to conclude that a juvenile's activities are not merely burglary but reflect "a much greater problem." Had the report mentioned only the missing money and not the female clothing, a different set of assumptions would have been made concerning the "true nature" of the case.

Another resource used by probation officers in determining a youth's character is a personal interview with the juvenile and his parents. From such interviews, the probation officer makes inferences about what the youth is likely to do. In the following interview, the probation officer attempts to inquire into the sexual activities of 13-year-old Linda:

PROBATION OFFICER: How do you like school?
JUVENILE: I like school. I miss it.
PROBATION OFFICER: How are your grades?
JUVENILE: Not that bad. I usually get good grades, but since all this mess I haven't been able to do much concentrating.
PROBATION OFFICER: [*Question about*] best girlfriend or maybe one or two
JUVENILE: Lisa Manson, we ditched once together. Bonnie Berner too.
PROBATION OFFICER: Who is your best boy, not for loving, but for friends?
JUVENILE: . . . Charlie Dubay. (*The girl appears uneasy at this time.*)
PROBATION OFFICER: Who did you have intercourse with first?

JUVENILE: Ronnie Jones. I did it to keep him. He said he really didn't care. He wanted to just kiss me here and kiss me there.

PROBATION OFFICER: Have there been any other boys since the episode?

JUVENILE: No. That's all dropped.

PROBATION OFFICER: How did it all start?

JUVENILE: There was Robert Bean. We were talking about it at school and he said, "You gotta prove it." Well, I didn't want to lose him just like with Ronnie Jones. I was scared but didn't want them to think I was chicken. But I thought it was kinda cool.

PROBATION OFFICER: Did Gregg ever bother you?

JUVENILE: No, he just wanted to help me.

PROBATION OFFICER: You're not pregnant?

JUVENILE: No.

PROBATION OFFICER: Have you ever used anything to prevent pregnancy?

JUVENILE: Once he used one of those things.

PROBATION OFFICER: Did you ever feel scared about getting pregnant?

JUVENILE: No, I was always trying to get even with my parents.

PROBATION OFFICER: You sort of wanted to [get] even with them.

JUVENILE: Yes, I always wanted to get even with other people. My mother gets mad at me. I love my father. I know that's what's wrong with me. I talk about this with my parents. I don't know why. *(The manner of speaking appeared "sincere.")*[37]

Note that the probation officer begins with some questions about school to "determine" something about the girl's character, even though one might reasonably question what relationship there is between doing well in school and sexual activity. Apparently, the probation officer is working on the assumption that one who does well in school and likes school is a basically "good kid" whereas one who does not do well is potentially troublesome. The important point is that the probation officer can structure the questions so that the conclusions are predetermined.[38] By asking certain kinds of questions and omitting others, he makes only certain types of responses possible. Therefore, what goes down on paper as the official record of delinquency is in a large part the result of actions of the probation officer, not just actions of the juvenile.

As we pointed out in Chapter 3, some theories of juvenile delinquency center on the home life of the juvenile. Probation officers typically hold such theories, and as a result they interview the juvenile's parents to determine the character of the juvenile. Cicourel provides the following example of an interview with Linda's parents:

PROBATION OFFICER: How is she at home?

MOTHER: She's not wild. She just changes. She doesn't know why she's doing it. You say, "Why are you doing that?" and she doesn't know why.

PROBATION OFFICER: Does she feel sorry for what she did?

MOTHER: Always.

FATHER: What's happened to Linda is caused by an emotional factor. After these tests we should know what is wrong. She may need psychiatric help. Why this hearing if there is something wrong with her? We are more interested in her than the court.

MOTHER: She does this, but she doesn't know why.

PROBATION OFFICER: This [the hearing] is a legal proceeding, nothing more.

MOTHER: Then this is a routine thing?

PROBATION OFFICER: Yes. . . . that's all.

FATHER: Does she have to be a ward?

PROBATION OFFICER: I'll recommend that, and the judge may not agree. You can ask him to dismiss it.[39]

Note how the parents' account can serve as a resource to the probation officer in constructing what the juvenile is. The parents define the situation as one in which the girl needs some kind of psychiatric help, some form of guidance. The probation officer says the occasion is a "legal proceeding" and ignores the parents' definition of the situation. This is significant in that the juvenile justice system is supposedly designed for guidance, as suggested by the parents, but the probation officer treats it as a merely "legal" situation. If it were that and "nothing more," it would seem unnecessary to elicit further information from the parents. The interview with the parents, then, appears to be merely a ritual that can be used to document the "interest" the juvenile justice system has in the child's welfare. These perfunctory interviews with both parents and child may have little actual bearing on the probation officer's decision even though their express purpose is to find out about the juvenile so that a proper disposition can be made.

Finally, the probation officer makes a recommendation based on his contacts with the juvenile and the parents, the psychiatric reports, and all other material gathered pertaining to the juvenile. The following recommendation was made:

Linda's behavior is . . . extreme. She is either very happy and lively and giddy, or she withdraws completely and is very moody. She is quite capable of stealing or lying according to whatever pressure is put upon her. Linda has an IQ overall of 100. Her reading scores are down in the fourth-grade level. Her arithmetic is around sixth grade. At the present time, Linda is in the eighth grade. . . . She is not doing well and is constantly reminded by her teachers to get down to business. Dr. Moreau [psychiatrist] has stated that Linda has self-destructive impulses and fantasies to an alarming degree. He feels that this suggests a latent schizophrenic reaction, and intensive and prolonged psychotherapy is strongly recommended. The Officer has discussed with him his recommendation that this psychotherapy should be with her parents' participation and that institutionalization at this time could be harmful. The Officer in this discussion stated that the money factor here was going to be a problem. He, in turn, stated that the only other alternative would be to place Linda in an institutional setting, such as [the state mental hospital]. The Officer, in turn, talked this over with Mr. and Mrs. Peters, and, according to Mr. Peters, he felt that it would be best to place Linda under the Department of Mental Hygiene for a three- to six-month period with intensive therapy and then try her at home.[40]

From the interviews with Linda and her parents, the portrait of the girl is equivocal. To be "giddy" one moment and "moody" the next may indicate serious problems, but it could also describe behavior that is characteristic of 13-year-olds. However, the probation officer, with some urging from Linda's parents, agrees with the psychiatrist, in portraying the girl as in need of psychiatric help. This is not to say that the probation officer is incorrect but merely to point out that the picture of the girl's character is constructed from particulars that could be seen in an entirely different light. How any juvenile is viewed depends not so much on what resources are available for making sense out of the juvenile as on what interpretative schemes come to dominate the process. The information presented might be seen as pointing to a psychological problem, as in Linda's case, but it could be used to "see" evil, youthful revolt, a serious problem with the school system, or the blooming of a "flower child." All this is done not by following a set of prescribed rules but by interpreting the activities in terms of a set of prescriptions, policies, and theoretical guidelines.[41] The probation officer's recommendation, then, is not a mere reaction to objective information about an offense or an offender but the product of a complex process of interpretation. It is neither right nor wrong, bad nor good, just nor unjust, and it is certainly not unreal. It is merely the way the judgmental function of the probation officer is performed.

There is another important point to note in the probation officer's recommendation. The officer states that there may be a financial problem in arranging for psychotherapy. The only alternative is to have the girl committed to some kind of public mental institution. In the United States the lack of private finances limits the possibility of private psychiatric attention. In most other modern societies, people's ability to pay for medical services does not determine their chance of receiving such services, and it remains one of the true anachronisms of American life that wealthy patients can receive private psychiatric attention while their poorer counterparts must be locked up in state institutions. A child whose parents have money may be sent to a private institution, where he will probably receive much better care than can be provided by the overworked staff of a state facility. However, since some of these "schools," as they are called, have a *monthly* "tuition" of a thousand dollars or more, the children of low- and moderate-income families have practically no chance of receiving their services. Thus, as Goffman points out, whether one is labeled and committed is often contingent on the available resources of both the individual and the society.[42] In our society, whether a juvenile is labeled delinquent depends to a large extent on the ability of his parents to "buy" a nondelinquent disposition.

SUMMARY

In this chapter we have attempted to show the character of the juvenile justice process as it developed historically and as it is socially operated. In comparison with the ideal, we find that juvenile justice is lacking in its actual operation. The juvenile justice process is not a reaction to delinquency but an interaction among various incumbents in the juvenile justice system, certain juveniles, their parents, the schools, and other societal and community resources. By understanding the process in this fashion, we can see the interconnection between delinquents and the institutional process for dealing with delinquents.

In the next chapter, we shall look at juvenile corrections examining both its dominant patterns and the various experimental alternatives. Much of what we have said in the present chapter relates to what we will discuss in the next, and while reading the following chapter the implications of this chapter should become more apparent.

NOTES

1. Alan R. Coffey, *Juvenile Justice as a System: Law Enforcement to Rehabilitation* (Englewood Cliffs, N.J.: Prentice-Hall, 1974).
2. Arthur Rosett and Donald R. Cressey, *Justice by Consent: Plea Bargains in the American Courthouse* (Philadelphia: Lippincott, 1976).
3. Anthony Platt, *The Child-Savers: The Invention of Delinquency* (Chicago: University of Chicago Press, 1969).
4. *Ibid.*
5. Anthony Platt, "The Triumph of Benevolence: The Origins of the Juvenile Justice System in the United States," in Richard Quinney (ed.), *Criminal Justice in America: A Critical Understanding* (Boston: Little, Brown, 1974).
6. Coffey, p. 37.
7. President's Commission on Law Enforcement and Administration of Justice, *The Challenge of Crime in a Free Society* (Washington, D.C.: Government Printing Office, 1967), p. 3.
8. Platt, "The Triumph of Benevolence," p. 378.
9. *Ibid.*, pp. 366–372.
10. *Ibid.*, pp. 367–368.
11. Randall G. Shelden, " 'Diverting' Youth: Juvenile Justice in Historical Perspective," unpublished manuscript, mimeographed, State University New York, Cortland, 1977. Shelden argues that "diversion" is nothing new, and every reform in the handling of juveniles has been a "diversion" from a previous procedure. See also Randall G. Shelden, "Rescued from Evil: Origins of Juvenile Justice in Memphis, Tennessee, 1900–1917," unpublished manuscript, dittoed, State University New York, Cortland, 1977.
12. Shelden, "Rescued from Evil," p. 7.
13. *Commercial Appeal* (Memphis, Tenn., October 26, 1902), p. 4.
14. Shelden, "Rescued from Evil," p. 8.
15 *Ibid.*, p. 9.
16. *Commercial Appeal* (Memphis, Tenn., July 21, 1903), p. 7.
17. Edwin Lemert, "The Juvenile Court—Quest and Realities," in *Task Force Report: Juvenile Delinquency and Youth Crime, by the President's Commission on Law Enforcement and Administration of Justice* (Washington, D.C.: Government Printing Office, 1967), pp. 91–97.

18. Hazel B. Kerper, *Introduction to the Criminal Justice System* (St. Paul, Minn.: West, 1972).
19. Lemert.
20. *Ibid.*, p. 92.
21. Joel Handler, "The Juvenile Courts and the Adversary System: Problems of Function and Form," *Wisconsin Law Review, 54:*7–51 (Winter 1965).
22. Kerper, pp. 390–393.
23. Donald J. Black and Albert J. Reiss, Jr., "Police Control of Juveniles," *American Sociological Review, 35:*63–67 (February 1970).
24. Donald R. Cressey and Robert A. McDermott, *Diversion from the Juvenile Justice System,* Project Report for National Assessment of Juvenile Corrections (Ann Arbor: University of Michigan, June 1973).
25. *Ibid.*, pp. 19–20.
26. *Ibid.*, p. 15.
27. *Ibid.*, p. 44.
28. Kerper, p. 392.
29. *Ibid.*, p. 392.
30. Gene Kassebaum, *Delinquency and Social Policy* (Englewood Cliffs, N.J.: Prentice-Hall, 1974), pp. 104–105.
31. R. M. Emerson, *Judging Delinquents: Context and Process in Juvenile Court* (Chicago: Aldine-Atherton, 1969), p. 219.
32. Aaron Cicourel, *The Social Organization of Juvenile Justice* (New York: Wiley, 1968).
33. *Ibid.*, p. 331.
34. *Ibid.*, p. 244.
35. Howard C. Daudistel and William B. Sanders, "Police Discretion in Application of the Law," *Et Al, 3:*26–40 (1974).
36. Cicourel, p. 249.
37. *Ibid.*, p. 296.
38. *Ibid.*, p. 297.
39. *Ibid.*, p. 301.
40. *Ibid.*, p. 306.
41. Don H. Zimmerman, "The Practicalities of Rule Use," in Jack Douglas (ed.), *Understanding Everyday Life* (Chicago: Aldine, 1970), pp. 221–238.
42. Erving Goffman, *Stigma* (Englewood Cliffs, N.J.: Prentice-Hall, 1961).

12 Juvenile Corrections

INTRODUCTION

The juvenile correction system is undergoing rapid change as new practices skirt the traditional system through various diversion programs. In the President's Commission Report it was reported that in 1965 there were 62,773 juveniles in institutions,[1] while only eight years later, in 1973, the number of juveniles in detention and correctional facilities had dropped to 45,694.[2] Whether this downward trend will continue in the 1980s is unknown, but it is clear that fewer juveniles are being locked up than in earlier decades. New alternatives to traditional probation and incarceration are examined in Chapter 13, while this chapter explores what happens to juveniles when they are placed on probation or sent to detention. By seeing what transpires in the context of probation and incarceration, we will gain some understanding of why new alternatives have been sought.

In the main, we will look at the goals of juvenile corrections and compare these with actual practices and outcomes. Currently, there are three distinct views of what juvenile corrections are, or should be, doing.[3] First, many people view juvenile correctional facilities as warehouses where young offenders are "stored" until someone decides to let them out. From this perspective correctional institutions are neither good nor bad for juveniles but simply serve to keep the youths "off the streets" for a time. A second view, usually held to be the official position of correctional operations, is that juveniles should be "treated" for their delinquency in the same way one would be treated for an illness. According to this rehabilitative position, the correctional institutions should be designed to do more than merely store juveniles. By providing a "rehabilitative milieu," the institutions should attempt to transform delinquent youths into law-abiding citizens. A third perspective is that juvenile correctional institutions are nothing more than "crime schools," regardless of the good intentions of those who operate and administer them. In these institutions, juveniles are introduced to the delinquent population, tutored in delinquent perspectives, and come to develop a delinquent self-concept.

If we look at these perspectives in terms of the general objectives of incarceration, we can see certain relationships. Sutherland and Cressey[4] identify four broad objectives of imprisonment: reformation, incapacitation, retribution, and deterrence. *Reformation* refers to socializing delinquents so that they will not break the law again. This is the thrust of the rehabilitative perspective of juvenile corrections. *Incapacitation,* in this context, has to do with protecting society from the delinquents by locking them up. The warehouse approach sees this as the primary objective of juvenile corrections. *Retribution* refers to "getting even" or the "revenge" society is to have on troublemakers.

It is the ancient "eye for an eye" philosophy, which defines justice as making sure that the delinquent receives punishment equal in severity to the damage he or she has caused. None of the perspectives we have identified publicly advocates retribution as a goal of imprisonment, but the warehouse perspective might take credit for this kind of insight. Finally, corrections are supposed to act as a *deterrent* to others who might think of breaking the law. Locking up those who commit delinquent acts, it is believed, will discourage others from doing the same thing by making the probable consequences evident. Since juveniles do not want to be deprived of their freedom, locking up delinquents serves to deter other juveniles who might think of doing something wrong.

The "crime school" viewpoint runs counter to all these goals. In this view, the only positive function served by the juvenile corrections system is the temporary incapacitation of the delinquent. And even this does not really protect society, because when juveniles come out of the "crime schools" they are much more dangerous than when they entered. This is especially true of juvenile-status offenders, who have committed no crime for which an adult would be arrested. In the reformatories, they have opportunities to learn all the tricks of the criminal trade, which would probably have been denied them if they had not been locked up.

These viewpoints will serve as a frame of reference in our discussion of the probation and incarceration alternatives in juvenile justice. However, in a more general sense, we will view the correctional process as a "control mechanism" used by society to mold and restrain juveniles. It is important to remember that no matter how humanistic or draconian the measures used by the juvenile correctional system are, at the heart of its operation is the intent to have juveniles do what the system wants.

PROBATION

In Chapter 11 we saw that the probation department has considerable influence in the courts and that the probation intake officer virtually decided the fate of youths in the juvenile justice system. In his or her role of deciding preliminary dispositions (that is, deciding whether to counsel, warn, and release or place on informal probation, for example) and in writing social history reports, the probation officer is acting as a judge more than as a custodian. Here we will look at the work of the probation officer as he or she works with juveniles who have been placed on probation.

The proportion of juveniles who are placed on probation as compared with those placed in some form of secure detention is fairly high, since detention is reserved for repeat offenders and there has been a recent effort to keep children out of detention. In 1965 the ratio of children on probation to those in detention was 4.5 to 1, but since that time the number of children being incarcerated has declined steadily. Because of the introduction of new programs in the form of diversion alternatives, the probation to detention ratio may have remained about the same, but there is a much higher ratio of nondetention to detention dispositions than before.

Probation consists mainly of periodic meetings between the juvenile and his or her probation officer in which the officer generally asks how the juvenile is doing. Sometimes counseling is done, either professionally or informally, by the probation officer, but typically the officer is so harried by other duties (for example, writing social history reports and making contact with relatives of the juvenile) that this important part of probation cannot be accomplished. If the probation officer knows that the juvenile is having a specific problem at home, at school, or at work, he or she can serve as a mediator or can attempt to change the actions of the youth or the source of the problem if it is not the youth. Because there is a good deal of variation among departments in the size of caseloads and the types of juveniles who are typically placed on probation, the time the probation officer has available for counseling activities varies widely.[5]

The probation officer's ability to control the youth is pretty much limited to talk, whether it is counseling or threats. Probation can be rescinded on the recommendation of the probation officer, with the juvenile either freed or put into an institution, and this power certainly has the potential to compel the youth to respect the probation officer. But the promises of early release from probation and threats of incarceration are merely talk. As soon as the probation officer invokes the actions implied in his talk (that is, release from probation), the juvenile is legally outside of the officer's control.

The conditions of probation and the ability of a probation department to make sure that these conditions are met depend on the available resources of the department. The following recommendation illustrates the problems involved in carrying out a probation sentence.

It is respectfully recommended to the Court that if the allegations contained in the petition filed in behalf of Smithfield Elston are found to be true he be declared a ward of the Juvenile Court of County—, his care, custody and control to be placed with—, who is authorized and directed to release the minor in the direct custody of his mother under the following terms and conditions of probation:
1. That he violate no law or ordinance;
2. That he obey the reasonable directive of his mother or the Probation Officer at all times;
3. That he attend school regularly and obey all school rules and regulations;
4. That he not be out after dark unless accompanied by his mother or some adult person approved by her;
5. That he report once each month to the Probation Officer, either in person or in writing.[6]

The first three of the five conditions of probation are simply a reiteration of what is required of all juveniles. The curfew and the monthly report to the probation officer are the only social requirements of a youth on probation. The degree of guidance that can come from a monthly meeting or letter to the probation officer is probably minimal, and judging from probation officers' common complaints of being overburdened with cases, it is often nil. This state of affairs is a continual source of frustration and despair to probation officers who still hope to help juveniles and a source of cynicism for those who have given up any pretense of helping juveniles.

One problem in juvenile probation supervision is the total lack of understanding of the purpose of probation. There are different ideas of what constitutes proper probation work, and no philosophy unifies them. Blumberg[7] points out that probation philosophy is identical to that of social work, but this is not always the case. On the one hand probation is a punitive/control function to ensure the safety of the community and punishment of the offender. This is clearly contrary to the ideal of *parens patriae,* which holds that the function of juvenile justice is to do the "best" for the offender and to help him or her. Probation officers claim, however, that it is unrealistic and impractical to assume such lofty ideals. They point out that youths will "get away with murder" if they are not controlled, citing numerous examples of violent acts by juveniles. The other side of probation, ideally at least, holds that the juvenile offender needs guidance and assistance. Various psychiatric, psychological, and sociological counseling practices can be employed to this end, but juvenile probation is such a hodgepodge of various methods, including no methods at all, that it is virtually impossible to point to any single one and state that it represents this guiding side of probation supervision. A number of years ago Healy and Bronner defined probation as "a term that gives no clue to what is done by way of treatment,"[8] and there does not seem to be much evidence that things have changed since then. True, probation officers today are better educated, and numerous different probation strategies are utilized, but the underlying philosophy and direction are no clearer than when Healy and Bronner wrote in the 1920s.

Attempts have been made to clarify the goal of probation and give it direction. The American Correctional Association has attempted to provide such direction and has spelled out the operational goal of probation as follows:

> Probation's most important achievement is not control of the probationer under supervision but rather enabling the probationer to understand himself and gain strength in independent control over his own behavior.[9]

Obviously, this is another form of control, but it states unequivocally that the mechanism for obtaining that control is counseling, not fear of sanctions.

The details of the mechanism for control may vary, but as long as there is a clear treatment direction instead of a punitive one, then the approach is consistent with the stated goal.

The treatment or counseling approach is valuable, but not for the reasons most people assume. In discussing the "treatment" approach to probation Carter and his associates point out that there is evidence that *any* program under the auspices of treatment or counseling is working, because the probation officer can attribute successes to the treatment program and attribute failures to repeat juvenile offenders.[10] There is the underlying assumption that *anything* done by the probation officer is for the probationer's good, and since anything happening to the probationer as a result of the probation officer is glossed over as "treatment," success is due to the treatment. Since the treatment ideal operates under the assumptions of the "medical model,"[11] if a "proven" treatment fails to work, it is assumed that there is something wrong with the patient's makeup. The phrase "the patient failed to respond to the treatment" presumes *patient failure;* whereas when we say the *treatment failed,* we point to the failure of the method of treatment. Therefore, recidivism is blamed on client failure, not program failure.

With this logic, probation always works. Moreover, a large number of juveniles who are placed on probation will not be repeat offenders no matter what happens on probation. This group of juveniles is in part made up of children who are nearing adulthood, and as we saw in previous chapters, there is a general decline in delinquent acts as adolescents become legal adults. Other juveniles who will not be repeat offenders include those who are not caught up in delinquent behavior patterns but simply happened to get into trouble and were labeled. By the same token, there are those who are going to fail regardless of what probation does to them. Individual probation officers realize this better than anyone else. If an adolescent "goes straight" who is "straight" to begin with, probation officers on an individual basis will not take credit for the "recovery." At the same time, if a child is "bad" or comes from a "bad environment," probation officers point out that there was nothing they could do. However, organizationally, the probation department can show an increase or decrease in recidivism, and as long as the nonrecidivists outnumber the recidivists, it can claim that the probation program is working.

Some children are affected by probation in ways that will either help them or harm them. A probation officer who helps a child overcome a problem that led the juvenile to delinquency can be said to "cure" the child. If the probation disposition serves to stigmatize a juvenile, it can be said to harm the youth. The problem is difficult to assess, as Diana concluded in his survey of probation officers:

It may well be that few correctional personnel are really aware of whatever techniques they use, and it is very highly probable that only a small percentage of the total are qualified caseworkers. It is also highly probable, and certainly seems to be the case from this writer's experience, that the image that many probation officers have of themselves is a picture of a warm and understanding though objective person, a kind of watered-down or embryonic clinician. In any event the influence of a clinical, casework ideology, along with its confused and contradictory elements, has been pervasive. Convention papers, the literature and supervisors are filled with this ideology, so that it is constantly before the probation officer. It is no more than could be expected, then, if the probation officer feels that whatever he does and however he does it, it *is* treatment.[12]

Since there is nothing to state what is being evaluated in terms of a systematic approach or philosophical grounding, it is almost impossible to measure where success has been due to probation or to something independent of probation. However, there seems to be little evidence that probation is any more successful in changing delinquents than doing nothing at all.

Since the problem in evaluating the success of probation is largely due to the absence of a clearly stated plan of operation and guiding theory, we should turn to those situations where probation has had a clear and measurable program. Here though, we encounter the problem of only counting successes and attributing failure to the client. In discussing evaluation of probation programs, Glaser points out:

> Failure to count dropouts in determining success rates is most dramatic at addiction treatment agencies, but occurs also in other people-changing efforts. Lerman reports that a private residential center for boys which he studied in New York rejects seventeen applicants for every one it admits, and subsequently expels 31 percent of the admittees "resisting treatment" before they complete the center's program, which has had an average duration of sixteen months. An evaluation that does not take into account the rejectees and expellees could clearly be misleading.[13]

Obviously, using the "dropouts" as failed clients rather than as indicators of a failure in the program will not evaluate the program. In Chapter 14, we will discuss the further ramifications and techniques of evaluation research and its application to delinquency programs. For now, suffice it to be aware of the importance of clear theoretically based programs and applicable research to evaluate the programs.

JUVENILES IN INCARCERATION

One problem in coming to terms with juvenile corrections is the language used to describe the institutions and the juveniles placed in them. We have used "correctional facilities" and other terms that suggest that some form of rehabilitation is supposed to take place. However, as we have pointed out, whether they are called "temporary holding facilities," "reformatories," "training schools," or whatever, these institutions are often nothing more than prisons in which juveniles are housed; therefore, they will be referred to here as "incarceratories." We do not wish to imply that juvenile incarceratories are good or bad or that no rehabilitation, correction, or reformation takes place in them. We simply want to avoid the implication that merely because they are designated in the offical jargon by the process they are supposed to perform, they actually fulfill that function. The following account by the author of a visit to a Dutch juvenile incarceratory illustrates why this terminology is used:

> The most striking thing about the juvenile prison, as the Dutch called it, was its setting. They had converted a Nazi concentration camp into what we would call a reformatory. The same barbed-wire fences used by the Nazis, with curved cement poles for holding the wires, were still in place. The buildings, including a crematorium outside the fence, were the same ones used to house Jews and other political undesirables by the Nazis in the Second World War. The interiors of the buildings were not bad, and indeed the Dutch had done a great deal to liven up the inside of these heinous structures. There was an abundance of trees and shrubs, and were it not for the fact that it had once been a concentration camp, the setting itself was quite pleasant. The director of the prison referred to the boys as "inmates," and even though they were treated more like students, it was refreshing to hear what I considered honest terminology. There were more staff than there were inmates, and there appeared to be a maximum effort to help the boys—mostly with vocational training—but since the director of the prison was a psychologist, there were counseling programs as well. There was an attempt to be democratic in some of the decision making; they held weekly meetings and discussions where complaints were aired, and the prisoners could vote on a number of alternatives. There was little emphasis on control, and some boys joked that they had to remind the guards, who stood near the entrance, to keep others *out.* If any of the boys wanted to escape, they would have had little difficulty. Had the prison been in the United States and were the setting not that of a former Nazi concentration camp, it would probably be seen as a greatly enlightened and progressive "reformatory."

As this description suggests, everything about the operation of the Dutch juvenile incarceratory belied its name. One who merely heard the name and knew of the setting might have concluded that the Dutch are unreasonably harsh in their treatment of juvenile offenders. Getting behind appearances and the official bureaucratic/psychiatric/social work jargon better enables us to understand what juvenile incarceratories are. In order to examine juvenile corrections, we need to look at additional examples and conceptualize what is taking place in terms of organizational routines.

For reasons that will become clear later, the custodial-oriented incarceratories for juveniles operate pretty much in line with the custodial goal they espouse. We will look first at an institution at the rehabilitative end of the continuum. The name of our example, the Fricot (California) Ranch School for Boys connotes the type of place the institution was designed to be.

In general, the Fricot Ranch School operates under the "training school" concept of rehabilitation, attempting to provide some form of educational and moral training so that boys and girls who have gotten into trouble will be "cured" or "rehabilitated." Moreover, this is done through understanding and communication instead of control and repression. The daily routine at the Fricot Ranch School is as follows:

> Lights are turned on at 6:05 A.M. The group is on silence during dressing and washing up, then the boys line up in the hallway, where quiet talking is allowed until they leave for the dining room at 6:35. On the dining-hall ramp the boys stand silent at attention until the "At ease, quiet talking" order is given. In the dining room low talking is allowed, but no horseplay or trading of food. After breakfast the group is moved to the lodge yard, where the supervisor takes a count and runs a bathroom call. He selects crews to sweep and mop the lodge washroom, locker room, day room, dormitory, honor room hall and office, and supervises the work. At 8:25 the boys are ordered into formation; the supervisor takes another count and then accompanies the group to the academic school building. When classes are let out at 11:30 A.M., the boys go directly to the dining-hall ramp, met by their supervisor, who takes count before the group enters. After lunch the boys go to the lodge, usually for a quiet period in the day room or on their beds, sometimes going on a short hike or playing indoors. At 1:05 P.M. they are ordered into formation for a count, then move again to the school building, followed by the supervisor. School is dismissed for the day at 4:15, and the boys go directly to their lodge yard, met by their supervisor, who takes a count, then usually allows free play. By 4:30 P.M. the boys are moved into the lodge to wash up before dinner, and they leave the lodge about 5:05 P.M. to march to the dining hall. After the meal the group moves back to the lodge for a count, a bathroom call, and a brief period of free play outdoors or in the lodge. At 6:15 P.M. the group is split, following the preferences of the boys, for the evening activities, which may include a hike, organized games, or supervised crafts. Activities end at 8:00 P.M., when the boys are returned to the lodge. They brush their teeth, undress, put their shorts, socks, and T shirts into laundry bags, and take showers by groups. As soon as they have showered, the boys go to their beds, and there is "package call"—which means that those who have received from home packages of cookies, candy, and toys may enjoy these treats until 9:30, when all boys must be in their beds. No boy is allowed out of bed after 10:30 unless it is to go to the bathroom, and during the night the supervisor quietly moves through the lodge to take a count of the boys three times every hour.[14]

This routine is designed to provide close interpersonal relations between staff and the boys—the main emphasis of the "rehabilitation." However, there are a number of social forces working in the opposite direction. First of all, well-developed inmate groups form which exercise greater influence than the "therapeutic milieu."[15] Indeed, at the Fricot Ranch School, the supervisors had what might be called an "exploitative truce" with the leaders of the various cliques.[16] The supervisors had to keep on the good side of the clique leaders if they hoped to maintain control. Boys who were given a choice between being ostracized or beaten by the powerful clique leaders or following the directions of the supervisors would generally succumb to the peer pressure.

Secondly, if we look carefully at the routine, we can see it more as a means of control than of therapy and rehabilitation. The lining-up and marching-off patterns are means of moving people in batches commonly used in total institutions.[17] By providing for some activity at all times, the authorities have maximal control. In custodial types of institutions, where there are fewer planned activities, there is actually less control. Additionally, the activities functioned both as punishments and as exhausting devices. Boys who got out of line were made to take strenuous hikes and to participate in "sports."[18] In one incarceratory observed by the author, a supervisor explained that the purpose of the daily athletic schedule was not "therapy," nor did juvenile corrections professionals espouse the philosophy that there is a relationship between sports and character building. Instead, they believe that a hectic athletic program will tire the kids out and make them more easily controllable.

At this point the reader should be able to see the common thread running through all incarceratories regardless of the institutional policy. As we noted in passing, juvenile incarceratories are total institutions—that is, establishments that control all facets of the inmates' day-to-day existence.[19] Total organizations include prisons, the military, mental institutions, and convents. The emphasis in these organizations is on control of the clientele or membership. In institutions that admit to control as their primary end, such as those with a custodial policy, we are not surprised to find an emphasis on control. However, in institutions with a rehabilitative policy, we see a displacement of goals, for inevitably the goal of control comes to replace the goal of rehabilitation in the daily routine. At first, this would seem to contradict the benign policy of "guidance" and "rehabilitation," but in fact a treatment orientation, like traditional punishment, is nothing more than a form of control. The basic assumption behind any treatment program—necessarily, it would seem—is that the treaters are "right" and those who are to receive the treatment are "wrong." That is, the administrators of treatment see something wrong with those who are to be given treatment. In order to apply the treatment, those who are to receive it must be controlled, and the end of treatment is also control, in the form of self-control. Thus, both the means and the ends of treatment are control.

In order to have control, treatment-oriented incarceratories engage in manipulation of inmates by rewarding those who comply with institutional policy. Reciprocally, the inmates develop an "underlife" wherein they attempt to overcome the control of their keepers, whether it is custodial or treatment-oriented.[20] The authorities' response to the inmate subculture is further control mechanisms, and the counterresponse is further inmate manipulation for the scarce and controlled goods and services. This cycle completely destroys the efforts at treatment as the staff comes to be more and more concerned with basic custodial control.

Part of the problem with the various treatment policies is the assumption that the inmates are inert and blind to the attempts to change them. No matter how good their intentions are, treatment orientations are always frustrated to some degree by their charges' lack of cooperation. Inmates, however, are very much aware of what is happening. One inmate pointed out that treatment programs measure the success of an inmate in terms of how far he has "progressed" from the time he entered the program. Inmates who were as difficult as possible at the outset of treatment were able to demonstrate faster "progress" than inmates who immediately cooperated. Therefore, the inmates who at first "raised hell" and then later settled down and cooperated were regarded as "cured" much sooner. The con-wise inmates knew this while the novices did not; as a result, the treatment program was manipulated more effectively than it manipulated those who were being treated.*

Another problem with rehabilitation programs is in evaluating their effects. Improved postrelease behavior may be due merely to having been locked up, or it may be due to treatment or to changes in society. For example, a study in Florida found that after the introduction of a "guided group interaction" treatment program there was a 44-percent reduction in delinquent recidivism.[21] At first it appeared that this might be due to the introduction of the new treatment program. However, in comparing Florida's rate of delinquent recidivism with that of Arkansas, it was found that the Arkansas rate was about 10 percent lower. Since the Arkansas training schools had no "guided group interaction" program, it was difficult to believe that the effect of the programs was the significant causal variable.[22] Different juvenile adjudicatory programs, different styles of law enforcement, or any number of other factors might have contributed to the different rates of recidivism in Florida and Arkansas. Without improved research and evaluation methods, we are in the dark as to the effectiveness of the various programs.

In summary, the effectiveness of juvenile incarceratories, whatever they are called and whether they are guided by a custodial or a rehabilitative policy, is often to be questioned. Evaluation procedures are very poor, and attempts to appraise what these institutions are doing suggest that the evidence is equivocal not only as to their effectiveness but as to their actual operation. However, it is certain that incarceratories do not "cure" delinquency, and there is evidence that they are more a part of the problem than of the solution.

*I am grateful to George Muedeking for this example.

THE EXPERIENCE OF INCARCERATION

In order to understand what happens to incarcerated juveniles, we will examine some selected experiences of youths who are locked up. What we often fail to understand, even under the best conditions of detention, is that there is a subjective experience on the part of the juvenile aside from the intended experience. Matza spoke of the "sense of injustice" experienced by juveniles in their encounters with the juvenile justice system.[23] From the point of view of those who administered the "justice," the subjective experience and interpretations of the juveniles who believed the system to be unjust was not warranted. The administrators of justice *intended* the best for the juveniles, and because of benign intentions, it was supposed that no matter what the youth believed to be the case, the course of action taken by the administrators would have the desired effect. However, as George Herbert Mead correctly pointed out, experiences are self-mediating, and rather than taking an uncritical view of a set of "stimuli," we must consider the sense that is made from what individuals encounter.[24]

The juvenile's initial experience with incarceration is when he or she is arrested and sent to a detention center to await some disposition. The following is from a letter smuggled out of one such center:

> You get off the paddy wagon; you walk up the steps; ring the doorbell. You are told to sit; you sit, sit and you sit; you listen to the guards talk about dirty jokes at home and so forth until most leave. Then you sit, and sit and sit until the guard tells you to stand. After you stand, he checks your hair and your jacket, your shirt, underarms, and pants, stockings, shoes, and does a very bad job of it. He takes what he finds and your belt and puts it in a big envelope. If you have cigarettes, he says he has to confiscate them, so he takes them, takes one out and lights up and puts the rest in his top left-hand shirt pocket.
>
> Then, you sit down again and watch him smoke your cigarettes. Then he comes over and has a form and he asks you your name, age, date of birth, father's name, mother's name, who you live with, what is the address, if you are gay, if you are to take any medicine, and if so what and when.
>
> Then, you take that form to another guard who throws a towel in your face, points to the shower, and tells you to wipe up the floor when you are done. When you are done, he tells you to take a seat in a room. In the room there are about two dozen kids from the age of nine to eighteen, for crimes ranging from stealing three dime bars of candy to strong armed robbery or shooting a person. In all two dozen boys sit there and watch TV until 9 o'clock at night. At 9 o'clock, we get searched again as badly as before then we get in two's by height and march up to the second floor and strip and get into a bed, and you must not make a noise, if you do the guards tell you they will beat the shit out of you or put their foot up your ass. . . .
>
> . . . now I will tell you what I think of this Audy Home. It does not help children, I myself am good because I don't want the shit beat out of me or stand on a wall for 10 hours with no exaggeration. When you are in here it is easy to

quit smoking if you stay away from the guards for they will blow smoke in your face to tease you. And the TV, what good is it, because half the time the guards watch what *they* want, and in the gym you have to exercise. They make you do so many [exercises] you don't want to play basketball or anything else. I am not saying that because I am soft, because I did exercise for an hour a night when I was home, and when you play there are two checkerboards. One shuffleboard and three basketballs for more than 75 kids. It is a fucking shame and only the big boys get to do anything for the fact that they are big and the rest are small. When you sleep if someone talks then everyone has to stand for three hours or does a few hundred knee bends. Even if the person is revealed, you still do the punishment. At all hours of the night you are woken up because some guards are laughing or shouting at each other or they have the TV or radio on full blast. But some guards are nice. The food is good and you eat the right things but not enough of them or anything else. You are always ashamed if you bump into someone accidentally and say you are sorry and they hit you, you can't hit back because if you do anything, that is 15 hours standing up on the wall; if you say anything for yourself, forget it, you will be on the wall until you mix with the paint. It wouldn't be so bad if it wasn't so boring and unfair. I think at Audy Home that they are very unorganized, especially the school system. It has very good teachers, but they teach only a fourth-grade level. I think in all, it would help if the people who worked there cared.[25]

The description of the detention center was written by a 14-year-old white boy from the suburbs who was locked up because he left home several times for being mistreated. The punishments are extreme, but the institution is not meant to be a rehabilitation center. The superintendent said in 1969,

There are security measures in all sections because this is a security institution. Each section is so keyed that no one can enter or leave that section except the people in it. And the external security features are quite visible. We have security windows, we have a wall around the yard, and I think it is pretty obvious that this is a security institution.[26]

The experience of those locked up in such institutions is not so much one of "fear" as it is the sense of injustice fostered by the treatment received there. Arguments citing the deterrence values of such institutions are invalid, for as Matza points out, whenever there is a sense of injustice the moral bind of the law is loosened.[27] Since the incarcerated youths experience injustice in these institutions, upon release instead of having respect for law and justice, they experience the opposite. Therefore, they are far more likely to enter into drift and abandon any commitment to conventional values and laws than if they had experienced "justice" in their encounters with the juvenile justice system.

For girls, the sense of injustice is likely to be even greater in the juvenile correctional system. Catherine Milton and her associates pointed out that girls are more likely to be sent to detention once they enter the adjudication proceedings, and they are more likely to be given a detention disposition for juvenile-status offenses.[28] Most of the juvenile-status offenses involve pro-miscuity, co-habitation, spending the night with a member of the opposite sex, general sex innuendo, prostitution, and "association with undesirable friends."[29] Except for prostitution, none of these offenses are criminal. The following case history typifies the kind of girl who gets locked up:

Melissa was 15 when she was first arrested. She was living with her parents and her two sisters. Her father supported the family on his $7,000 annual salary. Melissa is an attractive young woman and until the time of her first arrest, was doing well in school. According to school officials she is intelligent, made excellent grades and had a good attitude about school.

Within a month's time Melissa was arrested twice. The first time her mother called the police requesting that they pick Melissa up because she refused to go to school, and because lately she had been "getting upset too easily and having lots of emotional scenes." When the police arrived Melissa had left the house. They found her a few minutes later walking in the rain a short distance away. She was arrested and charged with running away. Melissa explained to the police that she did not want to return home because her father beat her. She asked the police if she could go to live with an aunt. However, her mother would not give her approval because "it wouldn't look right." Melissa then spent eight days in detention before she was returned to her parents' home. A few days later the police received a call from Melissa asking that they please come get her because she had just had an "argument" with her father and she was afraid he would hurt her. When the police arrived, they arrested Melissa at her request and again charged her with running away.

This time Melissa waited in detention for two weeks until she was placed with a foster family and ordered to attend a day school for troubled girls where she could receive counseling. Melissa was unhappy at the new school and eventually was dismissed for fighting with other girls. A few days later she was also asked to leave her foster home for "abusing the telephone" and having a "belligerent and non-conforming attitude," according to her foster parents.

Melissa was then placed at St. Ann's, a residential parochial school for "difficult" boys and girls. After a month and a half she ran away from there. While on the street she tried unsuccessfully to find a new foster home so she would not be returned to St. Ann's. Apprehended by the police, she refused to go back to St. Ann's and was placed in detention where she remained for two weeks.

She was then placed in a community residential program but was soon dismissed for leaving without permission to attend a local fair and for spending time with an unknown young man. She was returned to the detention center for four months before being committed to the state training school for girls.[30]

From the point of view of the child who is placed in detention for "misbehavior" amounting to no more than a juvenile-status offense, the punishment seems to greatly outweigh the crime. This is especially true in the case of girls, for there has been a far greater proportion of girls in juvenile incarceratories for juvenile-status offenses than boys. A 1976 survey of state training schools showed that approximately 50 percent of the girls in state institutions and 17 percent of the boys were locked up because of juvenile-status offenses.[31] The injustice of the relatively harsh treatment of girls is compounded when we consider the traditional role of women in society. If we take school as basically preparatory for a career and examine the role of the housewife, we find that society has placed far more pressure on boys to attend school than girls.[32] Many women with a college degree become housewives, never employing their education. Why, then, are the sanctions for such juvenile-status offenses as truancy applied with more severity against girls? This contradiction is more than irony; it is injustice, and to the extent to which this injustice is experienced by juvenile girls, the moral bind of the law is loosened.

CONCLUSION

The correctional mechanisms of the juvenile justice system began with the idea of "helping" youths adjust to society in such a way that they would grow up to become productive members of society. Upon examination of this ideal from either a critical or humanistic perspective, it is clear that the "help" amounted to a form of social control, and one that is unevenly and ineffectively applied. Thus, rather than helping juveniles, the system has had the opposite effect; it has fostered a sense of injustice.

This is not to say that there are a number of features of juvenile justice that provide a far more lenient form of corrections, but the situation in juvenile corrections is not what was intended. Visions of turning juveniles into responsible adults—either for reasons of exploitation as suggested by the critical theorists or for humanistic reasons—remains merely a vision. There is an unknown relationship between non-recidivism and juvenile corrections, but upon examination of what transpires in juvenile incarceratories, the intended rehabilitative processes are not operating. Therefore, any "rehabilitation" in the form of non-recidivism cannot be said to be linked to the rehabilitation program.

In conclusion, the correctional aspects of the juvenile justice system are not "working" in any intended fashion envisioned by the reformers who created the system. This fact is known to those responsible for juvenile corrections as well as researchers in the field of corrections. Steps have been taken to remedy this situation, both in the form of new programs and general diversion from the juvenile justice system. In the following chapter, we will examine some of the new directions in attempting to control and reform juveniles.

NOTES

1. President's Commission on Law Enforcement and Administration of Justice, *The Challenge of Crime in A Free Society* (Washington, D.C.: Government Printing Office, 1967), p. 161.
2. U.S. Department of Justice, *Children in Custody: Advance Report on the Juvenile Detention and*

Correctional Facility Census of 1972–73 (Washington, D.C.: Government Printing Office, May 1975), p. 1.

3. Peter G. Garabedian and Don C. Gibbons (eds.), *Becoming Delinquent: Young Offenders and the Correctional System* (Chicago: Aldine, 1970), pp. 222–223.

4. Edwin H. Sutherland and Donald R. Cressey, *Criminology,* 10th ed. (Philadelphia: Lippincott, 1978), p. 533.

5. Robert M. Carter and Leslie T. Wilkins (eds.), *Probation, Parole: Selected Readings* (New York: Wiley, 1970).

6. Aaron Cicourel, *The Social Organization of Juvenile Justice* (New York: Wiley, 1968), p. 212.

7. Abraham Blumberg, *Criminal Justice* (Chicago: Quadrangle, 1967), p. 144.

8. William Healy and Augusta Bronner, *Delinquents and Criminals: Their Making and Unmaking* (New York: Macmillan, 1926), p. 82.

9. American Correctional Association, *Manual of Correctional Standards* (Washington, D.C.: American Correctional Association, 1966), pp. 107–108.

10. Robert M. Carter, Richard McGee, and Kim E. Nelson, *Corrections in America* (Philadelphia: Lippincott, 1975), p. 190.

11. Erving Goffman, *Asylums* (New York: Doubleday, 1961).

12. Lewis Diana, "What Is Probation?" *Journal of Criminal Law, Criminology and Police Science, 51:*189–204 (July–August 1960).

13. Daniel Glaser, *The Effectiveness of Prison and Parole Systems* (Indianapolis, Ind.: Bobbs-Merrill, 1969), p. 163.

14. Carl F. Jesness, *The Fricot Ranch Study* (Sacramento, Calif.: State of California, Department of the Youth Authority, 1965), p. 9.

15. Garabedian and Gibbons, p. 224.

16. Jesness.

17. Goffman.

18. Jesness.

19. Goffman.

20. *Ibid.*

21. Robert J. Grissom, "The Effect of Guided Group Interaction Programs on Juvenile Delinquent Recidivism," unpublished research paper, University of Florida, Gainesville, 1974.

22. *Ibid.,* pp. 64–67.

23. David Matza, *Delinquency and Drift* (New York: Wiley, 1964), pp. 101–106.

24. George Herbert Mead, *Mind, Self and Society* (Chicago: University of Chicago Press, 1934).

25. Patrick T. Murphy, *Our Kindly Parents—The State* (New York: Viking, 1974), pp. 109–112.

26. *Ibid.,* pp. 108–109.

27. Matza, p. 102.

28. Catherine Milton, Catherine Pierce, Mona Lyons and Betsy Hippensteel, *Little Sisters and the Law* (Washington, D.C.: U.S. Department of Justice, August, 1977), pp. 10–12.

29. *Ibid.,* p. 8.

30. *Ibid.,* p. 8.

31. *Ibid.,* p. 72.

32. Helena Znaniecki Lopata, "The Life Cycle of the Social Role of Housewife," *Sociology and Social Research, 50:*5–22, (1966).

13 New Directions in Delinquency Control

INTRODUCTION

This chapter explores alternatives to the traditional modes of delinquency control. For the purposes of this discussion we will consider juvenile probation and incarceration the traditional means of controlling delinquency, realizing, of course, that a number of innovations exist in some probation departments and detention facilities. The alternative programs we will discuss, however, are indicators of failure in the traditional juvenile justice system. The new programs often attempt to provide justice where the traditional ones have failed to do so. At the same time, the new programs point to the failure of traditional treatment to rehabilitate or control delinquents. Thus, we will examine the new efforts to deal with delinquency in terms of providing justice and rehabilitation for juveniles.

By 1976, the Office of Juvenile Justice and Delinquency Prevention listed 117 different federal programs designed to provide justice, or prevent or reduce delinquency.[1] These programs ranged from Foster Grandparents to a State and Community Highway Safety Program. Obviously, not all of the plans are directly linked to juvenile justice or delinquency prevention, and it would be inappropriate to merely list or outline all of the federal, state, and local programs. Instead, we will select some of them with an eye to evaluating their appropriateness to deal with the underlying causes of delinquency in a just manner. Unfortunately, not many of the programs have been evaluated by social scientists to determine their effectiveness or even whether the juvenile populations at whom programs are directed are delinquent. Therefore, we will take only selected programs whose general orientation is relevant to several similar programs and discuss their operation and merits.

EDUCATIONAL PROGRAMS

In certain respects, virtually every program for juveniles involves some sort of education or views education as a means of reducing delinquency. Here we will focus on programs specifically designed to prevent delinquency by providing educational programs that will enhance the opportunities of juveniles or to reorient their behavior. Many of the educational programs are aimed at a general target group, usually a disadvantaged or minority group with a high rate of official delinquency, while others are used in conjunction with either a specific group of delinquents in or out of detention or aimed at a typical form of delinquent activity, such as drug use.

Theoretical Orientation

Education programs rest on two different sociological theories, structural and cultural. The structural theories of Merton[2] and Cloward and Ohlin[3] point to structural blocks to success goals. Denied opportunities for success, some juveniles turn to illegitimate (delinquent) means to achieve the goals. Since education is virtually a requirement for success in contemporary society, these programs seek to remedy the lack of opportunity due to inadequate education.[4] Some programs are aimed at overcoming language barriers, such as bilingual programs, while others provide special education for disadvantaged children whose preschool preparation is inadequate for educational achievement. In addition, there are vocational education programs for juveniles who do not achieve or have little interest in academic subjects; special teachers corps for placing teachers in areas where skilled teachers are in short supply; programs to reduce the dropout rate; and a whole spectrum of educational efforts aimed at enhancing the opportunities of children whose position in society place them at an educational disadvantage.

A second guiding philosophy behind educational programs is represented by the subcultural theories of Miller,[5] Cohen,[6] and Cloward and Ohlin.[7] Cloward and Ohlin contributed to both structural and cultural understandings of delinquency. In the context of subcultural theories, education played the role of resocializing juveniles whose subcultural beliefs placed value on delinquent acts. In a very real sense, the education was meant to be a "moral education," instilling conventional values to replace delinquent ones. Thus while the early "child savers" stated that a moral education was part of the reform process,[8] the subcultural approach implies as much.

Taking the structural and cultural theories together and applying them to delinquency prevention in the form of special educational programs appeared promising. Those who were labeled culturally disadvantaged would be given a boost in their ability to compete legitimately while at the same time the programs would seek to reorient their views. Children who had failed because of language difficulties could now succeed, and children whose preschool background had been inadequate would be given a headstart. Social inequality would be eradicated, and everyone would be given an equal chance—or at least a more equal chance.

Applications and Results

The educational programs were in the form of numerous federally funded projects, some of which we have already mentioned. Bilingual programs, special preschool classes for disadvantaged children, and even special college entrance requirements and grants have been made available to those groups who are overrepresented in the delinquency population. From the point of view of the administrators, a lot was being done that previously had not been, and there clearly were greater opportunities to get ahead.

There is little evidence that the programs have been successful, however, for there has been no general decline in delinquency among disadvantaged youths, and those who have succeeded may have done so without the programs. The structure of society is such that there are only so many success positions to begin with, and if there is a general shift into these positions by one group, there will have to be a displacement of another group. Therefore, if structural frustration is at the heart of the matter, there is always going to be a group that is on the outside. Whether this group will continue to be overrepresented by minorities or not is a moot point if the main argument is a structural one: that is, that the *nature of the social structure induces delinquent behavior*. By shifting around who will be at a structural disadvantage begs the question, for unless there is a change in the structure there will be a constant pattern of delinquency. Only the players will change.

Second, as Matza[9] noted, what are considered delinquent subcultures are hardly as delinquent as the term suggests. Most people go through a delinquent phase in life, but the general orientation is a fairly conventional one. Therefore, the values in a subculture of delinquency are largely conventional ones, and most of the subcultural members enter into conventional noncriminal roles. Since special educational programs are generally directed at high-delinquency groups rather than at specific groups of delinquents, a certain success rate is given regardless of the programs' content because most people are not committed to delinquency in the first place. This is not to say that the programs do not provide some equity to those in disadvantaged positions, but rather that the programs assume a helplessness and proclivity toward delinquency in these groups that may not exist in reality.

The application of education programs to prevent or reduce delinquency in middle-class areas has been geared toward the use of drugs. The Drug Enforcement Administration provides through its Public Education on Drug Abuse program various forms of educational materials to be used in the schools to educate children about drugs. Moreover, state and local programs involving the police also provide the schools with literature, films, and speakers about drugs and drug abuse. However, as we pointed out in Chapter 8, the credibility of such effort may be nil, for the experience of the drug users may contradict what the education provides. Moreover, since drug use is largely initiated and continued in groups, there is a strong countervailing force in the form of peer association and shared experiences.

Perhaps the greatest criticism of these programs comes from the critical theorists. For example, Quinney and Wildeman[10] point out that all of the apparently benign applications of knowledge and education are masking efforts to control the oppressed. The capitalist structure rests on inequality because the means of production are privately owned, and the owners, or power elite, manipulate the masses for their own interests. Since the interests of those in power lie in maintaining the status quo and their privileged positions within the structure, any actions taken by the institutions the elite control are guided not by humanism but by self-interest. If, as the critical theorists point out, structural inequities are at the root of delinquency, then why try to change the behavior of the individuals without changing the structure? Delinquency-prevention programs that have changed the opportunity structure for disadvantaged youths have merely given some of this group a greater opportunity to succeed in the *existing* structure, but they have not altered the basic structure so that all members of society can achieve *equality*. The solution, according to the critical theorists, is to replace the capitalist system with a socialist system, thereby eliminating the contradictions and inequities of capitalism.[11]

If we assume a structuralist position, the critical theorists make a strong point. There are many similarities in the underlying assumptions between the structuralism of Parsons and Merton and that of Marx and the critical theorists. The most basic is that delinquency is rooted in the social structure, and only by a change in the structure can the problem of delinquency be solved. This is not to say that all of the structuralists reach the same conclusions, but they do share a number of basic assumptions.

Yet several problems are associated with the structuralists' position, whether Mertonian or Marxist. First, a number of disadvantaged groups—such as the elderly—commit hardly any crime or delinquency. Older people suffer from numerous structural disadvantages, yet they do not engage in many activities that violate the law. Similarly, women, who commit more crime than is often realized, do not commit the same amount of crime as men, who are in a far better position in the social structure. Furthermore, there is no cross-cultural data to show that as societies move toward socialism their delinquency rate decreases. Holland and Switzerland are examples of countries with low delinquency rates but with capitalistic economic structures.* Finally, different groups have different rates of crime and delinquency within the same economic structure. Orientals, for example, have had a generally lower crime and delinquency rate in the United States than either whites or other minority groups.

To the extent to which a program is grounded in some theory, the failure of the program is indicative of a failure in the theory. Administrative mismanagement and external variables (such as unexpected social upheavals) may not be accounted for and certainly do not reflect the ideal of the theory on which a program is based; and as such the "test" of the theory is not an appropriate or fair one. However, we cannot fail to question seriously the validity of a theory if a program based on implied tenets of a theory fails.

---

*While it is true that Holland has had socialist governments, it is not the case that the economic structure is essentially a socialist one. Royal Dutch Shell Oil is a thriving capitalist concern.

GANG INTERVENTION

As opposed to, but not in contradiction of, the structuralist approach, is something we can call the intervention approach. This idea is vaguely connected with the subcultural theories. Because of the visibility of juvenile gangs and public concern over gang activities—in addition, of course, to the very real problem of gang violence—gang delinquency has been recognized as a unique form of misconduct. One approach to the gang problem, which developed in the late fifties and was implemented in the sixties, was to intervene in the day-to-day lives of the gang members. Mobilization for Youth in New York, the Los Angeles Youth Project, the Chicago Area Project, and San Francisco's Youth for Service are some of the better-known examples of these "gang-prevention" programs.[12] Those who worked directly with the gang members were called "detached workers" or "street workers," and the gang-prevention programs were generally referred to as "street work" programs.

In the most general terms, the programs were designed as an alternative to juvenile corrections. It was hoped that sending detached workers to work with the gang on its own turf would decrease the amount of juvenile delinquency. According to Klein,[13] the rationales for this approach included the following:

1. Detached work is the only effective way to maintain contact with "hard-to-reach" gang membership.
2. Left to their own devices, gang members manage to mire themselves ever more deeply in a self-defeating netherworld of alienation and deprivation.
3. The societal costs, physical and financial, of gang activity require that special attention be paid to procedures that might reasonably be expected to decrease that activity.

A detached worker with delinquent gangs may accomplish the following goals:

1. Control (principally of gang fighting).
2. Treatment of individual problems.
3. Providing access to opportunities.
4. Value change.
5. Prevention of delinquency.

The general operation of these programs involved a detached worker "adopting" a gang and working with it—that is, helping to find jobs for gang members, encouraging them to stay in school, planning various social events such as dances, sports, trips, and other activities to keep them out of trouble, and acting as arbitrator or mediator in gang disputes.

The success of the programs was for the most part questionable. A number of the major projects had no evaluation program whatsoever, and it is difficult to say whether any observed change in the gang's behavior was due to the detached worker's presence or to some other factor. In those cases that were evaluated, most were not found to have reduced delinquency, and in at least one—the Group Guidance Project in Los Angeles—there was an *increase* in delinquency among gang members.[14] Most programs simply did not work. A major exception was the Ladino Hills Project, which attempted to break up the gang's cohesiveness, regarded as the major contributing factor in the boys' delinquency. By doing so it reduced the overall number of gang offenses by 35 percent.[15] However, the project did not reduce the number of offenses by individual gang members.

In some areas these projects were successful. Individual workers were able to stop a number of gang fights. In our discussion of gangs it will be remembered that gang members put a great deal of emphasis on appearing tough and brave; if they were ever put in a position where they had to fight or lose face, they would fight. The gang workers served as "face savers,"[16] providing warring gangs with an "out" to fighting, and thus were often able to stop the fights. The following account illustrates how this was done:

> After several days of "hassling" between the Generals and the Red Raiders, it was clear that the Generals would be waiting for the Red Raiders at 3:15 near a local school. At the Red Raider's club meeting on the eve of the promised clash, approximately 80 members appeared in an unusual show of strength. One might have thought there would be no avoiding an all-out gang fight, but I watched worker H. put together his counseling skills with his knowledge that most members were fearful and would accept a face-saving alternative.
>
> It took two hours of discussion and harangue, but H. convinced the boys that they should all gather at 3:30 the next day at a playground some *six blocks* away from the school. I went to the school at 3:00 the next day and saw some of the Generals waiting. I then went to the playground and counted over 40 Red Raiders making a *show of strength which could not lead to a dangerous fight.* They were in "the wrong place at the right time," with some even claiming that the Generals were "chicken" and "poop-butts" because of their failure to make an appearance. No one, of course, had informed the Generals that the Red Raiders would be at the playground. The Red Raiders were thus able to convince themselves that they had acted nobly by being visible and available, but they had also avoided a serious fight. Worker H. had played a tricky game, and he had won.[17]

Other than occasional successes in stopping fights and breaking up gangs, though, these projects generally failed to make a significant dent in gang delinquency. Attempting to understand why they failed, Klein points out that most of the projects either lacked theoretical perspectives or were based on a hodgepodge of theories.[18] Since theories are useful sources of direction when they are applied, the programs started without basic tools, or with such a motley assortment that they could never use them in a coordinated manner. Secondly, the scope of the problem was so great and the available resources so meager that the projects were doomed before they started. The conditions that led to the development and maintenance of the delinquent gangs could not be offset by a few workers in a few months. Thirdly, there was an absence of specifically appropriate techniques. Other than the techniques available for stopping gang fights (for example, truce meetings), which themselves were initially ad hoc measures taken by detached workers, there were either vague techniques that were difficult to operationalize (for example, talking to individual gang members) or none at all. Some of the techniques employed were inappropriate and served to increase the problems instead of reduce them. Often assigning a worker to a gang would actually increase the gang's cohesiveness; what had been a fairly loose gang would be brought together by the gang worker. Furthermore, being assigned a street worker was a sign of status for the gang members, for only the "baddest," toughest gangs got to have a gang worker. (These unanticipated consequences, it might be noted, were generally caused by benevolent motives on the part of the agencies that were attempting to "help" the gang boys, but it should be remembered that the unanticipated consequences of a "get tough" policy equally serve to increase delinquency.) Finally, the workers lacked any way to elicit cooperation from the gang boys or other agencies in the community. The detached worker was literally *detached.* He was generally an alien in the gang community, in periodic conflict with other agencies such as the police, the YMCA, boys' clubs, and other institutions in his working milieu. If the boys did not voluntarily cooperate, there was little he could do to make them do so, and the same was true of the other community agencies.

Having reviewed the meager successes and massive failures of the gang prevention programs, we are tempted to dismiss the whole thing as a well-intentioned idea that did not work. By this token, however, we might also junk the police, the courts, and the correctional system, because they too have failed to reduce delinquency. Over the years attempts have been made to improve the police, the courts, and the correctional facilities, and the crime rates for both adults and juveniles have continued to climb. Nevertheless, because the gang programs did have some successes that may not have been realized without them, it would be wrong to throw out the good along with the bad. By grounding gang prevention programs in theory instead of the vague practicalities of street work, we would have a much better chance of success.

DIVERSION

Throughout this book there have been a number of references to diversion and diversion programs for juveniles. Currently, diversion programs of one type or another are the predominant "new" approach to the problem of delinquency. As Cressey and McDermott have wryly noted,

Only a few years ago, most American chief probation officers and other juvenile justice administrators used the words "research" and "breakthrough" constantly if they wanted good marks from their superiors and their colleagues. In large cities, especially, ratings of "excellent" went to the men who frequently used this rhetoric and who developed the corresponding research programs. Now the word is "diversion," and it is diversion programs that win the accolades.[19]

Here we will examine the concept and practice of diversion in a number of forms and attempt to determine the extent to which it is something new and whether the programs reflect the theories on which it is based.

Theoretical Background

In its most elementary form diversion refers to keeping juveniles away from the formal juvenile processing system. The reason lies in the belief that the cure is worse than the problem. This is certainly nothing new, and as Randall Shelden has aptly noted:

> "diversion," in its various forms, has been used throughout history. Each "new" institution (reform schools, training schools, groups homes, etc.) has been established on the heels of the failure of old institutions which have become overcrowded, inhumane and costly. Each "new" institution has supposedly been more "humane" and would alleviate some of the problems created by existing institutions. In time, however, these institutions have become as harsh and overcrowded as those they have replaced.[20]

This is not to say there is no underlying theory to account for diversion of one sort or another, but rather it suggests that the solution has been tried before.

The 1967 Report of the President's Commission on Law Enforcement and Administration of Justice, *The Challenge of Crime in a Free Society,* recommended that special programs and agencies be established as an alternative to normal processing in the juvenile justice system. In its 1973 report, *A National Strategy to Reduce Crime,* the National Advisory Commission on Criminal Justice Standards and Goals echoed this recommendation. If agencies were established that could deal with various forms of delinquency, especially juvenile-status and petty offenses, juveniles would not have to suffer the undesirable consequences of juvenile corrections. More importantly, these new agencies would be able to provide real help and guidance instead of punishment couched in the rhetoric of "rehabilitation" and "reformation."

The Commission therefore recommended the establishment of Youth Service Bureaus in the communities to provide services for juveniles who get into trouble. Instead of being taken to a juvenile incarceratory, such juveniles would be diverted to the Youth Service Bureau for professional help. Juveniles arrested for less serious offenses or for the first time would not be sent to "crime schools," where they would come in to contact with juveniles who were committed to delinquent activities and identities.

The Youth Service Bureau (YSB) might merely be another name for reform school or juvenile hall, but there were important differences grounded in *specific* theories. The first difference between the YSB approach and the juvenile court concept lies in the minimal intervention by the YSB. Youths taken to the YSBs were to be counseled along with their families, and that would be the end of it. Second, there was stress on not establishing delinquent records for youths sent to YSBs. Finally, all of this was to be on a community level with the child remaining with the family. While it is true that the original juvenile court concept attempted to minimize the stigma of a delinquent record, the court was not even to be involved in the YSB concept, and there certainly was no assumption that the state could help juvenile-status offenders by packing them all away to a noncommunity center where they would be grouped with career delinquents.

The two underlying theories that gave the most recent form of diversion its unique flavor are labeling and differential association theory.[21] Labeling theory emphasized the process of stigmatizing a youth that is inherent in the juvenile justice system. Since most juveniles commit delinquencies, one of the main contributing factors to career delinquency and a delinquent identity was to be found not in the general social structure but in the juvenile justice system itself. By minimizing stigmatization, through minimal societal reaction in the form of the YSB, diversion sought to circumvent the labeling process and its accompanying problems. Moreover, since the initial thrust of the diversion programs were aimed at juvenile-status offenders, the emphasis was clearly on those whose involvement in delinquency was minimal.

Coupled with labeling theory, differential association theory made up the second half of the theoretical rationale for diversion. Since differential association stressed the learning of delinquent behavior patterns, it pointed out that if nondelinquent children (dependent children; juvenile-status offenders) were locked up with delinquent ones, there was a much greater chance that the nondelinquents would learn delinquent behavior patterns and thereby become delinquents themselves.

By themselves, differential association and labeling theories provide the necessary reason to develop a diversion program and certainly justify the concept of diversion. However, Edwin M. Schur developed what he called radical nonintervention.[22] Schur proposed that intervention should be minimized beyond even that of the YSB. Stressing labeling theory and control theory, especially Matza's theory of "drift," Schur pointed out that any intervention by the juvenile justice system, especially for juvenile-status offenses, could only lead to crystallizing a delinquent identity.[23] Schur, in what might be considered an inaccurate interpretation of differential association theory, stated that the cultural transmission theories (for example, differential association) assumed that only the lower classes commit delinquent acts.[24] Since self-report surveys showed that juveniles from every walk of life engage in delinquency, and that youths who were considered subcultural delinquents were not committed to delinquency as suggested by subcultural theories, it became evident that the reason so many youths from the lower classes were engaging in delinquency was that we *assumed* this to be the case and took actions to label the lower-class youths as delinquents. Schur, citing Matza, pointed out that most subcultural delinquents "mature out" of delinquent behavior patterns, and by intervening in their lives while in periodic situations of delinquency, all the system did was to reduce the possibility of the natural maturation process.[25]

TABLE 13–1. Reactions to Delinquency[a]

	Individual Treatment	Liberal Reform	Radical Nonintervention
Basic assumptions	Differentness of offenders; delinquency a symptom; psychosocial determinism	Delinquency concentrated in lower class; individual constrained—particularly by subcultural pressures; social determinism	Delinquency widespread throughout society; basic role of contingencies; neoantideterminism
Favored methodologies	Clinical; comparison of matched samples	Analysis of rate variations; ecological analysis; study of subcultures	Self-reports; observation; legal analysis
Focal point for research	The individual	Social class; local community	Interaction between the individual and the legal system (and other agencies of reaction)
Representative causal perspectives	Psychodynamic theories; family-oriented theories	Anomie theories; cultural transmission; opportunity theory	Labeling analysis; drift and situational theories
Prevention	Identification of "predelinquents"; probation and counseling	Street gang work; community programs; piecemeal socioeconomic reform	Deemphasis on singling out specific individuals; radical sociocultural change
Treatment	Therapy; training schools	Community programs; improving conditions in institutions	Voluntary treatment
Juvenile court	"Individualized justice"; rehabilitative ideal	Better training and caseloads; more attention to social factors	Narrow scope of juvenile court jurisdiction; increased formalization

[a] Edwin M. Schur, *Radical Non-intervention: Rethinking the Delinquency Problem* (Englewood Cliffs, N.J.: Prentice-Hall, 1973).

The difference between the diversion ideas prompted by labeling and differential association theories and diversion based on radical nonintervention as suggested by Schur is more than a matter of degree, for Schur took different theoretical assumptions about social processes and delinquency. However, both approaches to diversion point to the failure of the juvenile court to alter delinquent behavior and, indeed, blame the court for certain patterns of delinquency. Table 13-1 outlines Schur's position in relation to other approaches to delinquency.

A key difference between Schur's radical nonintervention and the programs listed under "liberal reform" lies in the area of treatment. An important aspect of the diversion programs to be developed under the idea of a Youth Service Bureau is referral to community agencies, as illustrated in Figure 13-1.

In contrast, under the concept of radical nonintervention, Schur proposes that treatment be voluntary, and even though there is an aspect of voluntarism under the YSB concept, there is a greater element of control than in radical nonintervention.

As characterized by Schur, the liberal reform idea of juvenile courts stresses "better training and reduced caseloads and more attention to social factors" in contrast to a "narrow scope of juvenile court jurisdiction and increased formalization." In this respect Schur misrepresents the so-called liberal reform position. In a collection of works relating to diversion, many of which come from the 1967 President's Commission on Law Enforcement and Administration of Justice, Carter and Klein show that a key element of diversion is to increase "procedural justice" (due process) and limit the scope of the juvenile court.[26]

In summary, there is not a great difference between the "radical" approach suggested by Schur and the YSB concept. It would not be misleading to say that the underlying theory of the diversion movement has been somewhere between liberal reform and radical nonintervention. Essentially, the position of diversion is that it is better to keep children out of the juvenile justice system than to expose them to all of the problems the system creates.

APPLICATIONS OF DIVERSION

The most notable effect of diversion programs has been to reduce the number of juvenile-status offenders in detention. This has been due largely to the enactment of state laws forbidding the "secure detention" or incarceration of first-time juvenile-status offenders. Such action would satisfy the applied concepts of differential association theory in that juvenile-status offenders would be less likely to come into contact with committed delinquents and delinquent behavior patterns. At the same time, such actions would partially satisfy the labeling concepts being applied in that the child arrested for a

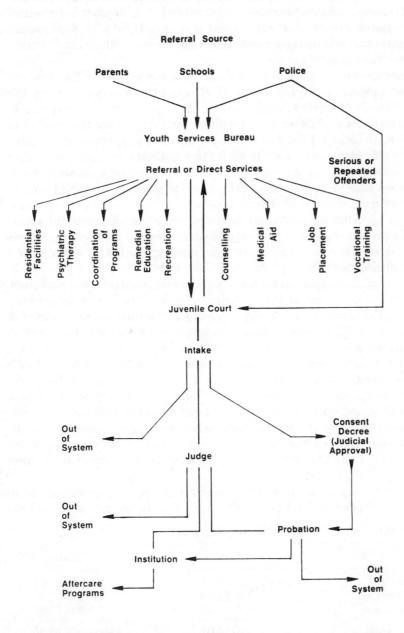

Referral Source

Parents   Schools   Police

Youth Services Bureau

Referral or Direct Services   Serious or Repeated Offenders

Residential Facilities Psychiatric Therapy Coordination of Programs Remedial Education Recreation Counselling Medical Aid Job Placement Vocational Training

Juvenile Court

Intake

Out of System   Consent Decree (Judicial Approval)

Judge

Out of System   Probation

Institution   Out of System

Aftercare Programs

Figure 13-1. From President's Commission on Law Enforcement and Administration of Justice, *The Challenge of Crime in a Free Society* (Washington, D.C.: Government Printing Office, 1967), p. 89.

status offense would not be labeled a delinquent either officially or by association. However, since a juvenile *can* be labeled a delinquent for repeated juvenile-status offenses, the initial arrest is recorded officially; thus there is a "prelabel" that sets up the juvenile for being labeled a delinquent in subsequent encounters with the law.

In order to examine the success of diversion programs, we will look at one that was implemented so that it could be compared with a control group. The Sacramento 601 Diversion Project was one of the early diversion programs to be instituted. Four goals were set for the project: (1) reduce the number of cases going to court; (2) decrease overnight detentions; (3) reduce the number of repeat offenders; and (4) accomplish these goals at a cost no greater than that required for regular processing of cases.[27] The first two goals were operational ones that made up the workings of the program, the third was an evaluative one, and the final goal was purely fiscal. The first two goals, reduction of detention and court petitions, were met. The control group, using the prediversion court petition procedures, sent 19.8 percent of its cases to court and put another 19.1 percent on informal probation for a total of 38.9 percent of the control group's referrals. The project group filed petitions in 3.7 percent of its cases and in 2.3 percent of the cases used informal probation, for a total of 6 percent of the diversion referrals.[28] Similarly, in reducing detention, the project (diversion) group had no detention for 86.1 percent of its referrals, and the control group had no detention for only 44.5 percent.

Recidivism was measured in a number of different ways, but the bottom line is the total percentage of juveniles who are rebooked. A total of 46.3 percent of the diversion group were recidivists, and 54.2 percent of the project group were rebooked for some offense. With a net reduction of about 8 percent, diversion showed some (but not much) improvement over the traditional juvenile justice system. However, when this slight reduction in recidivism is compared to the fiscal costs, the value of diversion increases significantly. Table 13-2 shows the average costs for the project and control groups.

Given the meager reduction in the diversion group, it would be difficult to conclude that labeling, control, or differential association theories have been

TABLE 13-2.   Average Total Cost per Youth[a]

	Project	Control
Handling	$113.60	$189.60
Detention	$ 98.98	$214.27
Placement	$ 61.43	$157.76
Total	$274.01	$561.63

[a]Roger Baron and Floyd Feeney, *Juvenile Diversion through Family Counseling* (Washington, D.C.: Government Printing Office, February 1976), pp. 14–15.

proven. It would even be difficult to conclude from the data provided that they have an impact. However, since the diversion project was consistent with the theories, we can be encouraged that there might be something in the sociological approach for understanding delinquency.

The most significant finding of the Sacramento project has to do with the reduced cost of diversion programs. Students of delinquency and sociologists usually do not concern themselves with developing theories or programs around the financial considerations necessary to implement them. Instead, they attempt to find the causes of delinquency and develop programs that will reduce the incidence of delinquency. In the real world of budget considerations and cost analysis, however, it is imperative that fiscal matters be analyzed. While we would prefer to work in a "pure" context independent of dollars and cents, those who wish to make changes in the existing structure must take financial considerations into account.

One recent program that has been tied in with diversion is the volunteer counselor concept. The Lincoln, Nebraska, Volunteer Probation Counselor Program developed in 1968 became an exemplary project of the Law Enforcement Assistance Administration.[29] The program used volunteers from a number of different sources who acted as counselors, supplementing regular probation officers. A program developed in Florida combined the volunteer concept, which the state had been using for some time anyway, with diversion.[30] Youths who were arrested for CINS (Children in Need of Supervision) violations and minor crimes (for example, shoplifting) were to be diverted to a volunteer who acted something like a "big brother" or "big sister." Most of the volunteers were to be recruited from students in nearby universities and colleges, especially those majoring in the social sciences and psychology. Students were encouraged to volunteer by being offered academic credits for their participation.

The rationale behind volunteer programs, including the Florida diversion project, lies in community involvement, and in the case of students, counseling apprenticeship. At the same time, since there is a larger cohort to draw from, it is argued that the juveniles receive more attention and more individualized attention than is possible with a traditional probation staff. Moreover, all of this is done without the stigmatization of the youths or the association with career delinquents.

The Florida volunteer diversion project is in progress at this writing and has not yet been evaluated, but the Nebraska volunteer program has been judged a success. The latter program showed a reduction of 62 percent in the offenses committed in the group who were participants in the volunteer program.[31] If the Florida project, which combined both of these effectively proven methods, is dealing with a comparable group under comparable conditions, we would expect a good deal of success.

SUMMARY

We have considered a number of alternatives to traditional treatment programs for juveniles. For our purposes in understanding delinquency as well as for practical purposes, we have seen that two important sociological tools stand out: theory and methodology. On the one hand, theory has provided practitioners with a guide to developing programs that get to the heart of the matter—namely, the causes of delinquency. By developing theoretically sound programs, the practitioner not only can accomplish the practical goals of reducing delinquency but can also test the validity of theory. If the practical goals are not met and the tenets of the theory have been incorporated into the program, then the theory has not been confirmed. It then becomes necessary either to reformulate the theory or redesign the program to better implement the elements of the theory. If the theory is well researched and is properly used, the program should succeed. Therefore, we can see that rigorous testing of theory is as important as evaluation of the program. This is where methodology comes in. With an empirical methodology the sociologist is able to test and develop theory from initial observations and hunches to a set of interrelated propositions that focus on a comprehensive explanation of delinquency. Once the theory is tested, it can be implemented into social policy and practical programs, which themselves are evaluated with the same methodological tools.

As we have seen, not all programs are evaluated, or there is some question as to which concepts are relevant theoretically in a program. In Chapter 14 we will examine the stages and problems in the evaluation of programs and their underlying theory. The point is to show that any practical program is linked to both theory and method and that the success of one is linked to the success of the other.

NOTES

1. Office of Juvenile Justice and Delinquency Prevention, *Federal Juvenile Delinquency Programs: First Analysis and Evaluation,* Vols. 1 and 2 (Washington, D.C.: Government Printing Office, 1976), p. 5.
2. Robert K. Merton, *Social Theory and Social Structure* (New York: Free Press, 1957).
3. Richard A. Cloward and Lloyd E. Ohlin, *Delinquency and Opportunity: A Theory of Delinquent Gangs* (New York: Free Press, 1960).
4. The actual programs were geared to improve the opportunity of the individual by preparing him/her to deal with the opportunity structure, but there was little change in the structure itself.
5. Walter Miller, "Lower Class Culture as a Generating Milieu of Gang Delinquency," *Journal of Social Issues, 14* (3):5–19 (1958).
6. Albert Cohen, *Delinquent Boys* (New York: Free Press, 1955).
7. Cloward and Ohlin.

8. Anthony Platt, *The Child Savers: The Invention of Delinquency* (Chicago: University of Chicago Press, 1969).

9. David Matza, *Delinquency and Drift* (New York: Wiley, 1964).

10. Richard Quinney and John Wildeman, *The Problem of Crime,* 2d ed. (New York: Harper & Row, 1977), p. 138.

11. *Ibid.*, p. 166.

12. Malcolm Klein, *Street Gangs and Street Workers* (Englewood Cliffs, N.J.: Prentice-Hall, 1971), pp. 44–45.

13. *Ibid.*, pp. 147–148.

14. *Ibid.*, p. 50.

15. *Ibid.*, p. 51.

16. Erving Goffman, *Interaction Ritual* (New York: Doubleday, 1967), pp. 5–45.

17. Klein, p. 149.

18. *Ibid.*, pp. 51–55.

19. Donald R. Cressey and Robert A. McDermott, *Diversion from the Juvenile Justice System.* Project Report for National Assessment of Juvenile Corrections (Ann Arbor: University of Michigan, June 1973), p. 1.

20. Randall G. Shelden, "Diverting Youth: Juvenile Justice in Historical Perspective," unpublished research manuscript, State University New York, Cortland, 1977, p. 1.

21. Cressey and McDermott, p. 2.

22. Edwin M. Schur, *Radical Non-Intervention: Rethinking the Delinquency Problem* (Englewood Cliffs, N.J.: Prentice-Hall, 1973).

23. *Ibid.*, p. 121.

24. *Ibid.*, pp. 156–157.

25. *Ibid.*, pp. 135–139.

26. Robert Carter and Malcolm Klein, *Back on the Streets* (Englewood Cliffs, N.J.: Prentice-Hall, 1976).

27. Roger Baron and Floyd Feeney, *Juvenile Diversion through Family Counseling* (Washington, D.C.: Government Printing Office, February 1976).

28. *Ibid.*, pp. 8–9.

29. Richard Ku, Richard Moore, and Keith Griffiths, *The Volunteer Probation Counselor Program, Lincoln, Nebraska* (Washington, D.C.: Government Printing Office, n.d.).

30. The volunteer concept was as much an economic measure as it was a device to involve members of the community. By having volunteers to house runaways, it was unnecessary to have to pay for special facilities and staff them. In the Florida program there was a chronic shortage and a high turnover of volunteers.

31. Ku, Moore, and Griffith, p. 8.

14 Sociological Theory, Evaluation Research, and Delinquency Programs

INTRODUCTION

A common complaint among students is that sociologists talk about delinquency but they don't do anything about it. Sociologists develop theories that explain delinquency, but they do not apply that knowledge to reduce or prevent delinquency. In a strict sense it is true that sociologists do nothing more than develop and test sociological theory, leaving the implementation of their theories to others. But it is not the job of sociologists to apply theory, and if it were, there would probably be a good deal of public resistance. For example, critical theorists believe the root cause of delinquency is the capitalist structure of American society, and if given a free hand to deal with juvenile delinquency, they would begin by replacing capitalism with socialism. Such action would obviously not be tolerated, but the example suggests why the application of sociological theory is in the hands of the policy makers —those who wield power—and not the theorists.

On the other hand, when policy makers ask sociologists to develop programs based on their theories, then sociologists are in a position to *apply* theory in the form of workable programs. At the same time, sociologists use their methodological techniques to test whether or not a program is effective.

This chapter examines how sociological theory and methodology can be applied to solve certain problems of delinquency in society. First, we will look at the relationship between theory and delinquency programs to see the critically important role of theory. Second, we will examine the role of sociological methods in evaluation research. Third, we will show how evaluation research is conducted, with an eye to both theory and methodology. Finally, we will see how important it is for sociologists to maintain their focus on developing theory, both for the "pure" sociological goals of creating better understanding of social processes and the "applied" goals of dealing with delinquency.

SOCIOLOGICAL THEORY AND DELINQUENCY PROGRAMS

Virtually any program designed to deal with delinquency has an underlying theory. The theory may involve nothing more than common sense, or it may be systematic and scientific, but there is always an *idea* of some sort that states or implies why things are the way they are. Some ideas are nothing more than prejudices and dogmas that persist in the face of evidence to the contrary, while others are part of a logical set of propositions based on observations, research, and testing.

Earlier in this book we saw a number of sociological theories and research that either supported or refuted the ideas put forth by the theory. Each theory had us consider different aspects of delinquency or the social world that contributes to delinquency. For example, the concept of stigmatization in labeling theory forced us to ask about the relationship between delinquency and the societal reaction to delinquency. On the other hand, differential association theory had us examine social relationships that lead to delinquency. Different theories have us focus on different aspects of the world in search of answers to the questions they raise. Some of these searches take us up blind alleys; others lead to solutions.

To the extent to which a theory provides answers to questions, the concepts and ideas of a theory can be applied to solve problems. Some of the solutions, based on the propositions of the theory, require changes in the entire social and economic structure, as is the case with critical theory. Other theories, especially psychological and social psychological ones, point to some problem with the individual or the individual's milieu. Finally, there are theories of the middle range.[1] For sociologists, middle-range theories deal with a level of abstraction that can be readily verified through research. Labeling, differential association, and control theories are all theories of the middle range. They examine processes and structures in society on a level that can be measured and observed. From such theories many of the programs discussed in Chapter 13 were developed.

To see the specific relevance of a theory to a delinquency program, we will take a brief look again at how diversion was developed out of differential association and labeling theories and show how the concepts of stigma, label, and differential association were necessary foundations for the program. First, there was *not* some automatic realization that the juvenile justice system itself has something to do with fostering juvenile delinquency. After all, the juvenile justice system purportedly *helps* juveniles who have, because of personality deficiencies or disadvantaged backgrounds, committed delinquent acts. However, with the introduction of such concepts as stigma and labeling, researchers were compelled to examine the juvenile justice system. At the same time, researchers who had been looking at association patterns and delinquency in the community began to examine the association patterns forced on juveniles who were placed in detention together. Their findings were especially interesting when the researchers examined the association between predelinquents (juvenile-status offenders) and delinquents who were locked up together. Given the concept of differential association, it was reasoned that the delinquents would pass on delinquent behavior patterns to nondelinquents. As a result, when attempting to arrive at a solution to the problem of delinquency, one of the first programs instituted in diversion was to keep status offenders out of detention so that they would not learn delinquent behavior patterns.

Retrospectively, much of what was done with the concepts of labeling and differential association theories was based on common sense. However, it was only because of the theories that researchers began looking in the places they did. Before the theories were formulated, the belief was widely held that the juvenile justice system helped juveniles, no matter what it did. After all, the causes of delinquency were seen to be largely independent of the system, and if the causes of delinquency were in the home or the environment, then the juvenile justice system *must* be helpful because it removed the juvenile from home and environment. However, by showing that associations forced on incarcerated juveniles and the labeling process of the juvenile justice system contributed to delinquency, it was possible to introduce new ideas and programs that would have otherwise been overlooked.

THE USE OF SOCIOLOGICAL METHODS IN EVALUATION RESEARCH ON DELINQUENCY

Evaluation research appears to many people to be a new and different tool, and many will point out the difference between doing "pure" and "applied" research, the former being used to test theories and the latter for evaluation. In many respects it is pointless to differentiate between pure and applied research *methodologies,* for even though one type of research evaluates theories and the other programs, the essential methodologies employed need not be different at all.

Testing Hypotheses and Goal Accomplishment

In just about any basic textbook on research methods, there is a set of steps given that generally apply to all research projects. The following five steps illustrate the overall process of a research project:

1. Choosing the research problem and stating the hypothesis.
2. Formulating the research design.
3. Gathering the data.
4. Coding and analyzing the data.
5. Interpreting the results so as to test the hypothesis.[2]

Essentially, the same steps are followed in both pure and applied research, but instead of stating and testing hypotheses, the evaluation researcher states and tests program goals. Moreover, to the extent to which the program procedures reflect theoretical concepts, the evaluation researcher is also testing hypotheses. Therefore, by knowing how to employ basic sociological methods, one should have no difficulty in conducting evaluation research.

In the following section we examine the steps in evaluation research and the special considerations which are taken that are not always necessary in pure sociological research. However, even though there are differences between pure and applied (evaluation) research, the two are essentially the same in terms of methodology and overall approach to gathering valid and reliable data.

Program Evaluation

Before a company produces a new product it conducts market research to determine whether the product has the potential to reap a worthwhile profit. For example, a company that decides to develop a new type of solar water heater must first determine whether or not the public will buy the device. A company may risk bankruptcy if it spends several million dollars developing and producing the water heater and then markets it only to find that the public will not buy it. On the other hand, if the company spends a few thousands dollars on market research and learns that the water heater will not sell, it has spent only a fraction of what it would have if it had gone ahead and produced the heater.

Of course, it would be even more disastrous for a company to develop a water heater on the basis of an untested theory. A company would be in serious difficulty if it bought the idea of a solar water heater from an inventor and mass produced the product only to find that it did not work. The firm would have made an even greater error than if it had neglected to market research a product before producing it.

The same relationship holds between sociological theory and program implementation. First, we test the basic theory to see whether it works. Next, we develop pilot projects based on the theory and test them. If the pilot projects work, we can begin to "mass produce" programs to eradicate delinquency based on the pilot projects. Our current juvenile justice system, unfortunately, went right from the idea to mass production, and it is little wonder we have an expensive failure. However, assuming we have tested our theory, we will now examine what is involved in the evaluation of delinquency-prevention programs.

Goal Measurement. The first thing necessary in a program is a statement of what one plans to accomplish.[3] In the most general terms, the goal may be to reduce delinquency, reduce juvenile incarceration, or improve juvenile rights in court. More specific goals are listed depending on the operation and intent of the program. For example, in Chapter 13 we saw that the detached worker's goals were (1) control (principally gang fighting); (2) treatment of individual problems; (3) access to opportunities; (4) value change; and (5) prevention of delinquency. Likewise, the Sacramento Diversion Project had specific goals: (1) reduce the number of cases going to court; (2) decrease overnight detentions; (3) reduce the number of repeat offenders; and (4) accomplish these goals at a cost no greater than required for regular processing of cases. The goals of the detached worker were broader and less specific than those of the diversion project, and there were differences in specific objectives.

In measuring goals it is necessary to define operationally what constitutes the action.[4] Essentially, this means that the goals have to be stated in such a way that we may observe or otherwise measure their accomplishment. For instance, in the detached worker's set of goals is "value change." Intuitively, we may know what we mean by values and what a change of values means, but how do we "see" values and their change. One possible operational definition of values may take a form as simple as a response on a questionnaire. In measuring values of "toughness" as opposed to values of "education," a questionnaire may compare which values are higher before and after the introduction of a detached street worker with a gang. The program may measure value change according to gang members giving education values a higher priority than "toughness" after the introduction of the street worker.

Such a measurement may seen naive, for after all, a questionnaire reflects words, not deeds. We may wish to have a more "solid" measure of value change, such as a change in the behavior of the juveniles in the gang. However, if we measure value change by a change in the behavior of juvenile gang members, we may not be measuring value change at all. In his work on sentiments and acts, Deutscher points out that stated attitudes (or values) may not reflect actions, and actions may not reflect values.[5] As we have seen, Matza pointed out that juveniles employ "techniques of neutralization" in accounting for their delinquent actions. For the most part subcultural delinquents hold conventional values, but in situations where they commit a delinquent act they neutralize the wrongness of the violation in accounting for it in such a way as to make the behavior consistent with conventional values. Therefore, even though the evaluator may assume that there is a direct relationship between values and acts, it is a mistake to measure a value by behavior that is not necessarily reflective of a value.

In comparing the goals of the detached gang workers and the diversion program, it is clear that the latter has far more specific and measurable goals. The goals are stated in such a way that they are operationally visible, and success or failure will be apparent. For example, the second goal is to reduce the number of overnight detentions. This goal is stated in such a way as to be easily measured. Simply by comparing the proportion of juveniles being sent to detention in the diversion program and the control group, this goal can be seen to be accomplished or not. Table 14-1 presents a comparison between the control group and the diversion group.

It is clear from the table that the project group had less overnight detention than the control group, and if we assume the control group represents the "normal" procedure for detaining juveniles, we can see that the program has accomplished the goal of decreasing overnight detention.

TABLE 14–1. Overnight Detention in Juvenile Hall as a Result of Initial Referral[a]

	Control (%)	Project (%)
No overnight detention	44.5	86.1
1 night	20.7	9.9
2–4 nights	19.2	3.0
5–39 nights	14.4	0.7
40–100 nights	1.1	0.3
Over 100 nights	0.0	0.0

[a]Roger Baron and Floyd Feeney, "Diversion through Family Counseling" (Washington, D.C.: Government Printing Office, February 1976).

On the basis of the comparison of the projects' goals, we may conclude that the objectives of the diversion program were better because they were more measurable. In one respect this is certainly the case, for it was clear from the way in which the goals were stated exactly what was intended and whether or not the goals were accomplished. However, there is a danger in assuming that because a program's goals are "measurable" they are inherently better. If program and project directors feel compelled to set up a program that can be measured, their activities will often focus on how to do measurable work instead of on how to solve a problem. If we allow measurability to dictate program activities, we have a case of the tail wagging the dog, for measurement is merely a means for evaluating goals; measurement itself should not be the goal.

To illustrate this point, consider a program that includes as an important goal to "raise the spirit of the community" or "foster community identity" in order to offset juvenile delinquency. We might well ask exactly what do we mean by "spirit," and what does "community identity" look like? Can we measure community spirit by facial gestures that express pride? How would we know whether the source of pride was personal or community-based? Is community identity measurable by attendance at neighborhood meetings? Do gang meetings constitute neighborhood meetings? These and other measurement questions often become so absurd that we lose sight of the conceptual goals. Rather than taking quantitative measures, we frequently have to take qualitative ones. Quantitative measures are valuable because the numbers they generate give us precise figures, but they are limited in that not everything can be meaningfully understood by numbers. Moreover, even if we do use quantitative statistics, we are still counting qualitative elements in society. Therefore, if the goals cannot be easily or meaningfully measured with quantitative methods, we should not hesitate to employ a qualitative methodology. Essentially, qualitative measures involve empirical descriptions of social processes, structures and action.[6] For example, we may want to examine a delinquent gang. Quantitatively, we could count the gang members, but qualitatively we would want to describe the gang's structure—including the various positions in the gang, the roles of these positions, and the strength of the structure over time. In a delinquency-prevention program, the goal may be to break up the structure of the gang or redirect its interests. Only by having qualitative measurements of the gang's structure and activities can we determine whether the program has had an impact.

For the most part we are not dealing with an either-or situation when it comes to qualitative and quantitative measures. There is every reason to employ multiple measures, using not only both quantitative and qualitative measures but different types of each.[7] In this way the evaluator can better determine whether the program being judged is really effective or not, or whether the evaluation merely reflects the measurements being employed.

Measurement of Program Implementation.   A seemingly obvious procedure in evaluation research is to determine whether or not the program has been properly put into action and the intended procedures are being carried out. As obvious as this may seem, this procedure is either overlooked or conducted in such a way as to undermine the goals of the program. In part this is due to a misapplication of quantitative measures by bureaucrats. For example, in a delinquency-prevention program dealing with gangs, the granting agency wanted "evidence" of the program's implementation. To gather this data it had the project workers fill out contact forms that documented contact between the workers and the gang members. Since the granting agency was able to count the contact forms that the workers sent in, they measured the success of the program's implementation by the number of forms they received. Thus, rather than focusing on programming group activities designed to reduce gang delinquency, the workers began spending time contacting gang members so that they could increase the number of contact forms to be sent to the granting agency.[8] Thus, the very measure that was used to determine the program's implementation served to undermine the very thing it purported to measure!

In a similar vein, Cressey and McDermott found that when diversion became popular, all types of traditional juvenile justice system activities suddenly came to be called diversion.[9] For example, informal probation was now diversion, and any police decision not to arrest a youth was no longer "police discretion" but instead "police diversion." The reason for such seemingly strange activities are rational when we consider the amount of money local agencies were receiving from the federal government for diversion programs. From the point of view of sociologists who were interested in whether their concepts and ideas were working in practice, however, such actions were inexcusable.

It has become increasingly clear that program implementation should be evaluated, along with the rest of any program, by outside evaluators who specialize in research methodology. There are several reasons for this, the least of which is the "watchdog" function to insure that the program personnel are doing their jobs. Program implementation and program evaluation are two entirely different sets of activities, and to the extent that those who implement a program are freed from evaluation procedures, both real and bureaucratic, the program has a chance of getting off the ground. Second, research methods constitute a specialized body of knowledge, and while there is nothing mysterious about methodology, evaluation research conducted by specialists is more likely to be conducted properly. Finally, while evaluation researchers are not totally objective, they are bound to be more objective than the practitioners who are involved in implementing a program. This is because the focus of the evaluation researcher is on the conceptual and scientific aspects of the program and not the program's success. Standing back, they are better able to see the entire picture and make judgments as to whether or not the program is being implemented as planned. In this role they should not be seen as "watchdogs" who are making sure that the bureaucratic functions and procedures are being met. Rather, they should be used by those who are implementing the project as a source of information concerning whether the program is developing as intended. If it is not, then the evaluators can point out what needs to be changed. Often time, effort, and money is wasted because of programmers' attempts to "cover themselves" from criticisms that they are not spending funds properly. This is the case when so-called safeguards or accountability forms force programmers knowingly to undermine a project. The instance of the gang workers running around filling out contact forms at the expense of generating group activities designed to reduce gang delinquency is a case in point. By freeing the project personnel from a myriad of forms and putting evaluation activities in the hands of researchers makes for not only better programs but better evaluation.

The Relationship Between Delinquency and Programs.   A third major purpose of evaluation research is to determine the relationship between the program and delinquency. If a program is started in an area in which delinquency declines shortly thereafter, the people involved in the project naturally want to take the credit. However, larger changes in society and in patterns of youthful involvement may drastically alter or negate any effect a program may have. For example, in Chapter 7 we saw that in the mid-1960s marijuana use became popular among middle-class youths. Suppose a delinquency-prevention program had been set up in a community just before the advent of middle-class juvenile drug use. If the program were a drug-abuse program and there was a sudden rise in drug use after its implementation, one might draw the erroneous conclusion that the program caused the increase in drug use! By the same token, if there is a general reduction in delinquency, it may not necessarily be because of a particular program but because of larger social changes. Many states have enacted laws decriminalizing juvenile-status offenses, and as we saw in the discussions of labeling and differential associa- tion theories, this should result in an overall reduction in delinquency. Therefore, if a nondiversion-delinquency-prevention program began simul- taneously with the enactment of such laws, the evaluation of the program would have to include the impact of the laws on delinquency *in addition to* any impact of the program itself.

A refrain often heard about social science research is that so many variables are present that it is impossible to determine what is a significant cause. While it is true that social scientists study a large number of variables, it is not the case that as a result we can learn nothing about social behavior. All of the variables tend to cancel one another out if we focus on the relevant matters and compare the program group with another group. In Chapter 13 we saw that the juveniles who were part of the Sacramento 601 Project had a lower recidivism rate than those in a comparable group. Assuming that the control and project groups were randomly selected from the same population and that other than the different treatment received by the project group there were no other differences, we can attribute the lower recidivism to the diver- sion program.

Sometimes during the course of operating a program for juveniles a number of serendipitous findings crop up. These accidental discoveries can sometimes tell us more about delinquency, both in theory and practice, than a theory or program that has been extensively researched. We saw that in the gang- prevention programs the gang members felt that they could build their "reps" by having a detached street worker. This accidental and unintended, but very useful, finding about gangs not only had the practical ramification of getting the gangs to accept detached workers but also showed the importance of "rep" in the world of juvenile gangs. Similarly, in the street gang programs, it was found that gang members *wanted* street workers to stop gang fights. It was assumed that the gangs really wanted to engage in lethal gang warfare, but instead it was learned that the gangs actively attempted to have the workers intervene in such a way that the gang would be able to save face and at the same time not have to fight. This knowledge provided the workers with an added resource for preventing gang fights and also led theorists to question certain beliefs they had about delinquent subcultural values.

The importance of serendipity in evaluation research cannot be overem- phasized, because it is through such spontaneous discoveries that we come closer to a true understanding of delinquency. Thus, even though evaluation research methods must be systematic and rigorous, they should not be so rigid as to overlook new unanticipated data, and programs must be flexible enough to incorporate such valuable information where applicable or at least take note of it for future programs.

There are certain costs for incorporating serendipitous findings in delin- quency-prevention programs. Perhaps the greatest cost is in evaluating a specific program and its concepts. If every unanticipated finding is immediately incorporated into the program and its evaluation, it becomes increasingly difficult to know what is being evaluated. Sometimes a new procedure may so affect the overall structure of a program that the program and its underlying concepts are all but invalidated. If there is a reduction in delinquency, the researchers may not know whether it is due to the original program, the new finding that was added on, or a combination of both.

As in other research, programs need to be pretested and small pilot projects introduced before launching a full-blown project. Ideally, the conceptual research in the development of theory should handle this, but there may be a considerable gap between theory and its application. Therefore, pretesting applied concepts in small pilot projects should serve to uncover relevant serendipitous findings and incorporate them into an overall system. Essentially this is what Denzin refers to as "sensitizing concepts,"[10] whereby the researcher tries out the concept in the research situation before coming up with an operational definition. Once applied concepts are sensitized to the actual program setting, one is less likely to be surprised later on with unanticipated findings that negate the original application.

Improved Programs Through Improved Theory

If a program fails to reduce delinquency, the reason is an invalid theory behind the program. If sociological theories are etiological ones in that they posit the causes of crime, either explicitly or implicitly, then any program that incorporates the theory is "buying the idea."[11] If the idea is invalid, barring unforeseen external factors, the program should be invalid. To say that the program was a "bad one" really begs the most basic question—namely, the question of theory. If we take punitive measures as reflecting a theory, we have to conclude that the "punitive theory" is a monumental flop. It does not work and none of the programs fostered by the "theory" have worked. Of course, punitive theory is more of an ideology than a true theory, and since ideologies are based more on sentiment than on empirical facts, we should not be too surprised that people are unwilling to give it up and seek an improvement. Sociological theory is not ideology, however, and it should not be treated as such. If a theory has been applied in practice and it can be shown that the theory failed "on the street," then there is no reason to insist that it is still valid. To do so is to preach ideology and not make use of science. We need to develop theory so that its validity can be shown to work in the mundane real world of delinquency. Theoretical research should proceed not only in the controlled setting of the social psychology laboratory and the sterile end of a questionnaire, but in the reality of juvenile delinquent situations. Once that reality is grasped and understood, theories should be developed, tested, retested, redeveloped, discarded, and redone until there is evidence of their validity. Then, and only then, are we in a position to test the theory in an applied program. If the theory fails in different applied programs, we start all over again—not with another program but with another theory.

When we finally arrive at the proper combination of theory and program we will see a decline in delinquency. The decline may be small or it may be a dramatic one. The theory and application may involve massive social restructuring or a simple yet overlooked consideration. Whatever the case, any change in the patterns of delinquency will depend on our ability to develop and test theory, the most basic process in sociology.

SUMMARY

The most important contribution that sociology has to offer the understanding of delinquency is in the development of systematic theory and the use of scientific methodology. This book has stressed the significance of theory, both as an abstract explanatory tool and as a foundation for developing programs to deal with delinquency. It is hoped that this last chapter has bridged the gap between theory and practice and has demonstrated the necessity of having good theory before we can even begin to have a viable approach to preventing or reducing delinquency.

In future generations we can expect changes in the patterns of delinquency, some for the better and some for the worse, but delinquency will probably always exist in some form. However, unless we can understand the dynamics underlying delinquency, we have no hope of controlling it. Our own juvenile experiments in delinquency should tell us, though, that the problem is certainly not insoluble.

NOTES

1. Robert K. Merton, *Social Theory and Social Structure* (New York: Free Press, 1957).
2. Kenneth D. Bailey, *Methods of Social Research* (New York: Free Press, 1978), pp. 4–11.
3. Janet P. Moursund, *Evaluation: An Introduction to Research Design* (Monterey, Calif.: Brooks/Cole, 1973), pp. 8–11.
4. *Ibid.,* pp. 18–20.
5. Irwin Deutscher, *What We Say/What We Do: Sentiments and Acts* (Glenview, Ill.: Scott, Foresman, 1973), pp. 12–14.
6. William B. Sanders, *The Sociologist as Detective,* 2d. ed. (New York: Holt, Rinehart and Winston, 1976), pp. 19–20.
7. Eugene Webb, Donald T. Campbell, Richard D. Schwartz, and Lee Sechrest, *Unobtrusive Measures: Nonreactive Measures in the Social Sciences* (Chicago: Rand McNally, 1966), p. 3. Norman Denzin, *The Research Act* (Chicago: Aldine, 1970), p. 297.

8. Malcolm Klein, *Street Gangs and Street Workers* (Englewood Cliffs, N.J.: Prentice-Hall, 1971), pp. 271–272.
9. Donald R. Cressey and Robert A. McDermott, *Diversion from the Juvenile Justice System,* Project Report for National Assessment of Juvenile Corrections (Ann Arbor: University of Michigan, June 1973).
10. Denzin, p. 14.
11. Edwin Sutherland and Donald R. Cressey, *Criminology,* 10th ed. (Philadelphia: Lippincott, 1978), p. 22.

Appendix

Juvenile
Delinquency
Self-Report
Survey
Instrument

The following questions pertain to activities you did when you were a juvenile, before 18 years of age in most states. It is a general set of questions to be used in estimating the proportion of a small sample, such as your class, that engaged in delinquency and to determine whether there are any differences between males and females and between various age cohorts. Remember, the questions refer only to what you did as a juvenile, not since that time.

Current Age ____   Sex: Male____Female____
1. Disobeyed your parents, defying them to their face.
        Yes____No____
2. Stole something from a store (shoplift).
        Yes____No____
3. Ran away from home overnight without your parents' permission.
        Yes____No____
4. Stole a car, even if you just drove it around and abandoned it.
        Yes____No____
5. Drove a car before you had a license or learner's permit.
        Yes____No____
6. Took money or other valuables from a person by using force or the threat of force.
        Yes____No____
7. Broke into a building and stole something.
        Yes____No____
8. Defaced, damaged, or destroyed property that did not belong to you or your family.
        Yes____No____
9. Drank alcoholic beverages without your parents' knowledge or permission.
        Yes____No____
10. Had sexual intercourse with someone of the opposite sex (if not married at the time).
        Yes____No____
11. Used illegal drugs, such as marijuana, LSD, cocaine.
        Yes____No____
12. Skipped school without a valid or legitimate excuse.
        Yes____No____

For a detailed discussion of self-report surveys and the questionnaire used by the National Youth Survey, see Delbert S. Elliott and Suzanne S. Ageton, "Reconciling Race and Class Differences in Self-Reported and Official Estimates of Delinquency," *American Sociological Review,* 45:95–110 (February 1980).

Index

G

Gagnon, John H., 157
Gangs, delinquent (*see* Delinquent gangs)
Gault decision, 238, 242, 243
Gibbons, Don C., 27, 30, 31, 102
Girls, amount of delinquency among, 47;
  and broken homes, 42–43; in gangs, 192,
  193, 194; runaway, 109; and sense of
  injustice, 265–267; and sex offenses,
  103–104; sexual behavior of, 103–104;
  shoplifting by, 3, 132–133, 134,
  135–136
Glaser, Daniel, 121, 259
Glueck, Eleanor, 36, 42
Glueck, Sheldon, 36, 42
Goals, culturally prescribed, 44–46
Goffman, Erving, 11, 35, 76, 81, 90, 109,
  111, 137, 140, 143, 204, 250
Goldman, Nathan, 13
Goode, Eric, 152, 154
Goring, Charles, 29
Grams, Paul, 42
Group Guidance Project, 275
Groups, auto theft by, 137;   and drug use;
  159, 165–167; property crimes committed
  by, 128, 129; shoplifting by, 137; *See also*
  Delinquent gangs
Guilt, assumption of, 235–238, 242

H

Hacker, James C., 63, 67, 69
Hakeem, Michael, 34
Handler, Joel, 238
Hanging groups, 187, 196
Haskell, Martin R., 192, 194, 197, 198
Healy, William, 33, 257
Heroin use, 173–175
Hindelang, Michael J., 121
Hippies, and drug use, 155–156, 159–160,
  162, 167, 170, 171
Hirschi, Travis, 64, 67–68, 121
Hits, 184, 206–208
Holland, 273
Homer, Louise, 109, 110, 116, 117
Homicides, 189–191, and differential
  association theory, 73; gang-related,
  189–191
Homosexuality, 104–106
Honor, and gangs, 93–94, 202–204, 206,
  216–217
Horowitz, Ruth, 94, 202, 205

I

Imprisonment, objectives of, 254–255
Incapacitation, definition of, 254
Incarceration, 97–99, 233–234, 235,
  259–263;   experience of, 264–267; length
  of, for juvenile-status offenses, 98
Incarceratories, custodial-oriented 260, 262;
  rehabilitative, 260–262; *See also specific
  type*
Informal probation, 241, 242–243
Informal processing model, 219
Injustice, sense of, 264–267
Inmate subculture, 263
Innovation, 45, 46
Insanity, claiming, 65
Intake officer, 239–242, 255
Intervention approach, 274
Interviews, with juveniles, 247–248;   with
  parents, 247–248

J

Jacobs, Jane, 208
Juvenile correctional facilities (*see*
  Incarceratories; *specific type facility*)
Juvenile corrections, 254–268;   as control
  mechanism, 255, 262–263
Juvenile court judges, 231;   caseloads of,
  237, 238, 241
Juvenile courts, establishment of, 231–233,
  235;   hearings in, time spent on,
  235–236; process of, 238–244; *See also*
  Juvenile justice
Juvenile delinquency, and age, 258;
  amount, distribution and measurement
  of, 11–16; changing patterns of, 16–18,
  89; criteria for adequate theory of,
  26–28; definitions of, 8–9, 186; and
  delinquency prevention programs,
  relationship between, 294–296; and
  drinking, 177–178; and IQ, 121, 122;
  legal aspects of, 4–7; as nonutilitarian
  behavior, 50–53; as a permanent
  phenomenon, 19; and school
  performance, 121–122; scope of, 2–4;
  situational perspective on, 19–20; social
  aspects of, 7–8; and social structure (*see*
  Sociogenic theories); as a transitory
  phenomenon, 18–20
Juvenile delinquent, definition of, 9–11
Juvenile detail, 223–228